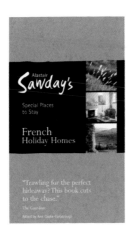

Sixth edition
Copyright © 2009 Alastair Sawday
Publishing Co. Ltd
Published in March 2010
ISBN-13: 978-1-906136-32-1

Alastair Sawday Publishing Co. Ltd,
The Old Farmyard, Yanley Lane,
Long Ashton, Bristol BS41 9LR, UK
Tel: +44 (0)1275 395430
Email: info@sawdays.co.uk
Web: www.sawdays.co.uk

The Globe Pequot Press,
P. O. Box 480, Guilford,
Connecticut 06437, USA
Tel: +1 203 458 4500
Email: info@globepequot.com
Web: www.globepequot.com

*We have made every effort to ensure the accuracy
of the information in this book at the time of
going to press. However, we cannot accept any
responsibility for any loss, injury or
inconvenience resulting from the use of
information contained therein.*

Series Editor Alastair Sawday
Editor Florence Oldfield
Assistant to Editor Angharad Barnes
Editorial Director Annie Shillito
Writing Alex Baker, Angharad Barnes,
Jo Boissevain, Ann Cooke-Yarborough,
Janet Edsforth-Stone, Monica Guy,
Susan Herrick Luraschi, Honor Peters
Inspections Katie Anderson,
Richard & Linda Armspach, Helen Barr,
Penny Dinwiddie, Janet Edsforth-Stone,
John & Jane Edwards, Georgina Gabriel,
Cristina Sánchez González,
Susan Herrick Luraschi, Judith Lott,
Diana Harris Sawday, Elizabeth Yates,
Thanks to those people who did a few inspections
Accounts Bridget Bishop,
Shona Adcock, Amy Lancastle
Editorial Sue Bourner,
Angharad Barnes, Jo Boissevain,
Roxy Dumble, Cristina Sánchez González,
Wendy Ogden, Polly Procter
Production Jules Richardson,
Rachel Coe, Tom Germain,
Anny Mortada
Sales & Marketing & PR Rob Richardson,
Sarah Bolton, Bethan Riach, Lisa Walklin
Web & IT Dominic Oakley
Chris Banks, Phil Clarke,
Mike Peake, Russell Wilkinson

Alastair Sawday has asserted his right to
be identified as the author of this work

Maps: Maidenhead Cartographic Services
Printing: Butler, Tanner & Dennis, Frome
UK distribution: Penguin UK, London

Alastair

Sawday's

Special Places to Stay

French Châteaux & Hotels

4 Contents

The buildings

Beautiful as they were, our old offices leaked heat, used electricity to heat water and rooms, flooded spaces with light to illuminate one person, and were not ours to alter.

So in 2005 we created our own eco-offices by converting some old barns to create a low-emissions building. We made the building energy-efficient through a variety of innovative and energy-saving building techniques, described below.

Insulation We went to great lengths to ensure that very little heat can escape, by laying thick insulating board under the roof and floor and adding further insulation underneath the roof and between the rafters. We then lined the whole of the inside of the building with plastic sheeting to ensure air-tightness.

Heating We installed a wood-pellet boiler from Austria, in order to be largely fossil-fuel free. The pellets are made from compressed sawdust, a waste product from timber mills that work only with sustainably managed forests. The heat is conveyed by water, throughout the building, via an under-floor system.

Water We installed a 6000-litre tank to collect rainwater from the roofs. This is pumped back, via an ultra-violet filter, to the lavatories, showers and basins. There are two solar thermal panels on the roof providing heat to the one (massively insulated) hot-water cylinder.

Lighting We have a carefully planned mix of low-energy lighting: task lighting and up-lighting. We also installed sun-pipes to reflect the outside light into the building.

Electricity All our electricity has long come from the Good Energy company and is 100% renewable.

Materials Virtually all materials are non-toxic or natural. Our carpets are made from (80%) Herdwick sheep-wool from National Trust farms in the Lake District.

Doors and windows Outside doors and new windows are wooden, double-glazed and beautifully constructed in Norway. Old windows have been double-glazed.

We have a building we are proud of, and architects and designers are fascinated by. But best of all, we are now in a better position to encourage our owners and readers to take sustainability more seriously.

What we do

Besides having moved the business to a low-carbon building, the company works in a number of ways to reduce its overall environmental footprint.

Our footprint We measure our footprint annually and use it to find ways of reducing our environmental impact. To help address unavoidable carbon emissions we try to put something back: since 2006 we have supported SCAD, an organisation that works with villagers in India to create sustainable development.

Photo: Tom Germain

Travel Staff are encouraged to car-share or cycle to work and we provide showers (rainwater-fed) and bike sheds. Our company cars run on LPG (liquid petroleum gas) or recycled cooking oil. We avoid flying and take the train for business trips wherever possible. All office travel is logged as part of our footprint and we count our freelance editors' and inspectors' miles too.

Our office Nearly all of our office waste is recycled; kitchen waste is composted and used in the office vegetable garden. Organic and fairtrade basic provisions are used in the staff kitchen and at in-house events, and green cleaning products are used throughout the office.

Working with owners We are proud that many of our Special Places help support their local economy and, through our Ethical Collection, we recognise owners who go the extra mile to serve locally sourced and organic food or those who have a positive impact on their environment or community.

Engaging readers We hope to raise awareness of the need for individuals to play their part; our Go Slow series places an emphasis on ethical travel and the Fragile Earth imprint consists of hard-hitting environmental titles. Our Ethical Collection informs readers about owners' ethical endeavours.

Ethical printing We print our books locally to support the British printing industry and to reduce our carbon footprint. We print our books on either FSC-certified or recycled paper, using vegetable or soy-based inks.

Our supply chain Our electricity is 100% renewable (supplied by Good Energy), and we put our savings with Triodos, a bank whose motives we trust. Most supplies are bought in bulk from a local ethical-trading co-operative.

For many years Alastair Sawday Publishing has been 'greening' the business in different ways. Our aim is to reduce our environmental footprint as far as possible, and almost every decision we make takes into account the environmental implications. In recognition of our efforts we won a Business Commitment to the Environment Award in 2005, and in 2006 a Queen's Award for Enterprise in the Sustainable Development category. In that year Alastair was voted ITN's 'Eco Hero'. In 2009 we were given the South West C+ Carbon Positive Consumer Choices Award for our Ethical Collection.

In 2008 and again in 2009 we won the Independent Publishers Guild Environmental Award. In 2009 we were also the IPG overall Independent Publisher and Trade Publisher of the Year. The judging panel were effusive in their praise, stating: "With green issues currently at the forefront of publishers' minds, Alastair Sawday Publishing was singled out in this category as a model for all independents to follow. Its efforts to reduce waste in its office and supply chain have reduced the company's environmental impact, and it works closely with staff to identify more areas of improvement. Here is a publisher who lives and breathes green. Alastair Sawday has all the right principles and is clearly committed to improving its practice further."

Becoming 'green' is a journey and, although we began long before most companies, we still have a long way to go. We don't plan to pursue growth for growth's sake. The Sawday's name – and thus our future – depends on maintaining our integrity. We promote special places – those that add beauty, authenticity and a touch of humanity to our lives. This is a niche, albeit a growing one, so we will spend time pursuing truly special places rather than chasing the mass market.

That said, we do plan to produce more titles as well as to diversify. We are expanding our Go Slow series to other European countries, and have launched *Green Europe*, both bold new publishing projects designed to raise the profile of low-impact tourism. Our Fragile Earth series is a growing collection of campaigning books about the environment: highlighting the perilous state of the world yet offering imaginative and radical solutions and some intriguing facts, these books will keep you up to date and well-armed for the battle with apathy.

Photos: Tom Germain

In spite of the gloomy financial news last year, the British cannot easily be deterred from going to France. France cannot be resisted. We are doing our best to reinforce her irresistibility. Not only have we come up with this 6th edition of *French Châteaux & Hotels* and an attractive mini guide to Paris, but we are also publishing two new lavishly illustrated titles, *French Vineyards* (published 2009) and *Go Slow France*.

That is hardly surprising, given the gloriously eclectic mix that France offers. You might be forgiven, however, after a peek at this edition, for thinking that the country has stood still. For the pages are alive with châteaux and manoirs, castles and domaines, 16th- and 17th-century auberges and old townhouse hotels – as if the Empire had returned and held up a velvet glove to the armies of change. But things are not quite as they seem, for the French are adept at adaptation.

Modern hoteliers need to come up with new ideas, new devices and new tastes while still offering relief from bewildering change. So how is a new generation of visitors reacting to France? I wager that most of them are as easily seduced by those old French hotels as I am. Who could fail to be gratified by a 12th-century château's many-mirrored bathroom with marble pillars, antique wooden throne and bell-chime flush? Nowadays there also may be an internet connection buried in the wall beside an 'oeil de boeuf' window, or a bubbling hot tub. Younger guests may well want comfort and instant gratification, but that is what the French do so well anyway. Swimming pools are everywhere, inside and out. Old buildings have been filled with new light, ancient walls washed with ochre and terracotta, vast and uncluttered spaces created beneath soaring arches and great domed ceilings. Things have moved on, but fires and ancient spaces satisfy deep, almost primitive, longings.

The chefs in French hotels are as brave as ever, many having moved out of cities to vaunt their skills in their home towns. They are modern, imaginative and daring, undaunted by tradition but deeply respectful of it. Within these pages we have cookery schools, gypsy caravans and treehouses – and some rather impressive past owners: Catherine de Medici and the Empress Josephine among others. Above all, we have people whose spirit we admire and celebrate and who, rest assured, would never yield to the bulldozer of 'progress' were it to threaten their character and individuality.

Alastair Sawday

In February 2009, as work began on this 6th edition of *French Châteaux & Hotels*, the French team from Bristol, where our offices are based, boarded Eurostar for a weekend in Paris.

In an attempt to distract myself from the couple playing sweet Valentines opposite, I picked up a newspaper and started to leaf through. "Sarkozy attacks focus on economic growth", read the headline. Against a backdrop of the French flag, an unusually animated-looking Sarkozy was arguing that the happiness and well-being of a country and its people were factors more indicative of a nation's progress than the state of its coffers.

While hard-nosed economists and politicians may think the president has gone potty, this argument, for all its

contradictions and shortcomings, is typical of what makes France so, well, French. This is, after all, a country renowned for its long holidays, its leisurely meal times, its celebratory approach to the good things in life. And it is this 'joie de vivre' that keeps us coming back time and time again.

The purpose of our trip to Paris? A French inspectors' gathering. In a hotel in the centre of the city we met up with the devoted team whose job it is to trek the length and breadth of France, visiting and revisiting all the manoirs, farms, auberges and châteaux that animate this guide. Early on in the proceedings the subject of 'what is special' came up for discussion – and soon became an outpouring of the inspectors' fondest memories from the past year. The Monsieur who ferried an inspector downriver on his longboat to catch a particularly spectacular sunset; the owners who whisked an inspector off on a tour of their vineyard, then treated her to a glass of wine amid the vines; an invitation to an open-air opera in the next village on a warm September's evening.

As I sat there listening I was reminded that, for our owners, their guests' satisfaction is as important as adding an extra percentage point to their profit margins, if not more so. In an industry overrun with people after an extra buck whenever they can get it, it's a comfort to know that our places are run by owners who really do go that 'extra mile'. They, too, measure their progress in well-being.

Photo left: Hôtel Design Sorbonne, entry 61
Photo right: Hostellerie du Val de Sault, entry 372

Back in the office, I delved into our reader feedback archives from the past year to see what other examples I could find of owners going beyond the call of duty; there were hundreds, and I would like to share a few of the best. The owners who celebrated a guest's mother's birthday with cake, wine and song the night before, knowing that they were leaving the next day; the owners who waited until the early hours, with dinner at the ready, to welcome weary guests who had spent half a day trying to track down lost luggage; the owner who spent a long evening in a hospital acting as translator after an excited five-year-old got a little too boisterous with a rope swing in the garden. The small acts of kindness are endless: a chilled bottle of wine on a special anniversary, a hot water bottle under the bedcovers on a chilly night, a wonderful recommendation for dinner in town – followed by a free pick-up home, so the guests could enjoy a tipple. But my personal favourite is the one about the couple who were picked up from the station in a donkey and cart as the family car was in for repairs… and they brought along a spare donkey for the luggage!

For every one of these tales that reaches us, I'm pretty sure there are dozens that don't. So please, keep writing: we love hearing and sharing your stories. Our owners deserve it.

Florence Oldfield

Photo, left: Hôtel La Désirade ©Ph.Ulliac Eliophot, entry 160
Photo, right: Château Juvenal, entry 368

It's simple. There are no rules, no boxes to tick. We choose places that we like and are fiercely subjective in our choices. We also recognise that one person's idea of special is not necessarily someone else's so there is a huge variety of places, and prices, in the book. Those who are familiar with our Special Places series know that we look for comfort, originality, authenticity, and reject the insincere, the anonymous and the banal. The way guests are treated comes as high on our list as the setting, the architecture, the atmosphere and the food.

Inspections

We visit every place in the guide to get a feel for how both house and owner tick. We don't take a clipboard and we don't have a list of what is acceptable and what is not. Instead, we chat for an hour or so with the owner or manager and look round. It's all very informal, but it gives us an excellent idea of who would enjoy staying there. If the visit happens to be the last of the day, we sometimes stay the night. Once in the book, properties are re-inspected every few years, so that we can keep things fresh and accurate.

Feedback

In between inspections we rely on feedback from our army of readers, as well as from staff members who are encouraged to visit properties across the series. This feedback is invaluable to us and we always follow up on comments.

So do tell us whether your stay has been a joy or not, if the atmosphere was great or stuffy, the owners and staff cheery or bored. The accuracy of the book depends on what you, and our inspectors, tell us. A lot of the new entries in each edition are recommended by our readers, so keep telling us about new places you've discovered too. Please use the forms on our website at www.sawdays.co.uk, or later in this book (page 445).

However, please do not tell us if your starter was cold, or the bedside light broken. Tell the owner, immediately, and get them to do something about it. Most owners, or staff, are more than happy to correct problems and will bend over backwards to help. Far better than bottling it up and then writing to us a week later!

Subscriptions

Owners pay to appear in this guide. Their fee goes towards the high costs of inspecting, of producing an all-colour book and of maintaining our website. We only include places that we find special for one reason or another, so it is not possible for anyone to buy their way onto these pages. Nor is it possible for the owner to write their own description. We will say if the bedrooms are small, or if a main road is near. We do our best to avoid misleading people.

Disclaimer

We make no claims to pure objectivity in choosing these places. They are here simply because we like them. Our opinions and tastes are ours alone and this book is a statement of them; we hope you will share them. We have done our utmost to get our facts right but apologise unreservedly for any mistakes that may have crept in. The latest information we have about each place can be found on our website, www.sawdays.co.uk.

You should know that we don't check such things as fire alarms, swimming pool security or any other regulation with which owners of properties receiving paying guests should comply. This is the responsibility of the owners.

Photo: Domaine de Pine, entry 263

Finding the right place for you

All these places are special in one way or another. All have been visited and then written about honestly so that you can take what you want and leave the rest. Those of you who swear by Sawday's books trust our write-ups precisely because we don't have a blanket standard; we include places simply because we like them. But we all have different priorities, so do read the descriptions carefully and pick out the places where you will be comfortable. If something is particularly important to you then check when you book: a simple question or two can avoid misunderstandings.

Maps

Each property is flagged with its entry number on the maps at the front. These maps are a great starting point for planning your trip, but please don't use them as anything other than a general guide – use a decent road map for real navigation. Most places will send you detailed instructions once you have booked your stay.

Ethical Collection

We're always keen to draw attention to owners who are striving to have a positive impact on the world, so you'll notice that some entries are flagged as being part of our 'Ethical Collection'. These places are working hard to reduce their environmental footprint, making significant contributions to their local community, or are passionate about serving local or organic food. Owners

have had to fill in a very detailed questionnaire before becoming part of this Collection – read more on page 446. This doesn't mean that other places in the guide are not taking similar initiatives – many are – but we may not yet know about them.

Symbols

Below each entry you will see some symbols, which are explained at the very back of the book. They are based on the information given to us by the owners. However, things do change: bikes may be under repair or a new pool may have been put in. Please use the symbols as a guide rather than an absolute statement of fact and double-check anything that is important to you – owners occasionally bend their own rules, so it's worth asking if you may take your dog even if they don't have the symbol.

Photo: Le Sainte Beuve, entry 67

Wheelchair access – Some hotels are keen to accept wheelchair users into their hotels and have made provision for them. However, this does not mean that wheelchair users will always be met with a perfect landscape. You may encounter ramps, a shallow step, gravelled paths, alternative routes into some rooms, a bathroom (not a wet room), perhaps even a lift. In short, there may be the odd hindrance and we urge you to call and make sure you will get what you need.

Limited mobility – The limited mobility symbol shows those places where at least one bedroom and bathroom is accessible without using stairs. The symbol is designed to satisfy those who walk slowly, with difficulty, or with the aid of a stick. A wheelchair may be able to navigate some areas, but these places are not fully wheelchair friendly. If you use a chair for longer distances, but are not too bad over shorter distances, you'll probably be OK; again, please ring and ask. There may be a step or two, a bath or a shower with a tray in a cubicle, a good distance between the car park and your room, slippery flagstones or a tight turn.

Pets – Our ▙ symbol shows places which are happy to accept pets. It means they can sleep in the bedroom with you, but not on the bed. It's really important to get this one right before you arrive, as many places make you keep dogs in the car. Check carefully: Spot's emotional wellbeing may depend on it.

Owners' pets – The ⋊ symbol is given when the owners have their own pet on the premises. It may not be a cat! But it is there to warn you that you may be greeted by a dog, serenaded by a parrot, or indeed sat upon by a cat.

Photo left: Port Rive Gauche, entry 316
Photo right: Arguibel, entry 266

Types of places

Hotels can vary from huge, humming and slick to those with only a few rooms that are run by owners at their own pace. In some you may not get room service or have your bags carried in and out; in older buildings there may be no lifts. In smaller hotels there may be a fixed menu for dinner with very little choice, so if you have dishes that leave you cold, it's important to say so when you book your meal. If you decide to stay at an inn remember that they can be noisy, especially at weekends. If these things are important to you, then do check when you book.

Rooms

Bedrooms – these are described as double, twin, single, family or suite. A double may contain a bed which is anything from 135cm wide to 180cm wide. A twin will contain two single beds (usually 90cm wide). A suite will have a separate sitting area, but it may not be in a different room. Family rooms can vary in size, as can the number of beds they hold, so do ask. And do not assume that every bedroom has a TV.

Bathrooms – all bedrooms have their own bathrooms unless we say that they don't. If you have your own bathroom but you have to leave the room to get to it we describe it as 'separate'. There are very few places in the book that have shared bathrooms and they are usually reserved for members of the same party. Again, we state this clearly.

Meals

Breakfast is included in the room price unless otherwise stated.

Some places serve lunch, most do Sunday lunch (often very well-priced), the vast majority offer dinner. In some places you can content yourself with bar meals, in others you can feast on five courses. Most offer three courses for €25-€50, either table d'hôtes or à la carte. Some have tasting menus, very occasionally you eat communally. Some large hotels (and some posh private houses) will bring dinner to your room if you prefer, or let you eat in the garden by candlelight. Always ask for what you want and sometimes, magically, it happens.

Prices and minimum stays

We quote the lowest price per night for two people in low season to the highest price in high season. Only a few places have designated single rooms; if no single rooms are listed, the price we quote refers to single occupancy of a double room. In many places prices rise even higher when local events bring people flooding to the area.

The half-board price quoted is per person per night unless stated otherwise, and includes dinner, usually three courses. Mostly you're offered a table d'hôte menu. Occasionally you eat à la carte and may find some dishes carry a small supplement. There are often great deals to be had, mostly mid-week in low season.
Most small hotels do not accept one-night bookings at weekends. Small country

hotels are rarely full during the week and the weekend trade keeps them going. If you ring in March for a Saturday night in July, you won't get it. If you ring at the last moment and they have a room, you will. Some places insist on three-night stays on bank holiday weekends.

Booking and cancellation

Most places ask for a deposit at the time of booking, either by cheque or credit/debit card. If you cancel – depending on how much notice you give – you can lose all or part of this deposit unless your room is re-let.

It is reasonable for hotels to take a deposit to secure a booking; they have learnt that if they don't, the commitment of the guest wanes and they may fail to turn up.

Some cancellation policies are more stringent than others. It is also worth noting that some owners will take the money directly from your credit/debit card without contacting you to discuss it. So ask them to explain their cancellation policy clearly before booking so you understand exactly where you stand; it may well avoid a nasty surprise. And consider taking out travel insurance (with a cancellation clause) if you're concerned.

Arrivals and departures

Housekeeping is usually done by 2pm, and your room will usually be available by mid-afternoon. Normally you will have to wave goodbye to it between 10am and 11am. Sometimes one can pay to linger. Some smaller places may be closed between 3pm and 6pm, so do try and agree an arrival time in advance or you may find nobody there.

Smoking

It is now illegal to smoke in public areas and few hotels in this guide permit smoking in bedrooms. Bars, restaurants and sitting rooms have all become smoke-free; smokers must make do with the garden.

Closed

When given in months this means for the whole of the month stated. So, 'Closed: November–March' means closed from 1 November to 31 March.

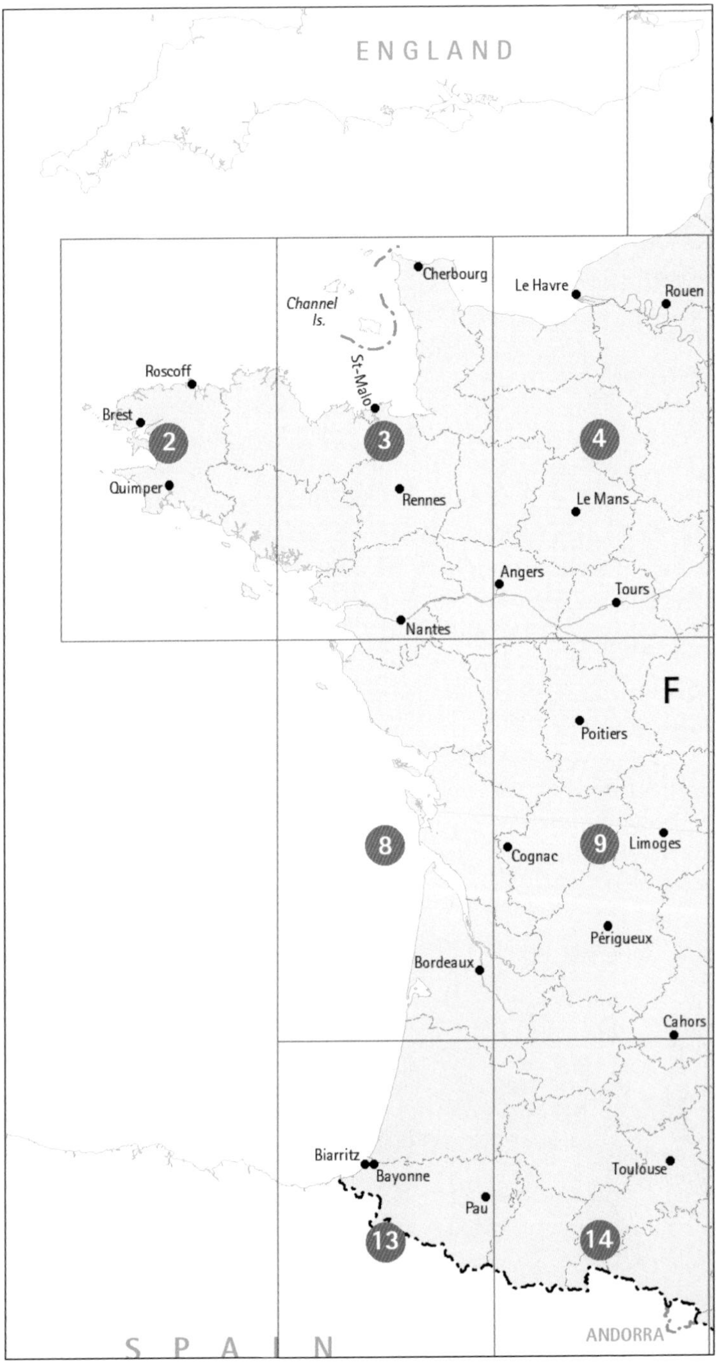

ENGLAND

Cherbourg

Le Havre

Rouen

Channel
Is.

St-Malo

Roscoff

2

3

4

Brest

Rennes

Le Mans

Quimper

Angers

Tours

Nantes

F

Poitiers

8

9

Limoges

Cognac

Périgueux

Bordeaux

Cahors

Biarritz

Toulouse

Bayonne

Pau

13

14

SPAIN

ANDORRA

©Maidenhead Cartographic, 2010

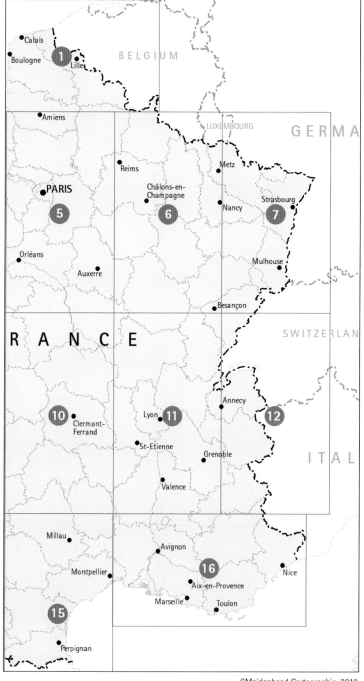

©Maidenhead Cartographic, 2010

Medical & emergency procedures

If you are an EC citizen, it's a good idea to have a European Health Insurance Card with you in case you need any medical treatment. It may not cover all the costs so you may want to take out private insurance as well.

To contact the emergency services dial 112: this is an EU-wide number and you can be confident that the person who answers the phone will speak English as well as French, and can connect you to the police, ambulance and fire/rescue services.

Other insurance

If you are driving, it is probably wise to insure the contents of your car.

Roads & driving

Current speed limits are: motorways 130 kph (80 mph), RN national trunk roads 110 kph (68 mph), other open roads 90 kph (56 mph), in towns 50 kph (30 mph). The road police are very active and can demand on-the-spot payment of fines.

Directions in towns

The French drive towards a destination and use road numbers far less than we do. Thus, to find your way à la française, know the general direction you want to go, ie the towns your route goes through, and when you see *Autres Directions* or *Toutes Directions* in a town, forget road numbers, just continue towards the place name you're heading for or through.

Photo: istock.com

Map 1   23

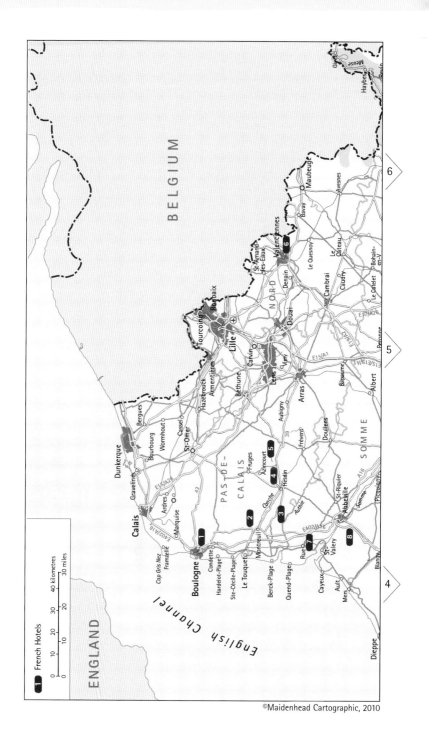

©Maidenhead Cartographic, 2010

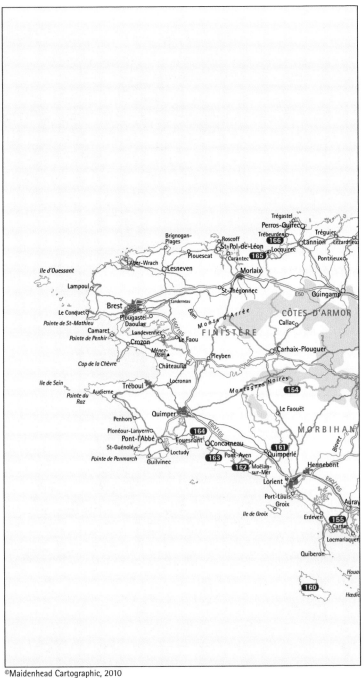

Map 3

25

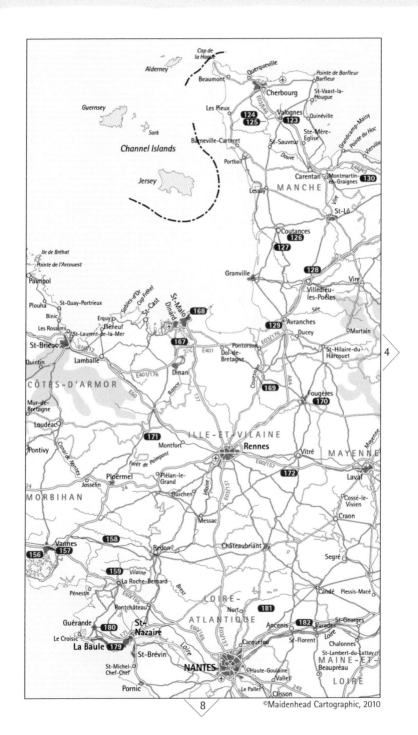

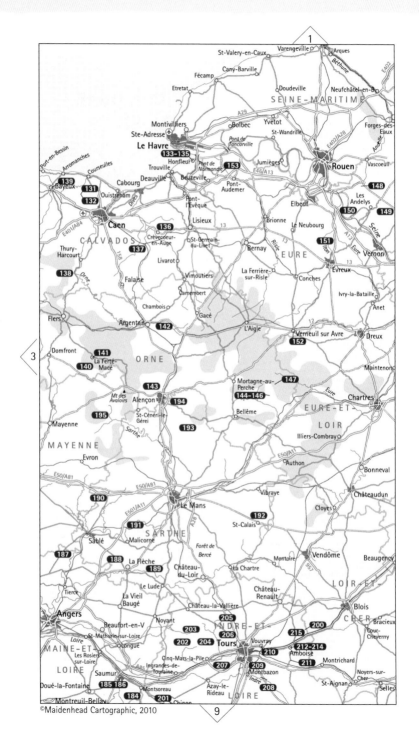

©Maidenhead Cartographic, 2010

Map 5   27

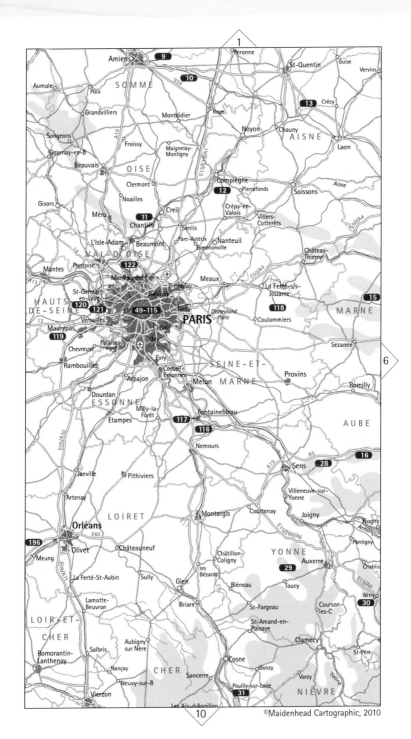

©Maidenhead Cartographic, 2010

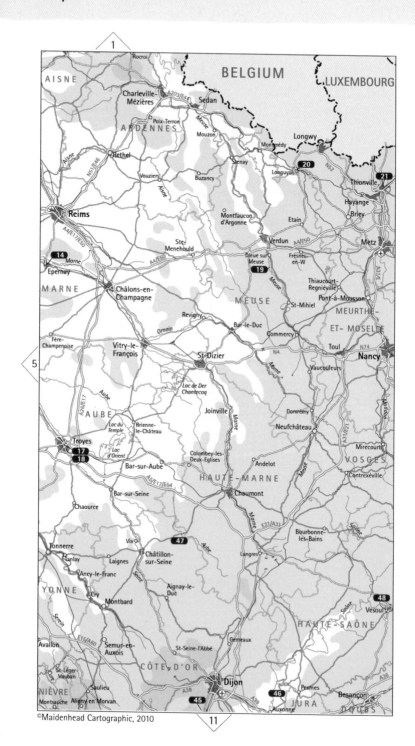

Map 7   29

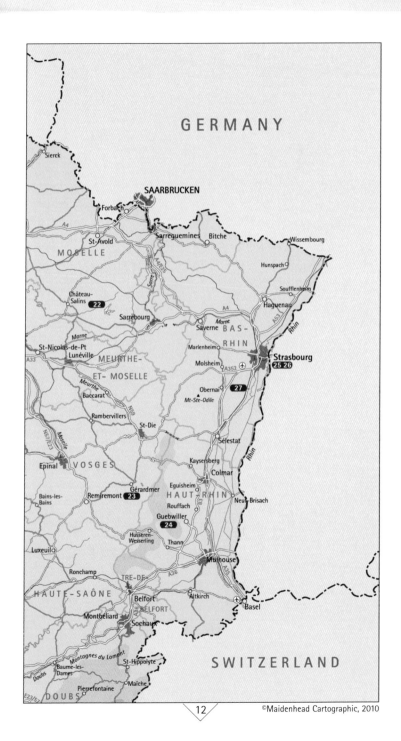

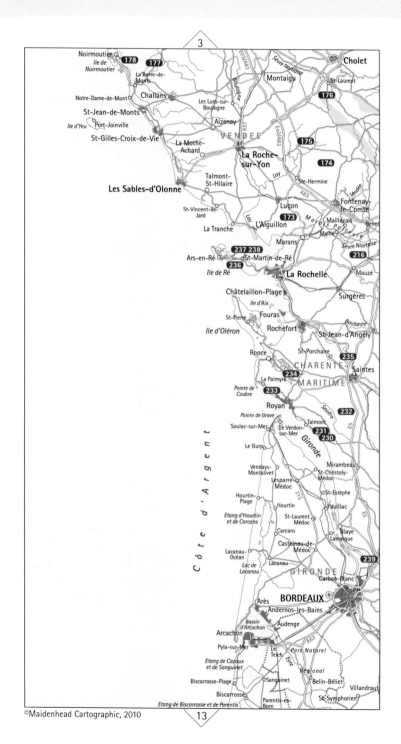

Map 9　　31

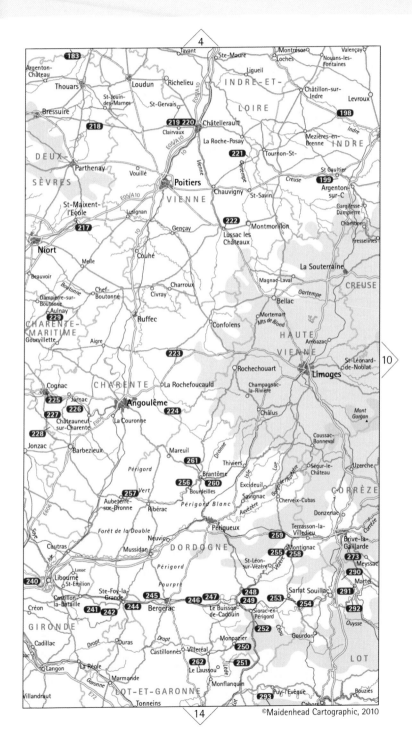

©Maidenhead Cartographic, 2010

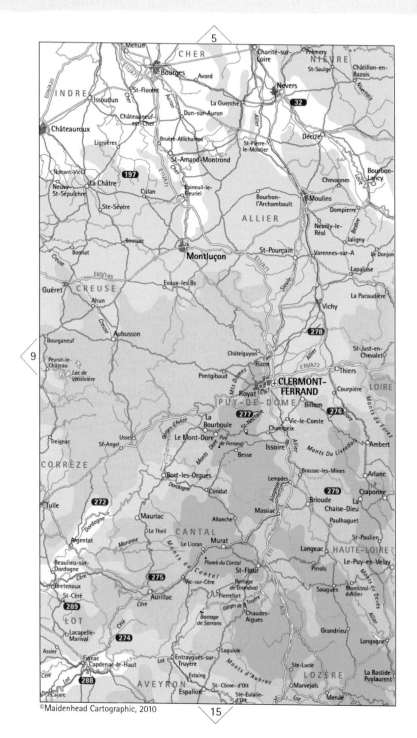

Map 11

33

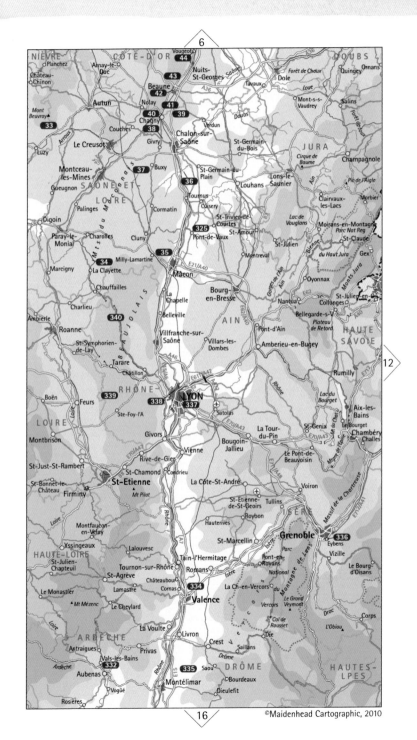

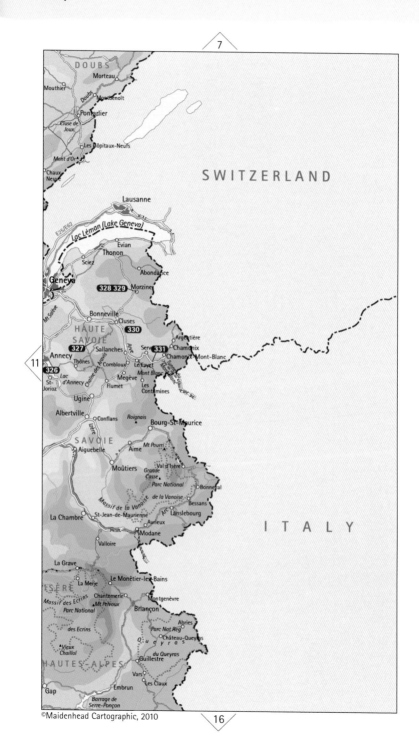

©Maidenhead Cartographic, 2010

Map 13   35

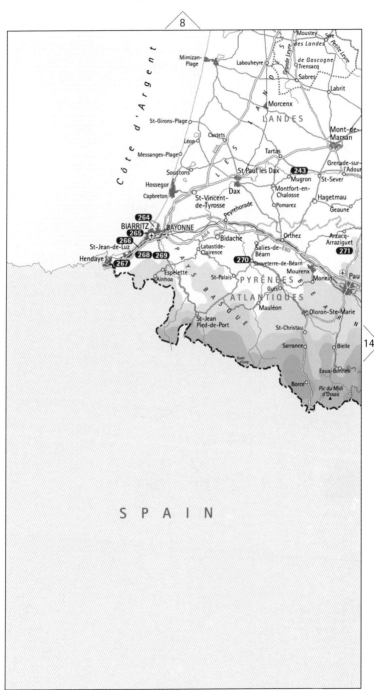

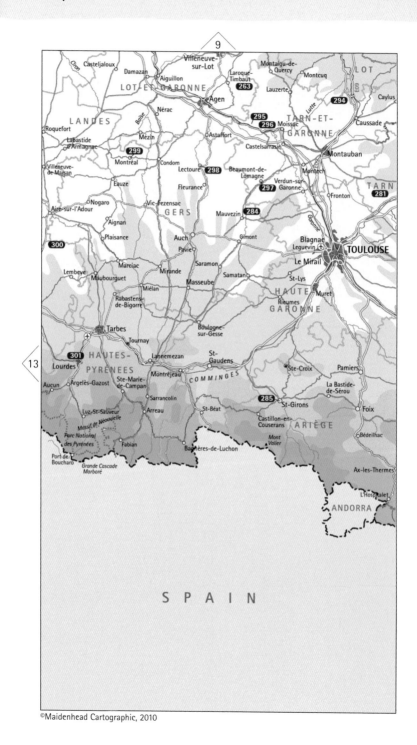

Map 15   37

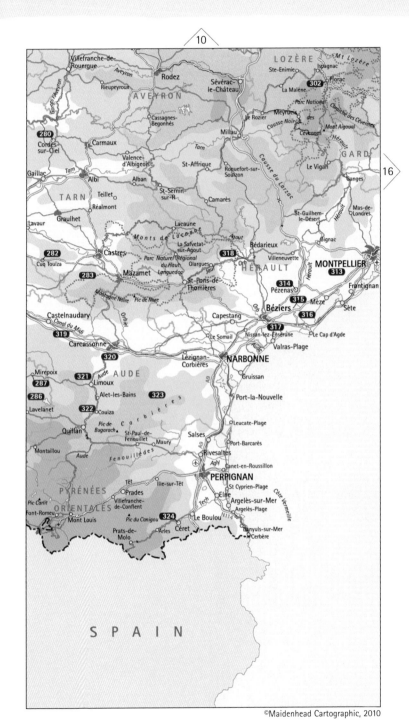

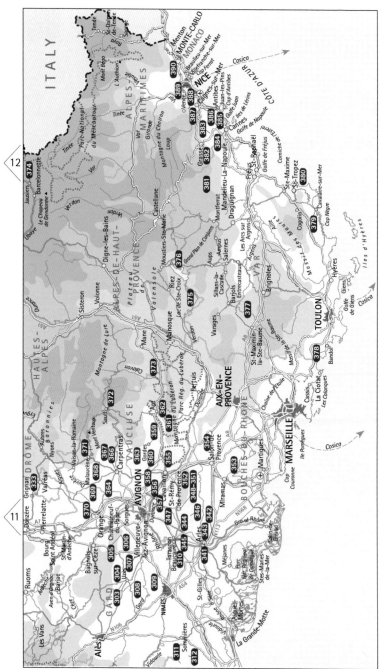

Photo: Prieuré Notre Dame d'Orsan, entry 197

The North • Picardy • Champagne – Ardenne

L'Enclos de l'Evêché

Up gracious steps you enter the 1850 mansion that almost rubs shoulders with Boulogne's basilica. All is polished parquet and hotel-like perfection, with the personal touch we so like. The charming young owners usher you up to bedrooms either on the first floor of the main house (preferable) or above the restaurant. Each one is airy, uncluttered and large, themed according to its name: 'Desvres' (a porcelain town), pretty and serene, all white painted furniture and blue toile de Jouy; 'Godefroy de Bouillon' (an 11th-century knight from Boulogne), rustic, with sand-blasted rafters and impeccable limewashed walls. Bathrooms are stocked with toiletries and towels, some have jacuzzis. Their restaurant, with a capacity for 40, now serves lunch and dinner – food takes priority here. Pascaline and Thierry serve in the evening, so another crew awaits you at breakfast, perhaps in the salon with the immense 19th-century sideboards. There's a suntrapped courtyard, a day room for TV and a choice of tables for breakfast – be as convivial or as peaceful as you like.

Price	€70–€135.	
Rooms	5: 2 doubles, 1 twin, 1 single, 1 family room for 4.	
Meals	Lunch & dinner €17.20. Restaurant closed Sun eve & Mon. Book ahead.	
Closed	Rarely.	
Directions	Follow signs to 'Vieille Ville' & car park 'Enclos de l'Evêché'. House next to car park & cathedral.	

Pascaline & Thierry Humez
6 rue de Pressy,
62200 Boulogne sur Mer, Pas-de-Calais
Tel   +33 (0)3 91 90 05 90
Email   contact@enclosdeleveche.com
Web   www.enclosdeleveche.com

Auberge d'Inxent

And, the lucky winner is… some people who collect bottle caps do win prizes. A sommelier in a restaurant in Lille, Jean-Marc won a Perrier contest on the luck of a draw. Off he tripped with his young wife and two children to a most emerald green valley and claimed a whitewashed, geranium-spilled, 18th-century country inn. Order a trout on their vine-covered terrace and back comes a live one in a bucket from their wonderful trout farm across the road by the river Course. Needless to say Jean-Marc's exceptional, reasonably priced wine list and creative use of local produce should lead to a prolonged stay (and the nearby ramparts of Montreuil Sur Mer are worth a visit). Inside all is wonky wooden beams, low ceilings, a battery of copper pans behind the original zinc countertop, red-checked tablecloths and the warmth and cosiness of a modest country kitchen with open fires on chilly days. The beamed-ceiling bedrooms have been furnished with cherrywood copies of antiques and some walls papered to look ragged; others wear old-fashioned stripes; all are comfortable.

Price	€68–€75.
Rooms	5: 3 doubles, 2 twins.
Meals	Breakfast €9.50. Lunch & dinner €16–€39. Restaurant closed same dates as hotel.
Closed	Wednesday; Tuesday only in July & August; 20 December–30 January; 1st week in July.
Directions	From Boulogne N1 for Samer. After Samer at 5km dir. Bernieulles, Beussent, Inxent.

	Laurence & Jean-Marc Six
	318 rue de la Vallée de la Course,
	62170 Inxent, Pas-de-Calais
Tel	+33 (0)3 21 90 71 19
Email	auberge.inxent@wanadoo.fr

Le Manoir

Wrought-iron gates, a gravel drive, a spreading lime and afternoon tea on the terrace: heaven. Jennifer (English) and Helmut (German) run their 18th-century manor house with a natural sense of fun and a fabulous eye for detail. There's space, too, in three reception rooms, big gracious bedrooms and 12 hectares of garden, orchard, potager and field; you can be as private or as sociable as you like. The salons exude an English country-house feel with their deep sofas and cream walls; the dining room, bathed in light from tall windows and furnished with round tables, is a perfect room for perfect breakfasts. As for the bedrooms, all are civilised spaces of subtle lighting and soft carpeting, delicious beds and dreamy colours, polished antiques and pretty porcelain. Throw open your elegant windows and the views – of manicured lawns, gravelled paths, dappled alleyways and countryside – will put a big smile on your face. No evening meals at Le Manoir but there's a wonderful restaurant on the edge of the village, and more in Montreuil. Beyond: beaches, riverside walks and birdwatching in abundance.

Price	€140–€150.
Rooms	4: 3 doubles, 1 twin.
Meals	Breakfast €10.
	Restaurants in village & Montreuil.
Closed	2 weeks in June; Christmas.
Directions	From A16 exit 25 for N939 Arras & Hesdin. Exit for Campagne les Hesdin. Look for Gouy St André; right at main x-roads; 1st iron gate on left.

Jennifer & Helmut Gorlich
34 rue Maresquel,
62870 Gouy St André, Pas-de-Calais

Tel	+33 (0)3 21 90 47 22
Email	helmut.gorlich@wanadoo.fr
Web	www.lemanoir-france.com

Les Trois Fontaines

Here is a long, low, plain Scandinavian style building dressed up to look like a typical French inn – and succeeding. It fits into the little market town (wonderful market on Thursday mornings) as if it had always been there. Arnaud Descamps is friendly and anxious to please. He took over in 1999 and concentrates on the quality of the food – only fresh produce – served in his panelled, chequer-floored dining room: the short menu changes every day and there's a special one for children. Bedrooms are in separate buildings overlooking the fine garden: six are brand new and are no-frills minimalist; ten are traditional French with quiet wallpapers and candlewick bedcovers. In the new wing, rooms are very comfortable, simply and decently clad with good quality pine, dark blue carpet, good lighting, pristine bed linen. All are sparkling clean and each room has its own table and chairs for summer breakfasts facing the garden. It is, indeed, a very typical small French hotel; it is quiet, good value and well placed for cross-channel visitors as well as the great beaches of Le Touquet and Berck.

Price	€59-€72.
Rooms	16 doubles.
Meals	Breakfast €7.
	Lunch & dinner €19-€35.
Closed	20 December-5 January.
Directions	Calais to Arras; after Montreuil, N39 for Hesdin. Follow signs to Marconne centre; hotel opp. the town hall.

	Arnaud Descamps
	16 rue d'Abbeville,
	62140 Marconne Hesdin, Pas-de-Calais
Tel	+33 (0)3 21 86 81 65
Email	hotel.3fontaines@wanadoo.fr
Web	www.hotel-les3fontaines.com

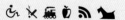

La Cour de Rémi

A raved-about bistro, seven delicious bedrooms, a romantic treehouse, a fine and tranquil domaine – such are the ingredients for a very spoiling weekend. In the expert hands of Sébastien these terracotta-roofed farm buildings have become informally but fabulously chic. A manger skirts the old stables, a glassed-over brick well glows softly in the three-tier former saddlery, floor-to-ceiling glass replaces high barn doors, grain storage attics have become vast beamed spaces with views to both sides, one suite has a jacuzzi, another has two baths side by side… but the cherry on top is surely the treehouse, wrapped spectacularly around a venerable sycamore four metres above ground, with a big decked balcony under the leaves. Breakfast can be delivered to your door as you consider your options: abbeys, châteaux, gardens, WWI sites, a bike ride, seal-spotting by the Somme. Whether you do all of these things or nothing at all, make sure you're back for Sébastien's 'râbles de lapin' or 'colvert rôti', served in the designer-chic, bistro-friendly dining room. La Cour de Rémi is sublime.

Price	€80-€95. Suites €140. Treehouse €160.
Rooms	8: 4 doubles, 3 suites, 1 treehouse.
Meals	Breakfast €10. Dinner €29. Wine €18-€100.
Closed	Christmas.
Directions	From A16 exit 25, D303 dir. Montreuil for 4km; right onto D939 dir. Hesdin & St Pol sur Ternoise; 22km, left onto D98 to Bermicourt; right in village. Signed.

Sébastien de la Borde
1 rue Baillet, 62130 Bermicourt,
Pas-de-Calais

Tel   +33 (0)3 21 03 33 33
Email   sebastien@lacourderemi.com
Web   www.lacourderemi.com

Auberge du Bon Fermier

Forget your high heels, for the cobblestones in the flowered courtyard continue right into the bar and restaurant of this 16th-century auberge. It is a maze of passageways, burnished beams and tiny staircases. A copper-bellied washbasin greets you at the top of the stairs leading to the rooms. Looking down from a glassed-in corridor, you can almost hear the clatter of hooves arriving in the courtyard, now a quiet terrace for afternoon tea and snacks. The rooms are all different, one with tapestried curtains and walls, another with red bricks and wooden struts, some not too well lit, all with baths and bathrobes. There are also two larger, lighter ground-floor rooms with post-modern lamps and tables. Downstairs, where a suit of armour guards a wooden reception dais, comes to life in the evenings when the main restaurant is lit by candles. The passengers jostling between Paris and Brussels were probably delighted to have been delayed in this bustling staging inn. Monsieur Beine takes enormous trouble to create new menus with his chef and most diners would raise a glass and make a toast in his direction.

Price	€110–€130. Singles €85–€105.
Rooms	16: 14 doubles, 2 singles.
Meals	Breakfast €9.50.
	Lunch & dinner €26–€47.
Closed	24 December.
Directions	From Cambrai A2 for Brussels, exit Valenciennes centre. Do not get off autoroute before. Continue for Valenciennes centre; signed.

	M. Beine
	64 rue de Famars,
	59300 Valenciennes, Nord
Tel	+33 (0)3 27 46 68 25
Email	beinethierry@hotmail.com
Web	www.bonfermier.com

Château de Noyelles

Past ornate iron gates in the village of Noyelles, at the head of the Baie de Somme, a 19th-century château – a pretty gâteau of layered peach and white in splendid gardens. Beyond, a seven-acre landscaped park with box-hedged orchards, neat lawns, rose beds and a terrace scattered with smart parasols. Rooms, some with suite-style connecting doors, are spread spaciously over three floors, with terraces for those on the first. Snug tower rooms on the third flaunt jaunty angles. Pine floors provide funky bases for claw-foot baths. Whites, pearly greys, oyster greens, hazy blues and sand two-toned paintwork and panelling make for sober, sophisticated and TV-free spaces; Chinese antiques and objects d'art – an opium pipe here, a courtesan's fan there – provide delightful detail. Three airy reception rooms and two drawing rooms please the eye with their considered variety: a Starck chair slipped into the classic, plush décor; deep crimson oh-so-comfy sofas set before a handsome marble fireplace. Fabulous seafood and lots to do locally tops everything off perfectly; easy to ignore the rush-hour traffic.

Price	€95–€185. Suites €175–€265.
Rooms	8: 3 doubles, 3 twins/doubles, 2 suites (some interconnect).
Meals	Breakfast €14. Picnic available. Dinner €30, book ahead. Wine €16–€40.
Closed	Never.
Directions	From Calais A16 exit 24 for Saint Valéry sur Somme & Le Crotoy; at r'bout D1001 for Abbeville & Forest Montiers; in Nouvion, right onto D111, 5km to village. Château in centre behind high iron gates.

François & Ludivine Blard
30 rue Maréchal Foch,
80860 Noyelles sur Mer, Somme

Tel	+33 (0)3 22 23 68 70
Email	info@chateaudenoyelles.com
Web	www.chateaudenoyelles.com

Château de Béhen

Horsey folk and families will be in clover – there are donkeys to stroke, bicycles to hire and ponies to ride. Surrounded by wooded parkland, the red-brick building with limestone trim started life as a summer residence, later its ground floor was extended. In the 1950s the Cuveliers moved in, adding paddocks and a pond for swans, deeply traditional decoration with strong colours and ornate oh-so-French flourishes. Today there are seven large bedrooms for guests, with solid oak floors and rugs, bedspreads plain or toile de Jouy, and furniture in Louis XV style. Two-tone panelling graces the first-floor rooms while those above have sloping ceilings and a beam or two. Bathrooms are hotel-perfect with double basins of mottled marble. Norbert-André, who managed stud pacers in Australia, has come home to cook; he does a grand job. Four-course table d'hôtes, at single tables if preferred, may include salt-marsh lamb or fish in cream sauce. Cheeses are local, vegetables are just-picked, banquets can be arranged. Lovely friendly people, perfect peace and 15 horses to ride.

Price	€115–€160.
	Suites & family rooms €168–€218.
Rooms	7: 2 doubles, 1 twin, 1 suite for 2,
	1 suite for 4, 2 family rooms for 4.
Meals	Dinner with wine, from €41;
	book 2 days ahead.
Closed	Rarely.
Directions	Calais A16 to Abbeville exit 23; A28 to
	Rouen. Exit 3 Monts Caubert to D928;
	800m, right to Béhen. Behind church,
	200m beyond, on right.

	Cuvelier Family
	8 rue du Château,
	80870 Béhen, Somme
Tel	+33 (0)3 22 31 58 30
Email	norbert-andre@cuvelier.com
Web	www.chateau-de-behen.com

Le Macassar

Le Macassar is named after the rare ebony used in the drawing room panelling – one exquisite example of too many to mention! This gem of a 19th-century townhouse was restyled in the Twenties and Thirties to please a pretty young wife – but it's more 'femme fatale' than blushing belle. Suave bathrooms, extra fine bed linen, feather duvets – only the best. The master suite is the epitome of Art Deco glamour, the ash and bird's-eye maple furniture set off by turquoise velvet walls, a carved stone fireplace and fine contemporary art. Now, under sloping beams, there is a wonderfully intimate and sophisticated new room decked in taupe, cocoa and pale blue, its exotic bathroom accessed through an ornate Moorish door. Downstairs are luxurious corners in which to lounge rakishly and admire the gorgeously varied art, the books and the glassware, the textures and the tones. Outside: an Italianate courtyard, a splashing fountain, a haze of lavender. Splendid breakfasts and aperitifs are included in the price, the hosts are truly charming and Amiens is close. An oasis of elegance and calm and in the heart of bustling Corbie.

Price	€175. Suites €195–€250.
Rooms	6: 1 double, 1 twin, 4 suites.
Meals	Hosted dinner with wine, €50 (Sundays only). Groups on request.
Closed	Rarely.
Directions	A16 exit 20 Amiens Nord; after tollgate, right at r'bout onto ring road (Rocade). Exit 36a Corbie; follow signs to Corbie 'centre ville'. On main square.

Miguel de Lemos
8 place de la République,
80800 Corbie, Somme

Tel	+33 (0)3 22 48 40 04
Email	info@lemacassar.com
Web	www.lemacassar.com

Entry 9   Map 5

Château d'Omiécourt

On a working estate, Omiécourt is a proudly grand 19th-century château and elegant family home (the Thézys have four children, mostly grown now), with tall slender windows and some really old trees. Friendly if formal, communicative and smiling, your hosts have worked hugely to restore their inheritance and create gracious French château guest rooms, each with an ornate fireplace and flooded with light. The 1900 room has a sweep of polished floor and a turn-of-the-century bed, the more modern Chambre des Ormieux sits brightly under the eaves in a separate 'maison'. Near the two pools (one outdoor, one in), it comes with a super new blue and white tiled bathroom and a guest kitchen on the ground floor. Enjoy a buffet supper in your room one night – aperitifs, candlelight, champagne – and a Michelin-starred dinner in Roye the next. Breakfast is continental and something of a feast. There are cookery classes for groups of six to ten, table football and table tennis for the children, and a boutique of pretty things. A house of goodwill, deeply traditional, naturally hospitable.

Price	€95. Apartment €125. Extra bed €20–€25.
Rooms	5: 2 doubles, 1 suite for 3, 2 family rooms.
Meals	Light supper in rooms, €10–€15. Restaurants 12km.
Closed	Rarely.
Directions	From A1 south for Paris; exit 13 onto N29 for St Quentin; in Villers Carbonnel right at lights onto N17 for 9km to Omiécourt; right in village, château on right.

Dominique & Véronique de Thézy
80320 Omiécourt, Somme

Tel	+33 (0)3 22 83 01 75
Email	contact@chateau-omiecourt.com
Web	www.chateau-omiecourt.com

Ferme de la Canardière

Forty kilometres north of Paris sits a long house of classic 18th-century stamp. Sabine, smiling and generous, is a professional cook and has just opened this immaculate guest house, its French windows gazing down the valley. Gleaming polished limestone floors lead to a light, airy sitting room with squashy leather sofas and huge stone fireplace. Tucked privately in one corner, light bouncing from creamy walls, are two big bright bedrooms that lead directly onto a terrace, narrow lawn and pool. A traditional draped bedhead in pretty putty and white ciel-de-lit is partnered by splendid horsey curtains and posters echoing equestrian glories. The twin – rich blue bedcovers, antique cherrywood tables – feels elegantly restrained and formal. Bathrooms tiled from top to bottom in blue and white are sybaritic. In the cook's kitchen, where Sabine produces her wonderful homemade breakfasts (ingredients from the family's cereal farm), you may also book into a cookery master class. This is deep in the heart of French racing country: who knows, you may get an insider tip for the French Derby. *No credit cards.*

Price	€150. Singles €130. Extra bed €25.
Rooms	2: 1 double, 1 twin.
Meals	Hosted dinner, 4 courses with wine, €30. Restaurants 10-minute walk.
Closed	Never.
Directions	From Chantilly N16 for Creil. Leaving Chantilly, cross bridge, 1st left opp. 'Arc de Triomphe' on Rue Guilleminot to viaduct; straight on, house on right above road.

Sabine Choain
20 rue du Viaduc,
60500 Gouvieux Chantilly, Oise
Tel   +33 (0)3 44 62 00 96
Email   contact@fermecanardiere.com
Web   www.fermecanardiere.com

Auberge à la Bonne Idée

Deep in the forest, the walled village is worth a visit and the Bonne Idée is where Parisiens and Belgians come to escape the excitement, knowing they will find a sound welcome, country peace and superb food. The inn, once a woodcutters' dive, still has masses of old timber and tiling in what could be called romantic-rustic style. Start with a drink by the fire in the bar, move to an elegant table in the dining room where bread warms by the great fire, and delve into a fine, gourmet meal. The emphasis is on food here – and in summer there's a terrace and space for children to play. Bedrooms, four in the main house, the rest in the converted stables, some still in their brown 70s garb, are gradually being renovated by the owners in a bright, stylish contemporary fashion, nicely adapted to the fabulous hulk of the building. A favourite would be the ochre-orange room with its mushroom, beige and white contrasting bedding and fine brick-coloured bathroom. Ideal for walking, cycling, riding and relaxing; Compiègne and the great castle of Pierrefonds are close.

Price	€80–€90. Apartments €105–€155.
Rooms	23: 20 doubles, 3 apartments for 2-4 (without kitchen).
Meals	Breakfast €12. Lunch & dinner €31–€75. Restaurant closed Sunday eve & Mondays in winter.
Closed	3 January-3 February 2010.
Directions	A1 exit 9 Verberie & Compiègne. Through Verberie, left on D332 for Compiègne for 5km; right on D85 for St Jean aux Bois.

Yves Giustiniani
3 rue des Meuniers,
60350 Saint Jean aux Bois, Oise

Tel	+33 (0)3 44 42 84 09
Email	a-la-bonne-idee.auberge@wanadoo.fr
Web	www.a-la-bonne-idee.fr

Domaine Le Parc

Down a sweeping horse-chestnut lined drive between tailored lawns you approach this 18th-century mansion built on castle foundations. The river Oise slides gently by. There are ten lawned and tree'd acres here, and at the back, a brick-walled belvedere terrace with soaring views over woodland, untamed countryside and river. Inside, wander at will – between a gracefully decorated dining room, breakfast room and library and a sitting room with gorgeous soft sofas. Up the spiral oak staircase are the bedrooms, classically and elegantly decorated, some with more of those views. Strong colours with floral fabrics stand out against striped or patterned fabric walls, luxurious bathrooms have Balneo baths; clusters of antique bottles on the window ledges and an antique hobby horse add whimsical touches to a formal décor. Dutch Jos has previously won stars for his cooking, Anne is a former maître d'hotel, both are consummate, multi-lingual hosts, and you dine on the terrace in summer. The local town is no picture but beyond are fortified churches and great Gothic cathedrals. *No credit cards.*

Price	€75–€95.
Rooms	5: 3 doubles, 2 twins.
Meals	Dinner €35.
Closed	20 December–5 January.
Directions	Between Saint-Quentin and Laon; A26 exit 12; in Dainzy 2nd right.

Jos & Anne Bergman
Rue de Quesny,
02800 Danizy, Aisne

Tel   +33 (0)3 23 56 55 23
Email   leparc.bergman@wanadoo.fr
Web   www.domaineleparc.com

La Villa Eugène

Surrounded by the 19th-century follies that gave the street its nickname – 'Faubourg de la Folie' – the former house of champagne magnate Eugène Mercier still feels remarkably like a family home. Indeed, the old family photos still line the staircase and the staff can tell you exactly which room belonged to whom. Then there's the décor, an enticing balance of 19th-century tradition and contemporary touches: walls the colour of whipped-cream, furniture Louis XVI or 'colonial' (dark wood and wicker), soft yielding curtains, gracious parquet floors. There's modernity in flat-screens and WiFi, and pampering in the bathrooms, all of which are a good size, with fluffy towels and luxurious products by Damana. The buffet breakfast is an array of homemade cakes, tarts, yogurts and breads, served either in the light-filled conservatory – whose mosaic floor has been lovingly restored – or in the garden, with its heated summer pool, colourful beds and resident rabbits hopping on the lawn. A wonderful launch pad for the three major Routes de Champagne – and 30 minutes from Reims and its mesmerising cathedral.

Price	€129–€344. Extra bed €25.
Rooms	15: 6 doubles, 2 twins, 7 suites.
Meals	Breakfast €17. Restaurants 2km.
Closed	Rarely.
Directions	From Paris, take A4 east, follow signs to Epernay.

Agnès Rafik
82-84 avenue de Champagne,
51200 Epernay, Marne

Tel	+33 (0)3 26 32 44 76
Email	info@villa-eugene.com
Web	www.villa-eugene.com

Château d'Etoges

Louis XIV was impressed by the gardens. Etoges, used as a stopover by French kings on journeys east, is a moated 17th-century château surrounded by fountain'd parkland, later transformed into a hotel by the family who have lived here for generations. We find it charming, from the oh-so-French rooms to the elegant food to the delicious fabrics and linen. Bedrooms glow with antiques and fresh flowers, some have four-posters and two have mezzanine beds over bathrooms – once for servants, now delightful for children. New is the handsome restaurant created from the Orangerie, with a majestic limestone fireplace and deep orange curtains. If you fancy breakfast in bed, it is brought to your lace-covered table: breads, croissants, jams, fruit. If you prefer to breakfast downstairs, take your pick from the buffet and drift onto the terrace. This intimate hotel is right in the middle of champagne tasting country; easy too for cycling and fishing, with a well-stocked lake a ten-minute drive. Return for a gentle paddle round the moat and an ayurvedic massage in the spa. Special.

Price	€140–€200. Suites €300.
Rooms	28: 26 twins/doubles, 2 suites.
Meals	Breakfast €14. Lunch & dinner €35–€75. Wine €20–€200. Children's meals €18.
Closed	24 January–18 February.
Directions	From Paris, A4 exit 18 at Ferté sous Jouarre, follow signs for Chalons en Champagne. In centre of Etoges.

	Mme Filliette-Neuville
	4 rue Richebourg,
	51270 Etoges, Marne
Tel	+33 (0)3 26 59 30 08
Email	contact@etoges.com
Web	www.etoges.com

Domaine du Moulin d'Eguebaude

The secluded old buildings house two owner-families, a restaurant, several guest rooms and 15 tons of live fish. Fishing folk gather on Sundays to catch trout in the spring water that feeds the ponds; groups come for speciality lunches. Four-course meals may include watercress soup, steamed trout with cider, a selection of local cheeses and cinnamon custard. For breakfast around the large table there are brioches, baguettes, croissants, yogurt, cottage cheese, fruit salad, cereals, apple juice and their own jams and honey. Created from an old mill 40 years ago, the compact bedrooms under the eaves are small-windowed, simply furnished and prettily decorated in rustic or 'grandmother' style. Further rooms in the cottage across the driveway have been newly built in the regional half-timbered style. At one end of their shop – packed with cottage-industry goodies (charcuterie, honey, jams, wine and champagnes) is a wide floor of thick glass under which immense fish can be seen swimming to and fro between the water tanks. Wonderful service and good English spoken. *No credit cards.*

Price	€61–€74.
Rooms	6: 2 doubles, 1 twin, 2 family rooms, 1 triple.
Meals	Dinner with wine, €24.
Closed	Christmas, New Year & occasionally.
Directions	From Paris A5 exit 19 on N60 to Estissac; right on to Rue Pierre Brossolette; mill at end of lane, 1km.

Ethical Collection: Food.
See page 446 for details

Alexandre & Sandrine Mesley
36 rue Pierre Brossolette,
10190 Estissac, Aube

Tel   +33 (0)3 25 40 42 18
Email   eguebaude@aol.com

Hôtel Champ des Oiseaux

Only the Museum of Modern Art stands between the cathedral and this amazingly pure group of 15th-century houses in the centre of lovely, unsung Troyes. The dazzling timbers, beams and rafters inside and out, the simplicity of the beautifully jointed stone paving, the wooden floors, the softly luminous natural materials, all will seduce you. The owners had their restoration done by craftsmen who knew the ancestral methods and made it look 'as good as 1460 new'. Corridors twist around the creeper-climbed courtyard and the little internal garden, staircases change their minds, the place is alive with its centuries. Each bedroom has a personality, some soberly sandy and brown, others frivolously floral; they vary in size and status but all are warmly discreet in their luxury and good furniture. Bathrooms are perfect modern boudoirs. The unexpected salon, a long, white barrel vault of ancient stones, the original stonemason's craft lovingly revealed, was once a cellar, and the courtyard is delightful for breakfast. The Boisseau family can be justifiably proud of their contribution to medieval Troyes.

Price	€135–€175. Suites €230.
Rooms	12: 9 twins/doubles, 3 suites for 2-3.
Meals	Breakfast €17. Restaurants nearby.
Closed	Never.
Directions	In centre of Troyes, very close to cathedral.

	Mme Boisseau
	20 rue Linard Gonthier,
	10000 Troyes, Aube
Tel	+33 (0)3 25 80 58 50
Email	message@champdesoiseaux.com
Web	www.champdesoiseaux.com

La Maison de Rhodes

An exceptional find, a 16th-century timber-framed mansion that once belonged to the Templars. Monsieur Thierry's breathtaking renovation has brought a clean contemporary style to ancient bricks and mortar. Highlights include an interior courtyard of cobble and grass and heavy wooden doors under the coachman's porch that give onto the street. The house sits plumb in the old quarter of Troyes, on the doorstep of the cathedral. Bedrooms are bona fide jaw-droppers – expect the best in minimalist luxury. Huge beds are dressed in white linen, ancient beams straddle the ceilings. Walls are either exposed rough stone, or smooth limestone, or a clever mix. Bathrooms, too, are outstanding; most are enormous and have terracotta floors, big bath tubs, fluffy robes. Views are to the cathedral spires, the courtyard or the formal gardens of the Museum of Modern Art, directly opposite. A perfect blend of old and new, an exhilarating architectural landscape. Troyes is full of wonders, though the bibulous may be tempted to venture beyond the city walls. The region is quite well-known for its local tipple – champagne.

Price	€160–€205. Suites €220–€255.
Rooms	11: 8 doubles, 3 suites for 2-4.
Meals	Breakfast €17. Dinner €30–€50. Restaurant closed Sundays.
Closed	Never.
Directions	In centre of Troyes, at the foot of the cathedral.

Thierry Carcassin
18 rue Linard-Gonthier,
10000 Troyes, Aube
Tel +33 (0)3 25 43 11 11
Email message@maisonderhodes.com
Web www.maisonderhodes.com

Lorraine • Alsace

Hostellerie du Château des Monthairons

If you seek peace and quiet in lovely large grounds, or a spot of fishing maybe – the river Meuse meanders through – this would be a fair choice. Monthairons served as an American military hospital in the First World War and become a base for the Germans in the Second. It is now run by three offshoots of the Thouvenin family, who did a major refurbishment in the Eighties. One couple looks after the restaurant and food, the other two are in charge of the hotel and grounds. Because of this personal touch, there's a homely feel in spite of the proportions. Bedrooms are smart, classic French and come in all sizes, some with duplex suites ideal for families; we'd love a room facing the park. The restaurant is elegant and full of flowers, a place for a fancy dinner not a quick bite. You can swim and canoe here, too; a former owner diverted the river especially and the neighbouring meadow is now known as the 'old river'. Organised actvities? They do several packages, put on introductions to fly-fishing, rides in a horse-drawn carriages, visits to Verdun. Return to be spoiled in the spa.

Price	€95–€180. Duplexes & suites €150–€180. Apts €230–€320.
Rooms	25: 12 doubles, 6 twins, 5 duplexes for 2-4, 2 apartments for 2-4.
Meals	Breakfast €14–€15. Lunch €25, weekdays only. Dinner €40–€92.
Closed	January–11 February.
Directions	From Paris A4 exit 30 Voie Sacrée; dir. St Mihiel until Lemmes. At end of Lemmes, last road on left. Cont. to Ancemont; at last x-roads right to the château.

Mme Pierrat
26 rue de Verdun, Le Petit Monthairon,
55320 Les Monthairons, Meuse

Tel	+33 (0)3 29 87 78 55
Email	accueil@chateaudesmonthairons.fr
Web	www.chateaudesmonthairons.fr

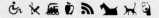

Le Mas & La Lorraine

Not a luxurious address – as is seen in the price – but a proud one, and solidly French. The hotel is a nostalgic reminder of a lost era – the great days of steam. It stands across the square from the station and was built in 1925; the Italian Express stopped here. These days it is more of a restaurant-with-rooms, the emphasis clearly on the menus. Owner chef Gérard Tisserant is a fine old gentleman, proud of a lifetime of restaurant catering in fine food, receptions and continuing culinary traditions, who still runs his kitchens and staff 'l'ancienne'. Course after course flies at you: coquilles Saint Jacques, foie gras, fillet de veau, gratin d'ananas à la crème de coco, in a large restaurant that is warmly inviting and where an open fire roars in winter. Every now and then live music nights are held and you dine to the accompaniment of classical guitar or jazz piano. Downstairs: off-white armchairs and huge bay windows in the sitting room; upstairs, bedrooms that are clean, decent and functional, suitable for a stopover. Belgium and Luxembourg are close – go by train!

Price	€64–€73.
Rooms	14: 5 doubles, 6 twins, 2 family rooms for 4, 1 triple.
Meals	Breakfast €8. Lunch & dinner €23–€69.
Closed	January.
Directions	From A4, exit 30 onto D603 then D618 to Longuyon. Hotel opposite railway station.

	Gérard Tisserant
	65 rue Augistrou,
	54260 Longuyon, Meurthe-et-Moselle
Tel	+33 (0)3 82 26 50 07
Email	mas.lorraine@wanadoo.fr
Web	www.lorraineetmas.com

L'Horizon

The house is only 50 years old but its arcading anchors it and Virginia has crept all over it, clothing its façade in lively warm character. Here is comfortable living in graceful surroundings, as in an elegant private house. A huge terrace envelops the ground floor; from here, from the restaurant (smart décor, excellent food) and from some of the balcony rooms on the first floor you have plunging views over Thionville and an astounding, glittering cityscape at night. By day the town is less pretty. Despite the surprising hall with its marbled flooring and glamorous tented ceiling, the bedrooms are classic French chic (though carpets may be a little worn here and there and some rooms are smaller than others). Bathrooms border on the luxurious, some are positively glamorous. Above all, you will warm to your charming hosts. Monsieur is passionate about Second World War history: the Maginot Line is all around and Thionville is on the Liberty Road that is marked every kilometre from Cherbourg to Bastogne. He speaks good English, is fascinating on the subject and we highly recommend his tours.

Price	€98–€145.
Rooms	12 doubles.
Meals	Breakfast €11. Lunch & dinner €39–€53. Restaurant closed Saturdays & Monday lunchtimes.
Closed	January.
Directions	From A31 exit 40 Thionville. Follow signs for Bel Air Hospital north of town. At hospital left up hill leaving town. Hotel 400m on left.

Jean-Pascal & Anne-Marie Speck
50 route du Crève-Cœur,
57100 Thionville, Moselle

Tel	+33 (0)3 82 88 53 65
Email	hotel@lhorizon.fr
Web	www.lhorizon.fr

Château d'Alteville

Exploring distance from Strasbourg, Nancy, Metz, a house with more than a whiff of history. The château was built for one of Napoleon's generals, and the two paintings that hang in the Louis XVI salon were gifts from the Emperor. Monsieur's family has farmed here for five generations; now he and Agnieszka welcome guests with huge kindness. Bedrooms are authentically French and solidly traditional, with carved armoires, Voltaire armchairs, perhaps a draped bedhead or a small chandelier. Parkland views float in through the windows; bathrooms are functional but adequate. Downstairs is more stylish: a library/billiard room, a multi-fenestrated salon room hung with portraits and a dining room where splendid dinners are served by candlelight in the company of your lively, interesting hosts. Recline on the soundproofed terrace at the back and gaze on the château-esque grounds, or pull on your hiking boots and follow your nose though woodland, circumnavigating the odd lake. Madame, soul of the house, cooks with skill and fills the place with flowers. Special, and well-priced.

Price	€68–€91.
Rooms	5: 4 doubles, 1 twin.
Meals	Dinner €31–€38.50. Wine €10.
Closed	Mid-October to mid-April.
Directions	From Nancy N74 for Sarreguemines & Château Salins. At Burthecourt x-roads, D38 to Dieuze; D999 south 5km; left on D199F; right D199G to château.

David & Agnieszka Barthélémy
Tarquimpol,
57260 Dieuze, Moselle
Tel   +33 (0)3 87 05 46 63
Email   chateau.alteville@free.fr

Ethical Collection: Environment;
Community; Food.
See page 446 for details

Auberge de la Poulcière

Come in April and you'll find yourself in a sea of wild daffodils. The area is famous for them and Gerardmer's annual Fête des Jonquilles lures plenty of visitors. The auberge, a 1775 farmhouse, stands at 800m and has been simply and delightfully renovated, with a brand new façade. Friendly Madame, an English teacher, ensures that each of the suites has comfort and space; bright bedspreads and old painted wardrobes contrast with dark stone floors, bathrooms have Italian showers and a luxurious feel, and every suite has a kitchenette. Best of all, generous windows open to captivating views. You get your own outside sitting area, too – a wooden balcony or a generous slice of the decked terrace. This is skiing country and you can walk or ski straight from the house. As for Gerardmer, it buzzes with entertainments on and off the lake and prides in having the oldest tourist office in France. The famous Jardin de Berchigranges is nearby. Return at the end of a busy day for dinner: the restaurant is, by all accounts, excellent, and promises a rich 'menu gastronomique'.

Price	€90. €110 for 3. Half-board €75 p.p.
Rooms	7 suites: 6 for 2, 1 for 3, all with kitchenette.
Meals	Breakfast €13. Dinner €25–€38. Wine €12–€60.
Closed	20 October; 25 December.
Directions	From Gerardmer D486 dir. La Bresse. After Rochesson/La Bresse intersection stay on D486; left after 150m, then immediately right. Signed.

Jocelyne & Michel Bouguerne–Arnould
10 chemin du Bouchot,
88400 Gerardmer, Vosges

Tel	+33 (0)3 29 42 04 33
Email	contact@auberge-poulciere.com
Web	www.auberge-poulciere.com

Hostellerie Saint Barnabé

It feels good here. The young owners of this angular, 100-year-old, flower-decked hotel are spontaneously smiley, chatty and attentive. He is the chef – trained with France's best and chef at Château d'Isenbourg for some years, so food is important here, and good. She is the perfect adviser on what to do between the Vosges hills and the Alsace plain: there are typical villages and wine-growers to visit, bike rides and good fishing places (they also have mini-golf on the spot). The ferny woods are full of paths and burbling brooks and there's skiing in season. There are two sorts of guest rooms: in the main house they are big, decorated with care and individuality (the yellow and white room has an iron-frame canopied bed, the red and white one twin head cushions and super-soft quilts), with smashing bathrooms and the odd balcony; in the separate building behind, they are smaller and more old-fashioned (and cheaper!) but are gradually being renovated. Here, bedroom doors all have typically Alsatian hand-painted, floral decoration. A great place for nature lovers and gourmets. Good value.

Price	€80–€207.
Rooms	26 twins/doubles.
Meals	Lunch €13, Monday-Saturday. Picnic on request. Dinner €19.50–€65.
Closed	3 days at Christmas; 3 weeks in January.
Directions	From N83 (between Belfort & Colmar) D430 for Guebwiller & Lautenbach. D429 for Buhl then Murbach. Hotel on left.

Clémence & Eric Orban
53 rue de Murbach,
68530 Murbach, Haut-Rhin

Tel	+33 (0)3 89 62 14 14
Email	hostellerie.st.barnabe@wanadoo.fr
Web	www.hostellerie-st-barnabe.com

Hôtel Cardinal de Rohan

Right in the historic centre, the old building that wraps itself around a courtyard in 17th-century Strasbourg style has been virtually rebuilt – with proper respect for its tall narrow neighbours. It has three rows of roof windows and tangles of geraniums down its façade, while inside is a warm, calm refuge; superb comfort, friendliness and attention to detail are the hallmarks here. Now the entire ground floor has been remodelled to create a spacious reception with small bar and sitting area, and a breakfast room in what was once the next door restaurant; all cleverly redesigned. Buffet breakfasts are civilised affairs with organic jams and fruit compotes sourced from the best suppliers, and outdoor tables spilling onto the pedestrianised street behind are planned for summer. Bedrooms too, from the slopey-ceilinged top-floor rooms down, have had facelifts; now each displays a warm colour scheme in plush carpeting and classical fabrics. Wardrobes in Louis XV style stand proudly beside modern pieces; mattresses are luxurious. Come in December for the famous Christmas market!

Price	€75–€149. Triples €159. Children under 12 free if in parents' room.
Rooms	36: 32 twins/doubles, 4 triples.
Meals	Breakfast €13. Restaurants nearby.
Closed	Rarely.
Directions	From ring road, exit Place de l'Etoile for Centre Ville & Cathédrale to underground car park (Place Gutenberg). Book ahead for private car park.

	Claude Hufajen
	17-19 rue du Maroquin,
	67000 Strasbourg, Bas-Rhin
Tel	+33 (0)3 88 32 85 11
Email	info@hotel-rohan.com
Web	www.hotel-rohan.com

Hôtel du Dragon

In old Strasbourg's hub, looking over river and cathedral, the Dragon is grandly, solidly 17th century on the outside, sleekly, refreshingly 20th century within. Built as a private mansion – Louis XIV stayed on his way to visit Marie-Antoinette in Austria – it became a hotel in the 1990s. The little courtyard received a classically pedimented porch and potted shrubs: a pretty place for an evening drink. They took a deeply contemporary approach inside – it is sober, minimalist-stylish and extraordinarily restful. Variegated grey and white are the basics: mushroom curtains on white walls, superb grey pinstripe carpeting, an arresting pattern of grey and white tiles in the bathrooms, muted mauve bedcovers for a dash of colour, and some good abstract paintings and sculptures here and there, displayed to great advantage. Some have river views and others see the cathedral's lovely spire. After 20 years as a mountain guide, Monsieur Zimmer returned to his native Strasbourg and has made the Dragon as welcoming as it is elegant. He is quiet and gentle and has a predilection for English-speaking guests.

Price	€89–€145. Apartments €174.
Rooms	32: 30 twins/doubles, 2 apartments for 4 (without kitchen).
Meals	Breakfast €11.50. Restaurants within walking distance.
Closed	Never.
Directions	Across river from Petite France, off Quai St Nicolas.

Jean Zimmer
2 rue de l'Ecarlate,
67000 Strasbourg, Bas-Rhin

Tel	+33 (0)3 88 35 79 80
Email	hotel@dragon.fr
Web	www.dragon.fr

Hôtel à la Ferme - L'Aigle d'Or

In a simple, colourful Alsatian village lies a superbly converted old farm, encircled by shrubs, roses, manicured hedges and a pretty bricked terrace. Bedrooms are splendid, a good size and comfortable, with polished floorboards, oriental rugs and fine beds, one carved in Alsatian style. The suites are in the outbuilding next door. In summer, choose a suite with an all-wood veranda; in winter, a cosy, part-panelled room in the main house: worth it for the scent of the baking. Delicious brioches and pastries are served in the wainscotted breakfast room warmed by an immense ceramic stove. Jean-Philippe's father mans the bar, his mother and grandmother help in the kitchen, Brigitte does front of house, Jean-Philippe is master chef and the food is outstanding. Chalked up on the board are escargots, foie gras, asparagus in season, choucroute, tarte flambé, apfelstrudel. One dining room is filled with ancient beams and antique cupboards, the other, elegantly contemporary, has old-gold velvet curtains and a fine inlaid wooden ceiling. A superb place run by a family that is professional, enthusiastic, endearing.

Price	€83–€135. Suites €114–€118.
Rooms	7: 3 doubles. Annexe: 4 suites for 2-4.
Meals	Breakfast €14. Lunch & dinner €32–€78 (except Monday eve & Tuesdays). Wine €25.
Closed	Rarely.
Directions	From Strasbourg A35 south, exit N83 dir. Colmar; 14km exit Erstein. Immediately right; 2km; right onto D288 for Osthouse. Signed in village.

Jean-Philippe & Brigitte Hellmann
10 rue du Château,
67150 Osthouse, Bas-Rhin

Tel	+33 (0)3 90 29 92 50
Email	info@hotelalaferme.com
Web	www.hotelalaferme.com

Burgundy • Franche Comté

Auberge des Vieux Moulins Banaux

Take a 16th-century mill straddling a rushing stream (and five minutes from a motorway), add a quartet of young, international, energetic talent, stir vigorously... and you have a recipe for success for a little auberge in Burgundy. Guillaume and his team started with the dining room and kitchen and completed a renovation in only a few years. The man in the kitchen serves great food: a saffron-sauced brochette of scallops with caramelised endives; slender panna cotta strawberry tarte accompanied by a sorbet of roses and strawberries. There are Sabien and Lukas (German), Tony (French) who alternate between dining room and reception; Guillaume (Franco-Dutch) pitches in everywhere. There is still carpeting on the corridor walls and, in some of the bedrooms, a 50s feel, but it is the food that is the priority here, and it is fabulous. Join a leisurely feast on the great dining terrace overlooking the large park and river, then try your hand at boules – or walk off lunch on the trail nearby. You are 45 minutes from the chablis vineyards – the position is perfect. The best rooms are on the first floor.

Price	€46–€67.50.
Rooms	15: 12 doubles, 1 suite, 2 triples.
Meals	Breakfast €8.25 Lunch & dinner €14.50–€27.50. Wine €15–€20. Restaurant closed Monday lunchtimes.
Closed	2010: 1-21 January; 1-10 June; 24 October-5 November; 19-27 December.
Directions	A5 exit 19 Villeneuve l'Archevêque; signed.

Guillaume Hamel
18 route des Moulins Banaux,
89190 Villeneuve l'Archêveque, Yonne

Tel	+33 (0)3 86 86 72 55
Email	contact@bourgognehotels.fr
Web	www.bourgognehotels.fr

Petit Manoir des Bruyères

Fruit trees, roses galore, aviaries of canaries and rare pheasant breeds: the gardens heave with floral splendour. As for the manoir, it is a rococo place unlike anything you've seen. Behind the creeper-clad façade with only the Burgundian roof as a clue is eye-boggling glamour: a vast beamed living room, an endless polished dining table, rows of tapestried chairs, many shiny ornaments. Upstairs, step out of the loo – once you've found the door in the trompe l'œil walls – to cupids, carvings, gildings, satyrs, velvet walls and clouds on the ceilings. There's a many-mirrored bathroom reflecting multiple magical images of you, marble pillars and gold-cushioned bath; a Louis XIV room with red/gold bathroom with gold/ivory taps; an antique wooden throne with bell-chime flush… and the biscuit is taken by the deeply, heavily pink suite with its carved fireplace, painted ceilings and corner columns – wild! But such is the enthusiasm of the hosts, the peace of the house and garden, the quality of comfort, food and wine, that we feel it's perfect for lovers of French extravaganza. Theatrical, delightful and joyous.

Price	€140-€220. Suites €140-€170. Cottage €1,000 per week.
Rooms	5 + 1: 3 doubles, 2 suites: 1 for 2, 1 for 2-3. Cottage for 2-4.
Meals	Hosted dinner €46, book ahead.
Closed	Never.
Directions	From Auxerre D965 to Villefargeau; right on C3 to Les Bruyères.

Pierre & Monique Joullié
89240 Villefargeau, Yonne
Tel   +33 (0)3 86 41 32 82
Email   jchambord@aol.com
Web   www.petit-manoir-bruyeres.com

Hôtel de la Beursaudière

Monsieur Lenoble's attention to detail is staggering. Not content with creating a buzzing, cheerful restaurant he has lovingly transformed a priory and farm buildings – stables, dovecotes, stone structures on varied levels, wooden verandas topped with red-patterned burgundian roof tiles – into a very seductive hotel. Each bedroom has a trade for a theme: a typewriter and old books for the 'writer'; antique irons for the 'laundress'; horse and ox collars for the 'ploughman'; vine-decorated wooden panels for the 'wine-grower'. The walls have been lightly skimmed in plaster in natural shades of ochre, pigeon-egg grey or light yellow. Floors are terracotta or flagstone, stone walls are painted, rafters exposed and windows round or cottage square with curtains of vintage linens and lace. Beds are king-size, mattresses are excellent and TVs are hidden in antique cabinets. Most bathrooms are open plan so as not to detract from the beams and volumes. There is even a sheltered sun lounge on the terrace only overlooked by sparrows. A nice place to sit and sample your chilled choice picked up in Chablis.

Price	€75–€115.
Rooms	11: 6 doubles, 5 twins.
Meals	Breakfast €10. Lunch & dinner €19–€43. Wine €15–€100.
Closed	Last 3 weeks in January.
Directions	A6 exit 21 Nitry; right to Nitry for 500m. Left at church to Vermenton for 200m. Signed.

	M & Mme Lenoble
	5-7 rue Hyacinthe Gautherin,
	89310 Nitry, Yonne
Tel	+33 (0)3 86 33 69 70
Email	message@beursaudiere.com
Web	www.beursaudiere.com

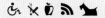

Le Coq Hardi

Anyone who loves France and what it stands for will coq-a-doodle-do. This small, modest hotel was built in the 30s to cater for the ever-increasing motoring tribe – from Paris to the Riviera. It experienced its heyday in the late 50s and 60s when the rich and famous would stop over for a night or two to wine and dine before heading down to St Tropez. These hotels and restaurants are now undergoing a revival; a reminder of when the pace of life was slower and food a priority. Here, summer meals are served on a lime-tree'd (though ordinarily furnished) terrace overlooking the Loire – and how! New chef patron Dominique Fonseca comes fresh from the kitchens of the Ritz, Paris and has the talent and ambition to continue this much-loved restaurant's standards; many stay for the food alone. Under the Fonsecas' ownership bedrooms have been refreshed and improved, with white bedcovers and plain pale colours; bathrooms still sport the colours of the 70s. Outside, expanses of neatly cut grass slope down to river's edge, and rose beds are neatly pruned and trimmed; it's a pretty setting for summer dining.

Price	€75–€90.
Rooms	9: 8 doubles, 1 suite.
Meals	Breakfast €11. Lunch & dinner €23–€57. Restaurant closed Sunday eve & Mondays October-April.
Closed	Mid-December to mid-January.
Directions	From A77 exit 25 & cont. thro' Pouilly sur Loire. Hotel opposite Cave Cooperative.

Françoise & Dominique Fonseca
42 avenue de la Tuilerie,
58150 Pouilly sur Loire, Nièvre
Tel   +33 (0)3 86 39 12 99
Email   lecoqhardi@orange.fr
Web   www.lecoqhardi.fr

Château de Prye

The Queen of Poland, Marie-Casimire, lived here at the tail end of the 17th century – in this château extraordinaire, this architectural curiosity. The rooms are vast, the marble stables are palatial and the corridors heave with antlers and stag heads from previous ancestors; the history is intriguing. The young Marquis and Marquise, recently installed, have joyfully taken up the challenge of running both château and estate (they breed Charolais cattle) and host their national and international guests with grace and ease. Each cavernous bedroom is furnished with antiques – a triple-mirrored wardrobe from the Thirties, a Breton carved bedstead, a vintage oil-fuelled heater; bathrooms are en suite. Take a peek at the château kitchen with its wonderful old range and copper saucepans... from here breakfast is dispatched to a boudoir-like room with pretty white wainscotting. This turreted, neo-Gothic château, its woodlands, gentle river and age-old trees of exotic and distant origins are contained within seven kilometres of walls... relish the fairy tale.
Sawday's self-catering also.

Price	€110-€185.
Rooms	4: 2 doubles, 2 suites for 2-4.
Meals	Dinner €35, book ahead.
	Wine €8-€105.
Closed	Mid-October to mid-April.
Directions	Nevers-Château-Chinon exit 36; D18 thro' Sauvigny les Bois. Gates between 2 pavilions open & close manually.

Magdalena & Antoine-Emmanuel
du Bourg de Bozas
58160 La Fermeté, Nièvre

Tel	+33 (0)3 86 58 42 64
Email	info@chateaudeprye.com
Web	www.chateaudeprye.com

Château de Villette

Coen and Catherine – he Dutch, she Belgian – fell in love with this little château in 2002, did it up together, then had their wedding here. They've opened just four rooms to guests (forming two suites) so they can spoil you properly. And get to know you over dinner. (Though, should you prefer a romantic dinner for two, they'll understand.) Deep in the Parc de Morvan, the château was built in 1782 as a summer retreat. Bedrooms, charmingly decorated by Catherine, are large, light and airy, with warm colours and polished floors. They are dressed in château-style finery with canopied four-poster or draped bedheads (except for the twin sleigh bed in one of the family rooms). Bathrooms are as they should be – new claw-foot baths carry exquisite antique taps – and views sail out of great windows to meadows and woodland beyond. Your five-course dinner is served in a candlelit dining room or outside. The grounds are perfect for duck and pheasant shoots. Families would love it here; Beaune and the vineyards lie temptingly close.

Price	€165–€235. Suite €295–€365.
Rooms	4: 1 double, 1 twin, 2 family rooms for 3. Rooms interconnect to form 2 suites for 5.
Meals	Dinner €48, book ahead. Wine €18–€100.
Closed	Rarely.
Directions	From N6 exit Beaune for Autun. N81 for Moulins for 18km, right to Poil. Thro' village, 2nd left. Signed.

	Catherine & Coen Stork
	58170 Poil, Nièvre
Tel	+33 (0)3 86 30 09 13
Email	catherinestork@chateaudevillette.eu
Web	www.chateaudevillette.eu

Château de Vaulx

It was described in 1886 as "well-proportioned and elegant in its simplicity". It is as lovely now and in the most beautiful position, high on a hill, with views that stretch to distant purple mountains. Marty, your host, and the animals of the property (Nema the Jack Russell, Zelda the golden retriever, Urga the filly, Otto the donkey… plus hens, the sheep and beehives) welcome you to this spacious domain. There's a fully panelled drawing room with chandeliers, a huge dining room with fresh flowers, two lovely big bedrooms, two suites, and an apartment for five. Sleep peacefully: not a hint of traffic rumble. The gardens have been spruced up, the lawns manicured, the box balls tightly topiaried; stroll down the romantic avenues in dappled sunlight. The vegetable garden provides food for delicious table d'hôtes, the views are glorious, the birds twitter, there's countryside all around and plenty of places to visit, including a 13th-century bell tower in the village. In La Clayette is Bernard Dufoux, one of the best chocolate makers in France; in Sainte Christophe is a weekly cattle market. Wonderful.

Price	€95–€115. Suites €145. Apartment €165.
Rooms	5: 2 doubles, 2 family suites for 4, 1 apartment for 5.
Meals	Dinner €30. Wine €18. Restaurant 3km.
Closed	Rarely.
Directions	From Charolles, D985 for Clayette 8km. 1km after crossing railway, 2nd road signed Vaulx. Up to top of hill, right at junc. Bell on iron gate.

Marty Freriksen
71800 Saint Julien de Civry,
Saône-et-Loire

Tel	+33 (0)3 85 70 64 03
Email	marty@chateaudevaulx.com
Web	www.chateaudevaulx.com

Château des Poccards

It is all most comforting and welcoming, staying in the Tuscan-style villa built in 1805 to woo an Italian beauty living in Burgundy. Now run by a husband and wife team ever on the go, the cream and ochre villa with five bedrooms has become an exemplary place to stay. After a day's sampling the great restaurants of Lyon Mâcou, exploring the wine routes of Beaune or the shops of Geneva, what could be nicer than to return to a big retro tub in a bathroom that sparkles with uplighters and oozes warm towels? Bedrooms are all generously big and different, with pretty terracotta floors and pale-papered walls, cream beds, elegant furnishings and *tout confort*. Some have windows to all sides so you feel you're in the tree tops – bliss when the sun streams in. In the mature park, a serene pool with wooden loungers and vineyard views. Families would be happy here, as would romancers. Wonderful breakfasts are supplied by Catherine and Ivan at white-clothed tables in a gracious room; a piano in the corner, windows to a terrace, a sumptuous parquet floor. Good value for money. *No credit cards.*

Price	€107-€147.
Rooms	5 doubles. Some rooms connect.
Meals	Restaurants 10-minute drive.
Closed	December-February.
Directions	A6 exit 28 to Sennecé les Maçon. Left to Laizé & Blagny. At stop, 1st left to Hurigny; 1st right Rue de la Brasse; château 100m on left.

	Catherine & Ivan Fizaine
	120 route des Poccards,
	71870 Hurigny, Saône-et-Loire
Tel	+33 (0)3 85 32 08 27
Email	chateau.des.poccards@wanadoo.fr
Web	www.chateau-des-poccards.com

Maison Nièpce

All the modern necessities, of course, but otherwise little has changed since the old inn was turned into a family mansion by the uncle of Joseph (Nicephore) Nièpce, inventor of photography. It's a bit like staying in a charming museum – a place of candlelight, atmosphere and 18th-century elegance, plus a dash of antique grime. The owners and their golden retriever live in one great wing and guests in the other, while two odoriferous cats roam freely. First-floor passageways run hither and thither to graceful rooms with good beds and bathrooms, fine antiques and oriental rugs. On the slopey-ceilinged second floor, La Chambre Nièpce can link up to form a three-room apartment with bathroom. A display of arms in one bedroom and an oven for baking bullets in another recall the Revolution; a third, less bellicose, has serried ranks of books. Plump for a room at the back, quieter than those on the street, and gaze down on the big and enchanting walled garden. Breakfast and dinner (usually table d'hôtes) are in the fascinating dining room, aglow with copper pans.

Price	€50–€120. Apartment €500 per week.
Rooms	5 + 1: 1 double, 4 twins. Apartment for 4.
Meals	Breakfast €8. Dinner €23, book ahead.
Closed	Rarely.
Directions	20km south of Chalon sur Saone, N6 dir. Macon; left on leaving village.

Huguette & Jehan Moreau de Melen
8 avenue du 4 Septembre,
71240 Sennecy le Grand,
Saône-et-Loire

Tel	+33 (0)3 85 44 76 44
Email	moreau.jehan@wanadoo.fr
Web	www.maisonniepce.com

L'Orangerie

Ring the bell on the gate and enter gardens that are secluded, charming, full of colour and the babble of the brook. Being in the heart of Burgundy country you are immersed in silence in a valley of vines. Light spills into the sitting room entrance through vine-clad arched windows, while cream walls and Indian rugs add to the simple elegance of this *maison de maître*. Antiques and travel are the owners' passion, and David's gentle Irish brogue is enchanting (no surprise to hear he has interviewed European royalty for a prestigious magazine). The grand staircase in the centre of this gracious house would not be out of place on a 1930s luxury cruise liner, while interesting paintings and stylish oriental fabrics add up to a mix of styles that work beautifully together. Bedrooms vary in size and have lovely seersucker linen and antique prints; bathrooms are classically tasteful. Terraced lawns lead down to the heated pool, the meadows and trees, breakfasts are superb, and the wonderful Voie Verte cycle route, along the former railway, runs nearby. *Cash or French cheque only. Minimum stay two nights.*

Price	€75–€105.
Rooms	5 twins/doubles.
Meals	Hosted dinner with wine, €25–€40, on request.
Closed	Mid-November to mid-March.
Directions	From A6, exit Chalon Sud on N80 for Le Creusot; exit Moroges. Signed from village centre.

	David Eades & Niels Lierow
	20 rue des Lavoirs, Vingelles,
	71390 Moroges, Saône-et-Loire
Tel	+33 (0)3 85 47 91 94
Email	info@orangerie-moroges.com
Web	www.orangerie-moroges.com

Entry 37   Map 11

Côté Park

In the little wine town of Givry is a 17th-century mansion with tall proud windows and terraced wings that merges deliciously into an old stone chapel and outbuildings: a 'community' architecture of human dimensions. Lovely bubbly Anne-Marie and her doctor husband have devoted years to the estate's renovation and have created a chambres d'hôtes of luxury and charm. The main house is sheltered from the road by two entrance courtyards (one once the master's, the other the tradesmen's) over which two guest rooms gaze; all four bedrooms are light, spacious, cosy, opulent, uncluttered and inviting. We fell in love with the two-bedroom Jean d'Arcy suite, its big rosy terracotta floor topped by an oriental rug, its windows overlooking fabulous French gardens in which are spread elegant flowerbeds with box trims, wide sandy pathways, tree-shaded depths and a pool to one side. You breakfast at white iron-work tables in a parquet-floored breakfast room off which an irreproachably classical salon lies; formal yes, and gracious, but the delightful Anne-Marie makes you feel beautifully at home.

Price	€130–€150. Singles €110–€130.
Rooms	4: 2 doubles, 1 suite for 5, 1 suite for 6.
Meals	Restaurants within walking distance.
Closed	Rarely.
Directions	A6 exit Chalon Nord dir. Autun for 5km, then dir. Germolles Givry. At entrance to Givry 1st left (rue du Puit Brechet); 2nd right to Rue Georges Clemenceau.

Anne-Marie Guillermin
16 & 18 rue Georges Clemenceau,
71640 Givry, Saône-et-Loire

Tel	+33 (0)3 85 94 88 91
Email	cotepark@gmail.com
Web	www.cotepark.com

La Dominotte

On the edge of an old Burgundian village is a mellow farmhouse where grapes were gathered, pressed and stored; you can see the traces of the barrels on the breakfast room wall. They are less visible in the evening with low lighting and candles, when a board announces the daily specials. This room – stylishly simple in that perfect Dutch way – leads onto the garden; bliss to lie out here by the discreetly hedged pool. You are surrounded by vineyards and vast sloping hills – La Dominotte is a working winery still. Multi-lingual, hugely helpful and welcoming, Mart and Marij have been here for over a decade and are a font of knowledge on all things Burgundian, gastronomy in particular. After a ten-minute drive you reach the famous villages of Montrachet, Meursault and Pommard, while Beaune is a short cycle ride away; borrow the bikes. The doubles are on the ground floor of the old barn, more for sleeping in than lounging, but comfortable and characterful with their exposed rafters and slit windows. The views (of garden and pool) are from the big airy family room upstairs, with extra long beds!

Price	€95–€136. Family room €160.
Rooms	11: 10 doubles, 1 family room for 4 (with kitchen).
Meals	Late afternoon snacks. Hosted dinner €22–€25 twice weekly. Restaurant 400m.
Closed	22 November–1 April.
Directions	A6 Dijon & Beaune exit 24.1 to Bligny les Beaune onto D113, then to Demigny D18. Left at T-junc. after Casino; 3rd left to end of village; last house on right.

Mme Franssen
Rue de Jasoupe le Bas,
71150 Demigny, Saône-et-Loire

Tel	+33 (0)3 85 49 43 56
Email	info@la-dominotte.com
Web	www.la-dominotte.com

 Entry 39 Map 11

Château de Chassagne-Montrachet

You are in top wine country. The driveway passes through a small vineyard to the business-like château – winery in the middle, chambres d'hôte to the right. The stark 19th-century exterior does not prepare you for the modernism within: the sweeping wooden stairway, the slate and pink-marble floor, the stunning leather furniture, the billiard room with bamboo decoration and underfloor lighting. The refreshing irreverence continues upstairs; you might spot a Jacobsen 'egg' chair, feast on the sumptuousness of purple walls and oak floor or enter a room of zen-like calm. Windows show the vineyards floating away to the hills of the Massif Central or the Saône valley; on a good day you can see the Alps. Bathrooms are ravishingly contemporary; most have tubs surrounded by wooden decking, one has a double sink of rough-cast bronze mounted on rock – half basin, half art. You breakfast at two large steel tables on sculpted chairs by a wonderful fireplace and floor-to-ceiling doors. The château restaurant is 300 metres away and there's excellent walking in the hills. *Wine tour included, by arrangement.*

Price	€250.
Rooms	5 doubles.
Meals	Lunch €40–€50, with fine wines for tasting.
Closed	Never.
Directions	From Beaune, N74 exit Chassagne-Montrachet; château signed at village entrance.

Francine Picard
5 rue du Château,
21190 Chassagne Montrachet, Côte-d'Or
Tel   +33 (0)3 80 21 98 57
Email   contact@michelpicard.com
Web   www.michelpicard.com

Le Clos

Breakfast on the terrace overlooking the neat and pretty *jardin de curé*, then choose your suntrap in the garden – full of hidden corners. Or, under the shade of big trees, wander among the quaint agricultural machinery that sculpturally dots the lawns. The rustic white-shuttered farmhouse has been renovated with tender loving care to reveal exposed limestone walls and massive rafters. There's a charming country breakfast room and a light and lofty lounge, whose ancient tiles have been garnished with oriental rugs and sofas. Bedrooms are large, with matching floral bed linen and curtains, new carpets, substantial antiques, and the odd exotic touch. Bathrooms sparkle and there are no half measures: big bath tubs, walk-in showers, an abundance of towels and robes. No restaurant, but have a drink at the bar and and a chat with Alain – a professional hotelier with a dry sense of humour. The pretty residential village is deep in wine country – and when you've had your fill of burgundies and beaunes, there are mustards to try in a nearby village!

Price	€80–€115. Duplex suites €140–€200.
Rooms	24: 19 twins/doubles, 5 duplex suites.
Meals	Breakfast €12. Restaurants 100m & 3km.
Closed	December-January.
Directions	From Lyon A6 exit 24.1 towards Beaune Centre; 300m r'bout to Montagny lès Beaune on D113. Signed.

M & Mme Oudot
22 rue Gravières,
21200 Montagny lès Beaune, Côte-d'Or

Tel	+33 (0)3 80 25 97 98
Email	hotelleclos@wanadoo.fr
Web	www.hotelleclos.com

La Terre d'Or

This is five minutes from Beaune and Jean-Louis enthusiastically shares his love of Burgundy with you in many ways. Learn how the elegant vintages are made, link up with a Burgundian chef, be steered towards local vestiges of Roman art. All this by bike, horseback, jeep or hot-air balloon. Jean-Louis and Christine own three wonderful houses, each surrounded by a terraced garden and century-old trees. Their own house, with five large and lovely guest bedrooms, is contemporary and multi-levelled while the stone cottage is traditional, aimed at self-catering parties. The Martins restored noble old beams and rosy tommette floors, then added stylish lighting, crisp linen and polished country pieces (including wine-growers' chairs). Expect a serene and sunny décor, independent entrances, and, for the honeymoon suite, a private piece of garden. Bliss to relax on the main terrace and gaze across vineyards to the ramparts of old Beaune. Beyond is an inviting pool; down a wildflower path is a family-run restaurant. Stay three nights or more. *Group price for themed holidays (wine, cooking, culture).*

Price	€125-€205. Cottage €390.
Rooms	5 + 1: 4 doubles, 1 twin. 1 cottage for 2-6.
Meals	Breakfast €13. Picnic available. Restaurant 400m.
Closed	Rarely.
Directions	From Beaune, D970 for Auxerre & Bouze les Bèaunes. After 2km, right to La Montagne; well signed.

Christine & Jean-Louis Martin
Rue Izembart La Montagne,
21200 Beaune, Côte-d'Or

Tel	+33 (0)3 80 25 90 90
Email	jlmartin@laterredor.com
Web	www.laterredor.com

Château de Chorey

Typically Burgundian, this robust, sturdy collection of buildings under high slate roofs dates from the 13th and 17th centuries. Complete with towers, ancient yews and dovecots, flanked on both sides by a 34-acre vineyard producing prestigious premier cru wines, it has views that sail over a noble moated domaine. Interiors are handsome, formal and absolutely French with rich reds and rusts, mustards, golds and raspberry pinks; suave sobriety presides over period furniture, ornate wallpapering, polished wooden floors, high windows heavily draped and regal beds swathed in canopies matched to quilted spreads. Bathrooms are immaculate. Landings with Venetian mosaic floors lead to venerable stone stairs and down through doorways with ornately carved lintels (one sporting the family crest) and perfectly tailored arched panelling. A sitting room impresses with a monumental fireplace; the dining room, with high overhead beams, is where wholesome breakfasts are set before wide arched windows, overlooking the vines and interior courtyard. Wine tours and tastings are a must; Beaune oozes gastronomic delights.

Price	€165–€195. Suites €220–€260. Triple €225. Extra bed €30.
Rooms	5: 2 doubles, 2 suites for 2-4, 1 triple.
Meals	Restaurant 1km.
Closed	End October-Easter.
Directions	From A6 south dir. Lyon exit 24 (Beaune St Nicolas); at r'bout, 1st right; right at next r'bout onto D974 dir. Dijon. 1st right to Chorey lès Beaune. Château 1st on left after x-roads at village entrance.

François Germain
2 rue Jacques Germain,
21200 Chorey les Beaune, Côte-d'Or

Tel   +33 (0)3 80 22 06 05
Email   contact@chateau-de-chorey-les-beaune.fr
Web   www.chateau-de-chorey-les-beaune.fr

Hôtel de Vougeot

Rows of vines sweep down an incline, surround the regal Château de Clos de Vougeot (shown above) in tones of pale yellow stone like a sepia photograph, and come to an abrupt halt at the back doorstep of this modest converted townhouse. For centuries Clos de Vougeot was considered the finest of all burgundies; the Cisterian monks planted some of the vines in the 12th century. Thirty hogsheads were sent to Rome in 1371 to celebrate the election of Pope Gregory XI; the gift-bearing abbot was soon made a cardinal. The cloister, cellar and enormous presses are among the most interesting examples of architecture in Burgundy. The best rooms here have views of both the château and the vines. You are on your own here with a key to come and go as you like. Everything has been kept simple and clean; the rough outlines of the dark timbers are a nice contrast to the white walls, light coloured bedspreads, new parquet floors and teak furniture. Splash out on one of the huge rooms. A copious buffet breakfast served under the ground floor stone arches will be a perfect start to your day.

Price	€58–€110.
Rooms	16: 12 doubles, 1 triple, 2 quadruples, 1 room for 5.
Meals	Buffet breakfast €9.50. Cold platter €20.
Closed	20 December–20 January.
Directions	A31 exit 1 Nuits St Georges, D974 dir. Vougeot. Hotel in village.

Alain Senterre
18 rue du Vieux Château,
21640 Vougeot, Côte-d'Or

Tel	+33 (0)3 80 62 01 15
Email	contact@hotel-vougeot.com
Web	www.hotel-vougeot.com

Castel de Très Girard

Nuits Saint Georges, Gevrey Chambertin, Clos de Vougeot, Vosne Romanée – all tongue-twisters in the best sense of the word and all strewn in your path as you travel down the trunk road from Dijon. Why not stop here and be greeted by this friendly team who handle everything in the nicest manner? The warmth comes not only from the embers in the fireplace by the leather club chairs but from the whole atmosphere of this renovated wine press and 18th-century Burgundian manor. There are confident touches of burgundy reds (naturally) in the carpeted bedrooms, plus padded leather headboards, cream walls and just enough golden stone and beam exposed to give the large hotelly bedrooms character; small vestibules ensure ultimate peace. Even the gleaming white bathrooms have views over the rooftops or to the Côte de Nuits vineyards. Outside is a grassed and swimming pool'd garden, sheltered from the carpark by immaculate hedging. Now plans are afoot for the restaurant to expand. Food has always played a major role at the Castel de Très Girard, and is matched by wines from the region's best producers.

Price	€91–€170.
	Suites & triples €168–€240.
Rooms	9: 3 doubles, 2 suites, 4 triples.
Meals	Buffet breakfast €17.
	Lunch €19.50–€58. Dinner €35–€58.
	Restaurant closed Mon, & Sun in
	winter.
Closed	15 February-7 March.
Directions	20km from Dijon; A31 exit Dijon Sud
	for Nuits St Georges on N74, then
	right to Morey St Denis. Signed.

Didier Petitcolas
7 rue Très Girard,
21220 Morey St Denis, Côte-d'Or

Tel	+33 (0)3 80 34 33 09
Email	info@castel-tres-girard.com
Web	www.castel-tres-girard.com

Château de Flammerans

All is fresh, luxurious, relaxing – and Guy has the perfect pinch of passion for Burgundian cuisine even though he hails from Cantal. Ask to see the 18th-century kitchen with its original painted ceiling where he teaches the secrets of jambon persillé or fricassée d'escargot. The billiard room and the library are just off the entrance hall with its superb 19th-century ceramic tiles and a handsome iron banister leads upstairs. You may breakfast on the large balcony overlooking the park, in the sitting room with its creamy walls, oriental rugs, green and gold upholstered easy chairs, or in the elegant dining room. Bedrooms are big and uncluttered with working fireplaces and mineral water on the side tables. You'll find robes in the gorgeous bathrooms along with weathered marbled floors from the south of France. If you are lucky, you'll catch one of the concerts – maybe baroque or jazz – that Guy and Catherine organise. Sit and dream on a bench in a shady glen, gaze at the magnificent red oaks, discover the glistening ponds (one was used to clean the carriage wheels). A pleasing place. *Sawday's self-catering also.*

Price	€88–€178. Suites €158–€198.
Rooms	6: 3 doubles, 1 twin, 2 suites.
Meals	Light lunches available. Hosted dinner with drinks, €45; book ahead.
Closed	Never.
Directions	A39 exit 5 to Auxonne; D20 for 6km to Flammerans. Signed.

Guy & Catherine Barrier
21130 Flammerans, Côte-d'Or

Tel	+33 (0)3 80 27 05 70
Email	info@chateaudeflammerans.com
Web	www.chateaudeflammerans.com

Le Château de Courban

This ambitiously renovated 19th-century mansion – with a 17th-century dovecot in the courtyard testament to an even older heritage – was transformed into its current incarnation by Jerome's father, perfectionist Pierre Vandendriessche. Most of the 22 rooms are in the original mansion and flaunt a wide variety of styles, from the bold and bright to the floral and cosy, all tastefully harmonised and generously comfortable: recessed bedheads, draped four-posters, crisp colour schemes and carefully chosen prints. Newer outbuildings vaunt more contemporary design, and have their own verandas. Bathrooms feature claw-foot tubs in some, walk-in showers with monsoon heads in others. Meals – excellent, reliable, robust Burgundian cuisine – can be taken in the expansive restaurant, the orangerie or the veranda; breakfast should be enjoyed in bed with the shutters wide open. An ivy-smothered wooden cottage conceals a delightful suite. Behind the house a large terrace precedes two pools – one slender and black, stretching across the garden – and a new spa where you can burn off lunch. Failing that there's an abutting bar.

Price	€105. Twins €95. Single €85. Suite €225. Triples €145. Quadruples €185–€265.
Rooms	22: 11 doubles, 4 twins, 1 single, 1 suite, 3 triples, 2 quadruples.
Meals	Breakfast €12.50. Dinner €35–€48. Wine €25–€110.
Closed	Christmas.
Directions	A26 to A5, exit 23 to D396 for 14km to Gevrolles; D996 thro' Montigny sur Aube, D995 to Courban; follow signs in village, entrance on left.

Jerome Vandendriessche
7 rue du Lavoir Courban,
21520 Courban, Côte-d'Or

Tel	+33 (0)3 80 93 78 69
Email	contact@chateaudecourban.com
Web	www.chateaudecourban.com

Château d'Epenoux

Next to the dear little 18th-century château stands a baroque chapel tenderly maintained by the ladies of the house. Susanne and Eva have given both the facelift they deserved – windows sparkle and floorboards gleam. Your thoughtful, friendly, unassuming hosts have opened up five airy bedrooms on the first floor to guests. All are generously big and different. The suite, prettily papered in blue, its twin beds draped with soft white duvets, has long windows overlooking majestic trees, copses and lawns; the large double is panelled in French green; fresh, feminine Mona Lisa is all deep pink walls and a cream sofa. Sparkling white bathrooms come with lashings of hot water. Sink into the wildly floral armchairs in the blue-carpeted salon for a pre-dinner aperitif, drift into the grand dining room with its glass chandelier for dinner: maybe some perfectly roasted duck and a well-chosen wine. Wander round the park afterwards and admire the ancient trees, or take a short drive to charming Vesoul, notable for its lake and recreational park, and intriguing Gothic façades in the old quarter.

Price	€98-€110. Apartment €110-€140. All prices per night.
Rooms	6: 4 doubles, 1 suite, 1 apartment.
Meals	Dinner €27. Wine €12-€38.
Closed	2-7 January.
Directions	From Chaumont, N19 to Vesoul; D10 for approx. 4km. Château on left at entrance to village of Epenoux.

Eva Holz & Susanne Hubbuch
70000 Pusy et Epenoux, Haute-Saône

Tel	+33 (0)3 84 75 19 60
Email	chateau.epenoux@orange.fr
Web	www.chateau-epenoux.com

Paris – Île de France

Hôtel Britannique

Breakfast on the balcony under the trees? Hard to imagine such a lanquid oasis in the historic heart of the city, only a tiny leap to the banks of the Seine, noble Notre Dame and the Louvre. Originally run by the British Baxters, the hotel is now owned by an ex-naval man with a passion for Turner. The great painter's *Jessica* greets you in the lobby, copies of his oils and watercolours adorn the laquered grey corridors, and the *Fighting Temeraire* dominates the deeply comfortable salon. Baldaquins discreetly drape over good beds, thick curtains in caramel and cream or cranberry and eggshell echo the colours in the thin-striped carpets, bathrooms shine like sugar *bon-bons* in their mint greens and blackcurrant reds. Higher floors have views over roofs, all have thirsty bathrobes and flatscreen TVs. It's lively and fun in the daytime, quietish at night. The basement breakfast room is a honey-warm, rustic country kitchen. There is great attention to detail here; it is simply comfortable with no ancient flourishes and a friendly reception staff in stripy waistcoats.

Price	€160–€221. Suite €279–€325.
Rooms	40: 39 twins/doubles, 1 suite.
Meals	Buffet breakfast €13. Restaurants nearby.
Closed	Never.
Directions	Metro: Châtelet. RER: Châtelet-Les Halles.

Jean-Francis Danjou
20 avenue Victoria,
75001 Paris

Tel	+33 (0)1 42 33 74 59
Email	mailbox@hotel-britannique.fr
Web	www.hotel-britannique.fr

Le Relais du Louvre

Look down the throats of gargoyles, soak up the history. The Revolutionaries printed their newsletter in the cellar; the place inspired Puccini's Café Momus in *Bohême*. It is utterly delightful and so are the charming young managers who greet you from the antique desk. Everywhere, antiques and oriental rugs complement the modernity of firm beds and perfect bathrooms. Front rooms look onto the church's Gothic flights of fancy and along to the austerely neo-classical Louvre; others give onto a light-filled patio. Top-floor junior suites have space for a non-convertible sofa (no cluttering up), pastel walls, exuberant upholstery and heaps of light from mansard windows. The apartment is big and beautiful with fireplace, books, music, old engravings and a superb veranda kitchen. Smaller rooms are luminous, fresh and restful — yellow, a favourite colour, brings sunny moods into small spaces. You feel softly secluded and coddled everywhere. The sense of service is highly developed and as there is no breakfast room, breakfast comes to you. *On each floor, two rooms can make a family suite.*

Price	€170-€215. Singles €125. Suites €244-€270. Apartment €435. All prices per night.
Rooms	20 + 1: 13 twins/doubles, 5 singles, 2 suites. 1 apt for 5.
Meals	Breakfast €13 (served in bedroom only, until 2pm). Lunch & dinner €10-€30, on request. Wine €7.
Closed	Never.
Directions	Metro: Louvre-Rivoli (1), Pont Neuf (7). RER: Châtelet-Les Halles. Buses: 67, 69, 72, 74, 85. Parking: Private car park on request, €25.

Sophie Aulnette
19 rue des Prêtres,
St Germain l'Auxerrois, 75001 Paris

Tel	+33 (0)1 40 41 96 42
Email	contact@relaisdulouvre.com
Web	www.relaisdulouvre.com

Hôtel Molière

This is an enchantingly French hotel with a sensitive mixture of urban and country comforts. The big lobby/salon is smart and rather grand with its *faux-marbre* columns, potted palms and beige bucket chairs, and the staff at reception are very competent, very friendly; the young owners infuse the place with their intelligent enthusiasm. The breakfast room is a delight, and red and white striped blinds frame the leafy, cobbled courtyard. There's also a small, deep-chaired salon round the corner for your quiet moments. Bedrooms are just as pretty with judicious use of nostalgic Jouy prints on walls and coordinated checks on quilts – or vice versa, or stripes, or sprigs... The Jouy colours go perfectly with the occasional antique: red and yellow, grey and green, blue and ivory, a little old writing desk, an unusual chair. Bathrooms, some vast, some snug, are modern; those in the suites, listed for renovation, bask in their old-fashioned built-in fittings and mosaic tiles. Interesting paintings and ornaments give the hotel a well-cared-for feel. Everyone loves the Molière.

Price	€170–€190. Singles €145–€170. Suites €220–€300. Triples €220.
Rooms	32: 14 doubles, 8 twins, 5 singles, 3 suites for 4, 2 triples.
Meals	Breakfast €14. Restaurants nearby.
Closed	Never.
Directions	Metro: Palais Royal-Musée du Louvre (1, 7), Pyramides (7, 14). RER & Roissybus: Auber, Opéra. Buses: 21, 24, 27, 29, 39, 48, 72, 81, 95. Parking: Pyramides.

	Patricia & Rémy Perraud
	21 rue Molière, 75001 Paris
Tel	+33 (0)1 42 96 22 01
Email	info@hotel-moliere.fr
Web	www.hotel-moliere.fr

Hôtel Le Relais Saint Honoré

Unique, the rue Saint Honoré is a delight: once past the gardens of the Presidential Palace it becomes human-sized and unpasteurised, as it meanders along the Tuileries, crosses the Place Colette and then charges into an area of higgledy-piggledy streets and iconoclastic shops, some of which have been there forever. The Relais, once a brasserie frequented by Jean Cocteau, dates from 1650. After months of careful renovation there are 13 small but perfect rooms and two larger suites. No patching-over here: every detail has been overseen by Paul Bogaert, a knowlegeable and experienced hotelier. Some are invisible – the finest mattresses and softest fleece blankets enveloped in fine cotton – others less so. The beams, removed and stored for over a year, have been painted lapis lazuli blue, bamboo green or cranberry red to pick up nuances from exquisitely patterned fabrics on curtains and bedheads. The bathrooms have huge mirrors, heated towel rails and everything works; breakfast is classic French or with cereals. No ostentation, no frills, just pure comfort with a caring staff.

Price	€206. Suites €305–€345.
Rooms	15: 13 twins/doubles, 2 suites.
Meals	Breakfast €13 (served in bedroom only). Restaurants nearby.
Closed	Never.
Directions	Metro: Tuileries (1), Pyramides (7, 14). RER: Musée d'Orsay. Buses: 68, 72. Parking: Marché Saint Honoré.

	Paul Bogaert
	308 rue Saint Honoré, 75001 Paris
Tel	+33 (0)1 42 96 06 06
Email	relaissainthonore@wanadoo.fr
Web	www.relaissainthonore.com

Garden Saint Martin

In a corner of genuine people's Paris that has attracted trendy cafés and hip young shoppers, this budget hotel stands between the tranquil St Martin Canal and the mad dash of the Place de la République. It has always been a hostelry, one of a row of harmonious, unpretentious 1890s buildings, with an old bakery on the corner. Beyond the semi-veranda breakfast space, the green flowering patio is just the spot for summer mornings beneath the giant sun-yellow parasols; bedrooms in the garden building give onto this. All rooms and bathrooms are gradually being renovated: clean, spring-like décor, primrose-painted furniture, pine-slatted walls to replace mock-wood cladding. Shower rooms are tiny, and some doubles so small the bed fills the width of the room. One of the quadruples has a bit of timber framing in the middle and from some front rooms you can see down to the barges and boats cruising along above road level; the canal is charming on a summer's evening. Don't miss Chez Prune, a lively bar and restaurant on a terrace overlooking the water.

Price	€60–€100. Singles €72. Triples €108.
Rooms	32: 11 doubles, 10 twins, 6 singles, 5 triples.
Meals	Buffet breakfast €8. Restaurants nearby.
Closed	Never.
Directions	Metro: République (3, 5, 8, 9, 11). RER: Gare du Nord. Buses: 54, 56, 75. Parking: Boulevard Magenta (consult hotel).

M & Mme Depardieu
35 rue Yves Toudic, 75010 Paris

Tel	+33 (0)1 42 40 17 72
Email	gardensaintmartin@orange.fr
Web	www.hotel-gardensaintmartin-paris.com

Hôtel de la Bretonnerie

The position is hard to beat: the Pompidou Centre to the left, the Place de Vosges to the right, and the funky Marais on your doorstep. Beneath the Bretonnerie's 17th-century timbered frame is a welcoming raspberry and moss nest downstairs and gracious sleeping quarters up. There is space and shape to the lobby and the wrought-iron, wooden-railed staircase is an elegant reminder of that Parisian talent for grandeur on a human scale. The breakfast room, in a lovely bare-stone vaulted cellar, has subdued lighting that adds to the Jacobean hideaway feel: there is a second vault below! Bedrooms are reached along twisty split-level corridors and are all different: some in rich colours with old pieces, others with heavy wall fabrics and a country feel, a few with giant structural timbers. One large two-windowed corner room has yellow Jouy-style 'brocade' walls, a rich brown carpet, square yellow quilts on pure white (an idea used throughout), a big marble bathroom. Another fine suite has oodles of pink chintz, old furniture and... space. Note: no air con but stand-up fans. The staff are delightful.

Price	€135–€165. Suite €190. Family rooms €190–€215.
Rooms	29: 22 twins/doubles, 1 suite, 6 family rooms for 3-4.
Meals	Breakfast €9.50. Restaurants nearby.
Closed	Never.
Directions	Metro: Hôtel de Ville (1, 11). RER: Châtelet-Les Halles. Buses: 47, 72, 74, 75. Parking: Baudoyer, Lobau.

Philippe Bidal
22 rue Sainte Croix de la Bretonnerie,
75004 Paris

Tel	+33 (0)1 48 87 77 63
Email	hotel@bretonnerie.com
Web	www.hotelbretonnerie.com

Hôtel du 7è Art

The 'Seventh Art' is French for cinema. The director's chair is yours where black and white images of film are lovingly tended, as eternally youthful as the stars of yesteryear. Besides a pleasingly quirky little hotel, there is a lively bar where log fires burn in winter. The charming young owners have thought of everything, including a laundry room and a trio of fitness machines to maintain your Hollywood muscles in decadent Paris. Black and white is the theme – viz. that checked floor in the bar/breakfast room – and old film posters decorate the walls. Up the black carpeted stairs, the bedrooms are small and un-showily decorated – some hessian walls, some pine slatting, brown carpets – and have… white and black bathrooms with the occasional star-studded shower curtain! Some rooms are tiny – the largest are on the top floor – and some have ceiling fans. The atmosphere is peaceful (the bar closes at midnight), the street is full of antique shops and the oldest part of Paris is all around you. Nowhere in Paris does funky modern so well. *No lift. WIFI in reception only.*

Price	€95–€150. Single €75.
Rooms	23: 15 doubles, 7 twins, 1 single. Extra beds available.
Meals	Continental-plus breakfast €8. Restaurants nearby.
Closed	Never.
Directions	Metro: St Paul (1), Pont Marie (7), Sully Morland (7). RER: Châtelet-Les Halles. Buses: 69, 96. Parking: Pont Marie, Rue Saint Antoine.

Michel & Yolène Kenig
20 rue Saint Paul, 75004 Paris

Tel	+33 (0)1 44 54 85 00
Email	hotel7art@wanadoo.fr
Web	www.paris-hotel-7art.com

Hôtel du Jeu de Paume

The Île Saint Louis is the most exclusive 17th-century village in Paris and this renovated 'tennis court' – three storeys soar to the roof timbers – is one of its most exceptional sights. Add genuine care from mother-and-daughter owners, fresh flowers, time for everyone and super staff. Provençal in style, smallish rooms give onto quiet courtyards, have rich fabrics, pale walls, good bathrooms, old beams, stones, faded parquet. Some rooms have tiny staircases and tiny cupboards below; some show the building's beautiful beamed skeleton, some have little terraces; the new apartments over the street have tall windows, space and style. We love it – for its sense of history, eccentricities, aesthetic ironies, peaceful humour and feel of home; and for its unconventional attitudes and relaxed yet thoroughly efficient staff. The serene spacious lobby/lounge has Art Deco sofas round a carved fireplace and Scoop the soft gold dog; breakfast is beneath the magnificent timbers by the surrealistic columns; work-out in vaulted cellars. *Let Madame Prache know if your stay spans an anniversary.*

Price	€285-€360. Singles €185-€255. Suites €560. Apartments €600-€900. All prices per night.
Rooms	30 + 2: 20 twins/doubles, 7 singles, 3 suites. 2 apartments for 4-6.
Meals	Breakfast €18. Restaurants nearby.
Closed	15 June-1 September.
Directions	Metro: Pont Marie (7), Cité (4), St Paul (1). RER: St Michel-Notre Dame. Bus: 67. Parking: Pont Marie.

Elyane Prache & Nathalie Heckel
54 rue St Louis en l'Ile, 75004 Paris

Tel	+33 (0)1 43 26 14 18
Email	info@jeudepaumehotel.com
Web	www.jeudepaumehotel.com

Hôtel Abbatial Saint Germain

Relaxed and affable, Michel Sahuc is an enthusiast and his style informs his hotel: the receptionist may choose the music playing over the desk and nearby sitting area but the salon with its long caramel coloured leather sofas is quiet. Rooms are mostly a decent size, some special ones are on a corner, and almost all have two windows. They have just been redecorated: a brown and white swirly patterned carpet sets the colour theme with half-moon wooden headboards or long panelling behind the beds, new quilted coverlets and thick taffeta-like curtains in muted bronze. It's all spic and span and the new lighting arrangements are more than considerate of the nocturnal reader; some bathrooms have sliding doors and rain-head showers. A few rooms at the top have fabulous views swinging round from the colonnade of the Pantheon on its hill to the north rose of Notre Dame on her island, all within a few minutes' walk. The lush foliage on the trees fronting the hotel and a scattering of small neighbourhood bistros are a plus. A friendly and unpretentious place.

Price	€160–€195. Singles €140. Triples €220.
Rooms	43: 22 doubles, 13 twins, 5 singles, 3 triples.
Meals	Continental buffet breakfast €12. Restaurants nearby.
Closed	Never.
Directions	Metro: Maubert Mutualité (10). RER: St Michel-Notre Dame. Buses: 47, 63, 86, 87. Parking: St Germain.

Michel Sahuc
46 boulevard St Germain, 75005 Paris
Tel   +33 (0)1 46 34 02 12
Email resa@abbatial-paris-hotel.com
Web   www.abbatial.com

Hôtel Agora Saint Germain

Deep in the heart of the Latin Quarter – one of the oldest centres of learning in Europe – is a quiet place to stay a few steps from the animation of St Germain, the student buzz of St Michel and the rafts of history that carry Notre Dame beyond. Enter reception, très moderne, with crisp lighting and modish wallpaper on one wall, opening to a pretty glassed-in planted patio – greeting enough. Then you'll be welcomed by the charming receptionist or Madame Sahuc herself, youthful and bright. She has recently renovated with style: a gold and beige wallpaper in the corridors, solid blond wood doors, muted bronze curtains with bedcovers to match, sparkling chrome trimmed bathrooms with floating basins. There is an atmosphere of relaxed, feminine attention to detail. The old-stone basement breakfast room is comfortable with high-backed leather chairs and orange table dressings – and heavenly croissants and raisin rolls from Kayser, one of the master bakers of Paris. Next door, a lively outdoor market is a morning's entertainment on Tuesday, Thursday and Saturday. A good reliable address.

Price	€189-€195. Singles €149. Family room €210.
Rooms	39: 2 doubles, 9 twins, 27 singles, 1 family room for 3.
Meals	Continental buffet breakfast €11. Restaurants nearby.
Closed	Never.
Directions	Metro: Maubert Mutualité (10). RER: St Michel-Notre Dame. Buses: 47, 63, 86, 87, 24. Parking: St Germain.

	Pascale Sahuc
	42 rue des Bernardins, 75005 Paris
Tel	+33 (0)1 46 34 13 00
Email	resa@agora-paris-hotel.com
Web	www.hotelagorasaintgermain.com

Hôtel du Collège de France

This hotel has an atmosphere of solid, well-established family comfort: exposed stones, lots of wood, soft armchairs by the fireplace in the red salon, good lighting. You will be greeted by the delightful young manager and by a less animated and considerably older Joan of Arc. The breakfast room, off the lobby, is warmly red too, with old Parisian prints and a Madonna. Bedrooms are mostly not very big but each has a full-length mirror and a thoroughly practical desk unit. If you want a feeling of space, ask for one with French windows opening to a small balcony. The décor is quite colourful in places with coordinated botanical fabrics, and soft quilts – it is careful and restful, beds are new and bathrooms are fine. The staircase is worth visiting just for its round timbers and windows encrusted with autumn leaves; rooms at the top are worth the walk up from the fifth floor. Above all, a genuinely friendly reception is assured. Generous breakfasts and good value on a quiet street away from the bustle of the main student drags – and you may receive useful intellectual vibrations from the Collège as a bonus.

Price	€90–€145.
Rooms	29: 23 doubles, 6 twins.
Meals	Buffet breakfast €10. Restaurants nearby.
Closed	Never.
Directions	Metro: St Michel (4), Maubert Mutualité (10). RER: St Michel-Notre Dame. Buses: 21, 24, 27, 38, 63, 85, 86, 87. Parking: Maubert Mutualité.

Jean Marc
7 rue Thénard, 75005 Paris
Tel   +33 (0)1 43 26 78 36
Email   info@hotelcdf.com
Web   www.hotel-collegedefrance.com

Hôtel des 3 Collèges

Young Jonathan has taken over from his mother and is eager to please: he has whipped up an easy-to-use bus guide (a much more pleasurable way of getting around Paris than the metro), a list of neighbourhood restaurants and can arrange tickets for the Orsay and Luxembourg museums. Two prices are now available for breakfast: a quick bite for those on the run, a more elaborate repast for those who want a slow start – watching the world rush past the big windows of the open-sided ground floor. The walls are hung with ancient maps showing the Latin Quarter through the ages: the building's foundations were probably laid when Lutetia was capital of Roman Gaul and a 22-metre well still holds water. Bedrooms are spotless and simple, with white furniture and pastel-hued piqué bedcovers; there are splashes of colours in the curtains and good functional bathrooms have Roger & Gallet toiletries plus a clothes line. It is a very pleasant place to stay right beneath the looming wall of the Sorbonne where tomorrow's leaders are as yet learning their future trades. Good service, good value, great spot.

Price	€102–€150. Singles €82. Triples €150–€170.
Rooms	44: 27 doubles, 5 twins, 10 singles, 2 triples.
Meals	Breakfast €4.20–€8. Restaurants nearby.
Closed	Never.
Directions	Metro: Cluny La Sorbonne (10), St Michel (4). RER: Luxembourg, St Michel-Notre Dame. Buses: 21, 27, 38, 63, 82, 84, 86, 87. Parking: Rue Soufflot.

Jonathan Wyplosz
16 rue Cujas, 75005 Paris

Tel	+33 (0)1 43 54 67 30
Email	hotel@3colleges.com
Web	www.3colleges.com

Hôtel Design Sorbonne

How do you cajole a tired little hotel in a perfect location – across from the Sorbonne at the back of a cobbled porchway – into the 21st century? Pascale and Corinne Moncelli, who own a selection of the most interesting hotels on the Left Bank, have done it with luxurious fabrics, humour and a bit of faux-baroque. First they brought in daylight with a glass and metal cage for the reception which used to hide behind a pillar. Now the tiny lobby glows in a halo of turquoise and brown fabric wrapped in new panelling, a perfect setting for two luminous, lime-green armchairs (and art books you may borrow). A bright, curvy flourish of fuchsia on the walls and banana and black upholstered benches along the breakfast room will jolt you into wakefulness even before coffee is served. Rooms remain small and lighting moody, but splendid silky wallpaper, thick chocolate carpeting, real showers and a fresh new décor bring a sense of well-being. The ultra-modern touch is an iMac in every room with free access to your favourite film. The Moncellis sponsor young artists; some of their photographs are on display for your pleasure.

Price	€70–€350.
Rooms	38 doubles.
Meals	Breakfast €12 (€15 in bedroom). Restaurants nearby.
Closed	Never.
Directions	Metro: Cluny-Sorbonne. RER: Luxembourg. Buses: 21, 27, 38, 63, 82, 84, 86, 97. Parking: Rue Soufflot.

David Germain
6 rue Victor Cousin, 75005 Paris

Tel	+33 (0)1 43 59 58 08
Email	reservation@hotelsorbonne.com
Web	www.hotelsorbonne.com

Hôtel du Panthéon

Sainte Geneviève managed to save the Parisians from Attila in 451 and was declared their patron saint. This is her neighbourhood: her abbey is now a prestigious lycée; a tiny squiggle of a street and wonderful library opposite the hotel bear her name; the intriguing Saint Etienne du Mont on the other side of the square guards her relics. Is it the expanse of the red-draped windows, the fireplace, or the slightly sunken feel of the salon that gives such an intimate perspective on the town hall, the noble columns of the Panthéon and the hustle-bustle of the streets? It all has the feeling of an 18th-century townhouse; you expect the clatter of horses' hooves. Rooms, not large, are Louis XV 'country style' with beamed ceilings and exquisite patterned fabric on the walls; the beds, some four-postered and canopied or tucked in alcoves, are kept virginal white, their skirts, bedheads and coverlets in another pattern. The curtains frame views onto the Panthéon looming majestically in the centre of the square. Bathrooms are luxurious – one is even bigger than the room. The welcome is perfect.

Price	€99–€310. Family rooms €184–€470.
Rooms	36: 34 twins/doubles, 2 family rooms for 2-3.
Meals	Breakfast €13. Restaurants nearby.
Closed	Never.
Directions	Metro: Cardinal Lemoine (10). RER: Luxembourg, St Michel-Notre Dame. Buses: 21, 27, 38, 58, 82, 84, 85, 89. Parking: Rue Soufflot.

	Mathieu Paygamban
	19 place du Panthéon, 75005 Paris
Tel	+33 (0)1 43 54 32 95
Email	reservation@hoteldupantheon.com
Web	www.hoteldupantheon.com

Hôtel des Grands Hommes

You reach the hotel by crossing the expanse of the round neo-classical Place du Panthéon; then the doors of the hotel slide open and you slip into a knock-out Empire style. Urns, columns and classical curlicues set the tone, while in an intimate alcove the plush of velvet-covered settees and aubergine and blueberry-striped curtains invite discreet conversations. Burnished mahogany panels show off exquisite yellow vases perched on sconces. It is all subdued and elegant. The Grands Hommes refers to the illustrious men honoured in the Panthéon. (Marie Curie, added in 1995, was the first woman.) The great dome has a surreal proximity to the hotel, a reason for André Breton and his 'automatic writing' acolytes to hang out in the early 1900s – from the ground floor where breakfast is served to the top-floor rooms with their big terraces, some with views to the Sacré Cœur. Rooms are jewel boxes of canopied beds in alcoves, Pompeii-like frescoes, exquisite crystal chandeliers, toile de Jouy, yellow beams, pale pink ceilings. It's all pure magic, especially at nightfall when Paris takes on her glow.

Price	€108–€310. Suites €215–€430. Family rooms €184–€282.
Rooms	31: 23 twins/doubles, 3 suites, 5 family rooms for 3.
Meals	Breakfast €13. Restaurants nearby.
Closed	Never.
Directions	Metro: Cardinal Lemoine (10). RER: Luxembourg, St Michel-Notre Dame. Buses: 21, 27, 38, 58, 82, 84, 85, 89. Parking: Rue Soufflot.

	Mme Hery
	17 place du Panthéon, 75005 Paris
Tel	+33 (0)1 46 34 19 60
Email	reservation@hoteldesgrandshommes.com
Web	www.hoteldesgrandshommes.com

Hôtel Résidence Les Gobelins

All here is quiet, attentive and unassuming – street, hotel, owners. And the patio is a treat. Workers in the great Gobelins tapestry shops lived in this area and it was never very smart, but nearby is the entertaining, slightly bohemian rue Mouffetard – little eating houses, big mosque (try the hamman!), lively market, left-wing culture. The lounge, with country-cushioned wicker furniture, and the bright yellow airy breakfast room decorated with much-loved black and white photographs of Paris and Parisians, lie round that honeysuckle-hung courtyard where guests can sit in peace. Bedrooms and bathrooms are simple, spotless and well-equipped – a writing table and chair, a decent cupboard, an excellent shower – and have space (though singles are compact, as are some doubles); all is restful and harmonious. Bright white bedspreads sparkle and the green and dark red rattan furniture is ageing with grace. All rooms are quiet and light. The Poiriers' gentle unobtrusive friendliness reminds us that the family used to keep a *pension de famille*. And the dog answers to Jeannie.

Price	€89-€95.
Rooms	32 doubles.
Meals	Breakfast €8.50. Restaurant 100m.
Closed	Never.
Directions	Metro: Gobelins (7).
	RER: Port Royal.
	Buses: 27, 47, 83, 91.
	Parking: Place d'Italie.

Jennifer & Philippe Poirier
9 rue des Gobelins, 75013 Paris

Tel	+33 (0)1 47 07 26 90
Email	hotelgobelins@noos.fr
Web	www.hotelgobelins.com

Hôtel Les Jardins du Luxembourg

Freud once trampled this still peaceful cul-de-sac when he stayed in 1885 – and we know that the curtains round his bed were yellow: his disciple Ernest Jones relates that he applied chemical tests to make sure they did not contain arsenic. Now there are curtains at the windows only, some falling nicely to the floor; original beams are still on view under the eaves. Rooms are small, balconies minute, furnishings immaculate. We can imagine Freud sitting in front of the fireplace (still there) in the little salon; Art Deco chairs and brass lights over paintings give it an intimate feel, and the daily papers come free. The reception area, by contrast, is a big open space, with a handsome mahogany desk that doubles as a bar. Facing it is a long wrought-iron park bench with colourful cushions to remind us that the Luxembourg Gardens are just across the street. Keep your eye out for the delightful ochre and orange checkerboard tiles in the breakfast room and joyful little trompe l'oeil lizards and vine wreaths in the bathrooms, some of which have free-standing basins, four-legged bath tubs and mirror-speckled walls.

Price	€135–€170. Single €143.
Rooms	26: 18 doubles, 7 twins, 1 single.
Meals	Breakfast €11. Restaurants nearby.
Closed	Never.
Directions	Metro: Cluny la Sorbonne (10). RER: Luxembourg. Buses: 21, 27, 38, 82, 84, 85, 89. Parking: Private parking available.

	Hélène Touber
	5 Impasse Royer Collard, 75005 Paris
Tel	+33 (0)1 40 46 08 88
Email	jardinslux@wanadoo.fr
Web	www.les-jardins-du-luxembourg.com

Hôtel Raspail Montparnasse

Below the satisfyingly genuine 1924 frontage, the old doors spring towards you as you approach – 20th-century magic. There's old-style generosity in the high Art Deco lobby with its ceiling fans, leather chairs and play of squares and curves. The intimate hideaway bar with its leopard skin stools is a reminder of all night conversations about art and love, or the art of love... enjoy a coffee over the international papers. In the newly renovated bedrooms gauze curtains soften the daylight and elegant side tables match the handsome two-toned wooden headboards and desks. Fine fabrics and unfussy quilts add to the sober style. To each floor a colour: quiet grey, sunny ochre, powder-puff blue; to each landing a stained-glass window. Obviously, the higher the price, the bigger the room, but even the 'standards' have a decent desk and an armchair; some have the added perk of a glittering Eiffel Tower view at night. Montparnasse still bustles crazily down below and owner Christiane has heaps of ideas on where to shop and dine. A friendly and efficient welcome is the first and final flourish.

Price	€129-€220. Suites €225-€280.
Rooms	38: 36 twins/doubles, 2 suites.
Meals	Breakfast €10. Restaurants nearby.
Closed	Never.
Directions	Metro: Vavin (4), Raspail (4, 6). RER: Port Royal. Buses: 58, 68, 82, 91. Parking: Boulevard du Montparnasse.

	Christiane Martinent
	203 boulevard Raspail, 75014 Paris
Tel	+33 (0)1 43 20 62 86
Email	raspailm@wanadoo.fr
Web	www.hotelraspailmontparnasse.com

Le Sainte Beuve

This beautifully decorated hotel, well-known and loved during the wilder days of Montparnasse, exudes an atmosphere of unstuffy designer luxury – quiet good taste in gentle tones and thick fabrics. The harmoniously hued lobby/salon, which doubles as a breakfast room, has superb silk curtains, a winter fire in the marble fireplace, modern paintings and old prints. It is all small and intimate and the attentive, efficient staff are a vital element in your sense of well-being. Bedrooms come in ancient and modern finery: lots of pale walls, soft colours and textured fabrics, colourful chintzes and paisleys, at least one antique per room – a leather-topped desk, a walnut dressing-table, a polished armoire – and 18th/19th-century pictures in rich old frames. The Sainte Beuve room is the largest and it's dazzling. Bathrooms are superbly modern with bathrobes and fine toiletries. Start the day with a feast of croissants and brioches from the famous Mulot bakery... then you can run it off in the Luxembourg Gardens. End the day with très tasty food at teensy Le Timbre, in the same street.

Price	€155-€365. Suite €315-€365.
Rooms	22: 5 doubles, 16 twins, 1 suite for 2.
Meals	Breakfast €15. Restaurants nearby.
Closed	Rarely.
Directions	Metro: Notre Dame des Champs (12), Vavin (4). RER: Port-Royal. Parking: Montparnasse.

M & Mme Ferrero
9 rue Sainte-Beuve, 75006 Paris

Tel	+33 (0)1 45 48 20 07
Email	saintebeuve@wanadoo.fr
Web	www.hotelsaintebeuveparis.com

Pension Les Marronniers

It's an honest-to-goodness *pension de famille*, one of the very last, so if you're young and penniless or old and nostalgic, head for Marie's quintessentially French family place overlooking the Luxembourg Gardens. It's been in her family since the 1930s and is as personal and cluttered as anything in Balzac. There are countless pictures, portraits and photographs, statues and plants galore, notices from inmates on flower pots and mantelpieces, a cuckoo clock that was silenced 20 years ago and a superbly-carved, grass-green armoire topped with a motley crew of candlesticks. Marie coddles her guests (some return year after year) and loves cooking for them: she clearly enjoys food herself, especially vegetarian, and makes sure others do too. She is also down-to-earth, compassionate, perceptive and hard-working – a remarkable woman. The bedrooms for short-stayers have less personality than the dining and drawing room, rather as if they have been furnished with what was left over, and some share washing facilities. But what counts is the wonderful welcome, the tradition and the food.

Price	Half-board €40–€67 p.p. Weekly & monthly rentals.
Rooms	12: 6 twins/doubles; 6 twins/doubles sharing bath.
Meals	Half-board only, except Saturdays & Sundays (brunch on Saturdays).
Closed	Never.
Directions	Metro: Vavin (4), Notre Dame des Champs (12). RER: Luxembourg. Buses: 58, 82, 83. Parking: Rue Auguste Comte.

Marie Poirier
78 rue d'Assas, 75006 Paris

Tel	+33 (0)1 43 26 37 71
Email	infos@pension-marronniers.com
Web	www.pension-marronniers.com

Trianon Rive Gauche

Cosy, functional, on the Rive Gauche and near everything – three steps from the Sorbonne, three minutes from the Jardins de Luxembourg. A pair of buildings (one built in 1860, one Art Deco) run up eight storeys linked by a staircase that wraps its graceful self around the old-world cage-style lift... and the rooms on the top floor get the great views: gaze over Parisian rooftops to the Eiffel Tower and the Sacré Coeur. All has been refurbished inside. Step into a flashy black, white and silver reception, manned by delightful staff, with sofas unholstered in neo-baroque prints and a fabulous round mirror overseeing the space. There's an airy beige-tiled breakfast room for a buffet start to the day (or you can have coffee and croissants in your room) and a big basement bar that is on its way. Comfortable bedrooms, not huge but a fair size for Paris, have fabric-covered walls in dark orange and mustard, wall to wall carpeting in thin stripes, brown quilted bedspreads and heavy drapes. Reproduction old masters hang on the walls; bathrooms, though tiny, are sparklier. Paris lies at your feet.

Price	€109–€198. Singles €101–€165. Triples €165–€245. Quads €250–€270.
Rooms	110: 60 doubles, 34 twins, 5 singles, 9 triples, 2 quadruples.
Meals	Buffet breakfast €14 (continental breakfast included). Restaurants nearby.
Closed	Never.
Directions	Metro: Cluny, Odéon (10), St Michel (4). RER: Luxembourg (B). Buses: 21, 27, 38, 82. Parking: Rue de l'École de Médecine or Rue Soufflot.

Perrine Henneveux
1 bis & 3 rue de Vaugirard,
75006 Paris

Tel	+33 (0)1 43 29 88 10
Email	trianon.rg@wanadoo.fr
Web	www.hoteltrianonrivegauche.com

Hôtel Mayet

Youthful and fun, the Mayet emerged light-hearted and comfortable from its makeover and Laurence Raymond's touch is everywhere apparent. On the delectable old oak lobby floor, the desk is an office unit lookalike with two black meeting-room lamps overhead. To left and right, artists have been at bright, drippy mural work, the deep sofas are richly natural, the venetian blinds softly luminous. Here reigns smiling Hélène: she's been with Laurence for years and delights in the Mayet's brave look. Walk down to breakfast: every step is carpeted a different, vibrant colour; the stone vault houses self-service shelves and a long colourful table on a stripey floor. In cafeteria style, the croissants, breads and jams are tasty and fresh, and you can spoil your partner with breakfast in bed. Two vending machines are at your service with snacks and drinks while the day's restaurant recommendations are up on a blackboard. Compact bedrooms are in grey, white and dark red, with 'office' furniture, fans not air con, and excellent bedding. A quietish street in a great neighbourhood and, as we said, huge fun.

Price	€120–€140.
Rooms	23 twins/doubles.
Meals	Self-service breakfast included. Restaurants nearby.
Closed	August & Christmas.
Directions	Metro: Duroc (10, 13), Vaneau (10). RER: Invalides, St Michel-Notre Dame. Buses: 28, 39, 70, 82, 87, 89, 92. Parking: Bon Marché.

Laurence Raymond & Hélène Jacquet
3 rue Mayet, 75006 Paris

Tel   +33 (0)1 47 83 21 35
Email   hotel@mayet.com
Web   www.mayet.com

Le Madison

Discreet behind a row of trees opposite the vastly celebrated Deux Magots café, the Madison's Art Deco façade is as supremely Parisian as its antique-filled salons. The enlightened owner likes sharing his collections: a fine portrait of his mother as a young girl dominates the velour-clothed breakfast tables while a porcelain cockerel crows from its pedestal. This is a very stylish city hotel with top-quality fabrics and fittings, yet it's like no other: adventurous imagination guides the rich choice of colours and textures, bathrooms have stunning Italian tiling, luminous glass crescents clasp drapes, lift doors carry wonderful artists' impressions of the great names of St Germain and staff have just the right mix of polite class and friendly cheerfulness. All rooms are different, bursting with personality. In a big blue, beige and green room over the boulevard, a lovely green china lamp on a nice old desk and a deep red marble bathroom; next door, a small raspberry, yellow and royal blue room, vital and provocative; in the top-floor suite, a triumph of space and wraparound views.

Price	€235–€395. Singles €175–€195. Suites €415–€435.
Rooms	52: 46 twins/doubles, 3 singles, 3 suites.
Meals	Restaurants nearby.
Closed	Never.
Directions	Metro: St Germain des Prés. RER: Saint Michel.

	Caroline Demon
	143 boulevard Saint Germain, 75006 Paris
Tel	+33 (0)1 40 51 60 00
Email	resa@hotel-madison.com
Web	www.hotel-madison.com

Hôtel Saint Paul Rive Gauche

An exceptionally welcoming place with a flickering fire in the sitting room, a day-lit interior patio and Sputnik the sleeping cat. With the Luxembourg Gardens a stroll away, bustling Saint Germain at the end of the street, and exceptional service and attention to detail, it's the favourite of many guests. Expect crisp white duvets with a mohair throw for a splash of colour, a thick tiger-stripe carpet underfoot, new spotless bathrooms with real shower heads, Roger & Gallet soaps and comforting towel heaters. Bedrooms come in different sizes and that includes small – as with most Paris hotels; those in the back have handsome views onto the prestigious Lycée St Louis with its classical façade, those in front look onto the ever fascinating Rue Monsieur le Prince. There are beamed ceilings, sleigh beds, faux ostrich bedheads, clever corner armoires, a family antique placed here or there, even two baldaquin beds on the lower floors with the high ceilings. The fourth generation of a Franco-British family has made the Saint Paul a welcoming marriage of French elegance and English comfort.

Price	€168–€218. Singles €154. Family rooms €268–€298.
Rooms	31: 21 doubles, 7 twins/doubles, 3 family rooms for 3-4. Some rooms interconnect.
Meals	Buffet breakfast €13. Restaurants nearby.
Closed	Never.
Directions	Metro: Odéon (4,10). RER: Luxembourg. Buses: 21, 27, 38, 58, 63, 82, 84, 85, 86, 87, 89, 96. Parking: École de Médecine, St Sulpice.

Marianne Oberlin
43 rue Monsieur le Prince,
75006 Paris

Tel	+33 (0)1 43 26 98 64
Email	contact@hotelsaintpaulparis.com
Web	www.hotelsaintpaulparis.com

Hôtel Le Clos Médicis

You can see right into the lobby through what was a shop window; slip in from the excitable Boulevard St Michel and you hear muted jazz, feel soft air. In this place of quiet contemporary class, the attractive countersunk salon has a welcoming fire, deep brown armchairs, jungle pictures and a fine stone pillar; beyond it are a sunny Tuscan patio and a delightful young team at reception. To ground its very Parisian personality, the Hôtel Le Clos Médicis has opted for roots in provincial soil: a *clos* is a vineyard, and each room is named after a famous wine. Bedrooms have been redesigned by fashionable names in strong silent colours – rich red and blue, white, ginger and brown – real fabrics with wide contrasting borders, deep-framed mirrors and sophisticated wildlife prints. One room has a private terrace, another is a nicely arranged duplex; all are soundproofed and, if not always very big, are most comfortable. Bathrooms are still impeccable. The details have all been thought through. Add that lively sense of hospitality, and it's all you could hope for, and possibly more.

Price	€180–€270. Singles from €150. Duplex & family room €310–€435.
Rooms	38: 16 doubles, 20 twins/doubles, 1 duplex, 1 family room for 3.
Meals	Buffet breakfast €13. Restaurants nearby.
Closed	Never.
Directions	Metro: Odéon (4,10). RER: Luxembourg. Buses: 21, 38, 82, 84, 85, 89. Parking: Rue Soufflot.

Olivier Méallet
56 rue Monsieur le Prince,
75006 Paris

Tel	+33 (0)1 43 29 10 80
Email	message@hotelclosmedicisparis.com
Web	www.hotelclosmedicisparis.com

Hôtel Michelet Odéon

An inexpensive find in an extraordinary setting. Now that the scaffolding has been shed from L'Odéon, exposing the theatre's fine 18th-century pillars and scrubbed neoclassical façade, the excellent Michelet Odéon, right next door, is clearly visible. It, too, has come through a remarkable transformation thanks to Delphine Mouton whose grandparents once owned this hotel. The breakfast room off the day-lit lobby sets the tone: big padded cushions line a wall in chocolate brown, taupe and redcurrant; a row of black and white vintage photos sits above and reflects the light; it's simple and sober with a warm mix of colour and materials. Upstairs she skilfully uses earth tones with a zebra-patterned rug, silky taffeta curtains and thick bedspreads; one wall is lit in rose pink, khaki, mauve, butterscotch beige or aniseed green. There is space for potions in the modern bathrooms; all are sparkling-tiled in white with a discreet mosaic trim. From some rooms you can see the theatre, from others the Luxembourg Gardens. Best of all? There are Velib bikes for hire just around the corner – hop into the saddle and go!

Price	€122.50–€132.50. Single €100. Suites €220. Family rooms €175–€195.
Rooms	42: 35 twins/doubles, 1 single, 2 suites for 4, 4 family rooms: 3 for 3, 1 for 4.
Meals	Breakfast €14. Restaurants nearby.
Closed	Never.
Directions	Metro: Odéon (4,10). RER: Luxembourg. Buses: 21, 27, 38, 58, 84, 85, 89, 63, 87. Parking: Marché St Germain des Prés.

Delphine Mouton
6 place de l'Odéon,
75006 Paris

Tel	+33 (0)1 53 10 05 60
Email	hotel@micheletodeon.com
Web	www.hotelmicheletodeon.com

Hôtel Jardin de l'Odéon

When the cubists 'discovered' African art, revered were most things ethnic. Hence the marriage of tall ebony Egyptian scribes, an Ashanti statue and the reclining nude à la Picasso overlooking the clean lines of the Art Deco salon. The airy lounge and breakfast area with its velvet striped chairs and bistro benches continue the 30s feel. Just beyond, the tranquil sounds of a splashing fountain emerge from a jasmine-planted terrace; bathed in morning sun, it will tempt you to prolong your breakfast moment. Curtains and bedcovers mix and match handsome check and stripe fabric in reds, toffees and blues. Some suites have the bathtub in the room, those at the back have views of the patio (and birdsong), others exquisite private terraces large enough for a table and chairs; those on the street glimpse the columns of the magically lit Odéon. Effervescent, smiley Sylvia places orchids in the salon and lights candles at night; she will see to it that you are well taken care of. All this on a quiet, tiny street leading down to the bustle of St Germain or up to the Jardins de Luxembourg. A sweet retreat.

Price	€70–€370. Family rooms €166–€450.
Rooms	41: 19 doubles, 17 twins, 1 single, 4 family rooms.
Meals	Breakfast €13. Restaurants nearby.
Closed	Never.
Directions	Metro: Odeon (4,10), Luxembourg. RER: St Michel-Notre Dame. Buses: 21, 27, 38, 58, 63, 82, 84, 85, 86, 87, 89. Parking: École de Médecine.

	Sylvia Harrault
	7 rue Casimir Delavigne,
	75006 Paris
Tel	+33 (0)1 53 10 28 50
Email	reservation@hoteljardinodeonparis.com
Web	www.hoteljardinodeonparis.com

Grand Hôtel des Balcons

Les Balcons has the lot: an idea of service that produces tea on winter afternoons, a clothes line over the bath, and a daily feast of a breakfast (sumptuous cooked spread, fresh fruit salad), that's free on your birthday. Owners and staff appear to work with lightness and pleasure. Having decorated her Art Nouveau hotel by taking inspiration from the floral 1890s staircase windows, Denise Corroyer now teaches *ikebana* and flowers the house – brilliantly – while her son Jean-François and his wife charmingly manage. Rooms are simple yet pleasing. The five big family rooms have smart décor and pretty modern lamps, parquet floors and two windows, decent bathrooms (two basins, pretty tiles) and loads of space. Other rooms are tiny but purpose-made table units use the space judiciously, amusing prints decorate the walls and front rooms have balconies with planted window boxes. At the back, you may be woken by the birds. An eagle eye is kept on maintenance, beds are firm, colours and fabrics simple and bright. Remarkable value, super people, and bang in the heart of the Latin Quarter.

Price	€110-€175. Singles €85-€175. Family rooms €220.
Rooms	50: 25 doubles, 14 twins, 6 singles, 5 family rooms for 4.
Meals	Breakfast €12. Restaurants nearby.
Closed	Never.
Directions	Metro: Odéon (4, 10). RER: Luxembourg. Buses: 21, 24, 27, 58, 63, 86, 87, 95, 96. Parking: École de Médecine.

	Jean-François André 3 rue Casimir Delavigne, 75006 Paris
Tel	+33 (0)1 46 34 78 50
Email	grandhoteldesbalcons@orange.fr
Web	www.balcons.com

Hôtel Louis II

Inviting? The smell of fresh toast travels up to you in the morning. Quirky? All beds have been adjusted to the uneven old floors. Charming? Imagination has triumphed in this 18th-century house, often to dramatic effect, so that even the smallest rooms (some very snug) have huge personality. Two have dazzling wraparound trompe-l'œil pictures set into the timber frame, one has an antique door as a bedhead, all have WiFi, effective air con, perfect linen. Bath/shower rooms are small, brand new, sparkling white and fully equipped with large shower heads. On the top floor, you sleep under sloping rafters in a long room with sculpted gold sconces beside each bed. A lift descends to a refined breakfast in the golden elegance of the big salon with its magnificent fanning beams and rich double-sided curtains. Gilt-framed mirrors, a ship's figurehead, fine antique tables, and Turkey rugs on old terracotta tiles complete the picture. You will be enthusiastically welcomed here and properly cared for, embraced by the discreet charm of the Rive Gauche, a short walk from the Jardins du Luxembourg and the Carrefour de l'Odéon.

Price	€195–€220. Triples €310.
Rooms	22: 20 twins/doubles, 2 triples.
Meals	Breakfast €15. Restaurants nearby.
Closed	Never.
Directions	Metro: Odéon.
	RER: St Michel-Notre Dame.

Guillaume Jouvin
2 rue Saint Sulpice, 75006 Paris

Tel	+33 (0)1 46 33 13 80
Email	reservation@hotel-louis2.fr
Web	www.hotel-louis2.com

Hôtel Odéon Saint-Germain

Once across the threshold of this small hotel you will be swept away by the understated luxury, Parisian elegance and generous envelope of well-being. There is an honesty bar in the lobby along with black and white striped armchairs with red satin backs and a comfy toffee-coloured sofa facing an ancient stone fireplace and an open stone wall. A tiny lift brings you to the rooms, some with high ceilings and silk canopies, others with chaises longues for lounging, or a luscious panel of flower-patterned silk hung behind the leather headboards. Most of them have beamed ceilings painted in egg shell or off-white. Sounds are muffled, even the doors to the rooms have been padded for everyone's comfort. Attention to detail is evident, from the chocolates popped on the pillow at night to the L'Occitane products in the bathrooms; the staff are a delight. The owners were previously in the restaurant business so breakfast is a feast with homemade fruit compotes and cakes, prunes plumped in a cinnamon syrup and the best pastries that Paris can offer. Ask for one of the larger rooms, and book ahead.

Price	€145–€370.
Rooms	27: 15 doubles, 6 twins, 2 singles, 4 triples.
Meals	Breakfast €14. Restaurants nearby.
Closed	Never.
Directions	Metro: Odéon. RER: St Michel-Notre Dame.

M & Mme Triadou
13 rue Saint Sulpice, 75006 Paris

Tel	+33 (0)1 43 25 70 11
Email	mail@hotelosg.com
Web	www.hotelosg.com

Entry 78   Map 5

Hôtel Relais Saint Sulpice

Smack on the back doorstep of Saint Sulpice church, tucked into one of those tiny magic streets untouched by the passage of time, this is the perfect hideaway for sleuthing around for *Da Vinci Code* clues or spotting the literati of Saint Germain des Prés. You might almost miss the entrance if you are not careful; it's more an entryway into an aristocratic 18th-century home than a door to a hotel. The womb-like salon continues the lived-in feeling with screened mahogany bookcases, backlit objets lining the top shelves, a pair of 1940s armchairs and a couple of large Chinese jars; a big gilt mirror sits in a corner to reflect light from the high windows. No reception desk to speak of here, just a friendly spirit behind a small table to hand out keys to your small but cosy room. The attention to detail is impressive: you may spot a fringe-like frieze along the walls or an elegant wrought-iron bed and bistro table, while most bathrooms have trompe l'œil 'rugs' of colourful tiles. A huge glass roof and a bounty of greenery give a winter garden feel to the breakfast room. An exceptional address.

Price	€178–€270. €245 for 3.
Rooms	26: 19 doubles, 7 twins. Extra bed available.
Meals	Breakfast €12. Restaurants nearby.
Closed	Never.
Directions	Metro: Odéon (4, 10), Mabillon (10). RER: St Michel-Notre Dame, Luxembourg. Buses: 58, 63, 86, 70, 87, 96, 84. Parking: Place Saint Sulpice & Marché Saint-Germain.

	Hélène Touber
	3 rue Garancière, 75006 Paris
Tel	+33 (0)1 46 33 99 00
Email	relaisstsulpice@wanadoo.fr
Web	www.relais-saint-sulpice.com

Hôtel Le Clément

This cute little hotel has been in the same family for 100 years and Madame Charrade, the fourth generation, is the gentlest hotelier you could hope to meet. Charming and communicative, she takes care of her guests like family. More cosy living room than lobby is the inviting sitting area off the new breakfast room, with fireplace, gleaming wood panelling and bookshelves. From the higher floors, the view across the St Germain marketplace to the towers of St Sulpice church is super; these rooms at the top have loads of character with their sloping ceilings, if less space. Back rooms have no view, of course, except over the pretty planting at the bottom of one of the lightwells (the hotel occupies two connecting buildings), but peace is guaranteed. Madame's decorative style is southern cottage: small spriggy or floral prints, harmonious wallpapers, good colour combinations – midnight-blue and ivory, Provençal red and orange – and crisp, white piqué bedcovers; bathrooms are often tiled in colourful mosaic. A hotel of good value – from which reaching all the sights is a breeze.

Price	€126-€148. Family rooms & triples €165.	
Rooms	28: 12 doubles, 6 twins, 5 family rooms for 3, 5 triples.	
Meals	Buffet breakfast €11. Restaurants nearby.	
Closed	Never.	
Directions	Metro: St Germain des Prés (4), Mabillon (10). RER: Luxembourg. Buses: 63, 70, 85, 86, 95, 96. Parking: Opposite hotel.	

	M & Mme Charrade
	6 rue Clément, 75006 Paris
Tel	+33 (0)1 43 26 53 60
Email	info@hotel-clement.fr
Web	www.hotel-clement.fr

Grand Hôtel de l'Univers

Your taxi driver may suggest dropping you off on Boulevard St Germain which slices this one-way street in half; no matter, the lower bit, more a pavement than a street, is only ten giant steps long and finishes on the trendy Rue de Buci. As you've guessed, you are in an old part of town and the 15th-century effigy of a man leaning on his truncheon, found above the door, remains a mystery. Even seen through large windows on the street the big airy salon is a surprise with the theatricality of its 18th-century sofa, armchairs and antique dresser set against a huge wall of honey-coloured stone; the bar behind the reception is a much cosier affair. Rooms are delightful, quiet, and decorated with real flair; bathrooms are recent in marble and chrome. If size is important, opt for the superior rooms. Breakfast in the stone-vaulted cellar is a real treat, with eggs, sausages, fresh orange juice and delicious breads. Extra atmosphere comes from the backlit medieval sconces. There are rafters in the corridors here, and the two special deluxe rooms are worth the extra charge.

Price	€150–€280. Singles €130–€185.
Rooms	33 twins/doubles.
Meals	Buffet breakfast €10.
	Restaurants nearby.
Closed	Never.
Directions	Metro: Odéon (4,10).
	RER: St Michel-Notre Dame.
	Buses: 58, 63, 70, 86, 96.
	Parking: Rue Mazarine,
	St Germain des Prés.

	Eric Desfaudais
	6 rue Grégoire de Tours,
	75006 Paris
Tel	+33 (0)1 43 29 37 00
Email	grandhotelunivers@wanadoo.fr
Web	www.hotel-paris-univers.com

Hôtel Prince de Condé

In one of the smallest hotels in the city on one of the most sauntering streets – named after the great river to which it leads – you'll meet delightful staff and great attention to detail. Paris is full of vaulted cellars transformed into breakfast rooms but it is rare to find one done in such style. A red patterned carpet warms the exposed stone, little round tables invite intimacy and low-riding armchairs clothed in broad stripes and fun patterns are a lesson in comfort and cosiness – with an elegant porcelain service to match. There are canopies over beds, cloth-lined walls, double glazed windows and just the right English chair or Napoleon III desk to personalise a bedroom. The large suite on the top floor under the roof gets a royal bathroom: jacuzzi tub, double basins, swish Italian faucets. It's big enough to wear red and green medallion wall paper, sit a couple of plaid armchairs in a corner and still have room for a moss-green upholstered sofa and cushions trimmed in red cord. Lots of galleries for gazing and people for watching on Rue de Seine and the Rue Buci nearby. Just lovely.

Price	€150–€300. Suite €280.
Rooms	11: 10 twins/doubles, 1 suite for 2.
Meals	Breakfast €13. Restaurants nearby.
Closed	Never.
Directions	Metro: St Germain des Prés (4), Odéon (4,10), Pont Neuf (7), Mabillon (10). RER: St Michel-Notre Dame. Buses: 58, 70. Parking: Rue Mazarine.

	Hélène Touber
	39 rue de Seine,
	75006 Paris
Tel	+33 (0)1 43 26 71 56
Email	princedeconde@wanadoo.fr
Web	www.prince-de-conde.com

Welcome Hôtel

On one of the trendiest crossroads of Paris where the delightfully twisty, fashionable little un-cheap shopping streets and the legendary cafés of St Germain meet, the Welcome has that easy atmosphere created by a natural and unpretentious attitude to life and people. The ground-floor reception is tiny but there's a bit more space as you move up. On the first floor is the small, timbered, tapestried Louis XIII salon whence you can look down from the breakfast table onto the bustle below. Most of the bedrooms are smallish, too, and all give onto one or other of the streets, so choose between outside air and (not very efficient) double glazing. Among all sorts of angles and juttings-out, the variegated décor has in some rooms been revived with floral fabrics and bottle-green carpeting; furniture is functional wood and bathrooms are tiled. On the top floor you find sloping ceilings and beams: one bedroom is reached through its half-timbered bathroom. It's quirky, night-noisy and absolutely in the thick of things. Breakfast is a communal affair in the hallway.

Price	€76–€134.
Rooms	30 twins/doubles.
Meals	Breakfast €11. Restaurants nearby.
Closed	Never.
Directions	Metro: St Germain des Prés (4), Mabillon (10), Odéon (4, 10). RER: St Michel-Notre Dame. Buses: 39, 48, 58, 63, 70, 86, 87, 95. Parking: St Germain des Prés, St Sulpice.

	Perrine Henneveux
	66 rue de Seine, 75006 Paris
Tel	+33 (0)1 46 34 24 80
Email	welcome-hotel@wanadoo.fr
Web	www.welcomehotel-paris.com

Hôtel Prince de Conti

The narrow, peaceful Rue Guénégaud, just off the riverside, is one to savour slowly. Thankfully, most of the galleries and one-of-a-kind shops have been there almost as long as La Monnaie, the French Mint, now revamped with interesting exhibitions and gift shop. Even our favourite ethnic jewellery shop feels like a gallery as the owner knows the origin of every bead necklace. The Prince de Conti – the Princess lived here in 1670 – feels as authentic the moment your feet hit the lobby's parquet floor. The choice is eclectic but it works: a little sofa fits perfectly in the bay window, a faïence stove sits next to a chinoiserie bamboo chair, a lovely bronze figure in movement watches all from its three-legged pedestal. If you are splurging and want a view, ask for the suite on the top floor with its antique desk, checked armchairs and double-sinked bathroom; or a ground-level room with French windows opening to the interior courtyard. If you're on a budget, the 'standard' rooms on the courtyard will suit – ask for one with two windows – but the larger rooms are definitely worth the extra.

Price	€150–€300.
Rooms	28: 21 doubles, 5 twins, 2 duplexes for 3.
Meals	Breakfast €13. Restaurants nearby.
Closed	Never.
Directions	Metro: St Germain des Prés (4), Odéon (4,10), Pont Neuf (7). RER: St Michel-Notre Dame. Buses: 58, 70. Parking: Rue Mazarine.

	Hélène Touber
	8 rue Guénégaud, 75006 Paris
Tel	+33 (0)1 44 07 30 40
Email	princedeconti@wanadoo.fr
Web	www.prince-de-conti.com

Hôtel de Seine

Underneath the arches, through the big doors: it still feels like a private mansion and the welcome adds to this impression. There are two really French salons off the hall, fresh flowers, space, deep quiet. The breakfast room, presided over by a fine little Pan, aims to please all sorts with a large table for the sociable and several small tables for the less so; walls are clothed in Florentine-style fabric, chairs are blue and studded, antique corner cupboards glow, swags and tassles bobble but it's not cluttered. Bedrooms have class too, with their strong colour schemes, furniture that is gently painted Louis XVI or highly polished, cane-seated Directoire and, again, that sense of being in a home not an anonymous hotel. One room displays rather daring black paint and gilt edging in honour of the 1850s craze for all things Far Eastern; others have quirky layouts dictated by the old architecture. Elegant bathrooms are much mirrored and the higher floors naturally carry 18th-century timbers and the occasional balcony for rooftop views or bird's-eye vistas of Parisian façades. A very welcoming place to stay.

Price	€195–€205. Singles €175. Triples €230.
Rooms	30: 14 doubles, 8 twins, 4 singles, 4 triples.
Meals	Breakfast €12–€13. Restaurants nearby.
Closed	Never.
Directions	Metro: St Germain des Prés (4), Mabillon (10), Odéon (4, 10). RER: St Michel-Notre Dame. Buses: 39, 48, 58, 63, 70, 86, 87, 95. Parking: Rue Mazarine.

Perrine Henneveux
52 rue de Seine, 75006 Paris

Tel	+33 (0)1 46 34 22 80
Email	hotel-de-seine@wanadoo.fr
Web	www.hoteldeseine.com

Hôtel Saint Germain des Prés

There are two spirits afloat in Saint Germain. And because it sometimes feels that the bright-and-blinky has the upper hand, one flees to quiet reminders of another time, like the Place de Furstenberg with Delacroix's museum, or the tiny, almost hidden garden next to the church. Or take a room here, where the time button has hit pause. When we visited, there was an elegantly bejewelled matron – a regular guest – dressed in a stylish white beret chatting with the charming manager, Eric Desfaudais. Perched on one of the high-backed chairs, she matched the décor to perfection. Be seduced by the pale translucent beauty of the Murano chandelier over the reception desk, and the antique tapestry on the wall. The salon, which doubles as the breakfast room, is lit by a glass wall, with a winter garden and a painted mural; the red velvets and smart fabrics of the upholstered armchairs sit nicely against exposed stone walls. The lift is tiny, and so are the rooms, with a boudoir feel and beams galore. (If you're staying in mid summer, ask for one with wall-mounted air con.) But bathrooms are proper 21st century.

Price	€170–€290. Single €130. Suites €350.
Rooms	30: 27 twins/doubles, 1 single, 2 suites for 2.
Meals	Buffet breakfast €10. Restaurants nearby.
Closed	Never.
Directions	Metro: St Germain des Prés (4). RER: St Michel-Notre Dame. Buses: 39, 48, 63, 86, 87, 95. Parking: 169 boulevard St Germain.

	Eric Desfaudais
	36 rue Bonaparte, 75006 Paris
Tel	+33 (0)1 43 26 00 19
Email	hotel-saint-germain-des-pres@wanadoo.fr
Web	www.hotel-paris-saint-germain.com

Hôtel de Buci

On one of the little streets in the heart of St Germain, where tempting galleries, restaurants, antique shops, fashion houses, cafés and bars are encroaching on the much-loved market, stands the Buci, full of old-fashioned comfort and hospitality. In the basement breakfast room are ornate red sofas, in the salon, every portrait, lamp and chair tells a story, and off tiny sloping corridors are bedrooms that vary in peacefulness and size (if you wish to keep windows open in summer, choose one at the back). Expect checks, stripes and florals, canopies, pelmets and quilts, furniture old or repro and a different colour for each floor: sun yellow, redcurrant, cornflower blue, cream. The bathrooms are pretty and inviting, the monogrammed linen is crisp and white, and the WiFi works a treat. Come evening, the morning's gentle classical music turns to jazz to suit the 1930s mood. Best of all, the staff are helpful and delightful. This is a thoroughly reliable place to stay on one of the most fabulous little streets in Saint Germain – and well-priced to boot.

Price	€195-€335. Suites €330-€550.
Rooms	24: 12 doubles, 8 twins, 4 suites for 3-4.
Meals	Breakfast €17-€22. Restaurants nearby.
Closed	Never.
Directions	Metro: St Germain des Prés (4), Mabillon (10). RER: St Michel-Notre Dame. Buses: 58, 70. Parking: St Germain des Prés.

Christophe Falaise
22 rue Buci, 75006 Paris

Tel	+33 (0)1 55 42 74 74
Email	reservations@buci-hotel.com
Web	www.buci-hotel.com

Artus Hôtel

Attitude and plenty of it. The Artus already had a young, trendy art crowd who would stay at no other place, so the new owner – a collector – could afford to be bold. In sympathy with one of the many African art galleries in the area, two stunning primitive statues are displayed in the large windows on the street. A sweep of an entrance, bare except for the name of the hotel boldly embosssed in mosaic, leads you further back, past the slim crescent of a reception desk and into a cluster of bright bucket chairs kept close to the ground. It is all rather breathless and new. The challenge here is space; the rooms were never big, so functionality mixed with style, a minimum of colour and top-class textiles are what count. The final touch is the artistic detail in every room – whether an antique door or a modern doll-like sculpture on a wall, each is in the very best taste. Leather trims, red silk curtains, Murano basins, open bathrooms with smoked green glass, tweed curtains: it's refreshing and new. A lot has changed – except for the imperturbable Sangay, irreproachably manning the desk.

Price	€195–€305.
	Duplex & suite €395–€415.
Rooms	27: 20 doubles, 5 twins, 1 duplex,
	1 suite for 2.
Meals	Buffet breakfast included.
	Restaurants nearby.
Closed	Never.
Directions	Metro: St Germain des Prés (4),
	Mabillon (10), Odéon (4,10).
	RER: St Michel-Notre Dame.
	Buses: 58, 63, 70, 86, 87, 96.
	Parking: St Germain des Prés.

	Christophe Falaise
	34 rue de Buci, 75006 Paris
Tel	+33 (0)1 43 29 07 20
Email	info@artushotel.com
Web	www.artushotel.com

Hôtel d'Aubusson

Through the superb old doors into the flagstoned hall – touch the space, hear the quiet piano in the bar, see the promise of moulded, fountained magnificence through the patio doors, and unwind. It is an absolutely beautiful stone building, serene and elegant in its golden 17th-century proportions, properly modern in its renovation. Reading by the great hearth in the antique-furnished salon or breakfasting in the Aubusson-hung room beyond, you are cocooned in pure French style: a forest of beams high above your head, tall slim windows, superb parquet floors, monogrammed china. There are two lovely patios for summer drinks, a luxurious bar with piano entertainment in the evenings, a Louis XV internet point in a quiet corner. Bedrooms are big or very big, some with wonderful beams, all richly, unfussily furnished in custom-made Directoire-style mahogany, thick quiet fabrics, white and grey bathrooms (not huge but with all requisites). You are a short walk from Pont Neuf, the Louvre, Luxembourg Gardens, everything… in a grand house where guests are nurtured by the nicest staff. Quietness is a virtue.

Price	€255–€450. Duplexes €480. Suite €535.
Rooms	50: 46 doubles, 3 duplexes, 1 suite.
Meals	Breakfast: wake-up €7, buffet €23. Light meals with wine, from €39.
Closed	Never.
Directions	Metro: Odéon. RER: St Michel-Notre Dame, Pont-Neuf. Buses: 56, 63, 70, 86, 87, 96. Parking: At hotel.

Walter Waeterloos
33 rue Dauphine, 75006 Paris

Tel	+33 (0)1 43 29 43 43
Email	reservations@hoteldaubusson.com
Web	www.hoteldaubusson.com

Millésime Hôtel

"Our room had an impossible peacefulness – all we could hear was birdsong," writes a reader. Behind its imposing old doors, the Millésime is intimate, pretty, peaceful and welcoming. The reception is warmly Mediterranean, with brick-red and soft ochre sponging all over the lobby, deep sofas set on glowing parquet and a charming little patio for breakfast; three rooms open from the patio itself. This is a fine old building and the new owners have restored the 17th-century staircase with proper respect, in spite of the lift. Smartly carpeted bedrooms vary in size but are never too cramped, have pale yellow walls and good white and grey bathrooms. A variety of ancient-looking cast-iron lamps contrast with pretty, contemporary checks and stripes; original cord-crossed quilts embrace beds; two top-floor rooms have brilliant high-peaked ceilings and roof windows over historic towers and domes. The vaulted breakfast room is as charming as all the rest, and the Left Bank position is unsurpassed. Looking spic and span after a full renovation, this is decent value for the area.

Price	€190–€220. Suite €380.
Rooms	21: 20 doubles, 1 suite.
Meals	Breakfast €13–€16. Restaurants nearby.
Closed	Never.
Directions	Metro: St Germain des Prés. RER: St Michel-Notre Dame. Buses: 39, 48, 63, 86, 95. Parking: St Germain des Prés.

	Julien Lucas
	15 rue Jacob, 75006 Paris
Tel	+33 (0)1 44 07 97 97
Email	conciergerie@millesimehotel.com
Web	www.millesimehotel.com

Hôtel des Deux Continents

The hotel and its three ancient listed buildings sink discreetly into the background among the decorating and antique shops. Its public rooms are atmospheric with fresh flowers, beams, gilt frames, draperies and dark furniture, lightened at the front by the big street window and at the back by a little patio. Venus stands shyly among the greenery and tables are laid with fine white cloths and bright china against a green and gold backdrop. The geography is intriguing: two buildings look onto quiet inner courtyards, the larger, noisier rooms are at the front; choose the quadrangle side. All are done in contemporary-classic style with yards of fabric – walls, bedheads, covers, curtains, pelmets, the odd canopy – in occasionally surprising mixtures of colours and patterns; but it all 'works', as do the bronze lights and pretty old mirrors. In the last building (two storeys, no lift), the very smallest rooms are peaceful, charming and air-conditioned (the rest have fans). The whole place has masses of personality, the staff are young and welcoming and St Germain des Prés hums.

Price	€124–€185. Singles €101–€165. Triples €185–€230.
Rooms	41: 19 doubles, 10 twins, 8 singles, 4 triples.
Meals	Breakfast €11–€12. Restaurants nearby.
Closed	Never.
Directions	Metro: St Germain des Prés (4). RER B: St Michel-Notre Dame. Buses: 39, 48, 58, 63, 70, 86, 87, 95.

Perrine Henneveux
25 rue Jacob, 75006 Paris

Tel	+33 (0)1 43 26 72 46
Email	continents.hotel@wanadoo.fr
Web	www.hoteldes2continents.com

La Villa Saint Germain

Find soberly studied forms and colours: a big blocky black desk, soft silky curtains the colour of glazed chestnuts, a curvy steel stair rail, ochre-flecked stone floor slabs; gentle music too and a series of deep chairs in grey, brown and café latte, on a teak floor by the bar. Staff are appropriately young, bright and attentive, as is Jean-Philippe Nuel's décor. In the bedrooms, the drama of colour is wine red, brown and white, the gentleness is ivory, rich beige. Materials are rich and yielding – thick blue or burgundy red curtains folded back on their fine silk linings, 'crocodile'-skin bedheads in dark wooden frames, fluffy white duvets with dark grey and ivory woollen squares on top, all against a pair of sober scarlet walls. And the details: room numbers light-projected in front of the door, monogrammed linen, superb designer bathrooms in chrome and ground glass, big stone-framed mirrors. The bar is peaceful, the lift is speedy, and breakfast is down the 1930s-look stairs in a stylish space of rich red walls and engravings. It all feels really good and the cool Left Bank laps at your feet.

Price	€285–€370. Suites €470.
Rooms	31: 17 doubles, 10 twins, 4 suites for 2.
Meals	Buffet breakfast €22; continental €16. Restaurants nearby.
Closed	Never.
Directions	Metro: St Germain des Prés (4), Mabillon (10). RER: St Michel-Notre Dame. Buses: 39, 48, 58, 63, 70, 86, 95, 96. Parking: St Germain des Prés.

Christine Horbette
29 rue Jacob, 75006 Paris

Tel	+33 (0)1 43 26 60 00
Email	hotel@villa-saintgermain.com
Web	www.villa-saintgermain.com

Entry 92   Map 5

Hôtel du Danube

Built in the 1870s as a private mansion, this soft, civilised hotel rejoices in a dazzling black and red salon and a pale salmon patio where potted palms and a spreading rhododendron sit on quadrangles of teak and stone. Tables can be laid here for breakfast and elegant façades rise skywards. Croissants are also served in the breakfast room off the patio, where a delightful collection of blue china teapots sits on lighted shelves. The quietest rooms look over the patio – though voices can carry – or the smaller lightwell with its pretty trompe-l'oeil skyscape. Style and fittings vary widely, twisty corridors change levels, it's a warm, long-lived-in place. Superb 'superior' rooms have two windows, high ceilings, big closets, some very desirable antiques, armchairs and smart fabrics, yet they feel intimate and friendly. Recently renovated, bathrooms have trendy rectangle basins and large shower stalls with power showers. The 'standard' rooms are next on the list to be brought up to date. You will appreciate the bevy of young helpful staff at reception. Ask for one of the renovated rooms, with air con.

Price	€148-€235.
	Suite & family rooms €245.
Rooms	40: 28 doubles, 9 twins, 1 suite, 2 family rooms.
Meals	Breakfast €11. Restaurants nearby.
Closed	Never.
Directions	Metro: St Germain des Prés (4). RER: Musée d'Orsay. Buses: 39, 48, 63, 95, 96. Parking: St Germain des Prés.

Michel Sario
58 rue Jacob, 75006 Paris

Tel	+33 (0)1 42 60 34 70
Email	info@hoteldanube.fr
Web	www.hoteldanube.fr

Hôtel Lenox Saint Germain

The jazzmen-inlaid Lenox Club bar has atmosphere. It is used by publishers for drinks after work, by film stars for interviews, by writers for literary wrangles… great fun, very St Germain des Prés, and no longer the hotel breakfast room – which is now in the vaulted basement. Hotel entrance and lobby have been transformed into a symphony of pure 1930s style: strict lines straight and curved, plain natural materials, a fascinating frieze motif and a superb framed inlay of a panther. Upstairs are large rooms and (much) smaller ones, all different. Some have old furniture, some have more modern units, there are hand-painted cupboards and intriguing 1930s pieces. Colour schemes are mostly muted. Rooms on the little rue du Pré aux Clercs are quieter than the others; you may have the added luxury of a balcony. We really like the corner rooms with two windows and lots of light. Bathrooms are good and extra shelving for pots and paints is provided by little trolleys. A small, quaint, rather peaceful hotel, with a five-minute walk to museums and river, that makes you feel you belong.

Price	€140–€180. Suites €230–€330.
Rooms	34: 17 doubles, 12 twins, 5 suites.
Meals	Breakfast €11–€14. Bar snacks €5–€10. Wine €5. Restaurants nearby.
Closed	Never.
Directions	Metro: St Germain des Prés (4), Rue du Bac (12). RER: Musée d'Orsay. Buses: 39, 48, 63, 68, 69, 83, 94. Parking: Rue des Saints Pères, Rue du Bac.

Mme Laporte
9 rue de l'Université, 75007 Paris

Tel	+33 (0)1 42 96 10 95
Email	hotel@lenoxsaintgermain.com
Web	www.lenoxsaintgermain.com

Hôtel Bourgogne et Montana

Luxury of the four-star variety has now taken over the whole of this marvellous hotel
where the quiet, sober atmosphere may possibly reflect the serious work being done in the
nearby National Assembly – note the bountiful gendarmes! (An excellent area, convenient
for the Place de la Concorde, the Tuileries, the Louvre, the Musée d'Orsay.) The owner's
grandfather, a bored MP in the 1890s, drew those wicked caricatures of his solemn
colleagues; his own antiques and pictures are placed for your pleasure in the famous
raspberry rotunda, the primrose salon and the deeply tempting breakfast room that is full
of light and the most sinful buffet (included in the price). This combination of wit and
creature comforts is peculiarly French and civilised – as is the quaint little 'birdcage' lift.
Abandon yourself to the caress of fine damask and deep velvet, smart designer fabrics and
oh-so-French traditional Jouy prints. The bigger rooms and suites have space and antiques,
thick quilted upholstery and some extraordinary bathrooms with Italian tiles and bidets;
the smaller ones are like rich, embracing nests.

Price	€180-290. Singles €180-€200. Suites €360-€380.
Rooms	32: 23 twins/doubles, 3 singles, 6 suites.
Meals	Restaurants nearby.
Closed	Never.
Directions	Metro: Assemblée Nationale (12), Invalides (8,13). RER & Air France bus: Invalides. Buses: 63, 83, 93. Parking: Invalides.

Christophe Falaise
3 rue de Bourgogne, 75007 Paris

Tel	+33 (0)1 45 51 20 22
Email	bmontana@bourgogne-montana.com
Web	www.bourgogne-montana.com

Duc de Saint Simon

If Lauren Bacall chose this jewel over the Ritz, there has got to be a good reason: perhaps it was the hideaway feel. Terrifically peaceful on a tiny street, it opens with a discreet archway that would go unnoticed were it not for the lanterns and the wisteria over the cobblestone terrace. Or perhaps it is the elegant cosiness of the salon, enveloped in an extraordinary pleated yellow and red fabric with swagged garlands along the top, warm panelling and a tangerine fringed sofa and chairs. The Bacall 'suite' is pale yellows and puffy beige satins with a leafy view. The other rooms, four with private terraces, are not large but just as appealing in the originality of their décor and fabrics, the careful choice of the right antique desk or objet. Street-side rooms (just as peaceful) have air con, the rest have fans. Service is responsive and charming, you can walk to the Louvre and Notre Dame, and it's no problem at all if you arrive early: a leisurely drink at one of the garden tables serenaded by birdsong will put you in the right mood. Once you stay here you may never want to try anywhere else…

Price	€225–€290. Suites €385–€395.
Rooms	34: 29 twins/doubles, 5 suites for 2.
Meals	Breakfast €15. Restaurants nearby.
Closed	Never.
Directions	Metro: Rue du Bac (12).
	RER: St Michel-Notre Dame.
	Buses: 63, 68, 69, 83, 84, 94.
	Parking: Private parking available.

Gisela Siggelko
14 rue de Saint Simon, 75007 Paris

Tel	+33 (0)1 44 39 20 20
Email	duc.de.saint.simon@wanadoo.fr
Web	www.hotelducdesaintsimon.com

Hôtel des Marronniers

Another of the family's private mansion hotels, it stands between quiet courtyard and real garden. The almost dramatically Second Empire salon, all ruches and gilt, leads to a delectable old-style conservatory where red-cushioned iron chairs and marble-topped tables await you under the fruity 'chandeliers', reflecting the big shrubby garden – privilege indeed. Rooms vary: mostly smallish, they give onto the garden or the front courtyard – no need for double glazing. From the top floor you see higgledy-piggledy rooftops or the church tower; from all rooms you hear the chimes. The décor is based on coordinated fabrics (walls, curtains, canopies, beds), bright floral prints or Regency stripes serving as backdrop to an antique desk, a carved armoire or a pair of lemon-tree spray lights... lots of character here. Renovated bathrooms are most attractive, be they grey and ginger marble or white tiles with an original tropical island 'picture'. After so much light, the basement breakfast room is in soft, dark contrast for cool winter mornings. Or hie ye to the conservatory.

Price	€149–€190. Singles €105–€135. Triple & quadruple €230–€250.
Rooms	37: 24 doubles, 8 twins, 3 singles, 1 triple, 1 quadruple.
Meals	Breakfast €12–€14. Restaurants nearby.
Closed	Never.
Directions	Metro: St Germain des Prés (4). RER B: St Michel-Notre Dame. Buses: 39, 48, 63, 86, 95. Parking: St Germain des Prés.

	Perrine Henneveux
	21 rue Jacob, 75006 Paris
Tel	+33 (0)1 43 25 30 60
Email	hotel-des-marronniers@wanadoo.fr
Web	www.hoteldesmarronniers.com

Hôtel de Varenne

Step into the little green cul de sac with its ivy covered walls, hidden fountain and exquisite canopy over the entrance door and you will feel like Alice in Wonderland; you have tumbled into an oasis of peace and calm, far from the hustle bustle of the city streets. The front doors slide open, the reception desk is a friendly antique writing table, two bronze statues grace antique chests of drawers and a handsome gilt-studded balustrade leads you upstairs. There's a country air to the bedrooms as most of them look onto the quiet garden where breakfast or an evening drink is a delight. Most are a reasonable size for Paris and all have a desk and a chair. Monsieur Pommier is a man of detail and classic taste: green, gold, blue or wine red are the classic figured bedspreads while the striped curtains repeat the colour schemes. There are attractive framed prints of Parisian monuments and well-kept bathrooms with smooth moulded basins and plenty of shelf space. Four bigger rooms give onto the street. The charming staff will go out of their way to make your stay special.

Price	€127–€197.
Rooms	25: 15 doubles, 10 twins.
Meals	Breakfast €10. Restaurants nearby.
Closed	Never.
Directions	Metro: Varenne (13), Invalides (8, 13). RER & Air France bus: Invalides. Bus: 69. Parking: Invalides.

	Jean-Marc Pommier
	44 rue de Bourgogne, 75007 Paris
Tel	+33 (0)1 45 51 45 55
Email	info@hoteldevarenne.com
Web	www.hoteldevarenne.com

Eiffel Park Hotel

The Eiffel Park started as a clean-cut, shiny business hotel (telephones still in the loos), then had a change of heart. The softening involves Asian furniture and objets, an oriental rug on the granite hall floor, rattan colonial armchairs, a wonderful table made from a pair of Indian shutters and a gigantic Chinese urn. Pass a carved Indian gate to the small bar and salon with low-slung leather armchairs and photos of 50s French film stars, then enter the warmly Mediterranean Garcia-designed breakfast room. Most bedrooms reveal a rustic touch of the Far East in little chests and bedside tables that have been polished or hand-painted to match each room's colour scheme: blue and sunny gold maybe, or vibrant pink and red. Rooms are not big but quiet – this is a peaceful neighbourhood – some with quirky angles (connecting rooms can be arranged), some with parquet floors and toile de Jouy. Bathrooms are classic white. The crowning glory is the roof terrace where grapes grow, lavender perfumes the air and you can breakfast under parasols gazing across the rooftops. And there's home-grown honey for breakfast.

Price	€155–€310.
Rooms	35 twins/doubles.
Meals	Breakfast €20. Restaurants nearby.
Closed	Never.
Directions	Metro: La Tour Maubourg. RER & Air France bus: Invalides.

Françoise Testard
17 bis rue Amélie, 75007 Paris

Tel	+33 (0)1 45 55 10 01
Email	reservation@eiffelpark.com
Web	www.eiffelpark.com

Hôtel de Londres Eiffel

With La Grande Dame (the Eiffel Tower) outside your window, and the gilded lid over Napoleon's place of rest close by, here is a wonderfully sited, warm-coloured and warm-hearted hotel. The mixture of fine blinds and heavy curtains makes for a welcoming atmosphere in the lobby and round into the sitting/breakfast area where a purple, red and dark pink striped fabric gaily wraps the chairs. A country buffet and straw hats on a stand are a wink to a Provençal feel. Beyond, past a pair of plant and flower-filled lightwells, is the *pavillon* with six peaceful little bedrooms on two floors in sweet seclusion. They play variations on satiny quilts and curtains in pale violet or grenadine with softly striped fabric on the walls. Isabelle is rightly proud of her new renovations in the main building: good bath and shower rooms have well-lit wood-framed mirrors, beds are in alcoves, white and beige flowers dress windows and beds. With the guest book proudly displayed at the reception next to an eager and enthusiastic team, you will be very well looked after. And the RER can whisk you straight to Versailles.

Price	€110-€215. Singles €99-€165. Family room €250.
Rooms	30: 15 doubles, 7 twins, 7 singles, 1 family room for 3.
Meals	Breakfast €14. Restaurants nearby.
Closed	Never.
Directions	Metro: Ecole Militaire. RER: Pont de l'Alma. Buses: 69, 80, 87. Parking: Ecole Militaire.

	Isabelle Prigent
	1 rue Augereau, 75007 Paris
Tel	+33 (0)1 45 51 63 02
Email	info@londres-eiffel.com
Web	www.londres-eiffel.com

Hôtel Gavarni

The neat little Gavarni astonishes still, heaving itself up into the miniature luxury class on ropes of rich draperies, interesting pictures, heavenly bathrooms and superb finishes. From its ground floor of deep raspberry and yellow richness you may expect more delights. The suites and doubles at the top are big and stunning with their jacuzzi and massage shower panels, fine canopies and beautiful furniture – supremely French with Eiffel Tower views – yet never overdone. The first-floor rooms are less luxurious but the quality is the same: thick lovely carpets, finely stitched quilts, heavily draped curtains and good little pieces of furniture. The triumph is those cramped little bathrooms which have gained so much space with their utterly ingenious made-to-measure red 'granite' basin, shower and loo. Xavier, the dynamic young manager, is dedicated to making the Gavarni as 'green' as possible and a terrific organic, fairtrade breakfast is served on the patio; energy is renewable and only eco-friendly detergents are used. This is a superb combination of rich, strong modern style and pure traditional comfort.

Price	€160-€200. Singles €110-€170. Suites & family rooms €240-€500.
Rooms	25: 10 doubles, 6 twins, 4 suites, 5 family rooms for 3-4.
Meals	Breakfast €15. Restaurants nearby.
Closed	Never.
Directions	Metro: Passy (6), Trocadéro (6, 9). RER: Boulainvilliers. Buses: 22, 32. Parking: Garage Moderne, Rue de Passy.

Ethical Collection: Environment.
See page 446 for details.

Xavier Moraga
5 rue Gavarni, 75116 Paris
Tel   +33 (0)1 45 24 52 82
Email   reservation@gavarni.com
Web   www.gavarni.com

Hôtel Passy Eiffel

The first owner was a passionate bee-keeper so he perhaps picked a place with a bit of nature as a centrepiece. When you step off the smart shopping street you can certainly believe that Passy was just a little country village a hundred years ago. Breathe deeply in this calm atmosphere, a restful mix of old-fashioned and contemporary styles where nothing is overdone. Lounge in the glassed-in veranda where you can see a darling gardener's cottage across the tiny cobbled yard. There are two comfortable salons off the panelled hall which give onto the street through arching windows. Rooms are decorated in firm but unaggressive colours with floral quilts and curtains. The suite has four windows onto That Tower, beige carpets and grey moiré walls, a sofabed in the sitting area, a pretty period desk and a nice pale grey bathroom. Beams and timbers frame the upper floors; furniture is cane and wood; storage space behind mirrored folding doors is good. On the courtyard side, you look down onto the hotel's green patio and the next-door neighbour's very well-kept garden. Lovely staff, too.

Price	€160–€185.
	Suites & family rooms €210–€250.
Rooms	49: 40 twins/doubles, 5 singles,
	2 suites for 2, 2 family rooms for 3.
Meals	Breakfast €14. Restaurants nearby.
Closed	Never.
Directions	Metro: Passy (6).
	RER: Boulainvilliers.
	Buses: 22, 32.
	Parking: 19 rue de Passy.

Christine Horbette
10 rue de Passy, 75016 Paris

Tel	+33 (0)1 45 25 55 66
Email	contact@passyeiffel.com
Web	www.passyeiffel.com

✗ ⟋ ⅄

HotelHome Paris 16

Ah, a flat in Paris – with a difference. Laurence has combined hotel services with a family-like atmosphere and she picked the right spot. A quiet street, a classic 1900s building and Virginie at reception. A glass roof runs across a narrow courtyard lush with fern, green and black bamboo, acacia, jasmine, and honeysuckle – perfect for leisurely breakfast or afternoon tea. The tiniest lift in Paris will get your bags up or down (you follow) to the big rooms, each with a salon and a fabulous customised kitchenette. Charming are the marble fireplaces, antique ceramic radiators and moulded ceilings; modern are the ochre walls, bright carpets on parquet floors and armchairs in gay green and yellow plaid. Big family apartments on the top floor have two or three bedrooms; smaller rooms on the ground floor have views of the garden. Beds are made every day, linen and towels changed twice a week. Laundry machines are available as well as space to store suitcases. Returning guests leave a bag and wellies for their next visit. Delightful, dynamic Laurence knows what service means. *Special prices for Sawday guests.*

Price	€180–€340.
Rooms	17 apartments: 5 for 2-3, 10 for 4, 2 for 6.
Meals	Restaurants within walking distance.
Closed	Never.
Directions	Metro: Jasmin (9). RER: Boulainvilliers. Buses: 22, 52. Parking: Some private parking, enquire at hotel.

Laurence Vivant
36 rue George Sand, 75016 Paris

Tel	+33 (0)1 45 20 61 38
Email	hotelhome@wanadoo.fr
Web	www.hotelhome.fr

Hôtel Keppler

We don't feel we are taking a chance with this completely renovated luxury creation from young owner Jean-Marie Nouvel and decorator Pierre-Yves Rochon. They have re-invented a top-class hotel with all the bells and whistles in one of the ritziest parts of Paris, nicely near the Champs-Elysées yet far enough away to hear your own footsteps on the small side street. The bedrooms are outstanding. First of all, Rochon has expanded on the moulded ceiling and exaggerated a crenellated pattern around the rooms to soften the overhead lighting. Then the basic black and white theme is splashed with a touch or two of mauve, Chinese red or sun yellow as counterpoints. Thick white damask curtains contrast nicely with dark leather headboards and plaid bedcovers. An astonishing waterproof toile de Jouy, also in black and white, muffles the shine of marble tiles and basins in the bathrooms. There is a glass canopied salon, an intimate lounge bar and an architectural feat of daylight and garden in the open-sided breakfast space downstairs. Alain Lagarrigue is at the helm and a warm welcome is guaranteed.

Price	€265-€490. Suites €475-€1,000.
Rooms	39: 34 twins/doubles, 5 suites.
Meals	Buffet breakfast €22. Restaurants nearby.
Closed	Never.
Directions	Metro: Charles de Gaulle-Étoile. RER & Air France bus: Charles de Gaulle-Étoile. Buses: 22, 32, 73, 92. Parking: Avenue Marceau.

Alain Lagarrigue
10 rue Keppler, 75116 Paris

Tel	+33 (0)1 47 20 65 05
Email	hotel@keppler.fr
Web	www.keppler.fr

Hôtel François 1er

The François 1er is a house of taste and luxury whose attentive owners, along with decorator Pierre-Yves Rochon, chose period furniture, lamps and pictures in a brilliant mix of classic, baroque and contemporary. The salon and bar areas are intimate and warmly panelled; a glassed-in patio with year-round greenery, moulded ceilings, a Turkish rug on parquet, real books on coffee tables and faux books around the bar summon you to comfort and ease. Even though a portrait of François 1er greets you in the lobby, you'll quickly discover that Alain Lagarrigue is the real spirit of the house and seems to be everywhere at once. He prides himself on the well-kept rooms and rich varied fabrics; those stretched on the walls match the patterns on the fine beds to offset the average-size rooms. Some are incredible jewel boxes of intense poppy reds or elegant pale yellows. If other stimuli besides a hot drink can help you get the right start in the morning, the breakfast room is for you: a tropical theme of flowers and vines, fruits and frills all in reds and yellows, it is a joy. Porcelain patterns join in the fun.

Price	€260-€490. Suites €600-€1,000.
Rooms	40: 38 twins/doubles, 2 suites.
Meals	Breakfast €21. Restaurants nearby.
Closed	Never.
Directions	Metro: George V (1).
	RER & Air France bus: Charles de Gaulle-Étoile.
	Buses: 22, 32, 73, 92.
	Parking: George V.

Alain Lagarrigue
7 rue Magellan, 75008 Paris

Tel	+33 (0)1 47 23 44 04
Email	hotel@hotel-francois1er.fr
Web	www.the-paris-hotel.com

Hôtel des Champs-Elysées

Madame Monteil inherited the hotel, and the art of hospitality, from her grandparents and parents whose delightful pre-war pictures hang here. The Art Deco theme remains but recent renovations have brought things up to date and now it sparkles. The centrepiece is Madame's amazing collection of hat pins lovingly displayed in the main lobby. (Check in first because you will certainly get caught up in these beautiful pieces and you may never make it up to your room.) Once installed, you'll discover that photos of some of the more outstanding ones are featured over the beds. Like the hat pins, the rooms are not large but each is beautiful: luscious beaded taffeta curtains in swirly patterns replace doors to bathrooms; silver wallpaper and grey metallic headboards shimmer; quilted bronze bedcovers and chocolate carpeting breathe comfort. There are vintage glass lights on the walls and excellent reading lamps. Bathrooms have proper windows, the latest chrome bits and two shower heads apiece. Be sure to walk down the stairs; there is a different lady flapper on each of the elevator doors.

Price	€120–€365.
Rooms	26 doubles.
Meals	Breakfast €18. Restaurants nearby.
Closed	Never.
Directions	Metro: St Philippe du Roule (9), Franklin Roosevelt (1, 9). RER & Air France bus: Charles de Gaulle-Étoile. Buses: 22, 28, 32, 73, 80, 83, 93. Parking: Rue de Ponthieu.

	Marie-Joëlle Monteil
	2 rue d'Artois, 75008 Paris
Tel	+33 (0)1 43 59 11 42
Email	contact@hoteldce.com
Web	www.champselysees-paris-hotel.com

Hôtel Pergolèse

Once past the doors you exchange the trumpeting sculptures of nearby Arc de Triomphe for a festival of modern design where light and natural materials, custom-made furniture and minute details all add up. Édith Vidalenc worked with renowned designer Rena Dumas, creator of Hermès boutiques worldwide, to keep a sleek but warmly curvaceously human hotel. Her sense of hospitality informs it all: the faithful team at reception are leagues away from the frostiness that can pass for four-star treatment. Pastel tones are mutedly smart so the multi-coloured breakfast room is a slightly humorous wake-up nudge, the linen mats and fine silver a bow to tradition: not taking oneself too seriously while being really professional is the keynote here. Rooms, not vast but with good storage, are fresh and all furnished in pale wood and leather, thick curtains and soft white bedcovers: no distracting patterns or prints, just coloured plush cushions to soften. The star Pergolèse room is a small masterpiece in palest apricot with a few spots of colour and a superb open bathroom. Édith's assistant, Julia and her staff take good care of you.

Price	€175-€290. Suite €270-€390.
Rooms	40: 36 doubles (some interconnect), 3 singles, 1 suite.
Meals	Breakfast €12-€17. Restaurants nearby.
Closed	Never.
Directions	Metro: Argentine (1). RER A: Charles de Gaulle-Etoile; RER C: Porte Maillot. Air France bus: Porte Maillot. Parking: Avenue Foch/Porte Maillot.

	Édith Vidalenc
	3 rue Pergolèse, 75116 Paris
Tel	+33 (0)1 53 64 04 04
Email	hotel@pergolese.com
Web	www.parishotelpergolese.com

Hôtel de Banville

Deliciously Parisian, as is the owner, Marianne Moreau, the Banville has the elegance of inherited style (the small, charming Parisian lift), and the punch of ultra-modern fittings (the sober stone corridors and red doors are fantastically numbered and lit from below ground). You feel welcomed into a private château where gilt-edged Old Masters supervise the gracious salon with its buffed grand piano – and the owner sings on Tuesday nights. The designs are wondrous and fairy-lit. Ask for a room with an Eiffel Tower view: Marie, in subtle tones from palest eggshell to rich red loam, has a gauzily-canopied bed, a delicious little terrace and a brilliant bathroom with thick curtains for soft partitioning. Amélie is sunnily feminine in pale yellow and soft ginger; the three Pastourelles are freshly countrified in gingham and weathered blinds; Paul above has a handsome slate bathroom. Other rooms, full of light, gentle colours and intimacy, have an airy touch, perfectly chosen modern and period furniture and fabulous bathrooms. Staff are delightful – hospitality could have been born here. *Chauffeur for airport pick-up & private tours.*

Price	€310–€420.
Rooms	38: 37 twins/doubles, 1 suite.
Meals	Breakfast €20. Light meals €20–€30. Wine €6. Restaurants nearby.
Closed	Never.
Directions	Metro: Porte de Champerret (3), Pereire (3). RER: Pereire. Buses: 92, 84, 93. Parking: Rue de Courcelles.

	Marianne Moreau
	166 boulevard Berthier, 75017 Paris
Tel	+33 (0)1 42 67 70 16
Email	info@hotelbanville.fr
Web	www.hotelbanville.fr

New Orient Hôtel

Pretty, original and fun, the New Orient is close to lute-maker land – and the Batignolles Organic Food Market. Behind a superb bottle-green frontage flanked by carriage lamps with ivy geraniums pouring off the windowsills, Catherine and Sepp display their love of trawling country-house sales for furniture, pictures and mirrors and the mixed styles are sheer delight – Louis XVI, 1900s, Art Deco... There are brass beds and carved beds, one with little columns, one with lovely inlay and matching dressing table, a marble washstand or a pretty table and everywhere oriental-type or Mediterranean fabrics. The ground floor houses a painted telephone box, a carved dresser and a set of light country watercolours while a fine grandfather clock supervises the breakfast area with its rattan tables and pink/green cloths (don't miss out on the homemade hot chocolate!). All the balconies are lit (daytime and nightime) to display colourful box displays of seasonal flowers. Given the pervasive opulence of the 8th arrondissement, this is a wonderfully unassuming place with the nicest possible owners – and staff.

Price	€120–€160. Singles €95.
Rooms	30: 12 doubles, 8 twins, 10 singles.
Meals	Buffet breakfast €11; continental €7. Restaurants nearby.
Closed	Never.
Directions	Metro: Villiers (2, 3), Europe (3). RER & Roissybus: Auber, Opéra. Buses: 30, 53. Parking: Europe.

Catherine & Sepp Wehrlé
16 rue de Constantinople,
75008 Paris

Tel	+33 (0)1 45 22 21 64
Email	new.orient.hotel@wanadoo.fr
Web	www.hotelneworient.com

Hôtel Langlois - Croisés

Built as a bank in 1870, this splendid building soon became a special kind of 'hotel' and the best rooms carry wonderful legacies of the days of rich dark furniture and log fires: ceramic and marble fireplaces, superbly crafted cupboards, carved alcoves – one room even has a 'gazebo'. Not all rooms are as spectacular but many are a very decent size for Paris and bathrooms are fine, some enormous, most with windows. Fabrics fit too: heavy velvets, lots of red, some pretty pastel piqués; rooms are big enough to take it. In the attractive breakfast room there's yet another fireplace and a lovely antique birdcage housing two plaster birds. This is a peaceful and generous house and the owner wants deeply to keep the building's historical character, acquiring furniture and sculptures with 1900-1930 lines. Madame Bojena, a gentle and efficient presence, adds to the patina; she oversees a delightful staff. Take the stairs not the pre-war lift (characterful but impractical) and admire the fine paintings on the landings. There's double glazing, though the traffic dies down after 8pm, and the WiFi comes free.

Price	€140–€150. Suites €190.
Rooms	27: 19 doubles, 5 twins, 3 suites for 3-4.
Meals	Breakfast €13. Restaurants nearby.
Closed	Never.
Directions	Metro: Trinité-d'Estienne d'Orves (12). RER & Roissybus: Auber, Opéra. Buses: 26, 32, 42, 43, 68, 81. Parking: 300m, enquire at hotel.

	Mme Bojena
	63 rue St Lazare, 75009 Paris
Tel	+33 (0)1 48 74 78 24
Email	hotel-des-croises@wanadoo.fr
Web	www.hotel-langlois.com

Hôtel La Sanguine

Through a little lobby and up one flight to a house of flowers and easy friendliness. You will be welcomed by delightful, energetic people – family or long-standing staff – and Tokyo, the sausage dog. The atmosphere is one of quiet country-style comfort; find a desk and a couple of classical statues overlooking the floral breakfast tables and wander through to a little green patio. Carpets are thick, rooms are fresh and bright with good designer fabrics, upholstered chairs to complement colourful bedcovers, discreet personality, well-equipped marble bathrooms and umpteen red-chalk drawings to lend gentle interest; the little singles take one back to childhood and Beatrix Potter. Service here is infinitely human and attentive: in season, the owners make your breakfast jam with fruit from their orchard; Monsieur bakes your breakfast croissant then irons your monogrammed towels; Madame is full of good advice on what to see and do. Hard to believe that the powers of this world – ministers, fashion gurus, ambassadors – live just around the corner. *Wines & champagne for private consumption. No lift, 4 floors.*

Price	€99–€150. Family room €150–€300.
Rooms	31: 17 doubles, 5 twins, 8 singles, 1 family room for 3.
Meals	Breakfast €10. Restaurants nearby.
Closed	Never.
Directions	Metro: Madeleine (8, 12, 14), Concorde (1, 8, 12), Opéra (3,7), Auber (8). RER & Roissybus: Auber, Opéra. Buses: 42, 52, 84, 94. Parking: Madeleine, Concorde.

	M & Mme Plumerand
	6 rue de Surène, 75008 Paris
Tel	+33 (0)1 42 65 71 61
Email	hotelsanguine@free.fr
Web	www.hotel-la-sanguine.com

Le Relais Madeleine

If you are wondering where in Paris you can you relax in a warm bubbly tub and catch up on your favourite TV soap, go no further: the brand new Relais Madeleine has thought of that and just about everything else you would have had in mind for a perfect stay. There is a delightful patio for breakfast al fresco, a room with a sauna and small terrace, a marvellous suite for four on the top floor... all are carefully decorated in warm, floral fabrics, excellent pieces of furniture, top mattresses and the softest linens. This charming little street is a perfect balance between the business district and pleasant shopping areas around the Opéra and the Madeleine. As an extra treat, manager Paul Bogaert reveals his previous life as a talented autograph hunter during the early years of rock and roll. The famous musical hall where they all performed is right around the corner, so it's only right that nostalgia be on display. They are all there, along with their single covers: Chuck Berry, Jimi Hendrix, Donavan, Georgie Fame, Marianne Faithfull, the Yardbirds... what a treat.

Price	€175–€255. Suite €450.
Rooms	23: 21 doubles, 1 single, 1 suite.
Meals	Breakfast €13. Restaurants nearby.
Closed	Never.
Directions	Metro: Madeleine.
	RER & Roissybus: Auber.

	Paul Bogaert
	11 bis rue Godot de Mauroy,
	75009 Paris
Tel	+33 (0)1 47 42 22 40
Email	contact@relaismadeleine.fr
Web	www.relaismadeleine.fr

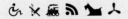

Hôtel Opéra Richepanse

On a little street off Rue Saint Honoré, a short walk from the Louvre, the Champs Elysées, the Tuileries, is this gem. The marquetry, the panelling, the smooth leather furniture and the mouldings of the lobby-salon were all custom-designed: expect a cool 1930s look and a courteous welcome. There's a minor concession to things 21st century in the atmospheric stone vault, where a sumptuous breakfast buffet is served: sausages and scrambled eggs, cold cuts, six different breads. A small lift transports you to bedrooms that are a fair size (though some are enormous, with floor-to-ceiling windows – a treat in Paris); ask for one of the quietest. There are new carpets, firm mattresses, clean-limbed Deco furniture and thick-textured fabrics for perfectly fitted bedcovers – no swags, no frills, no fuss. This gives space to appreciate the art that draws the eye and – in the magnificent great suites – original paintings. Bathrooms are excellent and trumpet the latest in basin design and triple bevelled mirrors. All feels clean-cut and rich, polished and pristine, and the service is attentive and generous.

Price	€250–€440. Suites €460–€590.
Rooms	38: 35 twins/doubles, 3 suites.
Meals	Breakfast €13–€18.
	Restaurants nearby.
Closed	Never.
Directions	Metro: Madeleine (8, 12, 14),
	Concorde (1, 12).
	RER & Roissybus: Auber, Opéra.
	Buses: 42, 52, 84, 94.
	Parking: Madeleine.

Édith Vidalenc
14 rue du Chevalier de St George,
75001 Paris

Tel	+33 (0)1 42 60 36 00
Email	hotel@richepanse.com
Web	www.richepanse.com

Hôtel Relais Montmartre

There are good reasons why artists still live in this village, tucked in behind that giant marshmellow of a church, the Sacré Coeur. It could be the views over the rooftops of Paris, or the meandering little streets, or Montmartre's transformation at dusk as the day's façades become bistro, bar and club. It deserves much more than an afternoon visit so book into this new little jewel and the secrets of this 'rediscovered' neighbourhood will be revealed. Just up from Amélie's celebrated café, tucked into a sweet side street, the entrance is discreet. Elegance and intimacy blend in the lobby with fireplace, antique desk and side table; the sofa, the large pouf, the period chairs and the curtains are an extraordinary mix of rich fabric; the small trellised patio set with sunny yellow garden furniture is the cherry on the cake. In the rooms, upholstered deep-cushioned armchairs complement the quilted headboards and bedcovers in dreamy pastels or reds, pinks and greens, mixing and matching with care. The mattresses are dreamy, the staff are attentive; this is simple luxury at its best.

Price	€160–€200.
Rooms	26 doubles.
Meals	Breakfast €13. Restaurants nearby.
Closed	Never.
Directions	Metro: Blanche (2), Place de Clichy (13, 2), Abbesses (12). RER: Gare du Nord. Buses: 30, 54, 80, 95. Parking: private parking, enquire at hotel.

Paul Bogaert
6 rue Constance,
75018 Paris

Tel	+33 (0)1 70 64 25 25
Email	contact@relaismontmartre.fr
Web	www.relaismontmartre.fr

Terrass Hôtel

The Terrass is the biggest (and highest) hotel in this book but its owner has so proper an idea of receiving guests that the atmosphere is as genuinely warm as at his smaller hotels. Antiques and tapestries, bronzes and old prints remove any sense of cold grandeur, a pianist plays in the club-like bar every evening, the breakfast buffet is a masterpiece in a room flooded with light that pours up the hill, the chef has an excellent reputation and you may have the fine-weather privilege of eating on the seventh-floor terrace looking across the whole city – this is four-star class indeed. The suites are superb (one has a private terrace): big and light with windows that fling you across the greenery of Montmartre cemetery, pale modern furniture and lovely matchings of green, blue, raspberry, beige, yellow textured fabrics. Other rooms have a more classic Louis XVI cane style and, of course, less space but all have delectable colours, different pictures and that rich, soft welcome of real taste and attention to detail. Buses, just across the street, sweep you down to Saint Germain des Prés or to the Opéra.

Price	€280–€330. Suites €380–€410.
Rooms	98: 83 twins/doubles, 15 suites.
Meals	Breakfast €17. Dinner from €23. Restaurant closed Sunday eve.
Closed	Never.
Directions	Metro: St Lazare, Gare du Nord. Buses: 80, 95.

Sabine Müller
12-14 rue Joseph de Maistre,
75018 Paris

Tel	+33 (0)1 46 06 72 85
Email	reservation@terrass-hotel.com
Web	www.terrass-hotel.com

Château de Bourron

Surrounded by perfectly clipped yew and box topinières, the early 17th-century château built on fortress foundations is hugely warm and inviting. Louis XV and his in-laws once met here; now it is owned by a charming young family. Inside is a feast of original Versailles parquet, oriental rugs and period pieces, exquisite fabrics and elegant tapestries. (Public rooms are reserved for receptions.) Pass the gold antique sedan chair, sentinel-like on the landing, and drift off to the east wing and guests' quarters. Rooms, in deep reds and golds, display pale marble bathrooms, gilt mirrors and Pierre Frey interiors: five-star stylishness in a château setting. On the first floor are a day room and a library, with panelled walls and shelves laden with leather-covered volumes. Outside, more treasures to uncover. The 80 acres of walled gardens and woodland are extraordinary… statues of Ceres and St Joseph, a chapel in one of two small pavilions, and the St Sévère spring supplying moat, canal and village wash house. Beyond lies the pretty village.

Price	€180–€500.
Rooms	4 twins/doubles.
Meals	Breakfast €15. Dinner €38.
Closed	25 & 31 December.
Directions	Paris-Lyon A6 exit Fontainebleau. At 'obelisk' r'bout N7 Nemours to Montargis; 8km. Right for Villiers-sous-Grez, follow Bourron Marlotte Centre. Ring interphone at wooden gates in 2nd courtyard.

Comte & Comtesse Guy de Cordon
14 bis rue du Maréchal Foch,
77780 Bourron Marlotte, Seine-et-Marne

Tel	+33 (0)1 64 78 39 39
Email	bourron@chateau-bourron.fr
Web	www.bourron.fr

Hôtel de Londres

Gaze on the Château de Fontainebleau, one of France's loveliest buildings, from your room in this 18th-century hostelry; it lies opposite. The hotel has been in the family for three generations; Philippe runs it quietly and considerately, with occasional help from his brother. The sitting room has an 18th-century classical look, also rich colours, comfy armchairs, plump cushions, grand flowers. The breakfast room – for simple breakfasts – has the feel of a small brasserie; both rooms have views to Fontainebleau. Bedrooms, on the upper floors, are similarly classical in style – smart, spotless and traditional; colours are bold, fabrics floral. A sense of timelessness pervades this peaceful place. You are also brilliantly placed for exploring the Forest of Fontainebleau, the hunting grounds of kings. As for the château, it was built around the keep of a smaller medieval building, completed in 1550 and has been added to over the years; the gallery of François I is considered one of the finest in Europe. You can visit free on Sundays and it's magnificently floodlit at night.

Price	€110-€170. Single €90-€130. Suites €150-€180. Triples €175.
Rooms	15: 5 doubles, 1 single, 7 suites, 2 triples.
Meals	Breakfast €12. Restaurants within walking distance.
Closed	12-18 August; 23 December-9 January.
Directions	A6 exit Fontainebleau for château. Hotel opposite château.

Philippe Colombier
1 place du Général de Gaulle,
77300 Fontainebleau, Seine-et-Marne
Tel   +33 (0)1 64 22 20 21
Email   hdelondres1850@aol.com
Web   www.hoteldelondres.com

Auberge de la Source

An auberge since 1763, this charming village restaurant-hotel was a favourite haunt of Monmartre bohèmes in the late 1800s, drawn to sublime Champagne countryside an hour from Paris. Today the auberge is intimate, classy, special. Outside, a wisteria-smothered terrace for al fresco dining. Over the lane, a heated pool with loungers and lavender, romantic sit-outs beneath a vast chestnut tree, a small bar, a summer sitting room. Inside, an exciting red entrance hall and a handsome restaurant lit by tall French windows. There are swathes of tiny tinkling fairy lights, light oak tables, armchairs upholstered in black, anthracite floors, teak cross beams, stainless steel cabochons and refined bistro food with exotic touches. Bedrooms, comfortable, comforting, are the biggest treat: tones of chocolate, tobacco, cream and white, and furnishings in decorative neo-classical style, wavy-fronted chests of drawers, wood-framed sofas in 'distressed' patina. After a hard day's champagne tasting, return to soft carpeting to pamper the feet and a whirlpool bath to soothe the limbs. Oh, and the staff are delightful.

Price	€98–€148. Suites €158–€198.
Rooms	8: 4 doubles, 4 suites.
Meals	Breakfast €12. Dinner €29–€39.
Closed	14 January–12 February.
Directions	From Paris, A4 dir. Metz, exit 18 thro' La Ferté sous Jarre to D407 dir. Monmirail for 6km. Right onto D68 to Saint Ouen sur Morin. Auberge in centre.

Laurent & Françoise Tizio-Cassou
8 place Saint Barthélémy,
77750 Saint Ouen sur Morin, Seine-et-Marne

Tel	+33 (0)1 60 24 80 61
Email	contact@aubergedelasource.fr
Web	www.aubergedelasource.fr

Saint Laurent

Cobbled, exceptionally pretty Monfort L'Amaury is home to some remarkable Renaissance stained-glass windows, a Ravel festival in October and this venerable private mansion. Built in the early 1600s, it later became a town hall; now it is an excellent hotel. The renovation is recent and thorough – lift, soundproofing, fine panelling – and in good taste. Old rafters reign in some bedrooms, the beams in the breakfast room are splendid, and skilful carpentry shows in headboards and cupboards of new oak. There are pure white walls and simple, elegant bedspreads, and ground-floor rooms with private terraces looking over the lawn where, under the big old linden trees, staff lay out chairs in summer. Each sedate bedroom bears the name of a plant or a tree from the Rambouillet forest. Fifty yards away, in a second townhouse, are three bedrooms, large and luxurious, with white-painted beams, marble bathrooms and comfy armchairs. Breakfasts are generous and include cooked ham and cheese. A peaceful stopover on the way to Paris – and Versailles, just 20 kilometres away.

Price	€99–€199.
Rooms	15: 12 doubles, 3 twins.
Meals	Breakfast €12. Restaurants within walking distance.
Closed	1-23 August.
Directions	From Paris, A13; A12; N12 to Dreux then Monfort L'Amaury. In Monfort, through gates for car park.

	Christiane Delabarre
	2 place Lebreton,
	78490 Monfort l'Amaury, Yvelines
Tel	+33 (0)1 34 57 06 66
Email	reception@hotelsaint-laurent.com
Web	www.hotelsaint-laurent.com

Entry 119   Map 5

Pavillon Henri IV

The historic and artistic credentials are impeccable. Dumas, Offenbach and Georges Sand stayed here; the Sun King was born in a room off the entrance hall. There's a fascinating mix of styles, too – Renaissance domed roof, Art Nouveau porch – and materials – ivory limestone, rosy brick. As for the views, the panorama sweeps across the valley of the Seine to Paris and La Défense. Relish them from the rooms, the restaurant, the terrace: feel on top of the world. Since the hotel changed ownership some years ago the bedrooms have been undergoing a gradual and welcome transformation, from classic sobriety to luxurious charm, while reception rooms are big and beautiful – white walls, shining parquet and mellow rugs, gilded antiques, moulded cornices, marble busts, sumptuous chandeliers and striking flowers. The dining is unquestionably lavish, and should you wish to walk off your indulgence afterwards, a wrought-iron gateway allows you into the vast walled and terraced gardens of Château de St Germain en Laye next door. Supremely enjoyable, wonderfully French.

Price	€130–€250. Suites €290–€550.
Rooms	42: 40 twins/doubles, 2 suites.
Meals	Breakfast €16. Lunch €49 (except July/Aug). Dinner à la carte, approx. €90.
Closed	Never.
Directions	A13 Paris-Rouen; exit St Germain en Laye on N186 to St Germain centre via Ave Général Leclerc. Over r'bout to Ave Gambetta; right at end to Rue Thiers. On left.

Charles Eric Hoffmann
19-21 rue Thiers,
78100 Saint Germain en Laye, Yvelines

Tel	+33 (0)1 39 10 15 15
Email	reservation@pavillonhenri4.fr
Web	www.pavillonhenri4.fr

Cazaudehore - La Forestière

The rose-strewn 'English' garden is like an island in the great forest of St Germain and it's hard to believe the buzzing metropolis is just a short train journey away. The first Cazaudehore built the restaurant in 1928, the second built the hotel in 1973, the third generation apply their imaginations to improving both and receiving their guests with elegant French charm. The buildings are camouflaged among the greenery, summer eating is deliciously shaded under rose-red parasols; hotel guests have the elegant, beamed dining room with its veranda to themselves (there are several seminar and reception rooms). Food and wine are the main focus – the wine-tasting dinners are renowned and the chef's seasonal menus are a delight, skilfully mixing tradition and invention: you will eat supremely well here. Bedrooms have been well renovated in a refined but unostentatious style with good fabrics, original gentle colour schemes – saffron, blue and green, for example – period furniture and prints, and masses of character. The perfect treat for an occasion. *Winter jazz dinners.*

Price	€205–€215. Suites €265–€285.
Rooms	30: 13 doubles, 12 twins, 5 suites.
Meals	Breakfast €20. Lunch & dinner with wine, €55–€70. Children's meals €23. Restaurant closed Mon & Sun eve Nov–Mar.
Closed	Never.
Directions	A13 for Rouen exit 6 for St Germain en Laye on N186. N184 for Pontoise. Hotel on left 2.5km after château. RER A from Paris, then 5 mins by taxi.

Philippe Cazaudehore
1 avenue Kennedy,
78100 Saint Germain en Laye, Yvelines

Tel	+33 (0)1 39 10 38 38
Email	cazaudehore@relaischateaux.com
Web	www.cazaudehore.fr

Hostellerie du Prieuré

Medieval Saint Prix, on the edge of the forest, feels delightfully rural. But from the village church you can see the Sacré Coeur: Paris is 15 minutes by train. This is an immaculate small hotel in a beautiful village, with bedrooms that are really quite something. Decorated with a flourish and a theme, from boudoir chic to eastern exotica, all have Middle Eastern carpets, gorgeous textiles, crisp sheets. There's purple-walled Aladdin with an octagonal Syrian table and a silver hand basin and mirror, and lovely Coloniale, with a bamboo four-poster and magnificent long views – to Paris, of course. Bathrooms are worth a wallow, thanks to scented oils and fine soaps. Yves and Frédérique are a warmly professional couple and breakfast is worth getting up for, served in the creamy-walled Café de la Côte with a long velvet banquette and 1900s-style bar. Reservations for dinner are essential as there are only a handful of tables. You will find gourmet dishes and an organic wine list is as long as your arm plus a choice of nine champagnes. All this on the edge of fine forest; take the bikes and explore.

Price	€115–€185.
Rooms	8: 2 doubles, 1 twin, 4 suites, 1 family room.
Meals	Breakfast €13. Lunch €35–€50 (except Mondays). Wine €20–€38. Restaurant closed Sundays.
Closed	2 weeks mid-August.
Directions	From Paris A15 for Cergy Pontoise, exit 115 dir. Taverny; exit St Leu La Forêt, St Prix on D139; 2nd street on right at r'bout; St Prix Village D144; left at lights dir. Chauvry D193.

Frédérique & Yves Farouze
74 rue Auguste Rey,
95390 Saint Prix, Val-d'Oise

Tel   +33 (0)1 34 27 51 51
Email   contact@hostelduprieure.com
Web   www.hostelduprieure.com

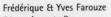

Entry 122   Map 5

Normandy

Le Manoir de Savigny

Walk around the grounds and you might catch deer nibbling on acorns or a coypu by the lily-covered lake. At the end of a poplar lined avenue, surrounded by meadows, it's hard to believe this handsome manor house is ten minutes from busy Valognes. Dating from the 16th century, it's part of an attractive group of farm buildings including an old cider press. The Bonnifets have kept original features – floor tiles, beamed ceilings, spiral stone staircase – blending them with strong colours and objets from their travels in Indonesia and Morocco. The result is a warm, relaxed, faintly exotic feel. Bedrooms are large and light-filled, with seagrass or rugs on stripped wood floors, pale plaster walls, striking beds – maybe brass or pretty wrought-iron – lacy bedcovers and a carefully chosen antique or two. Bathrooms are richly tiled, strikingly coloured, perhaps with a roll top or corner bath. Breakfast, in the sunny dining room with its vast fireplace, carved chairs and dark beams, is a generous spread. Well-placed for Cotentin's beaches, Bayeux, Cherbourg – or borrow bicycles and pack a picnic. *No credit cards.*

Price	€80–€100. Suite €145.
Rooms	5: 4 doubles, 1 suite for 5.
Meals	Restaurants 1.5–3km.
Closed	Rarely.
Directions	From Cherbourg N13 exit Valognes to St Sauveur le Vicomte on D2; D24 for Le Gibet. 50m 1st left dir. Savigny. 1km.

	Corrine & Éric Bonnifet
	50700 Valognes, Manche
Tel	+33 (0)2 33 08 37 75
Email	reservation@manoir-de-savigny.com
Web	www.manoir-de-savigny.com

Château de Pont Rilly

The Roucherays' passion, talent, attention to detail and good dose of patience have wrought a miracle of beauty and harmony. They have only been here 25 years (ten of which were spent with workers in their midst) but when a cubic metre of archives from the 18th century turned up giving itemized details on colour, paintwork, fabric... there was only one choice. It helps to be a restorer like Jean-Jacques who mixes his own paints, and a decorator like Annick who creates the bedspreads, curtains and cushions. Breakfast is served in the old kitchen with its monumental fireplace and original spit mechanism. The beds in the rooms above sit on rare Marie Antoinette parquet, tall windows are draped in white voile; one overlooks the front moat, paddocks and long drive, and a stone staircase leads up to the suite. Bath tubs are panelled, basins are set in stone surrounds. There are trout and eel in the stream, donkeys, sheep and goats in the paddocks and Léonne, a friendly peacock, shows up for the welcome. *Minimum stay three nights November-March in cottages.*

Price	€150.
	Cottages €650-€1,300 per week.
Rooms	4 + 3: 3 doubles, 1 suite for 3.
	3 cottages: 1 for 4, 1 for 6, 1 for 6-8.
Meals	Restaurants 3km.
Closed	Never.
Directions	From Cherbourg RN13 south. Approaching Valonges, exit 'Zone d'Armanville'. D62 to Sottevast. 5km to château, entrance on right.

Annick & Jean-Jacques Roucheray
50260 Négreville, Manche

Tel	+33 (0)2 33 40 47 50
Email	chateau-pont-rilly@wanadoo.fr
Web	www.chateau-pont-rilly.com

Château de Saint Blaise

You will be staying in the coach house, not the château. Everything will be perfect, right down to the bathroom flowers. When Ernst bought the coach house a few years back nothing remained of the building but the walls. He rescued two staircases, one stone, one spiral, and a balustrade from another place; you would never know the old building had lapsed from grace. The Grande Suite is a rich shade of dark blue, with a Napoleon III bed and draped curtains; one tall window overlooks the courtyard, with its pond of pink lilies and fish, the other looks onto fields. The Petite Suite is in blue and beige, with the same views and a narrow but elegant bed. You are served breakfast in a small, pretty room, with flowers on the table. It can be as late as you like and the staff will be delighted to light the fire in winter. There is fresh orange juice, coffee or tea and the eggs just as you like them. Guests are welcome in the large grounds, the wonderful walled garden and the deep blue and burgundy salon with gleaming leather chesterfield and chairs. Such attention to detail, such peaceful luxury.

Price	€220–€250.
Rooms	2 suites.
Meals	Restaurant 3km.
Closed	November–March.
Directions	N13 Cherbourg-Valognes, exit Bricquebec. D902 for 10km then right on route Les Gromonts. Château entrance 100m on left.

	Ernst Roost
	50260 Bricquebec, Manche
Tel	+33 (0)2 33 87 52 60
Email	info@chateaudesaintblaise.com
Web	www.chateaudesaintblaise.com

Le Castel

A classical Napoleon III château, large but not palatial, grand but not ornate, built as summer residence for a Parisian judge. He chose the position well: in deepest Normandy, amid four acres of parkland with views to rolling meadows and mooing cows. It may be private but it's not remote – this is 15 minutes to Coutances and the Normandy beaches, an hour from the Bayeux Tapestry and Mont Saint Michel. Jon creates a house-party atmosphere here and you can organise your own bash for special occasions – there's plenty of space: two salons scattered with French and oriental furniture (a white baby grand adding a Thirties' note) and paintings, wall hangings and tapestries throughout. French windows open to the terrace; eat here or, most convivially, at an oval walnut table amid porcelain, cut glass and candles. The menu (roast duck with raspberries, perhaps, pears in red wine) will delight. Bedrooms are in classic country-house mode: striped or silk wallpaper, polished French beds, an escritoire, a marble washstand. Cosy Burmese cats, a pet llama, charming hosts… bring the family, or have a house party! Great fun.

Price	€110-€155. Suite €210-€290. Cottage €550-€720 per week.
Rooms	5 + 1: 3 doubles, 1 twin, 1 family suite (1 double, 1 triple). Cottage for 2.
Meals	Dinner, 5 courses with coffee, €45.
Closed	Never.
Directions	From Montpinchon, D102 to Pavage. Right at junc., immediately left onto D252. Le Castel 2 minutes on left. Entrance 2nd white gate.

Jon Barnsley
50210 Montpinchon, Manche

Tel	+33 (0)2 33 17 00 45
Email	enquiries@le-castel-normandy.com
Web	www.le-castel-normandy.com

La Verte Campagne

Profoundly rural, surrounded by pastures and orchards, fronted by roses and clematis, is this very old (1702) auberge. From time to time, celebrities and politicians would escape here to relish the food and the deep peace. André is maitre d'hôtel, while Lynne is an excellent chef, responsible for the restaurant and fresh-from-the-oven pastries for breakfast. En suite bedrooms are comfortable and there are a clutch of 1960s collectors-item bathrooms that are all of a colour: one blue, one pink; the rest are plain white. The sitting room is cosy, with tapestry wall hangings, pictures from the area and a monumental stone fireplace with a wood-burning stove; off here, a tartan-walled, low-ceilinged bar and a tempting selection of fine whiskies. Oriental rugs add a stylish touch. The restaurant is romantic with another great stone fireplace and a log fire; specialities include preserved duck with honey, fresh fish from Granville and lamb from nearby Mont St Michel. Most come to eat well, make merry and tuck into bed! A real country auberge.

Price	€50–€78. Half-board €58–€65 p.p.	
Rooms	7: 4 doubles, 1 twin, 1 single, 1 triple.	
Meals	Breakfast €8. Lunch €13.50–€45. Picnic lunches €8.50. Dinner €24–€45. Restaurant closed Wednesdays.	
Closed	1–15 December.	
Directions	From Caen, A84 dir. Rennes, exit 37; 6km to Gavray. A7 junc. right, dir. Coutances on D7 for 9km. D49 dir. Montmartin sur Mer to Trelly; signed in village.	

André & Lynne Tamba
Le Hameau Chevalier,
50660 Trelly, Manche

Tel   +33 (0)2 33 47 65 33
Email lavertecampagne@wanadoo.fr
Web   www.lavertecampagne.com

Le Manoir de l'Acherie

A short way from the motorway is this hotel, deep in the Norman countryside, a lovely, ever-so-French discovery: an old granite house with immaculately tended gardens and an ancient granite cider press sunk into the lawn brimming over with red roses. At one side is a chapel, now bedrooms; on the other is an extension providing a sort of *cour d'honneur* entrance. Some of the furniture is authentically old though most is solid quality repro in the rustic Norman style; rooms are carpeted, bed covers are patterned, curtains are frilly. Mother and daughter Cécile handle the hotel and restaurant service, Stéphane runs the kitchen and continues to win prizes for his robust cuisine. Charcuterie is homemade, cider and calvados comes from the locality. The tables are dressed in prim, cream tablecloths; dark wooden beams, well worn floor tiles and a giant stone fireplace create a pleasant, cosy feel. The small number of people running this establishment and the quiet unstressed, unhurried but efficient way they do so, is admirable. Note that last orders in the restaurant are at 8.30pm.

Price	€55–€115. Singles €45. Suite €110.
Rooms	19: 9 doubles, 4 twins, 2 singles, 4 suites.
Meals	Breakfast €9. Lunch & dinner €18–€40. Restaurant closed Mon Sept-June; Sun eve mid-Oct to week before Easter.
Closed	2 weeks in November; February.
Directions	A84 exit 38 Brecey-Villedieu for Vire. Over 2nd r'bout for 2km; over main road opp. Président dairy.

Ethical Collection: Food.
See page 446 for details.

Stéphane & Cécile Poignavant
Sainte Cécile,
50800 Villedieu les Poêles, Manche

Tel	+33 (0)2 33 51 13 87
Email	manoir@manoir-acherie.fr
Web	www.manoir-acherie.fr

La Ramade

La Ramade, half a century old, was built in golden granite by a livestock merchant who made his fortune. Véronique took it on in 2001 and transformed it from B&B into charming hotel, fulfilling a long-held dream. Her individual interiors are a pleasing mix of modern and brocante finds – with her own Breton cradle sweetly displayed on the second floor. Bedrooms feel feminine and are named after flowers. Blue-carpeted Laurier has white-painted furniture and steps to a bathroom with a sunken bath, Coquelicot has a poppy theme and matching yellow curtains and towels. Pretty Eglantine has a canopied bed and afternoon sun streaming through large windows, Amaryllis – tailor-made for wheelchairs – a superb hydromassage shower. The grounds are filled with mature trees that give privacy from the road, and you are near Mont St Michel and the sea – a great spot for children who will love the guided tour across the great bay at low tide. Véronique now has added a lovely glassed-in veranda for breakfast, a tea room and a bar for samplings of the local pommeau – or a calvados before tucking into bed.

Price	€75-€122.
	Suite & family rooms €150-€185.
Rooms	11: 4 doubles, 3 twins, 1 suite,
	3 family rooms for 3-4.
Meals	Breakfast €10. Restaurants nearby.
Closed	January-6 February; 20-30 November.
Directions	From Avranches D973 for Granville;
	over river, then left on D911 for
	Jullouville; immediately on right.

Véronique Morvan Gilbert
2 rue de la Côte, Marcey les Grèves,
50300 Avranches, Manche

Tel   +33 (0)2 33 58 27 40
Email   hotel@laramade.fr
Web   www.laramade.fr

Château de Colombières

When the marshes were tidal, the château was an island fortress. Towers, turrets, 2.8m-thick walls, arrow slits, arches, moat: history jumps out at you. A long curving drive, a breathtaking first view, a bridge to a courtyard and there is Monsieur – charming, witty, dapper. The château has been in his wife's family for 300 years and he knows every inch by heart. Enter the grand 18th-century dining room, where breakfasts are served at a table under the gaze of an ancestress, rescuer of Colombières after the Revolution. The suites are three centuries older. One is reached via a rare circular elm-tread stair; its salon, vast, carpeted and inviting, has a monumental stone fireplace and a red and cream striped sofa; duck through the stone archway to the bedroom in the tower with the floral balaquined bed. The Louis XVI room is as lofty, as sumptuous, its fabrics pink, bold and coordinated, its bathroom with new green tiles and medieval tomettes. Garden arbours are equipped with chairs… wander at will, fish in the moat. It is a privilege to stay here – with Monsieur *tout compris*!

Price	€130–€180.
Rooms	3: 1 double, 2 suites for 4.
Meals	Breakfast €10; children €5. Restaurant 10km.
Closed	15 November–31 March.
Directions	From Bayeux D5 to Colombières, right on D29, left on D29A; signed.

Étienne de Maupeou d'Ableiges
14710 Colombières, Calvados

Tel	+33 (0)2 31 22 51 65
Email	colombieresaccueil@aliceadsl.fr
Web	www.chateaudecolombieres.com

Manoir de Mathan

A perfect size is this elegant manor house, introduced by a lovely crunching sound on the gravelled driveway and a 17th-century baroque arch. Finding this sober elegance in a typical Bessin farm, with its large courtyard and outbuildings, makes you wonder if all the farmers around here weren't aristocrats. Stay awhile and relax in the lounging chairs on the lawned grounds under the branches of mature trees. It's evident that the renovation was done with much loving thought and care; revealed and enhanced are the lovely beams and timbers, exposed stone walls, original fireplaces and spiral staircase. The large bedrooms were given proper space and light, bathrooms well integrated; it is classy but never overdone. The beds are big, the furniture regional but light and well-chosen, the windows large with over-the-field views. Some suites have canopied beds; some rooms are on the ground floor for easy access. Meals are a ten-minute stroll to the sister hotel up the road (La Rançonnière). Perfectly placed for Bayeux *and* near the landing beaches: you'll need two or three days to enjoy it all. *Check-in/out at sister hotel La Rançonnière (next page).*

Price	€110-€130. Suites €160-€260.
Rooms	20: 13 doubles, 7 suites.
Meals	Breakfast €12. Lunch & dinner at Ferme de la Rançonnière, €24-€48. Wine €15-€40.
Closed	Rarely.
Directions	From Caen exit 7 to Creully on D22 for 19km. Right at church for Arromanches on D65. 1st on right.

Vereecke & Sileghem Families
14480 Crépon, Calvados
Tel   +33 (0)2 31 22 21 73
Email   ranconniere@wanadoo.fr
Web   www.normandie-hotel.org

Ferme de la Rançonnière

A drive through the narrow crenellated archway into the vast grassy courtyard and history leaps out and grabs you. It was originally a fortified seigneurie – the tower dates from the 13th century – to protect against English reprisal sorties after William the Conqueror arrived in England. Inside are exposed timbers and stone walls. One amazing family suite has stone steps which lead down into a double bedroom then up a spiral staircase to a children's bedroom in a tower with tiny glazed windows. Rustic is the look; a butter churn in the corridor, large carved armoires and a well-worn kneading trough in a large family room remind you that this was a working farm. Off the main restaurant is a large, vaulted, stone-flagged sitting area with a log fire at one end making a perfect spot for after-dinner coffee. The bright breakfast room and terrace face south to catch the morning light. Young, efficient Isabelle Sileghem and her husband, with help from a devoted staff, keep this place humming. Book ahead for the best rooms. Entirely wonderful.

Price	€55–€130. Suites €160–€190.
Rooms	47: 21 twins/doubles, 16 triples. Manoir: 10 suites.
Meals	Breakfast €12. Lunch €24. Dinner €48. Wine €15–€40. Restaurant closed 3-25 January.
Closed	Rarely.
Directions	From Caen exit 7 to Creully on D22 for 19km. There, right at church for Arromanches on D65. In Crépon, hotel 1st on right.

Vereecke & Sileghem Families
Route de Creully, Arromanches,
14480 Crépon, Calvados

Tel	+33 (0)2 31 22 21 73
Email	ranconniere@wanadoo.fr
Web	www.ranconniere.fr

Les Maisons de Léa

You could almost do with a guide to hand, to steer you round the passageways, narrow stairs and twists and turns of this intriguing 16th-century building – once three fishermen's houses and a salt warehouse. Each of the houses, plus three across the way, has its own decorative style – romantic, nautical, Baltimore, country; the attention to detail is exquisite. Imagine dreamy fabrics, limewashed walls, fresh orchids, elegant omelettes on white china, cushions on painted wicker, toys and chairs for children and a booklet for each guest on the treasures of Honfleur. Look forward to fresh snacks when you want them, starred restaurants around the corner, and breakfast laid out in a yellow room with views to the big square and the Church of Sainte Catherine; on Saturdays, the food market leaps into action. Relax in the salons – one with a library, one with a fire – spoil yourself in the spa or the (free) hamman, self-cater in the delicious Petite Maison. No lift – that would spoil the charm – and a car park a few minutes' walk away, but staff will happily ferry bags to the upper floors. A total gem. *Hammam & massage available.*

Price	€120–€200.
	Suites & cottage €180–€325.
Rooms	29 + 1: 13 doubles, 10 twins, 6 suites.
	1 cottage for 5.
Meals	Breakfast €15. Light meals available.
	Restaurants within walking distance.
Closed	Rarely.
Directions	A13 exit Beauzeville; A29 exit Honfleur,
	right at r'bout with fountains; follow
	quai Sainte Catherine, cross bridge;
	left, Rue des Logettes.

Didier Lassarat
Place Ste Catherine,
14600 Honfleur, Calvados
Tel   +33 (0)2 31 14 49 49
Email   contact@lesmaisonsdelea.com
Web   www.lesmaisonsdelea.com

La Petite Folie

Fabulously situated for exploring Honfleur, these two townhouses double as havens from the artistic bustle. Most likely built for a sea captain in the 1830s, the commanding main one displays a façade heavily shuttered with grand mansarde windows. Its more modest but older neighbour is a gorgeous 14th-century home, containing three apartments (with kitchenettes) that march up three floors. American born Penny married Frenchman Thierry and they set out tailoring bedrooms lavishly and beautifully, each an enchanting mix of handsome bedsteads, plump duvets, lacquered armchairs, mahogany chests of drawers and whirls of different tones, even a touch of theatrical black-lace print wallpaper in one. The ground-floor sitting room, as wide as the house, offers red suede sofas at one end and a leather chesterfield at the other. The garden is a compact, neatly planted square of charm, its focal point a summerhouse with a Byzantine flourish and belvedere views out to sea. All this, and a delightful hostess. *Minimum stay two nights.*

Price	€135. Apartments €165–€185. All prices per night.
Rooms	5 + 3: 4 doubles, 1 twin. 3 apts: 2 for 2, 1 for 4. Extra bed available.
Meals	Restaurants nearby.
Closed	January.
Directions	From Paris A13 exit A29 for Honfleur; follow signs for centre, then 'Naturospace'. Cross bridge, cont. to Rue Haute; keep right of fork in road. 100m, cream house on right, green shutters.

Penny & Thierry Vincent
44 rue Haute,
14600 Honfleur, Calvados

Mobile	+33 (0)6 74 39 46 46
Email	info@lapetitefolie-honfleur.com
Web	www.lapetitefolie-honfleur.com

Hôtel Maison de Lucie

Named after Lucie Delarue Mardrus, the romantic novelist and poet who was born here, the 1850 house in the heart of Honfleur is shielded by a high wall. Sunshine illuminates panelled walls and leather sofas, the parquet'd salon has an Edwardian air, and bedrooms, elegantly colour-themed, now expand into an adjoining house, those on the second floor overlooking the estuary. Furnishings are immaculate — plum taffeta, burgundy velvet — beds are big and reading lamps won't spoil your eyes. Bathrooms are awash with potions and lotions, there are fresh orchids and vivid rugs, roll top baths and antique chests of drawers, and wide views over rooftops to the sea. Our favourite room rests under the eaves, but all are lovely. In the courtyard, the old caretaker's house is now a suite, its ground-floor sitting area furnished in a deliciously decadent 1930s manner; another room has a small new terraced courtyard area. Soak away your cares in the brick-walled jacuzzi; take your time over a great homemade breakfast of bacon, eggs, fruits, cheese — in bed or in the sun. Muriel's welcome is the icing on the cake.

Price	€150–€220. Suites €315.
Rooms	12: 10 doubles, 2 suites.
Meals	Breakfast €18. Restaurants 120m.
Closed	25 November–20 December; 7–18 January.
Directions	5 minutes from A13, signed from Église Sainte Catherine.

Muriel Daridon
44 rue Capucins,
14600 Honfleur, Calvados

Tel	+33 (0)2 31 14 40 40
Email	info@lamaisondelucie.com
Web	www.lamaisondelucie.com

Château Les Bruyères

Marcel Proust was indulged here when he visited the spa in Cabourg; he'd be pampered
still. Through the imposing gates, down the beech and chestnut avenue, past the
manicured lawns… expectations rise as you approach and are met on arrival. Monsieur
is chef de cuisine, Madame keeps thoroughbreds, their daughter spoils you with
massages and essential oils and the family has an obvious predeliction for beautiful
things. Château les Bruyères is a houseful of treasures and chinoiserie: orchids on the
dining table, modern art on the walls, plush red-carpeted corridors and fine repro
furniture; it is very civilised. In the salon are big rugs on black and white tiles, a flurry
of small armchairs and settees, a large open fire and glazed cabinets full of fine china. Ten
tickety-boo bedrooms await in the 19th-century château and a further four in the 18th-
century slate-hung manor that adjoins it; all ooze luxury and calm. Outside are several
acres of parkland in which hides a turquoise pool. *Gastronomic & pampering weekends.*

Price	€120–€210. Singles €85. Apartment €290–€360.
Rooms	14: 8 doubles, 2 twins, 2 singles, 1 triple, 1 apartment.
Meals	Breakfast €14. Dinner €39–€65. Wine €15–€50. Restaurant closed Mondays & Tuesdays October–May.
Closed	January.
Directions	A29 exit 'La Haie Tondue' for Falaise & Bonneboscq, then D16 to Cambremer. Opposite church, on left 150m.

	Philippe, Michèle & Julie Harfaux Route du Cadran, 14340 Cambremer, Calvados
Tel	+33 (0)2 31 32 22 45
Email	contact@chateaulesbruyeres.com
Web	www.chateaulesbruyeres.com

Château du Mesnil d'O

The approach to this 18th-century château lifts the spirit. Stone pillars and tall iron gates mark the entrance from the road, a tree-lined avenue set in five hectares of garden and parkland rolls you to the front door. The four bedrooms, one with listed wallpaper from 1905, are on the first floor up a beautiful staircase in white Caen with (listed) wrought-iron handrail and balustrade. A square landing with a long view over the park is the perfect place to spread your newspaper on a lovely old dining table; bookshelves bursting with literature line the length of one wall. Family portraits bring the corridor to life, along with the odd antique; fresh flowers are lovingly placed in bedrooms and on landings. A feast for the eye: blue velvet chairs, chevron parquet floor, panelled walls with painted scenes above the doors and a wonderful Louis XVI buffet displaying its collection of old plates – that's breakfast in the dining room. One might feel overawed by such splendour but the welcome makes the visitor feel instantly at home. You may be loath to leave. *No credit cards.*

Price	€110. Suite €170.
Rooms	4: 3 doubles, 1 suite for 4.
Meals	Restaurants within 5km.
Closed	Rarely.
Directions	From Caen N13 to Paris. In Vimont, right D47 then D40 for St Pierre sur Dives 7km; on right.

	Guy de Chabaneix
	14270 Vieux Fumé, Calvados
Tel	+33 (0)2 31 20 01 47
Email	lemesnildo@wanadoo.fr
Web	www.lemesnildo.com

Château La Cour

Warm and charming hosts, David and Lesley's attention to detail is impressive. Not everyone can take a 13th-century château, once part of the estate of the Ducs of Harcourt, and so successfully blend history with comfort. Expect a bold décor – striped yellow wallpaper with pink and blue curtains – and a subdued luxury: Lloyd Loom chairs, marble fireplaces, Egyptian cotton. One room has a curved wooden staircase that leads to a superb bathroom above. A house for feasting, too: fine English china, damask and candelabra set the table in the charming dining room. David grows for Lesley to cook, and his organic potager (seven varieties of potato, 50 of vegetable) is a delightful diversion. High stone walls shelter it from unkind winds, fruit trees shade the lawn, and long narrow beds make for easy harvesting. Lovely traditional bedrooms face south and look over the garden; the apartment is stunning. The Cravens are keen conservationists; barn owls nest in the end wall of the house and there is good birdwatching. The Normandy beaches, Bayeux and its tapestry are within easy reach. *No credit cards. Children over 12 welcome.*

Price	€140–€150. Apartment €750 per week.
Rooms	4 + 1: 3 doubles, 1 twin. Apartment for 2.
Meals	Hosted dinner with wine, €35–€50; book ahead.
Closed	Rarely.
Directions	D562 south from Thury Harcourt for 5km; right onto D133 for Culey le Patry; left onto D166; 2nd right onto D211. Château on right approaching village.

David & Lesley Craven
14220 Culey le Patry,
Calvados

Tel	+33 (0)2 31 79 19 37
Email	info@chateaulacour.com
Web	www.chateaulacour.com

Entry 138   Map 4

Hôtel Tardif

A mid 18th-century maison in the centre of Bayeux, an architectural jewel. It was built for a botanist who worked at Versailles; specimen trees still stand in the grounds. In those days, carriages would rumble through the archway and enter the central 'cours d'honneur'; still cobbled, it's an exquisite spot from which to glimpse a fascinating range of building styles. Delighted to share all he knows about this house and its history, Anthony, with impeccable English, is an exceptionally generous young host. Inside are white walls, parquet étoile floors and a curved and suspended staircase, one of only two in France. And such beautiful things: antiques and tapestries, brocade chairs and gilded mirrors, a grand piano and a chandelier from Compiègne where the Empress Josephine lived. Bedrooms are elegant, spacious and sober, in keeping with the history. One bedroom, on the first floor, is classified 'monument historique', its panelling immaculately revived in regulation browns and golds. Other rooms have cream stone walls; all are uncluttered and serene. What value! *New rooms open 2010.*

Price	€50–€160. Suite €150–€200. Extra person €20.
Rooms	7: 6 doubles, 1 suite for 4.
Meals	Breakfast €8. Restaurants within walking distance.
Closed	Christmas.
Directions	From RN13, exit 36 for Bayeux, follow signs to 'centre ville'; left at 1st r'bout, right at 2nd r'bout. Large green gate 300m on right. (Car access 57 rue Larcher.)

Anthony Voidie
Sci Relais de la Liberté,
16 rue de Nesmond, 14400 Bayeux,
Calvados

Tel	+33 (0)2 31 92 67 72
Email	hoteltardif@orange.fr
Web	www.hoteltardif.com

Bois Joli

This is bang in the middle of pretty, fashionable Bagnoles de L'Orne, a traditional spa town with waters that flow at 24 degrees; boating lake, casino and spa remain. Bois Joli was a *pension* built in the mid-1800s for those seeking the cure, and sits on the edge of the Fôret d'Andaine in an acre of lawn, shrubs and sequoias. Décor is traditional, understated, elegant. In the salon are comfortable chairs, books, newspapers, flowers in pewter vases and a piano you may play; in the dining room, fine rush-seated chairs and white napery. The food is good-looking and delicious: homemade brioche and orange pressé for breakfast; oysters, magret de pigeon and apricot tart for dinner. Slip off your shoes in a carpeted bedroom, immaculate with matching wallpaper and bedcover in toile de Jouy or pale flower, perhaps an old country wardrobe to add character. That lovely lake is a minute away and the hotel arranges mushroom-picking weekends in the woods. Staff are discreet and helpful, and you are surrounded by all the benefits of civilisation – golf, swimming, tennis and restaurants aplenty.

Price	€76–€150.
Rooms	20 twins/doubles.
Meals	Breakfast €11.
	Lunch & dinner €21–€63.
Closed	Never.
Directions	From Argentan, D916 for Mayenne, follow signs for Bagnoles Lac. Signed.

Yvette & Daniel Mariette
12 avenue Philippe du Rozier,
61140 Bagnoles de L'Orne, Orne
Tel   +33 (0)2 33 37 92 77
Email   boisjoli@wanadoo.fr
Web   www.hotelboisjoli.com

Auberge de la Source

Using reclaimed beams and stone, Christine and Serge built the auberge on the site of his parents' 18th-century apple press. Unfortunately that means no more cider, but they serve a superb one made just down the road. Both the restaurants – one smaller and cosier, the other with huge sliding windows – and the bedrooms were designed to make the most of the view down to the lake, which is the hub of a huge sports complex. Apart from windsurfing and a sailing school, there's riding, a climbing wall, archery, fishing and something called 'swing-golf', easy to learn, apparently. Children have a play area, pony rides, mini-golf and pedal boats. If you want real nature the forest is nearby where you will see huge stags without too much searching. The auberge has big rooms catering for families, all with huge beams and chunky antiques mixed in with more modern furniture. The food is simple, centring on steaks cooked over a wood fire, and fresh farm produce to go with them. A sensible choice for families with small children – or sporty teenagers. *This is a farming family; please book ahead for dinner.*

Price	€56–€96.
Rooms	5: 1 double, 4 family rooms.
Meals	Picnic €10. Lunch & dinner from €15, book ahead. Wine €5–€20.
Closed	Rarely.
Directions	From La Ferté Macé D908 for Domfront Mont St Michel. After 2km right to hotel; signed.

	Christine & Serge Volclair
	La Peleras,
	61600 La Ferté Macé, Orne
Tel	+33 (0)2 33 37 28 23
Email	auberge.lasource@orange.fr
Web	pagesperso-orange.fr/auberge.lasource/

Le Pavillon de Gouffern

More mansion than lodge, Gouffern was built 200 years ago by a wealthy gentleman with plenty of fellow hunters to entertain. But the scale of this elegant 'pavilion' is perfect for today's traveller. It stands in an estate of 80 hectares and guests can walk, cycle or ride in the private forest in peace and seclusion. Big windows let in lots of soft light to illuminate the newly renovated décor: hunting themes, an Edwardian salon with leather chairs and oak floors, an unfussy elegance that gives a sense of the quiet class of a good country house. Recently renovated bedrooms, some of them in the well-converted outbuildings, are big and eminently comfortable (smaller on the top floor), new bathrooms have all the necessary bits and meals are served in the handsome dining room – the food has been much praised. In the grounds, the delightful Doll's House, built for children of another age, is now an idyllic suite (honeymoon specials arranged)… and you may play billiards by the fire in the bar. A nearby stable delivers horses to the door and, if you are lucky, the chef will cook your freshly caught trout.

Price	€80-€200. Cottage €60-€160. Prices per night.
Rooms	19 + 1: 18 doubles, 1 single. Cottage for 2-4.
Meals	Breakfast €12. Picnic available. Lunch & dinner €25-€55.
Closed	24-25 December.
Directions	N26 exit Argentan. Hotel 7km from Argentan in forest of Silly en Gouffern; signed.

Karelle Jouaux & Vincent Thomas
61310 Silly en Gouffern, Orne

Tel	+33 (0)2 33 36 64 26
Email	pavillondegouffern@wanadoo.fr
Web	www.pavillondegouffern.com

La Louvière

It's a joy to discover this 18th-century manor house, a classic gentilhommière embraced by delicious grounds. Drive up an avenue of lime trees, step under the clematis-strewn pergolas, and enter the hall. Charming hostess Isabelle Groult says the old house has "une ambiance de soie": a chandelier sparkles above lace tablecloths in the dining room, pale chintz dresses elegant windows in the sunny *Grand Salon*, and the *Petit Salon*'s fireplace is flanked by charming chairs. Colours and fabrics match beautifully. Take an aperitif on the terrace, get sporty on the tennis court, and dream in the gardens, fragrant with roses and buzzing with bees. Patterned paving leads to a potager in which your dinner vegetables grow. Inside, an oak staircase curves up to the first-floor bedrooms, daintily, exquisitely romantic, decorated with fine fabrics and antiques; up again is Chambre d'Aurélie, tucked into the splendid 'charpente'. Chambre d'Alexandre is equally striking – and discreet. Everything you could want for a weekend is here: a heated pool, tennis court, small fishing lake, happiness and peace.

Price	€95–€130. Suite €135.
Rooms	4: 3 doubles, 1 suite for 4.
Meals	Dinner with wine & coffee, €32.
Closed	November–Easter.
Directions	From Alençon N12 west. In St Denis sur Sarthon right; signed La Roche Mabile for 2km to le Fault. Property signed on right.

Isabelle & Alain Groult
Le Fault,
61420 Saint Denis sur Sarthon, Orne

Tel	+33 (0)2 33 29 25 61
Email	isabelle@louviere.fr
Web	www.louviere.fr

Moulin de Villeray

The scale of this grand old 16th-century mill in pleasant riverside grounds is unexpected and thrilling. Emerge through a beguiling creeper-covered entrance to discover a big paddle wheel behind a huge arched window in a dining room that trumpets excellent food and unlimited French wines – the pride of Christian. Naturally there are beams galore, all stripped to natural tones to form a union with soft furnishings; in the sitting rooms, age-old flagstones with a patina of mushroom and fawn; in cosy, wood-clad bedrooms, beds dressed in checks, florals and plain natural tones. Beneath weathered old terracotta runs a storey of roof windows each providing plunging river views; ground-floor areas are an evocative mix of beam and exposed stone. A cavernous bread oven converted into an open fireplace is the epitome of warm rusticity and a fine symbol of this family's welcome and dedication. Enjoy the informality from beneath colourful umbrellas on the large terrace, or from the lawns that run all along the banks of the river. The village is untouched, the countryside magical. *Further rooms in château up the hill.*

Price	€95-€175. Suites €205-€255.
Rooms	26: 7 doubles, 12 twins, 7 suites (6 rooms are in village house next to Moulin).
Meals	Breakfast €15. Lunch €28-€69. Dinner €38-€69.
Closed	November-Easter (open for groups by arrangement & at New Year).
Directions	From Chartres on N23 dir. Nogent Le Rotrou. 14km after Montlandon, right on D203 to Condé Sur Huisne; D10 dir. Remalard for 3km, left to Villeray. Moulin at bottom of hill on right.

Christian Eelsen
Villeray, 61110 Condeau, Orne

Tel	+33 (0)2 33 73 30 22
Email	contact@domainedevilleray.com
Web	www.domainedevilleray.com

Château de Villeray

Perched to command acres of parkland, this Renaissance château, with its full complement of pepperpot towers, noble windows, belvederes and old moat, could scarcely be more French. For a place that has seen many of the highs and lows of French history, it invites you quite informally into oak-panelled reception rooms (a comfortable sitting room with open log fire) and, to the front, a splendid stone staircase lit by windows trimmed with stained glass. Another endearing touch is the frivolously pretty ceiling light in the restaurant at the watermill down the road (expect an agreeable mix of attentive service, haute cuisine and Christian's 'directoire' of French wines). Bedrooms spread in all shapes and sizes over the first two floors, united by a sense of easy elegance. Soft furnishings set neutral tones for Art Deco armchairs, polished boards, faded oriental rugs, the odd four-poster. Most bathrooms sport white tiles hand painted with the owner's own designs, one of many authentic touches. The deep country quiet is extraordinary. *Reception, pool & meals at Moulin de Villeray down the hill.*

Price	€95–€295. Suites €205–€395.
Rooms	13: 9 doubles, 4 suites for 2 (some interconnect).
Meals	Breakfast €15. Lunch & dinner €28–€69. Half-board only €47–€70 extra p.p., May to mid-Sept. Rest. closed Nov–Easter.
Closed	November–Easter; 1 week in January.
Directions	From Chartres on N23 dir. Nogent Le Rotrou. 14km after Montlandon, right D203 to Condé Sur Huisne; D10 dir. Remalard for 3km, left Villeray. Château on right.

Christian Eelsen
Villeray, 61110 Condeau, Orne

Tel	+33 (0)2 33 73 30 22
Email	contact@domainedevilleray.com
Web	www.domainedevilleray.com

Domaine de la Louveterie

From the forested road, the drive descends to glorious views over the hills of the Perche. And there is the house, a 17th-century longère in 32 acres of peacefulness, rescued and restored by Carol and Pietro. A charming couple, well travelled and fluent in several languages, they moved from Paris two years ago and are enchanted with their new life. A gravelled courtyard sets the scene (beyond are two gîtes). No short cuts have been taken in the renovation; no ostentation either — what you get is an overwhelming feeling of comfort and well-being. Pietro oversees pasture and woodland, potager and pool; Carol, a culinary photographer, stars in the kitchen. Good wines and food are ferried to a room where logs smoulder; hosts join guests for after-dinner coffee and digestifs. And so to bed... the Chambre Fifties is caught in a cosy time warp (in spite of the flat-screen TV), Chinoise and Voyage rest warmly under the eaves, and the suites spread themselves impressively over two floors, the grandest with wooden panelling, choice antiques and a real fire. *No credit cards. Ask about cookery & watercolour courses, & riding weekends.*

Price	€85–€110. Suites €130–€155. Apartments €580 per week.
Rooms	5 + 2: 3 doubles, 2 duplex suites for 2. 2 apts: 1 for 2, 1 for 3.
Meals	Dinner with wine, €38–€68.
Closed	Rarely.
Directions	From Rouen A13, A154, N154 to Evreux; N12 to Dreux; D828 then D928 to La Loupe. Ask for detailed directions.

Carol & Pietro Cossu-Descordes
61110 Moutiers au Perche, Orne

Tel	+33 (0)2 33 73 11 63
Email	domainedelalouveterie@wanadoo.fr
Web	www.domainedelalouveterie.com

Villa Fol Avril

Once a stopover for travellers passing on this peaceful road, the 19th-century relais de poste became a petrol station some years ago; now it's been rescued by the Sicres. Since leaving Paris, this energetic couple have added modern touches to authentic features and created a beautiful, bright hotel. Sunshine pours in through windows overlooking the pretty village's rosy-coloured roofs, and handcrafted furnishings pop up everywhere. Bedrooms are bold and individual, all with elaborately carved key fobs and something to make you go "ooh!" In one, an oak ladder leads to a high mezzanine – great fun for kids. The exposed timbers upstairs are magnificent and some remnants from the coach house's old life have been given a new lease of life: an ancient hayrack and shutters have become quirky headboards. Bathrooms are equally distinctive, with yellow tiles. Fresh local produce is served in the restaurant or on the garden terrace; look out for snails from the local 'escargoterie'. Venture into the Perche for plenty of surprises: forested walking tracks, fairytale manoirs and the famous Percheron horses.

Price	€70-€130.
	Family room & triple €110-€160.
Rooms	9: 5 doubles, 2 twins, 1 family room, 1 triple.
Meals	Breakfast €9. Dinner €25-€45. Wine €20-€60. Restaurants 8km.
Closed	Never.
Directions	From Nogent-le-Rotrou D918 dir. L'Aigle for 21km. Hotel in centre of Moutiers au Perche.

M & Mme Sicre
2 rue des Fers Chauds,
61110 Moutiers au Perche, Orne

Tel +33 (0)2 33 83 22 67
Email contact@villafolavril.fr
Web www.villafolavril.fr

Château de Bonnemare

You could almost imagine the Vicomte de Valmont and the Marquise de Merteuil plotting in the *grand salon*! A Renaissance gatehouse leads to a remarkable 17th-century *brique de St Jean* façade as you enter the grounds of this enticing 'monument historique'. Alain and Sylvie, generous and charming, have restored two elegant ground-floor rooms in the north wing, and two suites with listed decoration on the first floor. Breathtaking 'La Parade' announces a velvet swagged four-poster in an ornate alcove, a monumental fireplace and a single-bedded nursery; 'Louis XVI', decorated in 1777, reveals a pure French classical elegance, its exquisitely furnished yellow salon adjoining a vast bedroom with chandeliers and intricate mouldings. Bathrooms are pleasingly lavish — and modern. Breakfast in the vaulted Great Kitchen, its vast fireplace replete with a turbine-driven spit designed by da Vinci, means embroidered napkins, fresh fruits and flowers, pâtisserie and homemade jams. The estate walls enclose a small kingdom: chapel, farm, cider press, bakery, barns and 44 acres of park and woodland. Amazing.

Price	€92–€100. Suites €188–€246.
Rooms	4: 1 double, 3 suites for 2-3.
Meals	Restaurant 6km.
Closed	November–January.
Directions	From Paris A15 to Cergy-Pointoise. D14, then D6014 to Rouen. At r'bout in Fleury sur Andelle, dir. Radepont 4km. Exit Radepont, left to château, 3km outside village.

Sylvie Vandecandelaere
990 route de Bacqueville,
27380 Radepont, Eure

Tel   +33 (0)2 32 69 44 33
Email   svdc2@wanadoo.fr
Web   www.bonnemare.com

Château de Requiécourt

Discreetly in the heart of the landscaped settlement of Requiécourt — awash with cedars, horse chestnuts, sequoias, shrubs and ornamental lake — towers a wall. At the press of a button, tall gates swing open and invite you into the château grounds. Madame Milon, friendly and well-informed, receives you, then ushers you from smart reception counter to the bedrooms upstairs. Here, pastel colours and tall windows combine to create calm, light-filled spaces; elegant too, with crisp white bed linen and bare polished parquet. Paintings from local artists hang on pristine walls; dig into your pockets and you may take one home. Each room is different; Rose Velours, with its fourposter bed, pivoting antique wash basins and corner balcony surveying the park, is particularly pleasing. Back downstairs is a long oval table for breakfast and a furnished gravelled terrace the other side of the French windows. Kayak along the Epte, motor to Giverny in a vintage car — the tourist leaflets reveal all. With so much to do and Paris nearby you may find yourself booking for one night and staying for more. *Shiatsu available.*

Price	€85–€125.
Rooms	5: 4 doubles, 1 twin.
Meals	Restaurants within 10km.
Closed	Rarely.
Directions	From A13 junc. 16 to Vernon. D181 for Gisors, 14km; D9 to Cahaignes then Requiécourt. On village square, signed. Ring bell.

Emmanuelle Milon
Hameau de Requiécourt,
5 rue de la Chartreuse,
27420 Cahaignes, Eure

Tel	+33 (0)2 32 55 37 02
Email	welcome@chateauderequiecourt.com
Web	www.chateauderequiecourt.com

Entry 149   Map 4

Le Moulin de Connelles

Bring your boater, hop in a green and red-trimmed flatboat right out of a Monet painting and punt along a quiet arm of the Seine after a morning at Monet's garden, 30 minutes away. Watery greens, pinks and that scintillating veil of haze that is particular to this part of Normandy intensify the Impressionist mood. Then look up at the extraordinary half-timbered, chequer-boarded, turreted manor house and you will have to pinch yourself, hard. Part of the house is on an island; hidden paths lead through flowering bushes to a private pool. Young Karine keeps up the family tradition of quiet hospitality here while bringing the park and its flowerbeds up to snuff. Bedrooms and restaurant have been renovated with fine materials: oak, mosaics, weathered marble, granite and limestone. Step around to the garden and peek at rows of copper pots through the kitchen windows, reflections of the lovely meals served in the restaurant. Reserve a room with a balcony overlooking the river or splurge on the suite, with its jacuzzi for two in the tower. Bring your paintbrushes. *Boats for trips upriver.*

Price	€130–€170. Suites €170–€310.
Rooms	13: 7 doubles, 6 suites.
Meals	Breakfast €15. Lunch & dinner €35–€58. Children's meals €16.
Closed	Sunday evening; Monday October–April.
Directions	From A13 exit 18 Louviers on N15 towards Pont de l'Arche for 4km; right to St Pierre du Vauvray, Andé & Connelles; signed.

	Karine Petiteau
	40 route d'Amfreville sous les Monts, 27430 Connelles, Eure
Tel	+33 (0)2 32 59 53 33
Email	moulindeconnelles@wanadoo.fr
Web	www.moulin-de-connelles.fr

Château d'Emalleville

An elegant, listed 18th-century château, Emalleville has it all: perfectly landscaped and formal gardens, vast woodlands for walking (and autumn shooting), a tennis court, an ancient fallen mulberry that has rebuilt itself, a cosy suite in the converted beamed dovecote (a favourite) and fine rooms in the orange brick and limestone coach house and outbuilding. There is perfect toile de Jouy in some of the rooms and most beds are canopied. Contemporary touches here and there work nicely: photos and drawings dedicated to the dancer who took Paris by storm in 'Josephine', a colourful bullfighting theme in 'Seville', while 'Giverny' is floral and feminine. All open directly to the lawns. Tucked away behind the precious vegetable garden and orchard is the heated pool. Breakfast is served in the *salle de chasse*: try the mulberry or wild plum jam. The lady of the manor's exquisite taste has woven a magic from floor to ceiling, from Jouy print to antique wardrobe: you will feel like prince and princess here. And you're only 30 minutes' drive from Giverny.

Price	€100–€120. Suites €140–€230.
Rooms	8: 6 doubles, 2 suites for 2-5.
Meals	Restaurant 8km.
Closed	Never.
Directions	From Evreux, D155 for Louviers & Acquigny. Thro' Boulay Morin, 500m after village, left to Emalleville. 2nd road on right; château opp. church; ring bell.

Frédérique & Arnaud Tourtoulou
17 rue de l'Église,
27930 Emalleville, Eure

Tel	+33 (0)2 32 34 01 87
Email	tourtoulou@chateaudemalleville.com
Web	www.chateaudemalleville.com

Château de la Puisaye

Cats, dogs, horses, sheep and a fleet of farmyard fowl in 17-hectares of countryside heaven. Delightful ex-solicitor Diana moved to France with her French husband to indulge her love of horses. With its scattering of shuttered windows and classically pale façade, this Napoleon III château oozes 19th-century elegance. Large airy bedrooms are lightly furnished with antiques; huge mantelpiece mirrors and glass-panelled doors flood spaces with light; creamy paintwork, classic English wallpapers, marble fireplaces and snowy linen create an ordered calm. The salon and library have elaborate woodwork and the dining room, with its gleaming table and silver candlesticks, invites you to linger over breakfast, a feast of homemade pastries, jams and cooked dishes. Diana, a stylish cook, will prepare dinner on request, perhaps foie gras followed by truffle-stuffed guinea fowl; fruits and vegetables come from the potager, local markets and the 19th-century greenhouse. Lounge in the library over books, games, WiFi; borrow a bike and pedal the grounds; relax in the infra-red sauna amongst delicious aromatherapy oils.

Price	€95–€125. Suite €135–€180. Cottage €400–€790.
Rooms	5 + 1: 3 doubles, 1 twin, 1 suite for 4. Cottage for 8.
Meals	B&B only: breakfast included. Dinner €35; menu gourmand €55; Normandy platter with cider, €16.
Closed	One week in winter.
Directions	From Verneuil sur Avre on D839 to Chartres; D56 dir. Senonches for 1.5km; right onto C19 for château.

Bruno & Diana Costes
Lieu-dit La Puisaye,
27130 Verneuil sur Avre, Eure

Tel	+33 (0)2 32 58 65 35
Email	info@chateaudelapuisaye.com
Web	www.chateaudelapuisaye.com

Château de Saint Maclou la Campagne

Fabulous tales of drama, decadence, travels, travails, wealth and war surround this 17th-century château; these days the proud brick and limestone mansion is certainly more peaceful than in the past, yet every bit as deliciously luxurious. British hosts Robin and Nicola Gage welcome guests into an elegant wood-panelled drawing room where you can admire porcelains, portraits and family photos – and snuggle before a winter fire. Similarly graceful is the green dining room with its fine mahogany table; breakfast can be taken here or in the cosy semi-cellar amid brick walls and copper utensils. Waft up to generous bedrooms in apple green, mushroom, apricot or sunny yellow, each bearing antiques and an art collection spanning many years and styles. Bathrooms are thoroughly 21st-century. A dry moat encircles the château; beyond lie vast lawns interspersed with neat hedges, an orchard and a dovecote that once boasted 5,000 pigeons; beyond that, Normandy's cider apple countryside and beaches. A fascinating slice of history set in tranquil surroundings – and in the summer months you can rent the whole château.

Price	€100–€150. Whole house €5,000–€8,000 per week.
Rooms	4: 1 double, 3 twins/doubles. Whole house available.
Meals	Breakfast €12. Restaurant 300m.
Closed	Rarely.
Directions	A13 exit 28 for Beuzeville; at r'bout right onto D675, over next r'bout to Saint Maclou. Thro' village to traffic lights, then right. Entrance 200m on right.

	Robin Gage
	352 rue Emile Deson,
	27210 Saint Maclou, Eure
Tel	+33 (0)2 32 57 26 62
Email	rg@chateaudesaintmaclou.com
Web	www.chateaudesaintmaclou.com

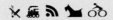

Brittany

Château du Launay

A dream of a place, another world, another time, beside bird-swept pond and quiet woods. Launay marries austere grandeur with simple luxury, fine old stones with contemporary art, rich minimalism with exotica. In the great white hall, a large decorated Indian marriage chest shares the Persian rug with two bronze stags. The staircase sweeps up, past fascinating art, to big light-filled rooms where beds are white, bathrooms are plainly, beautifully modern and light and colours are handled with consummate skill. The second floor is more exotic, the corridor punctuated with an Indian gate, the rooms slightly smaller but rich in carved colonial bed, polo-player armchairs, Moghul prints. For relaxation, choose the gilt-edged billiard room, the soberly leather-chaired, book-filled library or the stupendous drawing room with a piano (concerts are given) and many sitting corners. A house of a million marvels where you take unexpected journeys and may find yourself on a horse on old Roman roads or pike fishing on the pond. Your hosts are charming.

Price	€160–€180. Apartments €125–€140 (€750–€850 per week).
Rooms	8 + 2: 6 doubles, 2 twins. 2 apartments for 2-4.
Meals	Dinner €40. Wine €14–€30. Restaurant 5km.
Closed	January–February.
Directions	From Pontivy, D782 for 21km to Guémené; D1 for Gourin to Toubahado for 9km. Don't go to Ploërdut. In Toubahado right on C3 for Locuon for 3km. Entrance immed. after Launay sign.

M & Mme Bogrand
Launay,
56160 Ploërdut, Morbihan

Tel   +33 (0)2 97 39 46 32
Email   info@chateaudulaunay.fr
Web   www.chateaudulaunay.com

Hôtel Le Lodge Kerisper

Claudie and her young family moved from Paris to open this chic, charming, buckets-and-spade hotel. Huge mirrors reflect white walls, pale floors and seaside touches as you enter. There is more than a touch of the French 'Hamptons' about these converted stone buildings perched high above steep little lanes leading down to the harbour; sunhats, toys, kites and beach paraphernalia are the order of the day. The bedrooms in this cleverly adapted building, complete with giddy, architect designed conservatory on stilts, look inward to a small, prettily lawned garden and a pool, while antique gilt chairs chit-chat with modern sofas as you sip aperitifs at the ultra smart, zinc-topped bar. Bedrooms, many with terraces, are comfortably understated. Linen and voile curtains float on polished floors, white painted wood ceilings are discreetly contemporary. A hard day's cycling the coastal paths (or bikini gazing on a sandy beach) leads, inevitably, to supper at one of the pretty harbourside restaurants… fairy lights twinkle, halliards click and yachts bob gently in the stylish little port. *Spa & treatments.*

Price	€95–€255. Suites €180–€290.
Rooms	20: 12 doubles, 3 suites, 5 family suites.
Meals	Breakfast €15; children €8. Restaurant 100m.
Closed	4–26 January.
Directions	100m north of main harbour street in La Trinité sur Mer. Well signed.

Claudie & Philippe Favre
4 rue du Latz,
56470 La Trinité sur Mer, Morbihan

Tel	+33 (0)2 97 52 88 56
Email	contact@lodgekerisper.com
Web	www.lodge-kerisper.com

Le Parc er Gréo

The neat new building is a metaphor for Breton hospitality. The front is a high north wall – it may seem forbidding but once inside you know that it shelters house and garden from the wild elements, that fields, woods, sea and the coastal path are just yards away. Eric prepares itineraries for guests, boating is on the spot, swimming a little further away or in the pool. Warm colours, oriental rugs and fine family pieces sit easily on the tiled floors of the many-windowed ground floor. Eric's father's watercolours lend personality to all the rooms, and the unusual candlesticks in the hall and ancestral portraits, including a large Velazquez-style child in a great gilt frame, are most appealing. Salon and dining room open widely onto terrace and garden – wonderful places to relax or play with the children on the big lawn. Rooms, attractive in shades of red, green and salmon, are functionally furnished. Your hosts, their charming young family and their enthusiasm for their project – to stop being clients in boring hotels and do things properly themselves – make this an easy, friendly place to stay. *Eric's boat available to charter.*

Price	€70-€140. Suite €170-€290.	
Rooms	15: 7 doubles, 7 twins, 1 suite.	
Meals	Breakfast €14. Restaurants 3km.	
Closed	Mid-November to mid-March (occasionally open Christmas).	
Directions	From Vannes D101 for Île aux Moines. Ignore left turns to Arradon. Left to Le Moustoir then onto Le Gréo; follow signs.	

	Eric & Sophie Bermond
	9 rue Mané Guen, Le Gréo,
	56610 Arradon, Morbihan
Tel	+33 (0)2 97 44 73 03
Email	contact@parcergreo.com
Web	www.parcergreo.com

Villa Kerasy Hôtel & Spa

Bamboos and cherry trees, koi carp and stone statues – the presence of the East is strong. Influenced by an East India Company trading post nearby (now a small museum), Jean-Jacques has taken the Spice Route as a theme. The 1914 building, once a factory, is attractive enough from the outside; inside it is captivating. From the moment you pass the sentinel stone elephants you are enveloped in luxury. The bedrooms are all different, with muted, subtle colours, lovely fabrics, intriguing pictures, fresh flowers; five are new. Some overlook the railway, others the tiny but lovely Japanese garden. Thoughtfulness and attention to detail are apparent throughout – even the buddha has a fresh camellia dropped into his capacious lap; but there's no hint of pretentiousness. Jean-Jacques has experience in the hotel trade and knows exactly how to make you feel cherished without impinging on your space. The day begins with a fabulous breakfast and you're a ten-minute walk from the centre of Vannes, where there are any number of good shops and restaurants. Don't miss Saturday's market! *Ayurveda spa.*

Price	€118-€228. Suite €320-€380.
Rooms	15: 7 doubles, 7 twins, 1 suite for 2-4.
Meals	Breakfast €14. Restaurants 10-minute walk.
Closed	Mid-November to mid-December; January.
Directions	From N165 exit Vannes centre; follow signs to Hôpital or Gare SNCF; hotel signed.

	Jean-Jacques Violo
	20 avenue Favrel et Lincy,
	56000 Vannes, Morbihan
Tel	+33 (0)2 97 68 36 83
Email	info@villakerasy.com
Web	www.villakerasy.com

Château de Talhouët

The driveway through ancient tall trees and mysterious undergrowth is as impressive as the 16th-century Breton manor is imposing – and the views reach all the way to the Aze valley and the cliffs of Rochefort. Jean-Pol bought a ruin two decades ago and created this refuge of rare elegance and sophistication; he is fulfilling his dream. He is also restoring the grounds: woodland and wildflower meadow, grass parterres and walled gardens, English and French. Floors are wonderful – of stone worn to satin or polished wood with Persian rugs – and the sitting room is both companionable and vast at the same time; imagine old rose panelling, soft deep sofas, and an antique table groaning under the weight of books on art, architecture, design. Superb portraits, huge antique mirrors, Venetian Blackamore candle wall brackets, Delft vases – all are on an immense scale here. Jean-Pol joins you for a drink as you discuss the menu; the food is cooked by a talented young chef. Then to bed up an impressive stone stair, to sleep under fancy florals and softly painted beams. Be woken by birdsong and gentle views.

Price	€140–€225.
Rooms	8 doubles.
Meals	Dinner €47.
Closed	5 & 25 January; 15-30 November.
Directions	From Redon D775 through Allaire 9km; right D313 through Malansac to Rochefort en Terre; D774 for Malestroit 4km. Left onto small road, 2km. Entrance on left; château another 500m.

Jean-Pol Soulaine
56220 Rochefort en Terre, Morbihan

Tel   +33 (0)2 97 43 34 72
Email   chateaudetalhouet@libertysurf.fr
Web   www.chateaudetalhouet.com

Domaine de Bodeuc

A taste of Paris in the country. Jean and Sylvie, urban escapees, have restored, most glamorously, this 19th-century manor house in its own park surrounded by woodland. The roomy hall is dominated by a glass chandelier, wall colours are earthy and cool – mushrooms, aubergines – and a bold mix of good antiques with striking modern art gives a dramatic impression. Salons are small but bedrooms are large; whether in the house or stables, they are decked out in similar style giving a pleasing sense of space: beds large and crisply white with colourful spreads and proper sheets and blankets; bathrooms elegant and pampering. Relax with a drink on the small terrace overlooking the park or in the piano bar, dine well on locally sourced produce, venture out to one of the good local restaurants. It's supremely tranquil here, yet you're close to wild beaches, a huge choice of golf courses, and excellent shopping in the fortified port of Vannes. Wine tasting and mushroom weekends are planned for the future, along with the development of the organic potager and the original walled garden. *Balneotherapy on request.*

Price	€80–€166. Single €70–€95. Suite €132–€202. Family rooms €132–€180.
Rooms	14: 10 twins/doubles, 1 single, 1 suite, 2 family rooms for 3-4.
Meals	Breakfast €11.50. Dinner €29, book ahead. Wine €18–€53.
Closed	Mid-November to mid-December; mid-January to mid-March.
Directions	N165 from Nantes or Vannes, exit 16 (Nivillac) towards St Dolay. After 3km left in Izernac. From Rennes near Redon, right in Izernac, 4km before La Roche Bernard.

Sylvie & Jean Leterre
Route de Saint Dolay, Nivillac,
56130 La Roche Bernard, Morbihan
Tel   +33 (0)2 99 90 89 63
Email   contact@hotel-bodeuc.com
Web   www.hotel-bodeuc.com

Hôtel La Désirade

Everyone loves an island and this one, with its wild windswept coast, is especially enticing. Battered by storms in winter, it is hot and gorse-scented in summer and the roads are silent. La Désirade, sheltered in its parkland, is made up of a new village of colourwashed houses around a pool. If leafy gardens, comfortable hotelly bedrooms and super bathrooms (white bathrobes, lashings of hot water) don't bring instant relaxation, the spa and massages surely will. Breakfast is served buffet-style in the breakfast room or by the pool; dinner, formal but excellent, is in the hotel restaurant across the lane. The young chef specialises in local dishes and the presentation is impeccable; wines are first-class too. Research the island's possibilities curled up in a wicker chair in the reception salon with its unexpectedly blue fireplace: there are lots of illustrated books. You have 104 kilometres of coastal paths and cycle routes to choose from, while the beaches are a 20-minute walk away. Take your paintbox and you'll be in good company: Monet and Matisse both came to the island to paint.

Price	€125-€170. Family rooms €240-€340.
Rooms	32: 14 doubles, 14 twins, 4 family rooms for 4.
Meals	Breakfast €15.50. Dinner from €19.50. Wine €22-€99.
Closed	5 November-26 December; 3 January-27 March.
Directions	From Quiberon, ferry to Belle Île (45 min) then taxi or bus (7km). Well signed.

Pierre & Bénédicte Rebour
Le Petit Cosquet, Bangor,
56360 Belle Île en Mer, Morbihan

Tel	+33 (0)2 97 31 70 70
Email	hotel-la-desirade@wanadoo.fr
Web	www.hotel-la-desirade.com

Ethical Collection: Environment; Food.
See page 446 for details.

Château de Kerlarec

The plain exterior belies the 19th-century festival inside – it's astonishing. Murals of mountain valleys and Joan of Arc in stained glass announce the original Lorraine-born baron ("descended from Joan's brother") and the wallpaper looks great, considering it too was done in 1834. In the gold brocade-papered salon, Madame Avelange, an expert on interiors of the previous centuries, lavishes infinite care on every antique and painting. There may be furnishings from 1842 to 1865 in one room while in another, only Louis XV will do. The rooms are lavish. One suite is fresh in yellow and white with soft voile curtains at the window and draped from a coronet over the bed; the largest suite has an original peacock blue panelling. Expect excellent English along with porcelain and silver at breakfast. Specialities are homemade rhubarb and ginger, melon and star anise conserves. The set menu from local produce is innovative and original; clients who dine by candlelight once usually do again. Your enthusiastic hostess lavishes the same attention on her guests as on her house. Extraordinary. *No credit cards.*

Price	€115–€160.
Rooms	5 suites: 3 for 2, 2 for 2–3.
Meals	Dinner €30–€50. Wine €15–€40.
Closed	Never.
Directions	From Quimperlé D22 NE towards Pontivy for 6km; château on left – take care on entry.

Françoise & Dominique Avelange
29300 Arzano, Finistère

Tel	+33 (0)2 98 71 75 06
Email	chateau-de-kerlarec@wanadoo.fr
Web	www.chateau-de-kerlarec.com

Château-Hôtel Manoir de Kertalg

So many contrasts. Through thick woods of majestic trees and up a magical entrance drive, you expect the old château in its vast estate, but the hotel is actually in the big, blocky stables, built in 1890 for racehorses (who even had running water): it became a hotel in 1990 when the tower was added. The salon is formal and glitzy with its marbled floor, modern coffered ceiling, red plush chairs – and intriguing dreamscapes. You will be welcomed with polished affability by the charming young owner, and possibly by visitors come for tea and ice cream (a favourite summer outing). Even the 'small' bedrooms are big; walls are covered in lined fabric, cream with textured design, a combination of two fabrics above and below the dado rail. There is a feeling of being cocooned and wrapped up away from the world. The suite with the four-poster has windows looking out over both garden and château. The tower rooms are cosier but have space for a couple of armchairs. Wild woodland walks with hundreds of hydrangeas beckon and, yet, there's a helipad – somehow the two worlds meet and embrace.

Price	€115–€210. Duplex €260.
Rooms	9: 6 doubles, 2 twins, 1 duplex for 4.
Meals	Breakfast €15. Restaurants 2–8km.
Closed	November–Easter.
Directions	From N165 west exit Quimperlé Centre to Moëlan sur Mer. There, right at lights for Riec & follow signs (12km from N165).

M. Le Goamic
Route de Riec sur Belon,
29350 Moëlan sur Mer, Finistère

Tel	+33 (0)2 98 39 77 77
Email	kertalg@free.fr
Web	www.manoirdekertalg.com

Château de Kerminaouët

Down the long driveway, up steep steps into the panelled hall – bright with new paintings, sculptures, carvings and hand-crafted table – and into the home of Dutch owners Bob and Jacoline. Warm, friendly, hands-on, they are busily and happily engaged in their art (her bronze Celtic sculptures, his artworks in wood), their garden (designed on a Celtic knot, teeming with wild flowers and butterflies), and treating their guests to organically grown, well-sourced food; they do excellent table d'hôtes. The 19th-century château sits tall and upright overlooking a domain of 54 hectares, with views from the tower stretching to the Île de Glénan. Five of the bedrooms are in the château, old-fashioned and homely, enlivened by paintings, ceramics and inspirational views over gardens and forest. The apartment is on the ground floor of the 16th-century manor – which also houses a pair of bat colonies; in the lovely circular dovecot is a gîte. Madame nurtures the huge gardens with help from friends, farmers and artists in exchange for delightful lunches: this feels more B&B than hotel. *Ask about Indian massage & shiatsu.*

Price	€90–€180. Gîtes €350–€550 per week.
Rooms	5 + 2: 5 doubles. 2 gîtes for 2-4.
Meals	Breakfast €10 for self-caterers. Dinner €35.
Closed	Mid-December to February.
Directions	N165 Lorient & Quimper, exit Pont-Aven; at Pont-Aven dir. Concarneau on D783 route de Tregunc; after Croaz-Hent 1st left; signed. Entrance ahead.

Jacoline & Bob Dubois
Route de Kerminaouët,
29910 Tregunc, Finistère

Tel	+33 (0)2 98 50 19 68
Email	kerminaouet@wanadoo.fr
Web	www.chateaubretagne.info

Manoir du Stang

There is ancient grandeur in this 'hollow place' (*stang*) between the remarkable dovecote arch and the wild ponds. On the tamed side: a formal French courtyard, a blooming rose garden, an avenue of mature magnolia grandiflora, some masterly old stonework. But the welcome is utterly natural, the rooms not at all intimidating. The eighth generation of the Huberts like guests to feel at home in their family mansion with a choice antique here, an original fabric there, an invigoratingly pink bathroom to contrast with a gentle Louis Philippe chest – always solid, reliable comfort and enough space. Views are heart-warming, over courtyard, water and woods, the peace is total, bar the odd quack. Communal rooms are of stupendous proportions, as befits the receptions held here: the dining room can seat 60 in grey-panelled, pink-curtained splendour, its glass bays looking across to the gleaming ponds. Masses of things sit on the black and white salon floor – a raft of tables, fleets of high-backed chairs, a couple of sofas, glowing antique cupboards – and you still have space and monumental fireplaces.

Price	€75-€150.
Rooms	22: 20 twins/doubles, 2 family rooms.
Meals	Breakfast €10. Dinner for large groups only. Restaurants 1km.
Closed	20 September to mid-May; open by arrangement for groups only.
Directions	From Quimper N165 exit Concarneau & Fouesnant on D44, then D783 for Quimper. Entrance on left, private road. Parking a little way from hotel.

	Hubert Family
	29940 La Forêt Fouesnant, Finistère
Tel	+33 (0)2 98 56 96 38
Email	contact@manoirdustang.com
Web	www.manoirdustang.com

Grand Hôtel des Bains

Marine purity on the north Brittany coast: it's like a smart yacht club where you are an old member. The fearless design magician has waved a wand of natural spells – cotton, cane, wool, wool, seagrass: nothing synthetic, nothing pompous. Sober lines and restful colours leave space for the scenery, the sky pours in through walls of glass, the peaceful garden flows into rocks, beach and sea. Moss-green panelling lines the deep-chaired bar where a fire leaps in winter. Pale grey-panelled bedrooms have dark mushroom carpets and thick cottons in stripes and checks. Some have four-posters, some balconies, others are smaller, nearly all have the ever-changing sea view. Bathrooms are lovely – with bathrobes to wear to the magnificent indoor seawater pool and treatment spa. Staff are smiling and easy, the ivory-panelled dining room with its sand-coloured tablecloths is deeply tempting. Spectacular coastal paths, a choice of beaches, yoga and spa retreats, even a writer's workshop – the luxury of space, pure elegant simplicity and personal attention are yours. *Excellent wine cellar. Spa.*

Price	€154–€263.
Rooms	36 twins/doubles.
Meals	Dinner €35–€50.
Closed	Never.
Directions	From Rennes-Brest N12 exit Plouégat & Moysan, then Plestin les Grèves; cont. to Locquirec. Hotel in centre. Through gate to private car park.

Mme Nicol
15 bis rue de l'Église,
29241 Locquirec, Finistère

Tel	+33 (0)2 98 67 41 02
Email	reception@grand-hotel-des-bains.com
Web	www.grand-hotel-des-bains.com

Ti al Lannec

Heaps of English antiques yet it is superbly French, soft and fulsome: an Edwardian seaside residence perched on the cliff, its gardens tumbling down to rocky coves and sandy beaches; fall asleep to the waves and the breezes through the pines. (The beach club closes at midnight.) Inside, a mellow warmth envelops you in armfuls of drapes, swags and sprigs. Each room is a different shape, individually decorated as if in a private country mansion, with a sitting space, a writing table, a pretty bathroom and a view – to the sea (wonderful) or the cypresses. Expect florals, stripes, oriental rugs, white linen. Some bedrooms are big, with well-furnished white loggias, some are made for families with convertible bunk-bed sofas. Salons are cosily arranged with little lamps, mirrors, knick-knacks, old prints; the restaurant faces the sea and serves some pretty fancy food. The Jouanny family, immersed in the community and very mindful of their guests' welfare, have created a smart but human hotel. They also publish a daily in-house gazette and have created a lovely intimate spa alongside the indoor pool.

Price	€172-€409. Singles €92-€136.
Rooms	33: 22 twins/doubles, 3 singles, 8 family rooms for 3-5.
Meals	Breakfast €17. Lunch & dinner €26-€80. Children's meals €16-€23.
Closed	Mid-November to March.
Directions	From N12 Rennes-Brest road, exit 3km west of Guingamp for Lannion onto D767. In Lannion, follow signs to Trébeurden; signed.

Jouanny Family
14 allée de Mezo Guen,
22560 Trébeurden, Côtes-d'Armor

Tel	+33 (0)2 96 15 01 01
Email	contact@tiallannec.com
Web	www.tiallannec.com

Hôtel Manoir de Rigourdaine

At the end of the lane, firm on its hillside, Rigourdaine breathes space, sky, permanence. The square-yarded manor farm, originally a stronghold with moat and all requisite towers, now looks serenely out over wide estuary and rolling pastures, and offers a sheltering embrace. The reception/bar in the converted barn is a good place to meet the friendly, attentive master of the manor, properly pleased with his excellent conversion. A high open fireplace warms a sunken sitting well; the courtyard, a gravelled enclosure overlooking the estuary, is made for lounging in the sun; breakfast is at charming long tables topped with bright mats. Rooms are attractive too, in unfrilly good taste and comfort: Iranian rugs on plain carpets, coordinated contemporary-chic fabrics in pleasing colours, some fine old furniture, pale bathrooms with all essentials. Six ground-floor rooms have private terraces onto the kempt garden — ideal for sundowners. Good clean-cut rooms, atmosphere lent by old timbers and antiques, and always the long limpid view. Great for families, cyclists, sailors, walkers. *Sailing school in Plouër. Golf 10km.*

Price	€72–€89. Triples €87–€104. Quadruples €111–€119.
Rooms	19: 10 doubles, 4 twins, 3 triples, 2 quadruples.
Meals	Breakfast €8.50. Snacks & wine can be provided. Restaurants nearby.
Closed	Mid-November to Easter.
Directions	From St Malo N137 for Rennes. Right on N176 for Dinan & St Brieuc; over river Rance. Exit for Plouër sur Rance for Langrolay for 500m; lane to Rigourdaine.

Patrick Van Valenberg
Route de Langrolay,
22490 Plouër sur Rance, Côtes-d'Armor

Tel	+33 (0)2 96 86 89 96
Email	hotel.rigourdaine@wanadoo.fr
Web	www.hotel-rigourdaine.fr

Malouinière le Valmarin

The gracefully proportioned *malouinière* was built in the early 18th century by a wealthy ship owner. Very close to the ferry terminal, and in the centre of town, this hotel has an unexpectedly large rose-filled garden with sunloungers and tables dotted around under mature cedars and a copper beech. Most bedrooms – light-filled with high ceilings, tall windows carefully draped to match the bed covers – overlook the garden: lovely. Second-floor rooms have sloping ceilings and a cosier feel, with exposed beams, white walls and pale blue carpets and paintwork. There are lavender bags in the wardrobes, plenty of books in French and English, and breakfast at the small yellow and blue dining tables. Or, have a lie-in and ask for your café au lait in bed – before exploring the fabulous ramparts of the city or sunning on the nearby beaches. There are equestrian facilities and excellent thalassotherapy spas nearby or take an ocean ride to the islands of Jersey, Guernsey, Sark or Herm. Dinan, the 'Nice of the North', is a very short drive. Great value. *Secure parking available.*

Price	€100–€145.
Rooms	12: 8 twins/doubles, 4 family rooms for 3–4.
Meals	Breakfast €11. Restaurants nearby.
Closed	Call for out of season reservations.
Directions	In St Malo follow signs for St Servan & town centre. Left at r'bout 'Mouchoir Vert' for St Croix Church; right at church; 20m to hotel.

Françoise Nicolas-Quéric
7 rue Jean XXIII, St Servan,
35400 Saint Malo, Ille-et-Vilaine

Tel	+33 (0)2 99 81 94 76
Email	levalmarin@wanadoo.fr
Web	www.levalmarin.com

Château de la Ballue

Artists say this 1620s château inspires creativity: the moment you spot its graceful two-winged façade you'll fall under its spell. The formal gardens are incredible, so wonderfully recreated they are a historic monument open to the public, a reverie of bosquets and allées sprinkled with sculptures, gazing over Mont Saint Michel's green valleys. Recitals resonate in the courtyard, while inside, Purcell's odes float through elegant wood-panelled rooms sporting marble fireplaces, antique paintings, gilded mirrors and orchids. This is no museum piece, however, but a family home, and Madame and Monsieur are as passionate about it as they are laid-back. Drift off on dreamy canopied beds in rooms that are all different, all fabulous, from bold red 'Victor Hugo' to 'Florence', with its blue fern patterns and feathery toile. Three have *cabinets de toilette* rather than separate bathrooms – another period feature. Silver cutlery tinkles over a fine continental spread in the blue-panelled breakfast room; birds sing a glorious hymn in the *bosquet de musique*. Baroque, family-friendly, enchanting.

Price	€180-€195. Suite €220-€290. Triple €220-€235. Extra bed €40.
Rooms	5: 3 doubles, 1 suite for 2-4, 1 triple.
Meals	Breakfast €18. Restaurants 7km.
Closed	Rarely.
Directions	St Malo N137 towards Rennes, after 27km, left to Combourg; D796 to Bazouges la Perouse. Château well signed.

Mme Mathiot-Mathon
35560 Bazouges la Pérouse,
Ille-et-Vilaine

Tel	+33 (0)2 99 97 47 86
Email	chateau@la-ballue.com
Web	www.laballue.com

La Foltière

Come for the 'parc floral' – and Monsieur! He loves having guests, and these botanic gardens are his pride and joy. They date from 1830 when the château was built, designed to be fashionably informal. The château has the usual sweeping drive and imposing stairway and hall. Rooms are vast. The feel is hushed stately home, yet it's not at all precious and children are welcomed, even spoiled, with mazes and bridges, slides and surprises. Bedrooms, just five, have tall windows and are big enough to dance in: peachy 'Degas' with its own dressing room, deep-red 'Renoir' (these two interconnect); blue 'Monet' with its original porcelain loo; 'Sisley', a symphony in yellow; 'Pissaro', ideal for wheelchair users. Breakfast on homemade croissants (and, when Madame is around, Breton crêpes) or charcuterie and cheese. Then seek out the grounds – magnificent from March to October, a delight for all ages. Paths meander round the huge lake and past secret corners bursting with camellias and narcissi, azaleas and rhododendrons, old roses and banks of hydrangea. *Tea room & garden shop open afternoons.*

Price	€140-€150. Suite €170.
Rooms	5: 4 doubles, 1 suite.
Meals	Breakfast €12. Restaurants nearby.
Closed	20-28 December.
Directions	From Rennes & Caen A84; exit 30 for Fougères; Parc Floral 10km from Fougères towards Mont St Michel & St Malo.

Alain Jouno
35133 Le Châtellier, Ille-et-Vilaine
Tel   +33 (0)2 99 95 48 32
Email foltiere@parcfloralbretagne.com
Web   www.parcfloralbretagne.com

Château du Pin

Painter and photographer, the brave, artistic Ruans have launched with passionate enthusiasm into renovating a small château with a ruined chapel, antique stables and a thrilling atmosphere. Traces of seigneury date from the 15th century; the owners' sense of space and colour will triumph. The original staircase curves up to the 'literary' guest rooms – mauve/silver Proust, ochre/gold Georges Sand, theatrical suite Victor et Juliette, Oriental for Pierre Loti – and each shower is behind a great rafter. The vastly magnificent drawing/billiard room wears rich reds, has two large windows back and front plus a small window on a gable wall which sits on top of the mantlepiece; it's great fun. A small cottage with a romantic garden and interior courtyard sits in the nine-hectare park. Your gentle hosts love cooking: breakfast is a treat with crêpes, homemade jams and cakes, fruit and yogurt; they then share dinner and stimulating talk with you. This is a land of legends; the Brocéliande forest, the Emerald coast, the gulf of Morbihan, Dinard and Saint Malo all nearby for exploration.

Price	€85–€180. Suites €110–€270. Cottage €380–€520 per week.
Rooms	5 + 1: 2 twins/doubles, 1 suite for 2, 2 family suites for 4. Cottage for 3-4.
Meals	Breakfast €12. Dinner €30. Wine €10–€30.
Closed	Rarely.
Directions	From Rennes N12 west to Bédée 23km; D72 to Montfort sur Meu; D125 for St Méen le Grand; château 3km on left.

Catherine & Luc Ruan
35370 Iffendic près de Montfort,
Ille-et-Vilaine

Tel	+33 (0)2 99 09 34 05
Email	luc.ruan@wanadoo.fr
Web	www.chateaudupin-bretagne.com

🗡 🐾 🔊 🐾 🚲

Château des Tesnières

Wonderful, fairytale Château des Tesnières, with turrets that look like they could reach the stars, is set amid venerable trees, with far-reaching views and six hectares of parkland to explore. Inside is perfection. No chintz in sight, but contemporary design merging perfectly with 19th-century features and fireplaces, soft hues contrasting with rich colours and bathrooms stylishly dramatic, two with claw-foot baths. You might spot barn owls on the window ledge of Sud – they nest in the turret of this suite. Downstairs, the Louis XVI drawing room, library and dining room have elegant furniture, marble fireplaces, sofas so deep that you won't want to rise, gilt-edged mirrors, seagrass floors, parkland views. The energetic, enthusiastic Dutch owners have done a fabulous job restoring this place; prepare to be wickedly spoilt. Breakfast is a sumptuous feast, served in your private salon, in the dining room or on the terrace. In the surrounding area are numerous lovely walks, water sports on the Villaine river, and historic Vitre, a market town with an 18-hole golf course. Superbe!

Price	€110–€160.
Rooms	5: 1 double, 4 suites. Extra bed & cot available.
Meals	Restaurants in Vitré, 10-minute drive.
Closed	December–January.
Directions	From Vitré, D178 for La Guerche. 2nd r'bout, right to Torcé, D33; 3km, left; D108 to Domalain. Thro' estate to countryside, 2nd left.

John & Siebren Demandt Boon
35370 Torcé, Ille-et-Vilaine
Tel   +33 (0)2 99 49 65 02
Email   info@chateaudestesnieres.com
Web   www.chateaudestesnieres.com

Western Loire

Le Château de l'Abbaye

In endlessly flat countryside, set back from the main road in its own walled grounds, this 'castel romantique' has been graciously managed by Danielle Renard for more than 20 years. Now she is joined by the new generation: son Renaud-Pierre and daughter-in-law Korakot. So many visual enticements the moment you arrive: bibelots and boxes, photo frames and fresh flowers, small items embroidered by Korakot, furniture antique and new, even a vintage Belgian stove. Roosters are a family passion and can be found in every medium, shape and size; take a peep at the bulging scrapbooks of drawings sent in by previous guests and their children. Continental breakfast with homemade jams is served on the veranda in summer; dinner at candlelit tables reflects the best seasonal produce (French regional menus from Danielle, Thai from Korakot). Bedrooms, not huge, lie off the corridor on the second floor and are individually decorated to create cocoon-like spaces; extras include children's books and embroidered needlecases – typical touches from these charming, thoughtful hosts.

Price	€79-€159. Apartment €159. All prices per night.
Rooms	5 + 1: 2 doubles, 1 twin, 2 suites/family rooms for 3. Apartment for 2-4.
Meals	Breakfast €12. Dinner €36. Wine €18-€49.
Closed	Rarely.
Directions	A83 exit 7 to La Rochelle; through Moreilles, château at end of village with large red gate.

Danielle, Korakot &
Renaud–Pierre Renard
85450 Moreilles, Vendée

Tel	+33 (0)2 51 56 17 56
Email	daniellerenard@hotmail.com
Web	www.chateau-moreilles.com

Entry 173   Map 8

Château de la Cacaudère

The 19th-century, golden-stone château had been abandoned for 50 years when the Montalts discovered it. Madame has a fine eye for colour and a lightness of touch; music and châteaux are her passions. (She also produces fine fruit tarts for breakfast.) Original wood panelling is there but much of the furniture has been picked up on postings abroad – a wardrobe from a London auction house, a scroll-top bed from Korea – then put together with French flair. Bedrooms range from smallish to large with sumptuous sashed canopies; one has steps down to a pretty pink room for a child, another a reading room in a turret. Bathrooms are similarly stylish, one with an old curvy tub with Savoy taps, another with a trompe l'oeil ceiling of the sky. Pass the kitchen on your way to breakfast and catch a glimpse of polished copper pans – immaculate, spotless. There's a big, comfy sitting room with long windows looking to the garden; it's large and leafy, filled with copper beeches and pines, walled orchard and pool. Sheep graze peacefully, and there's an old garage for bikes and ping-pong. Delightful. *No credit cards. Minimum stay two nights.*

Price	€85–€130.
Rooms	5: 2 doubles, 1 twin, 1 family room for 3, 1 quadruple.
Meals	Barbecue available for guests' use. Restaurants 5km & 15km.
Closed	September–April.
Directions	From La Rochelle, A11 towards Poitiers for 8km; at r'bout exit N137 (E03) for Nantes to Ste Hermine, right at monument Clémenceau to centre ville.

M & Mme Montalt
Thouarsais-Bouildroux,
85410 La Caillère, Vendée
Tel +33 (0)2 51 51 59 27
Email chris.montalt@wanadoo.fr
Web www.chateau-sud-vendee.com

Manoir de Ponsay

The family manor, a listed building, goes back to 1492: note the coat of arms above the door. Now both castle and hotel are run generously, and singlehandedly, by charming young Laurent who was born here and his Roumanian wife Orelia. Outside is one of the oldest dovecotes in France, and a peaceful pool, a tiny sauna, table tennis and bikes; the grounds are open and safe, the meadows stretch to the horizon. Inside, a dignified room for candlelit feasts, a sitting room with billiards and a tapestry or two, a priest's hole for hiding revolutionaries (should any lurk), and a massive stone stair. This sweeps you up to five characterful suites, historic, traditional, their long windows overlooking the park, their armoires polished to perfection, their chintz bright, their fireplaces (when required) lit; the Chambre à Baldequin has an exquisite four-poster. In the wing (once the granary) are three further rooms, all good value. Dinner is prepared, served and taken with your hosts; special wines can be ordered from the cellar. Beyond: the summer extravaganzas at Puy de Fou draw a million spectators a year.

Price	€62–€120.
Rooms	8: 5 suites: 2 for 2, 1 for 3, 2 for 4. Wing: 1 double, 1 twin, 1 suite for 3.
Meals	Breakfast €9. Dinner €34.
Closed	November–April.
Directions	From Nantes A83 dir. Bordeaux; exit 6 Chantonnay & Bournezeau. D949B Poitiers to St Mars des Pres. Signed.

	Laurent de Ponsay
	85110 Chantonnay, Vendée
Tel	+33 (0)2 51 46 96 71
Email	manoir.de.ponsay@orange.fr
Web	www.manoirdeponsay.com

Entry 175   Map 8

Château de la Flocellière

You really need to see La Flocellière from a helicopter. The aerial view is the most striking; the battlement'd castle was built around 1090 and is listed. Hotel guests stay in the château, where bedrooms are vast, gracious and opulent, with huge windows on two sides onto the gardens and park. Overseeing this vast dominion is the Vicomtesse and her meticulous eye misses nothing, from the topiary in the grounds to the maids' attire. All is opulence and beauty and beeswax infuses every room. You can lounge around in the sitting room in the gallery, play a game of billiards, admire the magnificent potager below the ruined walls, visit the library or be taken on a full tour. This is living at its most sedate and children are welcome providing they behave impeccably. Snacks are no-go in the secluded swimming pool area ("a terrace, not a beach"). If you choose to dine, tables d'hotes for 14 takes place two to three times a week — your chance to meet the hosts. Weddings and receptions are not limited to weekends, and the setting is sensational. Historic, magnificent, hospitable.

Price	€125-€205. Family suites €225-€305. Houses €1,900 per week.
Rooms	5 + 2: 2 twins/doubles, 3 family suites for 2-4. 2 houses for 10-12.
Meals	Dinner with wine, €54-€61; book ahead.
Closed	Rarely.
Directions	From Paris, A11 for Angers, then A87 to La Roche sur Yon; exit 28 for Puy du Fou, then to Pouzauges until St Michel Mt Mercure. Left at 2nd lights to La Flocellière and main church; left on rue du Château.

Vicomte & Vicomtesse Patrice Vignial
85700 La Flocellière, Vendée

Tel	+33 (0)2 51 57 22 03
Email	flocelliere.chateau@wanadoo.fr
Web	www.chateaudelaflocelliere.com

Domaine Le Martinet

Enthusiastic young owners have taken on the Martinet, a modest country hotel that combines simple comforts with good food. Sleepy Bouin with its notable church is just down the road; the beach is eight miles away. The hotel restaurant is still run by chef and kitchen gardener Emmanuel, and his wife Chrystelle, the speciality is seafood and you will undoubtedly eat well. The new restaurant is housed in a lovely old salt granary with a timbered ceiling; the buffet breakfast is served in the main hotel, spilling onto the veranda in summer. As for the simple, comfortable bedrooms, they are divided between those in the main house and those in the garden, ten steps from the pool. Nicely converted from the old stables and forge, the latter sport wicker furniture and tiled floors. The apartments have fridges and sinks and a second bed on the mezzanine – made for families. The pleasant grounds, with old stone walls and a sundial, are large and dog-friendly, and the nearby Passage du Bois, the only road in Europe that can be crossed at low tide, leads to the Île de Noirmoutier, famous for butterflies.

Price	€56–€72. Triple €78. Apartments €110.
Rooms	30: 20 twins/doubles, 1 triple, 9 apartments for 2-4 & 4-6.
Meals	Buffet breakfast €8. Picnic €12. Lunch & dinner €17–€36.
Closed	Rarely.
Directions	51km south-west of Nantes on D751 past Bouaye; D758 through Bourgneuf en Retz towards Noirmoutier for 9km. Signed. Turn left into hotel before 'no entry' sign.

Camille & Charles Salaud
Place du Général Charette,
85230 Bouin, Vendée

Tel	+33 (0)2 51 49 23 23
Email	contact@domaine-lemartinet.com
Web	www.domaine-lemartinet.com

Hôtel Fleur de Sel

Noirmoutier has a personality all its own: this group of simple white buildings in its Mediterranean garden is typical. Built in the 1980s, it sits peacefully between sea and salt marsh, long sandy beach and little yachting harbour. It is perfect for family holidays, with tennis court, golf driving range, big pool and outdoor jacuzzi. Bedrooms are good too, some in classic cosy style with country pine furniture and fabrics, others more bracing with ship-shape yew furniture and yachting motifs; several have little ground-floor terraces. The delightful, caring owners have humour and intelligence; their daughter's paintings are sometimes shown here. The chef has worked with the very best in Paris and meals are served by courteous waiters in the airy, raftered dining room or on the oleander-lined terrace. It is all clean-cut, sun-warmed, impeccable and welcoming. There is a bridge, but try and come by the Passage du Gois causeway, open three hours round low tide: an unforgettable four kilometre drive 'through the sea' where shellfish-diggers cluster. The island is, of course, very popular in summer.

Price	€125–€215.
Rooms	35: 30 doubles, 5 family rooms.
Meals	Breakfast €12.50. Lunch €20. Dinner €29–€39.
Closed	4 November to mid-March.
Directions	From Nantes ring road south-west D723, D751, D758 to Beauvoir sur Mer. Road to Noirmoutier via Le Gois only possible at low tide; otherwise take bridge. Hotel 500m behind church.

Pierre Wattecamps
Rue des Saulniers,
85330 Noirmoutier en l'Ile, Vendée

Tel	+33 (0)2 51 39 09 07
Email	contact@fleurdesel.fr
Web	www.fleurdesel.fr

Hôtel Villa Flornoy

Villa it is, a large one, in a quiet road just back from the vast sandy beach and protected from the sea-front bustle. Built as a family boarding house in the 1920s, Flornoy still stands in the shade of a quieter age: high old trees, nooked and crannied seaside villas in stone, brick and wood. Inside it is just as peaceful. After being greeted by the delightful new and young owners – enjoy sitting in the salon: garden view, four tempting 'corners', well-chosen prints and the occasional interesting *objet*. Rooms – mostly a good size, a few with balconies – have a pretty, fresh feel, nothing frilly, just plain or Jouy-style wall fabrics, coordinated colours and patterns, good modern/traditional furniture, excellent beds and white bathrooms with fine new fittings. Sylvie has refreshed some rooms in tones of ivory and string adding wood panelling for a more by-the-seaside feel. It is simple, solid, attractive and in the morning you will enjoy a generous breakfast in the light dining room or under the trees in the green and blooming garden. Really good value and a relaxed welcome. *Walking distance to beach.*

Price	€60–€110. Triples €70–€122.
Rooms	30: 22 twins/doubles, 8 triples.
Meals	Breakfast €10. Dinner €20–€22. Restaurant closed October–March.
Closed	Mid-November to January.
Directions	Pornichet to 'centre ville', right onto Ave Général de Gaulle for 300m. Ave Flornoy on right, just after Hôtel de Ville on left.

	Sylvie & Sébastien Laurenson
	7 avenue Flornoy,
	44380 Pornichet, Loire-Atlantique
Tel	+33 (0)2 40 11 60 00
Email	contact@villa-flornoy.com
Web	www.villa-flornoy.com

Le Tricot

Sunshine pours in past cream shutters and bathes the house in light. In the living room, windows face east and west so dawn and sunset are heavenly; once the last rays ebb away, the marble fireplace, piano and coat of arms come into their own. The dining room is as impressive; doors lead out to the garden, there's a black and white tiled floor and a splendid portrait of the Duke of Anjou – later Philip V of Spain. Bedrooms have exquisite Japanese fabric on the walls, polished boards and old rugs; French antiques are dotted about. Bathrooms are new, with showers or deep tubs and oodles of towels. The pale stone house dates from 1642 and is the largest inside the city ramparts, surrounded by a walled garden of box-trimmed flowerbeds and mature trees. Guérande is a fascinating medieval city and all the sights are within walking distance, the beach just a short drive. The rest of the peninsula could occupy you for weeks; go sea fishing, ride, explore the bustling harbours – and do visit the salt marshes, its fascinating salt museum and waterways of The Grande Brière, a haven for bird life. *No credit cards.*

Price	€100-€145. Suite €180-€210.
Rooms	3: 1 double, 1 twin, 1 suite for 4.
Meals	Restaurants nearby.
Closed	Mid-November to March.
Directions	Enter Guérande thro' Porte Bizienne, 1st right on rue du Tricot; house on right at end of cul de sac.

Loïc & Andréa de Champsavin
8 rue du Tricot,
44350 Guérande, Loire-Atlantique
Tel   +33 (0)2 40 24 90 72
Email   chambresdhotes@letricot-guerande.com
Web   www.letricot-guerande.com

Château de Cop-Choux

The name refers to the old lime kilns on the estate and comes from 'couper la chaux' – so, nothing to do with cabbages. Where to start: the elegant house built just before the French Revolution with towers added on either side in the early 20th century, the huge park of 18 hectares, the pool, the rolling lawns and ancient trees? Or the 17 marble chimneys, the original parquet floors and your friendly hosts? Patrick has just taken over the château and is full of enthusiasm and plans for the future. The park is huge, with chestnut trees lining the approach. A river runs through the grounds which contain lakes for fishing, woods for taking a country ramble. The house is full of light; several rooms have windows on three sides; bedrooms are big and dreamy and named after herbs. Violette has filmy blue fabric floating at tall windows, Romarin has exquisite carved twin beds (and an interconnecting room), bathrooms are gorgeous. You can have a just-laid egg for breakfast in a pretty panelled room, or on the terrace; then amble across lawns to the pool. *Large cottage for six available for weekly rental.*

Price	€110–€120. Suite €150.
Rooms	5: 4 twins/doubles, 1 suite for 4.
Meals	Breakfast €8. Hosted dinner €38. Restaurants 12km.
Closed	Rarely.
Directions	A11 exit 20 for Ancenis; N23 for Nantes; D164 towards Nort sur Erdre for 11km, right after Pont Esnault. Signed.

Patrick Moreau
44850 Mouzeil, Loire-Atlantique

Tel	+33 (0)2 40 97 28 52
Email	chateau-cop-choux@orange.fr
Web	www.chateau-cop-choux.com

Le Palais Briau

A glorious Palladian house perched high on the hillside overlooking the Loire valley. Built in the 1850s by François Briau, an early industrialist who made his fortune building railways, the house is palatial, lovingly restored and saved from commercial modernisation by the present owners. Faithful to the era, they have even held on to Briau's original furniture and fittings (of which he was immensely proud). Madame radiates exuberance and charm; Monsieur is an artist and designer whose impeccable taste has been stamped on every interior. A remarkable colonnaded stair sweeps up to the guests' sitting and dining rooms – pure Napoleon III. Bedrooms are light and large with separate dressing-rooms; all have magnificent views on the park or Abbey. Exquisite wallpapers, brocade canopies above polished mahogany beds, fine linen, flowers – all elegant and glamorous. Bathrooms are sumptuous and Italian-tiled. The grounds too are fabulous: large areas are completely wild and overgrown and contain the remains of a vast orangerie; herons return to nest every year. Breathtaking.

Price	€120–€180. Singles €90.
Rooms	4: 3 doubles, 1 suite for 3 & child's bed.
Meals	Restaurants 1.5km.
Closed	24-25 December.
Directions	A11 after Angers, exit Beaupréau; N23 for Nantes. Left on r'bout at entrance of Varades; signed. Rue Madeleine is small road behind industrial area.

Thérèse & François Devouge
Rue de la Madeleine,
44370 Varades, Loire-Atlantique

Tel	+33 (0)2 40 83 45 00
Email	devouge@palais-briau.com
Web	www.palais-briau.com

Auberge du Port des Roches

If you can see yourself sitting at the edge of slow green water of an evening, perhaps watching out for the odd fish, this is the place for you. Not grand – this is the Loir not the Loire, an altogether less glamorous river – but we can hear you saying: "Oh, what a pretty spot". Valérie and Thierry have been here about thirteen years, are young, very friendly though a touch shy, and full of enthusiasm for their auberge. Their main business is probably the restaurant – they can seat about 50 people in two rooms and the riverside terrace heavy with roses and perfumed plants– but Valérie is justly proud of the effort she has put into the bedrooms and into the way everything positively sparkles. Rooms are not large but done in fresh colours, sky blue, for example, with crisp white bedcovers. At the front you will have a view over the Loir. A small lane does run past the hotel, but windows are double glazed. This is a very quiet, very French place to stay, within easy reach of the châteaux and very good value.

Price	€49-€64.
Rooms	12: 9 doubles, 2 twins, 1 family room for 3.
Meals	Breakfast €8. Picnic available. Lunch & dinner €24-€49. Restaurant closed Sun eve, Mon, & Tues lunchtimes.
Closed	February; 1 week in autumn.
Directions	From La Flèche, N23 to Le Mans for 5km; right on D13 to Luché Pringé. Through village for 2km, right on D214; signed.

Valérie & Thierry Lesiourd
Le Port des Roches,
72800 Luché Pringé, Sarthe

Tel   +33 (0)2 43 45 44 48

Château de l'Enclos

The Guillous welcome you to a grand château in an elegant setting. Proud owners of a red 1933 Citroen, they will happily introduce you to their parkland of fine trees (schools love the tree trail), llamas, sheep, donkeys and hens. Opt to stay in the treehouse and you find a circular, 40-step staircase to two lovely, cosy, resin-scented rooms and an octagonal deck. Live close to nature and toast the views at sunset; wake to a breakfast basket at the end of a pulley (perhaps even champagne). Back at the château, a staircase sweeps you up to handsome bedrooms of parquet floors and rich carpets and tall windows. Three have balconies. The charming salon opens to a stage-set-perfect garden, and you dine with your hosts in best table d'hôtes style. Brûlon, "petite cité de caractère", is so close you can stroll there and medieval Le Mans is not much further. A grand house, beautifully furnished and equipped, yet not in the least intimidating, thanks to Madame and Monsieur who adore English-speaking visitors and treat you like long lost friends. A lucky find. *No credit cards.*

Price	€110. Treehouse €160.
Rooms	4: 2 doubles, 1 twin, 1 treehouse for 2.
Meals	Dinner with wine, €45.
Closed	Never.
Directions	From A81 Le Mans-Laval; exit 1 to Brûlon. Château on right at end of town. Signed.

Annie-Claude & Jean-Claude Guillou
2 avenue de la Libération,
72350 Brûlon, Sarthe

Tel	+33 (0)2 43 92 17 85
Email	jean-claude.guillou5@wanadoo.fr
Web	www.chateau-enclos.com

Château de Vaulogé

A fairytale place! The Radinis, from Milan, wanted their children to have an international education so moved to Geneva, then found Vaulogé. Marisa and her daughter now run the hotel, and Marisa devotes herself to the garden, her latest project being the horseshoe-shaped potager for fresh dinner produce. The original part of the château was built in the 15th century: this is where the family lives. Later Vaulogé was remodelled in a troubadour style, giving it two circular towers with conical slate roofs; when the shock waves of the Revolution had faded, the aristocracy reclaimed their houses. If it's space you're after, stay in Casanova: a huge round tower room, with terracotta floor and amazing, near-vertical beams – excellent for propping books on. (There are plenty of books: Marisa feels a house is not properly furnished without them.) There are other round rooms – La Petite Tour is smaller, and ravishingly pretty. The whole place is enticing with flowers and little nooks and crannies, often put to good use as wardrobes or cupboards. The grounds are lovely, with lilies on the moat and a delicate stone chapel.

Price	€230. Suites €250.
Rooms	5: 1 double, 4 suites for 2.
Meals	Dinner with drinks, €60; book ahead.
Closed	2 January-31 March.
Directions	A11 exit 9 Le Mans Sud. D309 for Noyen via Louplande, Chemiré le Gaudin. 1.5km after Fercé sur Sarthe, right at small chapel.

Marisa Radini & Micol Tassan Din
72430 Fercé sur Sarthe, Sarthe
Tel   +33 (0)2 43 77 32 81
Email   vauloge@mail.com
Web   www.vauloge.com

Château de la Barre

Over the cattle grid, down through unfenced fields, to the majesty of this ancient parkland – dotted, in spring, with ewes and lambs. Continue and you wash up at an enchanting medieval château – in the family since 1404. Your hosts, she English, he French, greet guests warmly and usher you into the hall. The portraits and furniture in the *Grand Salon* are as they were in 1784, a Dutch dresser displays family treasures, there's an honesty bar in the Salon Rose, and young Kakou the parrot keeps his distance (he's shy of strangers!). Madame works hard, painting, sewing, welcoming, gardening and still has time to spend with her guests. Book in for wonderful dinners served on fine china; tip-toe up an ancient spiral stone stair to bed. Bedrooms have oriental rugs on top of parquet, rich fabrics and grand oils, pillows dressed in embroidered linen, Roger & Gallet soaps by antique tubs (or new jacuzzis), marble fireplaces and balconies with parkland views. There are guided tours to the Perche, Le Mans, the châteaux of Chenonceau and Langeais. One of the best. *Wine tasting & French courses. Children over eight welcome.*

Price	€180–€300. Suites €380–€450.
Rooms	5: 2 doubles, 3 suites for 3.
Meals	Breakfast €15. Hosted dinner with wine, €95; book ahead. Restaurants 3km & 12km.
Closed	15 January–10 February.
Directions	A11 Le Mans & Rennes, exit La Ferté-Bernard. D1 for St Calais. Château 3km before St Calais; right directly off D1.

Ethical Collection: Environment; Community; Food.
See page 446 for details.

Comte & Comtesse de Vanssay
72120 Conflans sur Anille, Sarthe

Tel	+33 (0)2 43 35 00 17
Email	info@chateaudelabarre.com
Web	www.chateaudelabarre.com

Château de Monhoudou

Your delightful hosts are keeping the ancestral home alive in a dignified manner – 19 generations on. Something special inhabits a place when it has been treasured by the same family for so long and you'll find it here. It's a jewel set in rolling parkland; sheep graze under mature trees, there are horses in the paddock, swans on the lake, the occasional call of peacock, deer or boar, and, now, past the ancient kitchen garden, a lovely large swimming pool. Endless scope too for biking and hiking. Inside are antiques on polished parquet, comfortable beds in large lovely rooms, bathrooms and loos in turrets, billiards and a small library, intriguing alcoves, hunting trophies and a dining room elegant with family silver. Dinner, prepared by Madame, can be a romantic affair for two or you can join other guests for home-prepared foie gras, coquilles Saint Jacques, duck with peaches, braised leeks, apple and calvados sorbet. Then bask in front of the log fire in the sitting room under the ancestors' gaze. Timeless tranquillity, friendly staff – and a charming little chapel upstairs.

Price	€110–€160.
Rooms	6: 4 doubles, 1 twin, 1 suite for 3.
Meals	Dinner with wine, €42.
Closed	Rarely.
Directions	From Alençon N138 S for Le Mans, approx. 14km; at La Hutte left D310 for 10km; right D19 through Courgains; left D132 to Monhoudou; signed.

	Michel & Marie-Christine de Monhoudou
	72260 Monhoudou, Sarthe
Tel	+33 (0)2 43 97 40 05
Email	info@monhoudou.com
Web	www.monhoudou.com

Entry 193   Map 4

Château de Saint Paterne

A 21st-century fairy tale: a 500-year-old château was abandoned by its owners for 30 years, then rediscovered by the heir who left sunny yellow Provence for cool green pastures to resurrect the old shell. He and his wife are a charming young couple and have redecorated with refreshing taste, respecting the style and history of the building, adding a zest of southern colour to panelled, antique-filled rooms, pretty country furniture before ancient fireplaces and hand-rendered, rough and 'imperfect' finishes – nothing stiff or fixed. Sitting, dining and first-floor bedrooms are in château-style; the Henri IV room (he had a mistress here, of course) has thrillingly painted beams; ancestors and objets adorn but don't clutter. The attic floor is fantasy among the rafters: nooks, corners and split levels, a striking green and red bathroom, another bath sunk below the floor. Your host, an excellent cook, uses exotic vegetables from his kitchen garden and calls his cookery courses Liaisons Délicieuses. An attractive mixture of past and present values and superb hosts. *Sawday's self-catering also.*

Price	€135–€160. Suites €190–€240.
Rooms	10: 4 doubles, 6 suites.
Meals	Breakfast €13. Dinner with aperitif & coffee, €47; book ahead. Wine €15–€49.
Closed	January–March; Christmas week.
Directions	A28 exit 19 dir. St Paterne then St Paterne centre; signed.

Charles-Henry & Segolène de Valbray
72610 Saint Paterne, Sarthe

Tel	+33 (0)2 33 27 54 71
Email	chateaudesaintpaterne@wanadoo.fr
Web	www.chateau-saintpaterne.com

Hôtel Oasis

Efficient anglophile Monsieur Chedor runs a happy ship. You couldn't fail to feel well cared for: bedrooms are spotless and well-equipped, there are leather settees in the bar and a personal trainer in the gym. The cosy, woody reception sets the tone, flaunting all the beams, joists, exposed stones and wafer-brick walls you'd expect from a restored farmhouse with outbuildings. Bedrooms are in the stable wing, some off a raftered corridor upstairs, some at ground-floor level. All have white walls and old timbers, attractive repro country furniture, comfy armchairs, writing desks and immaculate bathrooms. The bar has an English pubby feel and serves very decent food (there's also a fabulous pizzeria/grill in the courtyard), the lounge is snug with plants, pool and piano and the new breakfast room is a treat: red-clothed tables on a stone floor and a big stone fireplace crackling with logs in winter. A shame to stay just a night, there's so much to see in the area, from the 24-hour race at Le Mans to the 14th-century château at Carrouges. And you could squeeze in a round of mini-golf before breakfast. Excellent value.

Price	€45-€85. Family rooms €85.
Rooms	14: 9 doubles, 3 twins, 2 family rooms for 4.
Meals	Breakfast €7. Light meals available.
Closed	Never.
Directions	From N12 at Javron, D13 to Villaines La Juhel. On right entering village.

Steve Chedor
La Sourderie,
53700 Villaines la Juhel, Mayenne
Tel   +33 (0)2 43 03 28 67
Email oasis@oasis.fr
Web   www.oasis.fr

Loire Valley

Château La Touanne

At the end of a lushly tree-lined drive, elaborate gates frame a graceful, slate-roofed stone façade. Friendly Nicolas and Christine's kind informality permeates this peaceful 17th-century château. Downstairs, ancestral portraits guard antique furniture, gilt mirrors and fine porcelain; you have the run of the antler-decked billiard room, panelled green sitting room and chandeliered salon. Breakfast in the rose-clad orangery or the stately dining room, where table d'hôtes dinners are also held (the food and wine is locally sourced). Bedrooms are sumptuous: marble fireplaces, high ceilings, fine oak parquet. La Contemporaine, imperial purple and white, has a modern bathroom and regal free-standing bath. Chambre du Parc has ravishing views on three sides, framed by olive taffeta curtains; walls are papered in a beautiful Jacobean print. A gravelled terrace leads into tree-studded parkland, home to the estate farm, chapel, and an orchard concealing a heated pool. Stroll through meadows past a gothic tower to explore bosky riverside paths, borrow a boat from the boathouse. All just 90 minutes from Paris.

Price	€110–€160.
Rooms	4: 2 doubles, 1 twin/double, 1 triple.
Meals	Dinner with wine, €30.
Closed	15 November–March.
Directions	From Orléans A10 dir. Tours, exit 15; left at r'bout onto D2, thro' Le Bardon for 3km dir. Baccon. Château entrance on right.

Nicolas & Christine d'Aboville
45130 Baccon, Loiret

Tel	+33 (0)2 38 46 51 39
Email	chateau-latouanne@orange.fr
Web	www.chateau-latouanne.com

Prieuré Notre Dame d'Orsan

Art as nature or nature as art? Go ahead, pinch yourself, your feet are still on the ground even though your spirit has been miraculously lifted by the harmony and elegance of this priory and its gardens. Patrice, an architect and landscape designer, saved the house from abandonment 15 years ago; originally built in 1107 as a convent, it stands in rural France at its most unspoilt. The oldest remaining buildings, probably the refectory and dormitory, are from the 16th century and form three sides of a square, enclosing beautifully restored gardens, open to visitors. There is no 'hotel' feel to the place at all, and the visitors to the gardens don't make it feel busy either. The reception rooms on the first floor are an interconnecting series of sitting rooms integrating the professional kitchen at one end; contemporary unfussy chic. Dine on homemade bread and home-grown produce under a leafy pergola when it's warm. Bedrooms have pine-panelled walls with shutters, windows and doors painted in a soft grey-green. You will look out onto the wonderful garden; serenity and contemplation are yours.

Price	Half-board only €380–€520 p.p. Extra bed €50.
Rooms	6: 3 doubles, 3 triples.
Meals	Breakfast €18. Lunch €25. Dinner €64. Wine €32–€42.
Closed	November–March.
Directions	A71, exit Saint-Armand-Montrond dir. Lignières; D3 to Morlac, D70 to Ids Saint Roch. Left at D65. Hotel 50m.

Patrice Taravella
18170 Maisonnais, Cher

Tel	+33 (0)2 48 56 27 50
Email	prieuredorsan@wanadoo.fr
Web	www.prieuredorsan.com

Château de Boisrenault

Built by a 19th-century aristocrat as a wedding present for his daughter – well overdue, she'd had two sons by the time it was finished – this may be turreted, noble and imposing on the outside, but it's a family home within. Furniture, objects, pictures, all have a tale to tell and there's no shortage of hunting trophies and stags' heads on the walls. Reception rooms are lofty, with huge fireplaces. One sitting room has a baby grand; another, smaller and cosier, is lined with books. As for the bedrooms, each is an adventure in itself. Named after the family's children and grandchildren, they feature a hotchpotch of pieces from different periods, including some excellent antiques. A couple of stuffed pheasants make unusual lamps in Hadrien's room and offset the yellow walls; two apartments upstairs have their own equipped kitchens. A delicious pool is discreetly tucked away behind trees in the lovely grounds; table tennis and table football are a godsend on rainy days. Meals are taken at a vast table in the dining room; be sure to book if you'd like dinner. A good place for a family stay.

Price	€84–€110. Family rooms €110–€145. Apartments €440–€500 per week.
Rooms	7 + 2: 2 doubles, 1 twin, 4 family rooms: 3 for 3, 1 for 4. 2 apartments for 4-5.
Meals	Dinner €25; book ahead. Wine €16.
Closed	Rarely.
Directions	From A20 exit 11 D8 to Levroux; D926 for Buzançais. Château on left 3km before town.

	Florence du Manoir
	36500 Buzançais, Indre
Tel	+33 (0)2 54 84 03 01
Email	boisrenault@wanadoo.fr
Web	www.chateau-du-boisrenault.com

Beau Soleil

Perched on a verdant hillside, with a fine view across the valley to St Gaultier, this elegant 19th-century hunting lodge has a nostalgic Victorian feel. Friendly Ren and partner Willem have furnished and decorated in impeccable style, from the cosy, inviting sitting room with its deep, richly upholstered sofas to the two peaceful first-floor bedrooms with their carefully chosen antique pieces. Sumptuous canopy beds are heaped with pillows and dressed with embroidered linen; shower rooms are small but perfectly formed. In the sunny dining room, an oval table heaves with fresh pâtisserie, fruit and yogurt on blue and white china; on a fine day you can move to the charming veranda and drink in the view. There's a friendly, personal feel throughout this house, with its memorabilia from your hosts' South African travels, and little Jack Russell Barack who arrived during the US elections. The Victoriana continues outdoors, to the orderly potager and the box-edged rose garden. You're a short walk from woods, open fields and the restaurants of St Gaultier; the beautiful La Brenne Parc Naturel Régional is nearby.

Price	€130.
Rooms	2 doubles.
Meals	Restaurants within walking distance.
Closed	Rarely.
Directions	In St Gaultier, cross river to Thenay for 1km. After sharp right bend, 3-pronged fork, take middle road. House 200m on right.

Ren Rijpstra
4 rue Beau Soleil,
36800 Thenay, Indre
Tel   +33 (0)2 54 47 94 87
Email   w-r.beausoleil@orange.fr

Château du Portail

Replete with suave gallic style amid five acres of delicious orchard-cushioned rose gardens, this 14th-century moat-fringed château has been a home to successions of French nobility, and a more recent haunt of contemporary European royals. Five country-best bedrooms range from the cosily inviting Suite de la Tour to the opulent Toile King Room, with matching bedspreads and wallpaper. An abundance of polished Versailles floors, exposed beams, exquisite antiques (your host, the amicable Claude Hubert Le Carpentier, is a connoisseur), Baroque furniture, porcelains, thick oriental rugs, heavy curtains and huge marble fireplaces – lit in winter – make for an authentically regal mood in the library, dining room and grand salon. Mod cons like WiFi and 'American style' bathrooms tether you to the present. Enjoy a peaceful read and aperitif in the shade of weeping willows, picnic on the banks of the Loire, explore the region's vineyards by bike, horse or helicopter, or simply swoon along the 19th-century bridal walk and pretend you're in *Dangerous Liaisons*. Worth every sou.

Price	€150–€180. Suite €250.
Rooms	5: 3 doubles, 1 twin, 1 suite for 2-4.
Meals	Restaurant 10-minute drive.
Closed	Rarely.
Directions	A10 dir. Bordeaux; exit Amboise to N152, 25km to Veuves; on to Monteaux. In village follow signs for 'Mesland'. Château 1km after village, green & white sign at entrance on right.

Claude Hubert Le Carpentier
Route de Mesland,
41150 Monteaux, Loir-et-Cher

Tel	+33 (0)2 54 70 22 88
Email	chateauduportail@orange.fr
Web	www.chateauduportail.com

Entry 200   Map 4

Hôtel Diderot

In the large sunny courtyard, contentment radiates from the very walls; climbers romp merrily up pergolas, roses peek around the olive tree, tables and chairs rest in shady corners. You'll want to linger here over breakfast, and the 66 varieties of homemade jam are the perfect excuse. In winter you have a low-beamed and charming dining room with a vast fireplace lit on cool days – a survivor from the original 15th-century house. Bedrooms feel like beautiful rooms in a family home and each is different in style: Napoleon III, Art Deco, contemporary. All have simple, elegant fabrics, pretty pictures, fresh flowers, a good supply of books. Those facing the courtyard are light and airy, those at the back overlook a quiet street, darker but cool and appealing. Further (ground-floor) rooms in the new 'Pavillon' are modern with cheerful colours, those in the 'Annexe' are more functional. Françoise and brother Laurent are naturally, delightfully hospitable, and having lived in this town all their lives they know its history well. Castle, churches, restaurants and river lie just beyond the door.

Price	€55–€80.
Rooms	23: 15 doubles, 8 twins.
Meals	Breakfast €8.50. Restaurants within 10 minutes.
Closed	Last 2 weeks in January; 1 week in November.
Directions	From Paris, A10 exit 24 after Tours. D751 to Chinon; signed.

	Françoise & Laurent Dutheil
	4 rue de Buffon & 7 rue Diderot, 37500 Chinon, Indre-et-Loire
Tel	+33 (0)2 47 93 18 87
Email	hoteldiderot@wanadoo.fr
Web	www.hoteldiderot.com

Domaine du Château d'Hommes

A tit had just made its nest in the post box and Madame was hoping that the guests wouldn't disturb it. No hunting, no shooting on this 178-hectare estate; lots of deer and birdsong and a posse of baby wild boar when we visited. The courtyard setting is certainly splendid: the moat and the ruins of the old castle, with one little tower still standing, make a thoroughly romantic setting for this great house, originally the tithe barn built just outside the castle wall. Inside, a vast baronial hall and fireplace welcome you and the atmosphere becomes more formal with a huge dining table, candelabra at either end. Antique furniture in the bedrooms (beautifully Italian in one case) goes hand-in-hand with lavish, impeccable bathrooms. Two rooms give onto the fine courtyard bounded by outbuildings; two look out to open fields and woods. In contrast, honeymoon couples ask for the Tower Room where the view overlooks the moat. Watch the friendly donkey follow Monsieur when he takes his morning ride or relax on the large lawned area starring a huge walnut tree. Very peaceful, very charming. *Spa & jacuzzi.*

Price	€87–€117.
Rooms	5: 3 doubles, 2 twins.
Meals	Dinner with wine, €30; book ahead. Restaurant 4km.
Closed	Rarely.
Directions	From Le Mans for Château du Loir & Château La Vallière. Then to Rillé, then Hommes. TD64 for Gizeux. Château on right on leaving village.

Hardy Family
37340 Hommes, Indre-et-Loire

Tel	+33 (0)2 47 24 95 13
Email	levieuxchateaudehommes@wanadoo.fr
Web	www.le-vieux-chateau-de-hommes.com

Entry 202   Map 4

Château de la Bourdaisière

A princely experience: a history-laden estate with remarkable gardens and native woods, a Renaissance château on the foundations of a fortress, vaulted meeting rooms and a little boudoir for intimacy as well as a bright, floral breakfast room onto the garden. Guest rooms? Gabrielle d'Estrées is gorgeously feminine as befits a mistress of Henri IV, who wears rich, regal red; Jeanne D'Arc has amazing beams and a loo in a tower. Smaller rooms are less grand, but still generous and comfortable. The drawing room is the prince's own – he drops by, his books lie around, his antiques and paintings furnish it; the place is superlative yet human. The 55 hectares of walled park (note the ancient sequoias and cypresses) are open to the public for paying visits. There is a long and rather lovely Italian allée, with an arch entrance said to have been designed by Leonardo da Vinci, and a huge parterre of box in the shape of a fleur de lys. The prince has a passion for gardens, grows 200 aromatics and 650 types of tomato; wine tastings can be arranged in conjunction with a 'cuisine des gourmandizes'! Great staff, too.

Price	€135–€240. Apartments €270.
Rooms	20: 8 doubles, 3 twins, 1 family room for 3, 2 apartments for 3-5 (without kitchen). Pavilion: 6 doubles.
Meals	Breakfast €15. Dinner for groups only, €41; book ahead. Restaurant 3km.
Closed	2 November-26 March.
Directions	From A10 exit Tours Centre for Amboise, then D751 to Montlouis sur Loire; signed.

Prince Louis Albert de Broglie
25 rue de la Bourdaisière,
37270 Montlouis sur Loire, Indre-et-Loire

Tel	+33 (0)2 47 45 16 31
Email	contact@chateaulabourdaisiere.com
Web	www.labourdaisiere.com

Entry 203   Map 4

Château de l'Hérissaudière

Wander through wild cyclamen under giant sequoias, take a dip in the elegant pool, enjoy an aperitif on the flowery terrace. You could get used to country-house living here, French-style. Madame, charming, cultured, welcomes you as family to her home. The classic manor house, built in creamy tufa stone, wrapped in 18 acres of parkland, is all light, elegance and fresh flowers. Walls are hung with gilded mirrors and bold paintings, tables covered with interesting objets. Relax in the sunny salon or the clubby library with its books and games table. Bedrooms, overlooking the park, are large, gracious and subtly themed, perhaps with rich Louis XV furnishings or a blue and yellow Empire style. The Chinon suite, tucked away, is good for children; the former hunting room is wheelchair-friendly; bathrooms are grand with original tiling and marble floors. Breakfast is a gourmet feast. Madame offers light suppers, weekend summer buffets or will recommend local restaurants. Loire châteaux, golf and cycling trails (bikes to hire) are nearby; tennis, ping-pong, croquet are in the grounds. *Cash or cheque only. Sawday's self-catering also.*

Price	€120–€135. Suites €130–€180.
Rooms	5: 2 doubles, 3 suites.
Meals	Occasional light supper, €25.
Closed	Rarely.
Directions	Leave Tours for Angers & Laval. 7km after La Membrolle sur Choisille, left onto D48, dir. Langeais & Pernay.

Claudine Detilleux
37230 Pernay, Indre-et-Loire

Tel	+33 (0)2 47 55 95 28
Email	info@herissaudiere.com
Web	www.herissaudiere.com

Hostellerie de la Mère Hamard

Watch the world from your window, the locals clutching their baguettes on their way home from the boulangerie. You are in the middle of a little village and it's peaceful here – yet Tours is no more than a ten-minute drive. The old *hostellerie* sits opposite the church and was built as a presbytery in the 18th century; Monique and Patrick have done it all up in a light, modern way. The two ground-floor rooms are large, each has its own tasteful colour scheme and matching bed covers and curtains. The bathrooms are bright and crisp with pretty friezes, some with showers, others with bath. Smaller rooms on the first and second floors have pale walls and light, bright fabrics. The two largest rooms, over the restaurant in another building, are under the eaves with sofas that can double as beds. Dine on the terrace in summer: another reason to stay is the food, traditional but with original touches. Enjoy leek flan with mussels, roasted pigeon with stewed onions, a stuffed saddle of rabbit with crayfish. Popular with the locals: book your table at weekends.

Price	€76–€99. Extra person €15.
Rooms	11: 7 twins/doubles, 4 family rooms for 3.
Meals	Breakfast €11.50. Lunch & dinner €27–€53. Restaurant closed Sunday eve & Mondays. Restaurants 5km.
Closed	3-23 January; 15 February-5 March.
Directions	From Tours, N138 for Le Mans; left for Semblançay. Hotel in centre of village, opp. church.

M & Mme Pegué
37360 Semblançay,
Indre-et-Loire

Tel	+33 (0)2 47 56 62 04
Email	reservation@lamerehamard.com
Web	www.lamerehamard.com

Château de l'Aubrière

Even before the Comtesse greets you, the fairytale turrets and sweeping lawns drop polite hints that you are among the aristocracy. Yet the 1864 château has a family feel, its ornate towers good-humouredly at odds with the kids' bikes by the back door – evidence of the Lussacs' five children. Rest assured, it is sumptuous inside. The bedrooms are magnificent, each named after a Loire château — caress the beautiful old elm wardrobe in Langeais, sink into the deep blue and red comfort of enormous Chenonceau, compose your postcards at the Napoleon III writing desk of Villandry. One bathroom is faux-black marble with red carpets while others have jacuzzi baths; all sparkle with gilt-framed mirrors. Downstairs dine at individual tables surrounded by some magnificent portraits. Scallop salad, duck confit, vegetables from the garden and lavender ice cream may tempt you – but save room for bacon and green-tomato jam at breakfast. There's plenty to do here: swim in the heated pool, admire the formal gardens or explore the 15 hectares of grounds with views.

Price	€120-€160. Single €80. Suites €180-€230. Family suite €230 for 4. Triple €180-€210.	
Rooms	13: 4 doubles, 3 twins, 1 single, 3 suites, 1 family suite for 4-5, 1 triple.	
Meals	Breakfast €14. Dinner from €40. Restaurant closed Wednesdays.	
Closed	October-end April.	
Directions	A10 exit 19 to Tours Nord & Le Mans. Follow signs for Le Mans on D938; exit La Membrolle sur Choisille. Signed.	

Comte & Comtesse Régis de Lussac
Route de Fondettes,
37390 La Membrolle sur Choisille,
Indre-et-Loire

Tel	+33 (0)2 47 51 50 35
Email	aubriere@wanadoo.fr
Web	www.aubriere.fr

Château du Vau

Lanky, relaxed philosopher Bruno has turned his family château into a delightful, harmonious refuge for the world-weary traveller. The cosy, book-lined, deep-chaired sitting room is a place where you find yourself irresistibly drawn into long conversations about music, yoga, art... The sunny breakfast room is charming with its stone-coloured tiles and pretty fabrics. Generations of sliding children have polished the banisters on the stairs leading to the large, light bedrooms that are beautifully but unfussily decorated – splendid brass bedsteads, Turkish rugs on parquet floors, old family furniture, pictures and memorabilia – the spirit of zen can be felt in the search for pure authenticity. A flock of sheep graze peacefully in the newly planted orchard, and there's a dreadlocked donkey called Omega. Deer can often be seen bounding across the meadow. With 118 hectares of grounds it is very hard to imagine that you're only 15 minutes from the centre of Tours. On fine summer evenings you can take a supper tray à la Glyndebourne in a favourite corner of the vast grounds. *Golf course opposite.*

Price	€120.
Rooms	5: 3 doubles, 1 family room, 1 triple.
Meals	Dinner €26; with wine €42. By arrangement. Summer buffets in garden.
Closed	Rarely.
Directions	From Tours, A85 Saumur 1st exit for Ballan Miré; signs for Ferme Château de Vau & golf course at motorway exit. Entrance opp. golf course.

Bruno Clément
37510 Ballan Miré,
Indre-et-Loire
Tel   +33 (0)2 47 67 84 04
Email   info@chateau-du-vau.com
Web   www.chateau-du-vau.com

Château de Reignac

A remarkably balanced restoration is this four-star hotel, full of elegance and charm, where the 'old' is underplayed and the 'new' is discreet. So many personalities stayed or were connected with this château that Erick decided to theme the rooms adding a portrait or special object – and a biography. 'Lafayette', who inherited the château and visited until 1792, is a small suite with two bathrooms all in subtle greens and yellows with an attractive writing desk for your historical novel and a private terrace for a balmy evenings. 'Axel de Fersen', a Swedish nobleman who swooned for Marie Antoinette, is in pale blues and yellows with a statue of his beloved and a claw-foot bath. Lime and mauve work wonders in the *grand salon* – enormous sparkling mirrors and flower-dressed chimney – while the exotic smoking room/bar – Zanzibar – is in dark browns with cane furniture. Books can be borrowed from the properly sober library where an Egyptian theme runs through the art on the walls. The guests-only restaurant serves a daily changing menu, full of spicy, original touches. We think you will like it here.

Price	€170. Suites €200–€250. Apartment €350.
Rooms	12: 6 doubles, 2 twins, 3 suites for 3, 1 apartment for 4 (without kitchen).
Meals	Buffet breakfast €14. Dinner with wine, from €47.
Closed	January.
Directions	A10 to Bordeaux, exit 23 Tours Sud; N143 to Loches for 22km; Reignac on left; château next to church.

Erick Charrier
19 rue Louis de Barberin,
37310 Reignac sur Indre, Indre-et-Loire
Tel   +33 (0)2 47 94 14 10
Email   contact@lechateaudereignac.com
Web   www.lechateaudereignac.com

Domaine de la Tortinière

It seems unreal, this pepperpot-towered château on a hill above the Indre, the bird-filled woods where wild cyclamen lay a carpet in autumn and daffodils radiate their light in spring. Then there's the view across to the stony keep of Montbazon; this is an exceptional spot with tennis, a heated pool, fishing or rowing on the river, too. Bedrooms are decorated with flair and imagination, be they in the château or in one of the several outbuildings. One of these, an adorable Renaissance doll's house, has two smaller rooms and a split-level suite; the orchard pavilion, for playing shepherdesses, is big and beautifully furnished – the desk invites great writings. Bathrooms are luxurious, some smaller than others. For wet nights there's an underground passage to the orangery where you dine – with a dining terrace for summer. Soft lighting, panelled reception rooms, deep comfort and discreet friendliness here in this real family-run hotel: the warm, humorous owners are genuinely attentive, their sole aim to make your stay peaceful and harmonious. Discover the mills and villages of the Indre.

Price	€155–€260. Suites €350–€370.
Rooms	30: 7 doubles, 4 suites.
	Pavilions: 16 doubles, 3 suites.
Meals	Breakfast €17. Dinner €44–€74.
	Restaurant closed Sunday eve
	November–March.
Closed	18 December–March.
Directions	2km north of Montbazon. From Tours
	D910 south for Poitiers for 10km. In
	Les Gués, right at 2nd lights; signed.

Xavier & Anne Olivereau
Les Gués de Veigné,
37250 Montbazon, Indre-et-Loire

Tel	+33 (0)2 47 34 35 00
Email	domaine.tortiniere@wanadoo.fr
Web	www.tortiniere.com

Domaine des Bidaudières

Sylvie and Pascal Suzanne have made their mark on this classic, creamy-stoned ex-wine-grower's property. Unstuffy and outgoing, this stylish young couple lend sophistication to the place and produce a small quantity of their own wine, having planted new vineyards to the terraced rear. Cypress trees stand on the hillside behind and give an Italianate feel. Bedrooms are fresh and contemporary, each immaculate and carpeted and decorated in Designers Guild fabrics. All are light, south-facing and have valley views. The sitting room, where the kitchen used to be, was actually built into the rock – a hugely attractive, stone-floored room with a low rocky ceiling and an open fire at one end. Guests can idle away the afternoon in the elegant swimming pool on the lower terrace which lies alongside the carefully restored orangerie. Sun beds are separated by small bushes for more privacy. There is even a direct access to the pool via the lift in the main house. Families are welcome to stay in the more rustic 'troglodyte' apartment nearby. *Cash or euro cheque only.*

Price	€125. Suite €140. Cottage suites €110–€170. Apartment €140.
Rooms	8 + 1: 4 doubles, 1 twin, 1 suite for 3, 2 cottage suites for 4-5. Apartment for 5.
Meals	Restaurants 10-15km.
Closed	Rarely.
Directions	From Paris A10 exit 20 Vouvray onto N952 for Amboise. In Vouvray D46 for Vernou sur Brenne; 2nd street on left after r'bout.

Pascal Suzanne
Rue du Peu Morier,
37210 Vouvray, Indre-et-Loire

Tel	+33 (0)2 47 52 66 85
Email	contact@bidaudieres.com
Web	www.bidaudieres.com

Hôtel du Bon Laboureur et du Château

This little hotel, a stroll from the château of Chenonceaux, started life as a coaching inn in the 18th century. Now in the hands of the fourth generation, it has expanded into an adjoining building (the old village school) and into a somewhat grander building with a rather pretentious tower, known tongue-in-cheek as 'The Manor'. The bedrooms are light and airy with plenty of space and are kept in tip-top condition. In the 18th-century house there are four; up a narrow wooden staircase tiled in terracotta is a double in pretty cream and red toile de Jouy. The heart of the hotel is in the original building, with its elegant 18th-century style dining room and a simpler, more relaxed one next to it. In summer, tables with starched white cloths, candles and flowers are set on the terrace under the trees. A good spot for seeing the châteaux; Amboise, Chaumont, Chambord and others are within easy reach so you can make your visits and return with time for a swim and a cocktail before dinner. A large potager behind the hotel supplies vegetables. Charming owners, delightful cuisine.

Price	€115-€155. Suites €190-€260.
Rooms	25: 20 doubles, 5 suites.
Meals	Breakfast €14.50. Picnic €9. Lunch & dinner €30-€85. Restaurant closed Tuesday lunchtime.
Closed	Mid-November to mid-December; January.
Directions	From Blois, cross Loire onto D751 then D764 to Montrichard. Follow signs to Chenonceaux; on right.

Isabelle & Antoine Jeudi
6 rue du Docteur Bretonneau,
37150 Chenonceaux, Indre-et-Loire

Tel	+33 (0)2 47 23 90 02
Email	laboureur@wanadoo.fr
Web	www.bonlaboureur.com

Le Vieux Manoir

Just imagine visiting Amboise, doing a whistle-stop tour of the magnificent château, a spot of lunch, and then staying in a beautiful manoir from whose wine cellars runs a secret tunnel to the château's very grounds. Gloria ran a wonderful B&B in Boston before resettling in France with her husband to fulfil a dream of restoring a 17th-century jewel. Rooms are filled with fascinating French flea market finds and family antiques, and bedrooms bow to the ladies: Colette is beamed and bright in a red and white theme, Madame de Lafayette's hand basin sits in an antique dresser, bevelled mirrors and hand-made tiles sparkle in the bathrooms. There's a salon, a snooze-friendly library and a convivial conservatory for fine breakfasting which opens onto a cheery French-formal town garden. The little two-storey Maison de Gardien has become an impeccable cottage for four with a sitting room and a kitchen only Americans know how to do – perfect for families with children over five. A second cottage next to the gates, equally special, is suitable for all ages, including couples in search of a romantic escape.

Price	€115–€190. Cottages €210–€295.
Rooms	6 + 2: 5 doubles, 1 triple. 2 cottages for 2-4.
Meals	Restaurants in town.
Closed	November-February. Call for out of season reservations.
Directions	In Amboise, from Quai Général de Gaulle onto Ave des Martyrs at post office. Rue Rabelais left after 150m, one way, narrow.

Gloria & Bob Belknap
13 rue Rabelais,
37400 Amboise, Indre-et-Loire
Tel   +33 (0)2 47 30 41 27
Email   info@le-vieux-manoir.com
Web   www.le-vieux-manoir.com

Le Manoir Les Minimes

You can stay in either the manor itself or in the small pavilion across the courtyard. Every detail has been thought out with care, lovingly chosen antiques and objets placed to create a light sophistication. A far cry from the Minimes order who had a convent here until it was destroyed in the French Revolution; this noble townhouse took the site. Between majestic Loire and historic castle, the manor has 18th-century grace and generous windows that look onto its big courtyard, the castle and the lustrous river. The charmingly young and enthusiastic Eric Deforges was a fashion designer, hence his faultless eye for fabric, colour and detail. Exquisitely decorated rooms are big – slightly smaller on the top floor, with beams and river views from their dormers – and have luxurious bathrooms. The masterpiece is the suite where the toile de Jouy wall fabric seems to be one single piece. There is a terrace outside where you can take an aperitif in the late afternoon under yellow umbrellas, gazing up at the royal château of Amboise, while Olga, the elegant Brie sheepdog, sleeps in the sun nearby.

Price	€122-€190. Suites €270-€460.
Rooms	15: 13 twins/doubles, 2 suites.
Meals	Breakfast €13-€17. Will provide menus & make reservations for local restaurants within walking distance.
Closed	Never.
Directions	From A10 for Amboise. Over Loire, then right on D751 for town centre. Hotel on left approaching town centre.

Patrice Longet & Eric Deforges
34 quai Charles Guinot,
37400 Amboise, Indre-et-Loire
Tel   +33 (0)2 47 30 40 40
Email   reservation@manoirlesminimes.com
Web   www.manoirlesminimes.com

Château des Ormeaux

The view's the thing. From the turreted 19th-century château built around a 15th-century tower, you take in the glories of 27 hectares. Corner rooms on two floors – original panelling on the first floor, sloping ceilings on the second – have tiny little boudoirs off the main room in the turret. A decent size, bedrooms have elaborate bedcovers and drapes; bathrooms are grand in a turn-of-the-century way. One room, blue and gold, has a marble fireplace and an 'armoire à glace', a wall of mirrors hidden behind an apparently ordinary cupboard; another, decorated in ochre and maroon, a crystal chandelier and plushly canopied bed. Two new rooms have been carefully restored in the 18th-century manoir, with visible beams and lime rendering. Best of all, from wherever you stand (or swim) those valley views are superb. Everyone dines at a table laden with china, crystal and candles, on fabulous food served by your fabulous hosts – Eric, Emmanuel and Dominique – enhanced by background Bach. A hugely welcoming place.

Price	€120–€250.
Rooms	8: 5 doubles, 3 twins.
Meals	Restaurants 6km.
Closed	15 January–15 February.
Directions	From Paris A10 exit 18 Amboise, D31 for Amboise. Right at Autrèche onto D55 to Montreuil en Touraine; D5 to Nazelles; right on D1 for Noizay. Château at end of village after La Bardouillère.

Emmanuel Guenot & Eric Fontbonnat
Route de Noizay (D1),
Nazelles, 37530 Amboise, Indre-et-Loire

Tel	+33 (0)2 47 23 26 51
Email	contact@chateaudesormeaux.fr
Web	www.chateaudesormeaux.fr

Le Fleuray Hôtel & Restaurant

The Newington family have created a haven of peace in the middle of the countryside surrounded by fields and grazing cows. The raw material was ideal: a solid, handsome old manor house with duck pond and barns, mature trees and bushes – all that was needed to persuade them to settle. The rooms in the converted barns are just right for families; slightly cut off from the rest, their French windows open onto the garden thus creating individual patios. Those in the main building are slightly smaller but cosy and immaculate with queen-size or twin beds. There is a wonderful country-house mood at Le Fleuray: lightly floral sofas into which you can sink, bookcases, prints and flowers. Enjoy a heated pool and dining on the terrace in summer and aperitifs in front of a crackling fire in winter. Talented young French chef Romain Grasso, who has come to Le Fleuray with a fabulous pedigree, produces a delicately inventive and exquisitely presented cuisine; the restaurant is one of the most popular in the area. Expect a genuine welcome from your hosts; the guest book sings their praises.

Price	€78-€146. Suites & family rooms €138.
Rooms	21: 10 twins/doubles, 2 suites for 4-6, 9 family rooms for 2-5.
Meals	Breakfast €14. Dinner €29-€49. Children's meals €17.
Closed	Christmas & New Year.
Directions	From A10 exit 18 Amboise & Château Renault. D31 to Autrèche. Left on D55 to Dame Marie les Bois. Right on D74 for Cangey. 8km from exit.

Ethical Collection: Food.
See page 446 for details

	Newington Family
	Fleuray, Route D74,
	37530 Cangey-Amboise, Indre-et-Loire
Tel	+33 (0)2 47 56 09 25
Email	contact@lefleurayhotel.com
Web	www.lefleurayhotel.com

Entry 215   Map 4

Western Loire

Le Logis d'Antan

Blue shutters against pale walls, faded terracotta roofs – the long façade suggests a simple country elegance. Once a wine merchant's house, then part of a farm, it basks in gardens full of beeches and wild poppies, fruit trees and figs. There's even a little pavilion. Bruno and Annie, ex-journalists with a young family, have created a friendly, unpretentious atmosphere – you'll like their style. Meals (Bruno has been on a cookery course) are eaten at a table seating up to 16 in a typically French dining room – or out on the veranda in good weather. Upstairs, where a mezzanine and maze of passageways make for great hide-and-seek, you can prepare picnics in a communal kitchen. Up here, too, are two double rooms, one with a bunk-bedded children's annexe. The triples are on the ground floor: big, traditional rooms, with their own entrances off the drive. Les Pictons, overlooking the front lawn, has exposed stone walls and a grandfather clock; La Pibale, its own terrace. Bruno and Annie work closely with a company called Cycling for Softies, so grab the bikes and explore the country. *No credit cards.*

Price	€67–€84. Suite €101.
	Family rooms €67–€118.
Rooms	5: 1 double, 1 suite for 4,
	3 family rooms: 2 for 3, 1 for 4-5.
Meals	Dinner with wine, €27.
Closed	27 October–5 November.
Directions	From A10 (Paris-Bordeaux) exit 33.
	8km after toll, left to 'Vallans'. Logis
	on exit dir. Epannes.

Annie & Bruno Ragouilliaux–di Battista
140 rue Saint-Louis, 79270 Vallans,
Deux Sèvres
Tel   +33 (0)5 49 04 86 75
Email   info@logisdantan.com
Web   www.logisdantan.com

Le Logis Saint Martin

Run with efficiency by the Pellegrins this 17th-century *gentilhommerie* offers that most attractive combination for travellers – solidly comfortable rooms and superb food. It is set conveniently on the outskirts of town, beyond suburbia, in a little wooded valley with a small stream running just outside. The bedrooms are mostly smallish, beamed, traditionally furnished and very comfortable; the bigger rooms, with lovely old rafters, are on the top floor. The tower has been converted into a charming suite with a sitting area downstairs and a smallish stone-walled bedroom up steepish stairs. Food is the thing here – regional, seasonal and served with panache, in the colour-washed restaurant or the pleasantly shaded and tranquil garden. New chef Aline Jarriault has worked with the best and there is an innovative yet classic feel, matched by some tempting wines. Choose between the menu terroir and the menu gourmand – or pull out all the stops and work your way through the menu dégustation! As for Saint Maixent l'Ecole, it's a pretty market town not far from Poitiers and La Rochelle.

Price	€125–€310. Suite €310. Family room €185.
Rooms	12: 9 doubles, 1 twin, 1 suite, 1 family room for 3.
Meals	Breakfast €16. Lunch €27–€45. Dinner €45–€75. Restaurant closed Sat, Tues lunchtimes & Mon.
Closed	Never.
Directions	From Poitiers exit 31; N11 until St Maixent l'Ecole; follow signs for Niort, left at 4th set of lights; follow signs. 400m from lights.

Edouard & Botagoz Pellegrin
Chemin de Pissot,
79400 Saint Maixent l'Ecole, Deux Sèvres

Tel	+33 (0)5 49 05 58 68
Email	contact@logis-saint-martin.com
Web	www.logis-saint-martin.com

Entry 217 Map 9

Château de Saint Loup sur Thouet

This château inspired Perrault to write *Puss in Boots*! The Black Prince incarcerated John the Good here in 1356 and it was rebuilt in the 17th century by the Marquis of Carabas, whose magnificence so impressed the fairytale writer. Charles-Henri visited the château on Christmas Eve 1990, fell in love with it and ten days later had bought it. Saint Loup is a listed monument, open to the public, and its restoration is a monumental task. Using 18th-century plans, the count is also working on the 50 hectares of grounds and kitchen garden. Rooms are lofty and light in the château, medieval in the separate keep. The Black Prince room in the old kitchens has two vast fireplaces and thick red-stained beams, the Bishop's room in the château has a splendid canopied bed between two big windows overlooking the garden. It's all a romantic's dream, though a housemaid's nightmare. Enjoy aperitifs in the courtyard of the orangery on the other side of the moat; your charming hosts make sure guests meet each other before dinner (delicious and home-cooked). A jewel of a château, a happy and authentic home.

Price	€150–€220.
Rooms	18: 16 doubles, 2 singles. Whole château (& 8-bedroom keep) available.
Meals	Breakfast €15. Dinner with wine, €75.
Closed	Rarely.
Directions	From Airvault D46 to St Loup Lamairé. Château visible on entering village.

Comte Charles-Henri de Bartillat
79600 Saint Loup Lamairé,
Deux Sèvres

Tel	+33 (0)5 49 64 81 73
Email	st-loup@wanadoo.fr
Web	www.chateaudesaint-loup.com

Hôtel Le Pigeonnier du Perron

René Descartes once owned this little *seigneurie*; its deeds are 15th century. More a country guest house than a hotel, it's been in the family for 150 years. Father and son are fully occupied in their wine laboratory in Cahors; Emilie, in her 20s and fresh from hotel school, prepares good simple meals (some organic produce, some fish) and runs it all with Fridda. Family connections guarantee an excellent selection of wines from Cahors, but also from Poitou and the Val de Loire. Sun-ripe tomatoes, courgettes and peppers are home-grown along with essential herbs for the kitchen, and you can eat on the the stone-flagged terrace in summer. The modest farm buildings are grouped around a sunny courtyard, hollyhocks surge from every nook and cranny and there's a lovely new pool. Smallish bedrooms are simply, pleasantly decorated with the odd splash of colour, their floors pale pine, their walls soft-sponged – or of creamy exposed stone. One in the dovecote has a little balcony, many look over the fields and valley. Good value. *Advanced notice please for vegetarian fare.*

Price	€79–€87. Family rooms €117–€148.
Rooms	14: 11 doubles, 1 twin, 2 family rooms.
Meals	Dinner €19.
Closed	Rarely.
Directions	A10 exit 27 for Châtellerault Sud. 2nd r'bout for Cenon; thro' Cenon for Availles. 1st right after village sign. Signed on right after 1km.

Emilie Thiollet
Le Perron,
86530 Availles en Châtellerault, Vienne
Tel   +33 (0)5 49 19 76 08
Email   accueil@lepigeonnierduperron.com
Web   www.lepigeonnierduperron.com

Entry 219   Map 9

Maisons d'hôtes Villa Richelieu

Chatellerault is a small market town on the river Vienne, within easy reach of the Loire's glories. Villa Richelieu is a small hotel within easy reach of the town, run by a lively hostess who lives here with her family. Madame is welcoming, well-organised and runs a happy ship. Don't be deterred by the unprepossessing street. Once through the gates you enter a different world: welcome to Villas 61 and 63. The first (a barn built in 1901) has a country-cosy décor; the second, across the courtyard, has an 18th-century street-facing façade and is smartly contemporary. You can expect an excellent breakfast with yogurts and homemade jams and can have a dinner tray ordered in if you don't fancy the 15-minute stroll. Bedrooms in Villa 61, restful and homely, have seagrass matting, pine walls and sofabeds for families, while the smaller, more sophisticated rooms in No. 63 have a stylish intimacy. Take your pick! For relaxed moments there are sitting corners with books, games and computer, a sunny veranda for Villa 63 and a fenced pool in the courtyard. A friendly and inviting little hotel, run in the spirit of B&B.

Price	From €90. Suite €115. Family rooms €115 for 2, €130 for 3-4.
Rooms	9: 1 double, 1 suite for 4, 3 family rooms. Villa 63: 4 doubles.
Meals	Breakfast €7. Restaurant 15-minute walk. Dinner tray on request.
Closed	Never.
Directions	Exit A10 for Chatellerault Nord & La Roche Posay. At r'bout 1st right. Left at x-roads into Ave de Richelieu. House on right.

Ludiwime Alizon
61-63 avenue de Richelieu,
86150 Châtellerault, Vienne

Mobile	+33 (0)6 70 15 30 90
Email	info@villarichelieu.com
Web	www.villarichelieu.com

Le Relais du Lyon d'Or

In one of France's most beautiful medieval villages is this excellent little hotel. Diana, American, brings her previous hotel and restaurant experience; Dominique, French, is a fully-fledged wine expert and dealer who will suggest the perfect bottle for dinner. Each public room has been rebuilt round its old flagstones, doors and beams, then decorated in warm natural colours to enhance the architectural features and the natural beauty. Bedrooms have intriguing details and individual touches; rafters for the ones under the roof, high ceilings and beams for the others. Some are big, some are smaller; none are overdone and all have sparkling bathrooms. The menu is varied with an emphasis on traditional dishes and local produce, while breakfasts feature juice pressed from local fruits; in summer you eat on a pretty parasoled terrace. Masses to see and do: the Valley of the Frescoes with its abbey at Saint Savin, the weekly markets of medieval Chauvigny and Loches, the magnificent Parc de la Brenne, for birds, turtles, orchids. And then there's Poitiers…

Price	€75–€135. Suites €125–€135.
Rooms	10: 8 doubles, 1 suite for 4, 1 suite for 5.
Meals	Breakfast €12. Dinner €25–€40. Wine €22–€500. Lunch for groups by arrangement. Restaurant closed mid-Nov to mid-March.
Closed	Rarely.
Directions	A10 exit Châtellerault Nord D9/D725 east through La Roche Posay; D5 to Angles sur l'Anglin. In village centre.

Dominique Fuscien & Diana Hager
4 rue d'Enfer,
86260 Angles sur l'Anglin, Vienne

Tel   +33 (0)5 49 48 32 53
Email   contact@lyondor.com
Web   www.lyondor.com

Hôtel Les Orangeries

Even before you step inside, the long cool pool beneath the trees will convince you that these people have the finest sense of how to treat an old house and its surroundings. The deep wooden deck, the rustic stone walls, the giant flower baskets, the orange trees, the candles at night – all create tranquillity and harmony. The young owners (he an architect) fell in love with the place and applied all their talent to blending 18th-century elegance with contemporary charm. Stripped oak doors, exposed stone walls, cool stone floors glow with loving care, like valued old friends, and Olivia has given each bedroom its own sense of uncluttered harmony; those facing the main road are double-glazed and the split-level suites are a delight. The Gautiers' passions include the old-fashioned games they have resuscitated for you: croquet and skittles under the trees, two kinds of billiards, backgammon and mahjong. Olivia speaks wonderful English and her enthusiasm for house, garden and guests is catching. Food is delicious, organic; breakfast, in the garden in summer, is all you'd hope for the price. An exceptional place.

Price	€70–€140. Apartments €115–€185.
Rooms	15: 11 doubles, 4 apartments for 4–5 (without kitchen).
Meals	Breakfast from €12.50. Dinner from €22. Wine from €18.
Closed	Mid-January to mid-February.
Directions	From Poitiers N147 dir. Limoges to Lussac les Châteaux; 35km. Hotel on left on entering town.

Ethical Collection: Environment; Food.
See page 446 for details

Olivia & Jean–Philippe Gautier
12 avenue du Docteur Dupont,
86320 Lussac les Châteaux, Vienne
Tel   +33 (0)5 49 84 07 07
Email   orangeries@wanadoo.fr
Web   www.lesorangeries.fr

Château de Nieuil

François I built the château as a hunting lodge in the 16th century, but swapped Nieuil for a bigger plot when he opted for the grander Chambord on the Loire. A gambling Count sold it to grandparents of the Bodinauds. Its hunting days are now over and Luce and her husband have instead created an exciting hotel and a hommage to our feathered friends with a magical birdwatching walk round the outside of the moat. Each room is named after a bird and if you are not awoken by real ones, an alarm will sing 'your' song. The château is grand and beautifully decorated; one room has a small children's room up a spiral stair, another a tiny reading room in a turret; most look onto the handsome formal garden at the back. The stunning breakfast room has views of the vast grounds through stained-glass windows. Luce, a chef in her own right, has well trained a young trio who run the restaurant in the old stables. A chandelier hung with love letters and a stainless-steel bar are touches of modern elegance in this country retreat. Open-hearted, open-armed — these people love what they do, and it shows.

Price	€135–€280. Suites €260–€430. Gîtes from €550 per week. Gypsy caravan €200 per week.
Rooms	14 + 4: 11 twins/doubles, 3 suites. 3 gîtes, 1 gypsy caravan.
Meals	Breakfast €15. Lunch €25–€50. Dinner €46–€60. Restaurant closed Sun eve, Mon & Tues lunch Sept-June.
Closed	November.
Directions	From Angoulême N141 to La Rochefoucauld, then Chasseneuil. On for 6.5km; in Suaux, left on D739 to Nieuil. Signed.

M & Mme Bodinaud
16270 Nieuil, Charente

Tel	+33 (0)5 45 71 36 38
Email	chateaunieuilhotel@wanadoo.fr
Web	www.chateaunieuilhotel.com

Château de la Couronne

Behind the imposing façade lies an amazing hotel. Mark and Nicky swapped the worlds of fashion and TV to turn this 19th-century château in the gentle green Charente into a fine example of contemporary design, and a chic home-from-home hotel. From the gravelled courtyard, the wrought-iron front doors lead to a thrillingly modern space where 60s and 70s pieces co-exist with swirling glassware and ornate antiques. Three airy salons filled with fat candles, a baby grand piano (complete with sleeping cat), and a retro honesty bar open on to the rear terrace, where marble bistro tables look out to an elegant garden with topiary trees and a sleek black-walled swimming pool. Across the courtyard are a billiard room and a private cinema. The bedroom suites are a triumph – lofty white spaces with splashes of cherry-red and chartreuse. The big bathrooms are a sensual treat – some incorporating the chateau's turrets, some with two tubs, all delightfully individual. Quaint Marthon (a few shops, a sprinkling of restaurants and bars), is a stroll away. Angoulème will charm you.

Price	€145–€315. Whole house €2,000 (€12,000 per week).
Rooms	5 + 1: 5 suites (4 doubles, 1 twin). Whole house available (sleeps 26).
Meals	Breakfast €15; children €10. Restaurants in village.
Closed	Rarely.
Directions	Angoulème D939 to Périgueux; D4 to Marthon. Left in village centre to Montbron, left at war memorial. Château ahead.

Nicky Cooper & Mark Selwood
16380 Marthon, Charente

Tel	+33 (0)5 45 62 29 96
Email	info@chateaudelacouronne.com
Web	www.chateaudelacouronne.com

Château de l'Yeuse

A delightful conceit: a miniature folly of a Charente château, dazzlingly striped in brick and creamy stone, with a modern extension in flamboyant style. It is just five minutes from Cognac yet is wrapped in parkland with views to the Charente river – utterly charming. Bedrooms are in the newer part – with fun, trompe l'oeil-flourished corridors – large and light in bold country-house style and with ultra-modern bathrooms. Book a room overlooking the river. By contrast, the 'old' château is all classical proportions, elegant furnishings and traditional comfort. Wallow in the cigar salon with its deep armchairs and glass-fronted cabinets, work your way through the 100-year-old cognacs. It's posh frocks for dinner in the chandelier-hung dining room, all stiff white napery and black jacketed waiters. The excitement over chef Pascal Nebout's cuisine is palpable. Céline, the young manageress, energetic yet ever-calm, will advise on visiting distilleries and music festivals. Discover the secret garden, relax by the pool, find a shady terrace or treat yourself to a massage in the hamman. Sophisticated living.

Price	€105–€175. Suites €230–€353.
Rooms	24: 8 doubles, 13 twins/doubles, 3 suites.
Meals	Breakfast €18. Lunch €18–€25. Dinner €50–€85. Resaurant. closed Mon, Sat lunchtimes; Sunday & Monday eve out of season.
Closed	January.
Directions	From Paris A10 exit 34. Follow signs St Jean d'Angély & Cognac, then for Angoulème; D15 to St Brice & Quartier de l'Echassier.

Céline Desmazières & Pascal Nebout
65 rue de Bellevue, Châteaubernard,
16100 Cognac, Charente

Tel	+33 (0)5 45 36 82 60
Email	reservations.yeuse@wanadoo.fr
Web	www.yeuse.fr

Relais de St Preuil

Madame from Burgundy has lived in Asia and has come home to fulfil a dream: to run her own hotel in the Poitou Charentes. The Montembaults, in search of a big old property and a business adventure, ended up with a hamlet… Le Relais de St Preuil sits alone at the top of a hill surrounded by vineyards and sky and it's a fabulous setting. Hard work and dedication have resulted in an expertly run holiday complex and some very comfortably dressed rooms (all but one on the ground floor): expect shiny sleigh beds, cheerful fabrics, ethnic themes and a few stunning old rafters. And there's so much to do you could never be bored: a tennis court and big outdoor pool, a pool house with fitness room and sauna, mountain bikes, ping-pong and playground… all has been included, from in-room massages to generous pool towels. This would be a terrific place for a group of friends – or for a sociable family. Meet the guests at table d'hôtes over regional dishes delicately and deliciously flavoured with cognac and pineau des Charentes. The finest cognac vineyards surround you.

Price	€105-€185.
	Gîtes €400-€1,450 per week.
Rooms	8 + 2: 4 doubles, 2 twins, 2 suites.
	3 gîtes for 4-5.
Meals	Breakfast €13. Dinner €40.
Closed	February-April.
Directions	From Paris A10 dir. Poitiers;
	N10 dir. Angoulême, then Jarnac;
	D10 to Segonzac. St Preuil is hamlet
	on hilltop.

Christine Montembault
Lieu-dit Chez Riviere, St Preuil,
16130 Cognac, Charente
Tel   +33 (0)5 45 80 80 08
Email   contact@relais-de-saint-preuil.com
Web   www.relais-de-saint-preuil.com

Logis du Fresne

The Butler family came to France 100 years ago to make cognac and Tone's husband Christophe has been in the business all his life. They bought the old, elegant Logis and opened in 2003, fulfilling their vision of a refined place to stay with an intimate bed and breakfast feel. The façade is wonderful and inside just as good. The whole feel is light and fresh and the style turn-of-the-century Norwegian (the land of Tone's birth): old terracotta tiles on the ground floor, pale painted beams, a cosy library, an elegant salon. Bedrooms are as serene. Those on the first floor have uncluttered chic: a gilded mirror hangs above an open fire, an oriental rug graces a limed floor. Those above are more modern, and the two-room suite has its own stair. Bathrooms come well-lit and beautifully modern. Gardens and pool are a delight, and breakfasts on the terraces romantic – expect a fresh cut rose and quintessential silver tea set at tables forged in the village. The grounds, with a hidden pool and a 15th-century tower, look across to terracotta roof tops against a cornflower blue sky. Breathtaking.

Price	€100–€125. Suite €185. Half-board option available.
Rooms	11: 10 twins/doubles, 1 suite.
Meals	Breakfast €12. Dinner (outside caterers) €36. Wine €15–€36. Restaurants 4km.
Closed	November–February. Call for out of season group reservations.
Directions	From Cognac, D24 for Segonzac then D736 for Juillac le Coq. 500m after village on right.

	Tone Butler
	16130 Juillac le Coq, Charente
Tel	+33 (0)5 45 32 28 74
Email	logisdufresne@wanadoo.fr
Web	www.logisdufresne.com

Le Logis du Paradis

Mellow stones, chunky beams, sensuous fabrics… there's a timeless feel to the beautifully renovated Logis du Paradis, where Nick and Sally greet you as old friends. These early 18th-century buildings, a 'paradis' where the oldest and finest Cognac was stored, embrace a magnificent oval courtyard. In spacious, luxurious bedrooms you snuggle down in superbly comfortable king-size beds under white linen… and wake in anticipation of a delicious breakfast. There's a pool in the aromatic garden and a bar in the former distillery, shared with the other guests. Or you may pootle down empty country roads in one of Nick's classic cars (choose from a selection); what better way to discover Cognac's finest vineyards, and the Atlantic coast's beaches and villages, than in an old MG? Return to a stroll around the walled *parc* by the pretty river Ne before a four-course table d'hôtes dinner, enjoyed on the terrace in summer. Nick's generous table features market-fresh produce from the Charentes, washed down by fine wines, and polished off with a glass of the neighbour's superb XO Cognac. *Two gîtes in grounds.*

Price	€85–€110.
Rooms	5: 4 twins/doubles, 1 twin.
Meals	Lunch €19. Dinner €39, on request. Restaurants 4km.
Closed	Mid-January to March.
Directions	N10 south from Angoulême dir. Bordeaux. Before Barbezieux, D151 thro' Viville; cross D1 until La Magdeleine. 100m after chapel on left.

Ethical Collection: Community.
See page 446 for details

Nick Brimblecombe
La Magdeleine,
16300 Criteuil la Magdeleine, Charente
Tel   +33 (0)5 45 35 39 43
Email   info@logisduparadis.fr
Web   www.logisduparadis.com

Hôtel du Donjon

Centre ville is on the doorstep and surprisingly busy; the warm frontage expresses the charm of a country-style hotel. Armelle and Stephane left Normandy in search of adventure and stumbled across a townhouse in need of love and care. Now olive green woodwork and neatly trimmed privet announce the entrance. Your hosts are always to hand, the service is simple and friendly, people come and go and everything ticks over harmoniously. Polished staircases are lit with spots; corridors have creamy stone and exposed natural beams on split levels. The downstairs lobby, bustling, bright and scented with fresh cut garden flowers, has neutral furnishings and a central stone fireplace. Bedrooms are quiet and simple with views to the pretty terrace where honeysuckle creeps up the walls; the bedroom for guests with limited mobility is superbly equipped. Wine tasting tours can be arranged and, for animal lovers, there's the Charentais Donkey Protection Society to visit. Discover the rare 'dreadlocks' Poitou donkey: one of the region's best-kept secrets. A great little place.

Price	€55–€77.
Rooms	10: 7 doubles, 2 triples, 1 family room for 4.
Meals	Breakfast €7. Dinner €13. Restaurant 50m.
Closed	Never.
Directions	Paris to Bordeaux on A10, exit Niort Sud or Saint Jean d'Augely. D950 to Poitiers Saintes.

Armelle & Stephane Gras
4 rue des Hivers, 17470 Aulnay de Saintonge,
Charente-Maritime

Tel	+33 (0)5 46 33 67 67
Email	hoteldudonjon@wanadoo.fr
Web	www.hoteldudonjon.com

Entry 229   Map 9

Château des Salles

A pretty little château with great personality, Salles was built in 1454 and scarcely touched until 1860, when it was 'adapted to the fashion' (profoundly). One hundred years later, the enterprising Couillaud family brought the estate guest house, its vineyard and farm into the 20th century. Behind its fine old exterior it exudes light, harmony, colour and elegant informality with spiral stone stairs, boldly painted beams and warm, well-furnished bedrooms bathed in soft colours and gentle wallpapers. Salles is a friendly family affair: sister at guest house reception, brother at vines, mother at her easel – her watercolours hang in the public rooms, her flowers decorate bedroom doors – and in the kitchen. At dinner, refined food made with local and home-grown produce is served with estate wines. Sylvie Couillaud will help you plan your stay – she knows it all and is almost a mini tourist office. It's a congenial, welcoming house: people come back again and again and one guest said: "She welcomed us like family and sent us home with goodies from her vineyard". *Château produces pineau & cognac.*

Price	€90–€140.
Rooms	5 doubles.
Meals	Breakfast €11. Dinner €38. Wine €15–€20.
Closed	November–March.
Directions	From A10 exit 27 Mirambeau, then D730 towards Royan. Château is between Lorignac and Brie sous Mortagne; signed at D730 & D125 junction.

Sylvie Couillaud
17240 Saint Fort sur Gironde,
Charente-Maritime

Tel	+33 (0)5 46 49 95 10
Email	chateaudessalles@wanadoo.fr
Web	www.chateaudessalles.com

Blue Sturgeon

It feels good to be here from the moment you arrive, and the simple Marché-based food will leave a smile on your face – even if caviar isn't your thing. Tiny St Seurin was the first place in Europe to produce caviar, and it is served here with a flourish. Robert and Eileen, relaxed and talented hosts, have created five uncluttered bedrooms in hip-hotel style, in an old wine store that dates from the 1700s. Soothing neutrals serve as a backdrop for artist Robert's abstract tableaux, one of which hangs behind each of the beds; the windows are framed by curtains that let morning light filter through; bathrooms sport aromatic soaps and gels. The ground-floor rooms face the garden while the family suite has a double bed on the mezzanine, and a balcony overlooking the restaurant. This part of France sees more sunshine than the Côte d'Azur – come in winter and sink into leather chairs in front of the log fire. There's a free-standing plunge pool in the lush gardens, restaurants in the nearby village and a beach down the road. Excellent for couples – or foodie friends.

Price	€95–€120.
Rooms	5: 1 double, 3 twins/doubles, 1 family suite for 4-6.
Meals	Dinner €35. Wine €15–€27. Restaurants 10-min drive.
Closed	Rarely.
Directions	From Bordeaux A10 for Paris; exit 37 Royan on D730 14km; left D2 to St Fort & Gironde; right D145 thro' Mortagne & Gironde to St Seurin. House on left.

Robert Stansfield
3 rue de la Cave,
17120 St Seurin d'Uzet, Charente-Maritime

Tel	+33 (0)5 46 74 17 18
Email	reservations@bluesturgeon.com
Web	www.bluesturgeon.com

Château de la Tillade

You can tell that Michel and Solange like people and love entertaining. Their château sits at the end of an avenue of lime trees alongside the family vineyards that have produced grapes for cognac and pineau de Charentes for over two centuries. Much of the original distillery equipment is on display and well worth a visit. Your hosts make you feel instantly at ease in their comfortable, friendly home, even if you're secretly terrified of dropping the fine bone china. Solange's talents as an artist (she also holds painting courses in her art studio) are reflected in her choice of fabrics. Each bedroom is like a page out of Michel's memory book; one was his parents' room, the other where he had his early schooling – a pinky double with toile de Jouy paper. His grandmother's bed is fit for a princess, as is the claw-foot bath. The smartly striped, dusky grey tower room belonged to his mother, its own terrace looks down to the pretty pinks in the front garden. Meals are a delight, with good conversation (in English or French) round the family table while you are waited on lavishly but without stuffiness.

Price	€90–€120. Extra bed €23.
Rooms	4: 1 twin, 3 family rooms for 3-4 (one room with wc along corridor).
Meals	Dinner €38; book ahead.
Closed	Rarely.
Directions	From A10 exit 36 right for Gémozac. At r'bout. Gémozac bypass for Royan, right on D6 for Tesson. Entrance approx. 3km on left, signed (château not in village, but on D6).

Vicomte & Vicomtesse Michel de Salvert
Gémozac, 17260 Saint Simon de Pellouaille
Charente-Maritime

Tel	+33 (0)5 46 90 00 20
Email	contact@la-tillade.com
Web	www.la-tillade.com

Ma Maison de Mer

Sink into a cream sofa with a chilled après-plage beer and soak up the nautical chic. Built in the 1920s in a quiet tree-lined street (150m from a lovely beach, 400m from 'centre ville') Ma Maison has been renovated by bubbly Emma, who lives here with her young family. An intimate bar greets you as you enter and the open-plan living and dining rooms are separated by an elegant archway. Wooden floors are painted white as are the walls, drawing attention to Emma's vibrant paintings; further charming touches, from seashell collages and knitted cushions to a model gaff-rigged yacht, decorate every room. The same soothing shades are used in the bedrooms, fresh and inviting with their seagrass floors, cane chairs, taupe-coloured bedspreads and white linen. Some of the rooms have mosquito nets, others central ceiling fans. The four-course set menu changes daily so expect the freshest seafood – superb. If you need an excuse to stay, you can take a boat across the Gironde from Royan to sample the Medoc wines, there are summer festivals in lively Saint Palais and the area is rich with unspoilt beaches.

Price	€70–€155.
Rooms	5: 4 doubles, 1 twin.
Meals	Dinner with wine, €30, on request.
Closed	Rarely.
Directions	From A10 exit 5, Saintes to Royan on N150; in Royan D21 to St Palais; at r'bout, 4th exit, house on right. Signed.

Emma Hutchinson
21 avenue du Platin,
17420 Saint Palais sur Mer, Charente-Maritime
Tel   +33 (0)5 46 23 64 86
Email   reservations@mamaisondemer.com
Web   www.mamaisondemer.com

Le Moulin de Châlons

The Bouquets are a family of perfectionists, and their beautiful stone mill house sits gracefully at the water's edge, its sun terrace overlooking the mill race. The restaurant, with its crisp white dining tables and tankful of lobsters, has earned itself a reputation for finesse; the family hotel is charming. Enter a relaxed salon with a pretty stone fireplace, cosy leather chairs and fresh flowers peeping from vases. Spotless gleaming bedrooms with ultra-sound insulation (against the main road) are traditional; those in the new wing, designed by the Bouquets' charming daughter, ultra-modern. So you may choose between blue toile de Jouy and bold pebble stencils, or elegant antique settees and rust and grey spots and swirls. Bathrooms too are immaculate and gorgeous, the newest with a serene eastern feel. Neatly tendered gardens line the entrance while thoughtful resting places invite you to admire the birds bobbing downstream. Close by are the chic islands of Ré and Oleron; more traditional visitors may catch a slow boat up the Marais to the Venise Verte.

Price	€100–€130. Suites €125–€165. Family room €125–€145.
Rooms	10: 5 doubles, 2 twins, 2 suites for 2, 1 family room for 3.
Meals	Breakfast €13. Lunch & dinner €25–€48.
Closed	Rarely.
Directions	From Royan on D25; left on D733, right on D241. Moulin is 500m after leaving Gua.

Bouquet Family
2 rue du Bassin, 17600 Le Gua,
Charente-Maritime

Tel	+33 (0)5 46 22 82 72
Email	moulin-de-chalons@wanadoo.fr
Web	www.moulin-de-chalons.com

Entry 234   Map 8

Château Mouillepied

The stream-fed moat is now mostly dry but this is how the house got its name 'wet feet': springs still gurgle in the nearby meadows, sometimes flooded by the Charente. This lovely, spreading, mellow-stone château, whose tower dates from the 15th century, stands in wonderful grounds redolent with history; the old laundry, bread oven, dovecote and wine store still stand. Now energetic young owners have arrived on the scene, full of plans for an English cottage garden and a more traditional décor. Clean-lined IKEA pieces will be replaced with period armoires and gilt mirrors; plain fabrics exchanged for patterns and toile de Jouy. Bedrooms are large and airy, some with lovely old wooden floors, while those in the charming, rustic studio have the original chicken nesting holes in the stone. Breakfast is still served in the orangery overlooking the garden; and can also be delivered to the studio door. Pick up a fishing licence at the bakery and stroll along the banks of the Charente to visit the Roman city of Saintes – and another castle said to inspire *Puss in Boots*.

Price	€84–€160.
	Cottage €390–€680 per week.
Rooms	10 + 1: 4 doubles, 2 twins, 1 studio suite, 3 family rooms. Cottage for 2-3.
Meals	Restaurant 2km.
Closed	Rarely.
Directions	From A10 exit 35 at Saintes, N137 to Rochefort; right to Ecurat D119. Right for Taillebourg D236; D127 to Saint James; right to Saintes D128, right after 300m, signed.

Claire & Patrick Beladina
17350 Port d'Envaux, Charente-Maritime

Tel	+33 (0)5 46 90 49 88
Email	info@chateaumouillepied.com
Web	www.chateaumouillepied.com

Hôtel de l'Océan

Seasoned travellers, Martine and Noël tried to find a hotel that felt like a home. Although they had worked in antiques and interior design, they realised after a spell running a restaurant that this was what they should be doing – but where? They knew it had to be on an island; they stumbled upon a hotel on the Île de Ré and realised they had found it. Set back from the street in a quiet little town, the hotel has 28 bedrooms: some around an inner courtyard pungent with rosemary and lavender, others like tiny cottages among the hollyhocks. Children will love the curtained cabin bed set in a buttercup yellow alcove. Two brand new rooms in a wing are large and colonial looking, with very modern bathrooms and a calming zen feel. Floors are covered in sisal matting; ships, lighthouses and shells are dotted around against cool, soothing colours. After your pastis, your supper will involve fresh fish and herbs. The dining room is another success, with cream boards on walls and ceiling and palest greeny-grey carved chairs. It gets better every year. *Beach 15-minute walk.*

Price	€75–€180. Twins €85–€120. Triples €105–€160. Quadruple €165–€200.
Rooms	28: 21 doubles, 4 twins, 2 triples, 1 quadruple.
Meals	Breakfast €10. Lunch & dinner €24–€50. Wine €14–€40. Restaurant closed Wednesdays Oct–March.
Closed	January.
Directions	A10 exit Niort sud; N248 to La Rochelle, then N11 Rocade round La Rochelle for Pont Île de Ré; after bridge, south to Bois Plage. Hotel in town centre.

Martine & Noël Bourdet
172 rue St Martin,
17580 Le Bois Plage en Ré (Île de Ré),
Charente-Maritime

Tel	+33 (0)5 46 09 23 07
Email	info@re-hotel-ocean.com
Web	www.re-hotel-ocean.com

Hôtel de Toiras

It's the French hotel you dream of but rarely find. Exquisite is the first word, refined is the second, then you stop thinking and let the senses rule. Revel in the soul of this quayside hotel, inspired by the illustrious figure of Jean de Caylar de Saint Bonnet de Toiras who protected the island from the English in 1627. Thus the arts of navigation and hunting set the tone and imbue the rooms with memories of 17th-century ship owners' houses. Linking the old part with the new is a cool fragrant garden with three palms. Then a reception room that resembles a study, black and white tiles in an elegant living room/library, open fires, a small bar, soothing music, friendly, impeccable staff. Gracious bedrooms, some large, some small, are named after writers, botanists, socialites, sailors; the detail in fabrics, paintings, objets and books is both rich and meticulous. Food is delicious, and you can shop with the chef for a tailormade dinner. This is an island of big skies and bicycles: 60 miles of cycle paths criss-cross its vineyards and pine forests. Stop off at ocean-side Cabana Jim's for fresh oysters – bliss!

Price	€135–€510. Suites €320–€1,500.
Rooms	20: 11 doubles, 9 suites.
Meals	Breakfast €18–€20. Dinner from €65.
Closed	Never.
Directions	From La Rochelle, over bridge to Île de Ré; on quay. In summer, call for code.

Olivia Mathé
1 quai Job Foran,
17410 Saint Martin de Ré (Île de Ré),
Charente-Maritime
Tel   +33 (0)5 46 35 40 32
Email   contact@hotel-de-toiras.com
Web   www.hotel-de-toiras.com

Hôtel La Baronnie - Domaine du Bien-Etre

Civilised seclusion from seaside bustle. Down the side street off the port, through a pair of beautiful old iron gates, enter another world. Built as government premises in the 18th century, La Baronnie, smartly painted and prettily shuttered, has a delightful cobbled courtyard garden and honeysuckle, mint and jasmine to scent the air. Inside are fresh flowers, wooden panelling, tiled floors and an ornate iron staircase that sweeps you upstairs. Bedrooms, large and filled with light, are finely tuned in gorgeous colours with thick curtains and elegant cushions, pale rugs on stripped wooden floors, good antiques and garden or courtyard views. Next door is the as-inviting Domaine du Bien-Etre, its bedrooms exuding a gentle country chic, the quietest facing the gardens. The charming owners, Pierre and Florence, know their island well, the nature and the history, the endless beaches beyond, the cycle paths, the sand dunes and pines. As for Saint Martin, it's full of chic shops, restaurants and bars. Fun for a stylish weekend – or more. *Car park charge. Osteopath treatments available.*

Price	€130-€230.
Rooms	16: 5 doubles, 4 suites. Domaine du Bien-Etre: 5 twins/doubles, 2 family suites.
Meals	Breakfast €15. Restaurants nearby.
Closed	November-March.
Directions	Over bridge from La Rochelle to St Martin harbour. Street on left going down to port.

Pierre & Florence Pallardy
17-21 rue Baron de Chantal,
17410 Saint Martin de Ré (Île de Ré),
Charente-Maritime

Tel	+33 (0)5 46 09 21 29
Email	info@domainedelabaronnie.com
Web	www.domainedelabaronnie.com

Aquitaine

Château Julie

Even if bordeaux is not your favourite tipple, this is a superb place to stay. Viticulture is the business here and if you come at the right time you have a grandstand view. Château Julie is Dutch-owned, run by young Renée and Rinse – a practised cook in his own right, he makes food to match the fine house wine. Rebuilt in the 18th century to charming proportions, the house is surrounded by 80 hectares of land, half of them glistening with vines. Stay in the château, whose rooms are simple and uncluttered, with big bathrooms, views over the park and oodles of towels, or in the self-catering cottage opposite; it sleeps six comfortably, has a big kitchen and two shower rooms. Meals are served in the panelled dining room; coffee and armagnac are taken in the drawing room across the impressive hallway. In the day there's tennis, fishing in the lake, exploring the grounds. Rinse can also arrange for you to visit a sister château near Saint Emilion. A great place for an active break or a lazy afternoon reading in the shade of a tree. *Cash or French cheque only. French, Dutch, English & German spoken.*

Price	€75–€135. Family rooms €135. Cottage €600 per week.
Rooms	5 + 1: 3 twins/doubles, 2 family rooms: 1 for 3, 1 for 4. Cottage for 6.
Meals	Dinner €30. Wine €5–€17. Restaurant 6km.
Closed	Rarely.
Directions	A10 Paris & Bordeaux, past toll Virsac. 1st exit towards Angoulême; signed.

Renée & Rinse Sevenster
1 Naudonnet, 33240 Virsac
(Nr St André de Cubzac), Gironde
Tel   +33 (0)5 57 94 08 20
Email   contact@chateau-julie.com
Web   www.chateau-julie.com

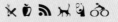

Château Lamothe Prince Noir

Turn off a suburban road into the pages of a fairy tale. A creeper-clad, stone château framed by two towers sits serenely in the middle of a moat. Knights on white chargers, at the very least Rapunzel, should soon appear…or possibly Edward, the Black Prince, who used it as a medieval hunting lodge. Slip between the trees, over the bridge and be welcomed by the Bastide family. Warm and charismatic, they have given the château a stylish opulence without detracting from its character. Large bedrooms have canopied beds, strong colours, antique bed linen and a rich but comfortable assortment of furniture. One suite has a Mexican theme, another, overlooking the moat, has murals of the seasons. Bathrooms are grand with gold taps, Venetian glass and most have windows. Breakfast on the rose-covered terrace or in the elegant, chandelier-hung salon. Light suppers or, for groups, slap-up dinners with family silver and lacy napery can be arranged. Visit Bordeaux, beaches, play golf, fish in the moat. The Bastides can arrange riding, wine tastings, even a massage. You will be treated as family guests.

Price	€180–€250. Single €85. Family room €310.
Rooms	8: 2 doubles, 1 single, 3 suites for 2, 1 suite for 3, 1 family room for 3–5.
Meals	Light supper with wine, €35–€45; book ahead. Restaurant 5-min. drive.
Closed	Rarely.
Directions	From Bordeaux N89 exit 5; D13 to St Sulpice. 2nd right across from bakery to stadium. Gate 800m on left. Signed.

Jacques & Luce Bastide
6 route du Stade,
33450 Saint Sulpice et Cameyrac, Gironde
Tel   +33 (0)5 56 30 82 16
Email   chat.lamothe@wanadoo.fr
Web   www.chateaulamotheprincenoir.com

Château de Carbonneau

Big château bedrooms bathed in light, a Napoleon III conservatory for quiet contemplation, gentle pastels over classic dados and big bathrooms gleaming with rich tiles – here is a quiet, self-assured family house and readers are full of praise. Good quality comes naturally, history stalks and there's space aplenty for three young Ferrières and a dozen guests. Outside are delightful grounds with a big fenced pool and 50 hectares of farmland, some of it planted with vines under the appellation Sainte Foy Bordeaux. The rest are used as grazing land for a small herd of Blondes d'Aquitaine. Visit Wilfred's winery and taste the talent handed down by his forebears; you may leave with a case or two. Jacquie, a relaxed but dynamic New Zealander, makes the meals, wields a canny paintbrush and has created a guest sitting room with two smart linen sofas and guide books aplenty. Breakfast is served on the main terrace in summer and Jacquie's dinners, enjoyed with the other guests, sound most tempting – salmon in filo with orange and mint dressing, chicken on a bed of courgettes.

Price	€90-€130.
Rooms	5: 2 doubles, 3 twins/doubles.
Meals	Dinner €25. Wine €8-€20.
Closed	December-February.
Directions	D936 to Castillion la Bataille-Bergerac; from Réaux, right to Gensac, Pessac; at r'bout, D18 to Ste Foy le Gde; 2km on right.

Jacquie Franc de Ferrière
33890 Pessac sur Dordogne,
Gironde
Tel   +33 (0)5 57 47 46 46
Email   carbonneau@orange.fr
Web   www.chateau-carbonneau.com

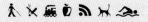

Château de Sanse

You are in Bordeaux wine country looking at a château more Tuscan than 18th-century French. The stunning entrance hall sets the tone: clean lines and a palette of pale creams and whites set off with splashes of mauve – fabulous. No fuss, no swags, only the necessary accessories: a teak desk, a wickerwork sofa strewn with white cushions. The off-white and oatmeal theme continues upstairs with sisal in the corridor and coir in some of the bedrooms — a play of texture rather than colour. Thought has been given to families – triples can be arranged and some rooms interconnect; there's a child-friendly pool and early suppers for the little ones. Most rooms have private balconies with lovely views, big enough to sit out on in comfort. Christian, talented and experienced, heads the kitchen and delivers some inventive dishes, but nothing overly pretentious or complicated. Enjoy such treats as terrine of foie gras *mi-cuit* with spiced bread and pear chutney, and lemon and ginger crème brulée. Peaceful seclusion and a special place – book early in season.

Price	€100–€150. Suites €165–€210.
Rooms	16: 12 twins/doubles, 4 suites.
Meals	Breakfast €12. Lunch from €20. Dinner from €35.
Closed	January–February.
Directions	A10 exit St André de Cubzac to Libourne dir. Castillon La Bataille; D17 right Pujols; D18 left Gensac; D15 right to Coubeyrac. Hotel signed on right.

Christelle Méot
33350 Sainte Radegonde,
Gironde

Tel	+33 (0)5 57 56 41 10
Email	contact@chateaudesanse.com
Web	www.chateaudesanse.com

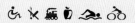

Entry 242   Map 9

Domaine de Sengresse

The characterful entrance hall sets the tone: raw silk dressing windows, a Steinway on a sparkling floor, oil paintings from Michèle's mother. This ravishing 17th-century domaine exudes a rare combination of elegance and rustic charm and, in the manner of the best country hotels, the owners' personality. Michèle and Rob moved from Somerset to the Landes in 2005, are there to look after you but never intrude, and happily share their houseful of riches. You'll love the bedrooms of luxury and light, the calm colours and the exposed beams, the peaceful gardens with hammocks and hidden corners, the elegant breakfasts on the terrace, the candlelit dinners beneath an ecclesiastical chandelier. The food is organic, home-grown, bountiful and delicious (and you may eat romantically à deux if you prefer). Breathtaking parkland surrounds you, there's a long avenue of trees, a pool by the beautiful stone barn and a children's library under the stairs. All this and the lovely Landes, with its markets for foodies and brocanteurs, its surfing dunes for beach bums and its small châteaux at Gaujacq and Amou.

Price	€95–€125. House €670–€1,450 per week.
Rooms	4 + 1: 3 doubles, 1 twin. House for 2–6.
Meals	Dinner with wine, from €25.
Closed	Rarely.
Directions	12km from N124 Dax & Mont de Marsan; exit Tartas for Mugron D924, 4km, right Mugron D332; right at junc. D3 to Mugron. 2nd right Gouts D18; entrance on right after Cap Blanc Kiwi sign.

Michèle & Rob McLusky
& Sasha Ibbotson
Route de Gouts,
40250 Souprosse, Landes

Tel	+33 (0)5 58 97 78 34
Email	sengresse@hotmail.fr
Web	www.sengresse.com

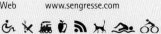

Château des Baudry

Steeped in 500 years of history, the four solid wings of this distinguished château enclose a grand central courtyard where water shimmers and tinkles and tiny fish flit. Entering through the hall, veer to the left for the salon, to the right, through large wood-panelled doors, for the intimate dining room: a room wrapped in blue wallpaper bearing a flower and ribbon motif. Seated at one of the tables, you'll discover that Hélène's wonderful cuisine 'à la grand-mère' is more than delicious; it's a reason to be here. To the north is the Italian-themed orangerie where breakfast is served among terracotta and citrus trees; to the south and east, guest rooms are large, traditional, framed by lofty beams and supported by equally solid stone piers. Fireplaces bring out the earthy colours, the glow of antiques and the softness of cotton and quilted coverings. From bedroom windows, views of formal Italianate gardens and a long drive of hornbeam hedges give way to more untouched countryside, even as pillars by the pool guide the eye to vistas of the Dordogne and Bordeaux landscapes beyond.

Price	€120–€150.
Rooms	4: 1 double, 3 twins/doubles.
Meals	Breakfast €12. Dinner €32. Wine €12–€32.
Closed	Rarely.
Directions	From Bergerac D936 for Bordeaux 12km to Gardonne; left D4 to Saussignac 5km, on D4 for Monestier. Château 2km from Saussignac, on left.

Hélène Boulet & François Passebon
24240 Monestier,
Dordogne
Tel   +33 (0)5 53 23 46 42
Email   chateaudesbaudry@orange.fr
Web   www.chateaudesbaudry.com

Ethical Collection: Environment; Food.
See page 446 for details

Château Les Farcies du Pech'

The neat and tidy winery a mile from Bergerac makes a leafy out-of-town stay. The tone is set by the impeccable cream and French-grey façade: here is a chambres d'hôte that is both elegant and homely. The Dubards, who took over ten years ago, live in a separate wing, work hard at their enterprise and are developing a shop to promote the wine. (You cannot go home empty-handed from one of the oldest vineyards in the world: this predates Bordeaux.) Inside, whitewashed walls rub shoulders with polished timbers, all is immaculate and not a thing out of place. Big, nicely proportioned bedrooms have high ceilings and gleaming floors, pale sponged walls, striped curtains, traditional lamps and the odd choice antique; windowless bath and shower rooms are halygon-lit. White cotton duvet covers trimmed with beige linen have matching pillows, but nothing is busy or overdone. Windows overlook gentle parkland and grazing deer, all feels settled, there's no one to rush you at breakfast and Madame Vidalencq, your courteous hostess, helps you plan your day.

Price	€100.
Rooms	5 doubles.
Meals	Restaurants nearby.
Closed	November-March.
Directions	From Bergerac N21 to Périgueux; right after Centre Leclerc. Signed 'Les Farcies'.

Serge Dubard
Les Farcies, 24100 Bergerac,
Dordogne

Tel	+33 (0)5 53 82 48 31
Email	vignobles-dubard@wanadoo.fr
Web	www.vignoblesdubard.com

Château Les Merles

The 19th-century French façade conceals an interior of Dutch minimalism suffused with light. Old and stylish new march hand in hand and a Dutch chef heads the kitchen bringing skill and finesse to the cooking: great spit roasts, Bergerac wines, fresh vegetables from the organic garden. A rustic-chic bistro (Philippe Starck chairs on charming old flags), a restaurant in the stables, two light-streamed sitting rooms, a bucolic nine-hole golf course to one side… A golfers' haven it is, but everyone would love it here. This family-run hotel – two sisters in charge – brims with generosity and professionalism. A black and white theme runs throughout – matt-black beds, white bedspreads, black frames, white lamp shades, black towels, white roses – the austerity offset by a rich gilt-framed mirror or a fuchsia fauteuil. Outside is a vast gravelled courtyard with striking white dining chairs and black parasols, a terrace looks south to the shimmering pool and the hills are braided with vines. Civilised, classy, welcoming. *Children's daycare available by arrangement.*

Price	€120-€160. Single €100-€145. Suites €150-€215. Apartment €220-€310.
Rooms	15: 11 twins/doubles, 1 single, 2 suites, 1 apartment for 4.
Meals	Breakfast €15. Lunch & dinner €20-€42.50.
Closed	Never.
Directions	From Bergerac D660 for Sarlat. At Tuilières, left onto D36 for Pressignac. Château 800m.

Judith Wagemakers
Tuilières, 24520 Mouleydier,
Dordogne

Tel	+33 (0)5 53 63 13 42
Email	info@lesmerles.com
Web	www.lesmerles.com

La Métairie

If you love horses you'll be in your element: you can relax on the terrace and watch them in the next field. You can also ride close by. La Métairie was built as a farm at the turn of the last century and converted into a hotel some 40 years ago, a U-shaped building smothered in wisteria and Virginia creeper. There's no road in sight and you really do feel 'away from it all' – yet the Dordogne and its cliff top villages are minutes away. Borrow bikes if you're feeling energetic! Bedrooms are small but cheerful, full of sunshiney yellows; beds are huge. They have room for a couple of comfy chairs, too. Bathrooms match – large and cheerful – and three ground-floor rooms have French doors and a semi-private patio. The pool is big enough for a proper swim and when you come out you can read under the trees – there are plenty right by the pool. In summer you can eat out here, or on the flowery terrace. The dining room has black and white floors, washed stone walls and well-spaced tables. Go ahead, indulge, order the four-course Périgourdine menu. You can swim it off later.

Price	€125–€160. Suite €190–€270. Half-board mandatory in high season; €48 extra p.p.
Rooms	10: 9 doubles, 1 suite.
Meals	Breakfast €16. Lunch €12–€50. Dinner €41; Périgourdine menu €50. Wine €25–€100.
Closed	November–March.
Directions	From Lalinde, D703 for Le Bugue. At Sauveboeuf, D31 through Mauzac; signed.

	M. Johner
	24150 Mauzac et Grand Castang, Dordogne
Tel	+33 (0)5 53 22 50 47
Email	metairie.la@wanadoo.fr
Web	www.la-metairie.com

Hôtel Les Glycines

Les Glycines has been providing lodging since 1862, when it was a *relais de poste*; Prince Charles stayed in the 60s with his Cambridge tutor. Sitting at the far end of town, in its own idyllic grounds near the river, it has been enlarged over the years with a swathe of new rooms in the old stables. Just past reception is a dining room that runs the breadth of the building, with views onto lush gardens planted by the son of a head gardener at Versailles. Meander down to the pool under arches laden with roses and honeysuckle or visit the flourishing potager. The Lombards took over ten years ago, threw themselves into decoration and have added a couple of panoramic terraces. Expect superb service from Monsieur and Madame and their close-knit team. Pascal leads the way in the kitchen, one of his specialities being roast veal with local ham and truffled polenta; the menus are rich, fabulous and matched by very good wines. The newest rooms ooze luxury and charm – natural fabrics, dreamy colours. The quietest are away from the busy road, the interconnecting rooms are perfect for families.

Price	€86–€162. Suites €186–€232. Extra bed €28.
Rooms	24: 17 twins/doubles, 7 suites.
Meals	Breakfast €14. Picnic lunch €10–€15. Lunch €19–€28. Dinner €39–€95. Restaurant closed Monday lunchtimes.
Closed	November–Easter.
Directions	From Périgueux, D47 to Sarlat. Over river, on left immediately before Les Eyzies station.

Pascal Lombard
4 avenue de Laugerie,
24620 Les Eyzies de Tayac, Dordogne
Tel   +33 (0)5 53 06 97 07
Email   glycines.dordogne@wanadoo.fr
Web   www.les-glycines-dordogne.com

Auberge de la Salvetat

Locals believe this area to be 'saved land' and there are 12th-century church ruins on the estate that pre-date the cloisters at Cadouin down the road. Part of the building that makes up the restaurant and some bedrooms was the presbytery and the views from the terrace are sublime: across the woods and pastures with not another building in sight. Bedrooms are not huge but perfectly comfortable and have terraces; those in the main house are the best and one has a mezzanine – good for families. The restaurant with its beamed and covered terrace is now overseen by Fabien, a chef with a local reputation for excellent, French country cooking, and Ann still makes the puddings. She and Steve are loving their change of career and everything is done with a smile; there's not a trace of pomposity here. Children will adore the space to play in the pretty gardens and the good-sized swimming pool; you may have to tear them away to do any sightseeing but there are some exciting water sports in the area and a different market almost every day. Walkers will be happy too: routes run from the door.

Price	€79-€95.
Rooms	14: 7 doubles, 3 twins, 4 family rooms for 3.
Meals	Breakfast €10. Lunch & dinner €20-€36. Wine €15-€30. Restaurant closed Sunday eve & Monday lunchtimes.
Closed	November-23 March.
Directions	2km from Cadouin on the Belvès road.

Steven & Ann Jordan
Route de Belvès,
24480 Cadouin, Dordogne
Tel   +33 (0)5 53 63 42 79
Email   contact@lasalvetat.com
Web   www.lasalvetat.com

Hôtel Edward 1er

Some people lie around the pool on their honeymoon; Arjan and Marije went hotel hunting on theirs. And they found one: a handsome 19th-century townhouse in a village voted one of the most beautiful in France. Now they are settled in nicely. Herbs are from the garden, vegetables and fruit are local, fish hales from Bordeaux and Arcachon; all is homemade here except bread and ice cream, and these are supplied by artisans. Marije creates the menus and has chosen mostly regional wines – Bergerac, Cahors, Monbazillac – to accompany the foie gras and duck cuisine. After you have explored the miraculously preserved 13th-century village, the four-sided fortress around a central square, the surrounding houses corbelled out with arches, the perfectly straight streets leading out from each side, you may want to compare Monpazier with the other medieval bastides; there are a dozen or so. Arjan has prepared bicycle itineraries and can point out the best place to paddle a canoe. Or you may just want to lounge around the pool, honeymoon-style! Romantic rooms await.

Price	€68-€184.
Rooms	12: 6 doubles, 5 twins, 1 single.
Meals	Breakfast €12. Dinner €29.50-€37.50. Wine €19-€50.
Closed	Mid-November to mid-March.
Directions	From St Cyprien D703 dir. Bergerac; left on D710 to Belvès; D53 to Monpazier.

Arjan & Marije Capelle
5 rue St Pierre,
24540 Monpazier, Dordogne

Tel	+33 (0)5 53 22 44 00
Email	info@hoteledward1er.com
Web	www.hoteledward1er.com

Le Prieuré du Château de Biron

The imposing Château de Biron, tossed back and forth between the English and the French for centuries, sits regally atop the highest point of the village, visible from miles around. Below and behind it is the church which gazes over the little village and hidden behind that, this 16th-century priory. Through the gate, across a tiny cobblestone courtyard, an ornate knocker on the nail-studded door sets a tone of enchantment. The original stone floor in the hallway under a low beamed ceiling leads to an elegant curved staircase. You can still see the original stone cooker and sink in the delightfully cosy living area; a door leads to the garden with heavenly views across the fields. Fireplaces take pride of place in the huge rooms on the first floor, along with exposed stone walls, the glow of antiques, fine linens and subtle colours of powder blue and pale gold. Rafters fly through the mostly white rooms under the roof, the views are stunning as are the bathrooms, double sinks and fluffy robes throughout. Harmonious, rich, elegant, welcoming, not to be missed. *Children over 12 welcome.*

Price	€120–€160. Apartment €950–€1,130 per week.
Rooms	5 + 1: 3 doubles, 2 family rooms for 3. Apartment for 3.
Meals	Dinner €25. Restaurant 50m.
Closed	Mid-November to April.
Directions	From St Cyprien, D703 dir. Bergerac; left on D710 to Belvès; D53 to Monpazier; D2 dir. Villeréal for 5km, left on D53 for Biron. Parking below château.

	Elisabeth Vedier Le Bourg, 24540 Biron, Dordogne
Tel	+33 (0)9 60 47 46 07
Email	leprieurebiron@yahoo.com
Web	www.leprieurebiron.com

Hôtel Clément V

In the pedestrianised old quarter of lovely lively Belves, a sturdy stone façade conceals a fetching little hotel. All nooks, crannies, twists and turns, it oozes history and character throughout: now the old stable block, linking the two main wings, has been colourwashed, opened up and sprinkled with lemon trees. Highly distinctive bedrooms range from those in the medieval vaults – including the moody, magical, atmospheric Papal Suite – to the lovely light-filled Abbess's Room that opens to a private terrace. Then there's Pierrot's Garret, its antique brass bed tucked under the rafters, Robert's Bachelor Pad (virtually a suite), and the family-spacious, coir-carpeted Tour d'Ivoire with a glowing mahogany bed and views of countryside that (to quote Henry Miller) is "close on earth to heaven". For winter cosiness there's a wood-burner in the conservatory and a vastly atmospheric fireplace in the salon; for summer, a pretty walled garden with twirly breakfast chairs and gay parasols. Come for truffle-hunting weekends and horse riding breaks – and châteaux by the hatful.

Price	€120–€180. Suites €200.
Rooms	10: 6 doubles, 1 twin, 3 suites.
Meals	Breakfast €12. Restaurant 100m.
Closed	Rarely.
Directions	From Bergerac D660 then D29; D710 to Belves. Hotel in town centre.

Muriel Fischer
15 rue Jacques Manchotte,
24170 Belvés, Dordogne

Tel	+33 (0)5 53 28 68 80
Email	contact@clement5.com
Web	www.clement5.com

La Villa Romaine

The 19th-century farmhouse and its two outbuildings are planted solidly in the ground; their neatly fitted limestone walls glow in the sun. They partially surround a vast courtyard that leads down to an infinity pool – and a wow of a view that sweeps the eye over Druid forests, green hills and a perched village on a cliff across the way. Plumb in the middle of the courtyard is an open-sided structure, once called the Halle aux Saumons; we now can only imagine the river running below, flowing silver with fish. Fine dining here, on fish or fowl, is the attraction, as well as the restaurant itself. It's a long airy room with beams and timbers, with a bar and a comfortable little sitting area with armchairs, some draped in pale linen, at the far end. Crisp white tablecloths set off sparkling table settings; French windows bring light and lead to a large terrace. Rooms, some in the outbuildings, some above the restaurant, are huge; the family suite with two bedrooms sleeps six. A choice of eight breakfast teas might give a clue to what is in store.

Price	€110–€160. Duplex €185–€250. Family suite €220–€300. Triples €160–€190.
Rooms	17: 12 twins/doubles, 1 duplex for 2-4, 1 family suite for 4-6, 3 triples.
Meals	Breakfast €13–€15. Dinner from €29. Restaurant closed mid-November to April.
Closed	Never.
Directions	From Sarlat to Gourdon & Cahors 6km. Signed.

David Vacelet & Emilie Velut
Saint Rome,
24200 Carsac Aillac, Dordogne

Tel	+33 (0)5 53 28 52 07
Email	contact@lavillaromaine.com
Web	www.lavillaromaine.com

Le Relais du Touron

Such a nice approach up the drive lined with box hedges and spiræa, surrounded by lawns and handsome trees. The reception is in the family house while all rooms and the dining room are now in the converted barn and stable block with the pool just below. A fireplace in the dining area keeps a cheery flame but in summer everyone gathers on the terrace under an open-sided timbered roof; the pool and garden beyond are flooded with light in the evening. Philippe and Chantal have built up a solid reputation for good, interesting food; choose the five-course half-board menu or go à la carte. Bedrooms have park and pool views and are decorated in straightforward style: plain carpets, bright bedcovers and curtains, decent lighting; bathrooms are sparkling new with handsome basins. The nearby road is well screened by thick trees and shrubs; indeed, the three-hectare garden, which also contains a small pond, is a great asset with lots of private corners to be explored. A delightful path of six kilometres will take you by foot or by bike right into Sarlat. Low-key, excellent value with a wonderful family welcome.

Price	€53–€69. Family room €96–€115.
Rooms	18: 12 doubles, 5 twins, 1 family room for 4.
Meals	Breakfast €9. Lunch & dinner €17.50–€36.
Closed	5 November–March.
Directions	From Sarlat D704 to Gourdon. Hotel signed on right before Carsac.

Viala Family
Le Touron,
24200 Carsac Aillac, Dordogne

Tel	+33 (0)5 53 28 16 70
Email	contact@lerelaisdutouron.com
Web	www.lerelaisdutouron.com

Auberge de Castel Merle

On the edge of a charming hamlet, a hidden paradise, a small inn atop a limestone knob that once held a castle of the Knights Templar. It has been in Anita's family for five generations; her archaeologist grandfather added stones from his own digs (Eyzies, the capital of prehistory, is nearby). Husband Christopher is also devoted to this atmospheric place and they have renovated the old buildings with consummate care, keeping the traditional look and using walnut from their land to restore bedheads and doors. Christopher is enthusiastic truffle hunter and head chef; this is wild boar country and 'sanglier' is one of his specialities. Flowery curtains, pelmets and painted flowers on the walls prettify the dining room; bedrooms have an unfussy country look: Provençal prints, stone walls. Some rooms overlook the courtyard, others the woods. As for the views: the glory of the place is its position, high above the valley of the Vézère with river, forests and castles beyond – best admired from a check-clothed table on the large leafy terrace. Hiking in the forests is a joy. *French lessons on request.*

Price	€45–€58.
Rooms	8: 7 doubles, 1 twin.
Meals	Breakfast €8. Dinner €15–€27. Half-board only in August. Restaurant closed lunchtimes.
Closed	October–March.
Directions	A89 to Montignac, then D706 for Les Eyzies. At Thonac left over bridge then right to Sergeac; signed.

Anita Castanet &
Christopher Millinship
24290 Sergeac, Dordogne

Tel	+33 (0)5 53 50 70 08
Email	hotelcastelmerle@yahoo.fr
Web	www.hotelcastelmerle.com

Hostellerie Les Griffons

The setting is impossibly lovely. Discover a handsome 16th-century house, once a mill, by a medieval bridge over the Dronne, irresistibly inviting with pale shutters… and town and château views that tip the dream beyond reality. One look at the website and you want to be there. Many of the old features have been nurtured – the big stone fireplaces, the lovely old windows; every beautifully decorated room has a medieval flavour. Some may find the mood on the first floor a touch sombre, though colours are fashionably bold; on the second, windows and timbers are white. From most bedrooms the views are special; bathrooms are fine rather than magnificent; local paintings add personality. You dine and breakfast stylishly by the river's edge in summer, a place where you would long to picnic if you were just passing through. The restaurant is superb (and the owner's son a pastry chef). Bourdeilles, downriver from lovely, summer-touristy Brantôme – 'Venice of the Perigord' – is enchanting. Come to be spoiled by Jacques, Frédérique and excellent staff, who treat guests as valued friends.

Price	€90–€115. Family rooms €135.
Rooms	10: 6 doubles, 2 twins, 2 family rooms for 3.
Meals	Breakfast €12. Lunch & dinner €30–€40. Wine €23–€60.
Closed	November–31 March.
Directions	From Périgueux dir. Angoulême; just before Brantôme, left for Bourdeilles (medieval village) for 5km. Hotel in village centre.

Frédérique & Jacques Dauba
24310 Bourdeilles, Dordogne

Tel	+33 (0)5 53 45 45 35
Email	info@griffons.fr
Web	www.griffons.fr

Entry 256   Map 9

Château Le Mas de Montet

A nose for fine living brought English owners Richard and John to this happy place. At the end of an avenue guarded by plane trees – serenely, gloriously French – is the château, slate-topped and turretted in Renaissance style. Once frequented by Mitterrand and his labradors – one suite is named in his honour – it has been extravagantly restored. Reception rooms lined with eau-de-nil brocade are sated with auction house finds, richness and softness bring instant seduction and bedrooms, named after Corneille, Voltaire, Madame de Lafayette, have all you'd hope for the price (British electrical sockets included!). Beds are big and supremely comfortable, four-posters canopied and draped, bathrooms Deco-white… the one in the tower has its own chandelier. Copious breakfasts are buffet style in the orangery restaurant. Later, dine in: the food is Perigordian and exquisite. Doors open in summer to a big terrace and 50 hectares of parkland with pool. Grand yet easy, this is the perfect place for stressed city souls to unwind… uncommercial, full of charm, heaped with readers' praise.

Price	€175–€225. Suites €225–€395.
Rooms	10: 4 doubles, 1 twin, 5 suites.
Meals	Breakfast €16. Lunch €20. Dinner €45. Wine €28–€135.
Closed	Never.
Directions	A10 then N10 to Angoulême, south towards Libourne, then Montmoreau, then Aubeterre. Signed on D2 & D20 between Aubeterre & Ribérac.

John Ridley & Richard Stimson
Petit Bersac,
24600 Ribérac, Dordogne

Tel	+33 (0)5 53 90 08 71
Email	reception@lemasdemontet.com
Web	www.lemasdemontet.com

Entry 257   Map 9

La Roseraie

Built as the country residence for a Parisian family, it is now a sparkling hotel. Experienced, enthusiastic hoteliers, the Nourrissons have brought their good chef with them. Pretty dining rooms dotted with yellow-clothed tables and posies set the scene for celery and truffle millefeuille and braised guinea fowl with pumpkin and chestnuts; such is their devotion to food there is an 'Initiation à la Gourmandise' menu for children. In summer you spill onto a terrace edged with clipped box… which leads to a garden of mature trees, roses and 19th-century formality, and a delicious palm-fringed pool. The gardens edge the river, prone to flood in winter (one good reason why La Roseraie closes in November). Bedrooms, comfortably pattern-carpeted with traditional furniture soon to be updated, have sweet river and garden views, while two apartments sit privately across the square revealing an unusual mix of the rustic and the frou-frou: fine old beams, stone walls, rococo-style chairs and a fancy four-poster. Medieval Montignac has it all – including the caves at Lascaux.

Price	€78–€130. Family rooms €140–€170. Apartments €270. Half-board €80–€150 p.p.
Rooms	16: 7 doubles, 3 twins, 4 family rooms for 4, 2 apartments for 4.
Meals	Breakfast €13. Lunch from €23. Dinner €24–€50. Wine €18–€75. Half-board only July & August.
Closed	November-Easter.
Directions	A20 & A89 to La Bachellerie; dir. Montignac, then Montignac centre.

Vincent & Isabelle Nourrisson
11 Place d'Armes,
24290 Montignac Lascaux, Dordogne
Tel   +33 (0)5 53 50 53 92
Email   hotelroseraie@wanadoo.fr
Web   www.laroseraie-hotel.com

La Commanderie

Off the medieval street, through the stone archway and the lightly-treed gardens, into the steep-roofed *commanderie*. The Commanders of the Order of Malta put up here 700 years ago en route to Santiago de Compostella and a low curved toll passage still forms part of the house, its black slate slabs gloriously intact. This is not so much a hotel as a houseful of guests overseen by diminutive Madame, a correct but considerate hostess. An uncontrived collection of antiques warms the friendly bedrooms, each with its own personality – convent-white walls are set off by touches of dark blue, ceilings soar, floors of varying ages and patterns are softened by Indian rugs, maybe there's a crucifix or a pink glass chandelier. Downstairs, guests gather at round tables set with antique cane chairs, floral curtains hang at tall windows and you get two choices per gastronomic course – just right for this unassuming, atmospheric place. There's a pool in the shade of the cedars and the Lascaux Caves are a mile down the road.

Price	€85.
Rooms	7: 5 doubles, 2 twins.
Meals	Breakfast €10. Lunch €20-€45. Dinner €25-€48. Restaurant closed Mondays.
Closed	Rarely.
Directions	N89 between Brive & Périgueux. At x-roads at Lardin, towards Condat, right to La Commanderie. Hotel 50m after church.

Mme Annick Roux
245 Condat sur Vezère, Dordogne
Tel   +33 (0)5 53 51 26 49
Email   hotellacommanderie@wanadoo.fr

Moulin de Vigonac

Wedge-shaped, like the prow of a ship, is this rare, immaculately renovated, 16th-century mill. It houses a little family restaurant where Monsieur does the cooking, Madame the serving and their son is front of house, all with charm. Over the bridge and on the parasoled terrace guests enjoy fresh, tasty, unpretentious food surrounded by water and ducks: avocado with crayfish tails, omelette aux truffes, rib of veal with wild mushrooms. In two wisteria-clad buildings ten bedrooms lie, light, airy, contemporary and positioned for maximum privacy. As perfectly executed as you'd expect, some have balconies, others terraces; all have superb mattresses, neutral colours and river views. Bathrooms are state of the art, the swishest with marble floors. Relax in summer surrounded by large lawns and formal terraced gardens, birds, butterflies and elegant trees. Slip into the pool, recline on a striped sunlounger. Watery, willowy Brantôme, stocked with tourists in summer, is a five-minute drive – hire a canoe and escape downriver, to unspoiled little Bourdeilles and its fortress-château.

Price	€120-€270.
Rooms	10: 6 doubles, 4 suites. Some rooms interconnect.
Meals	Breakfast €15. Dinner €45-€65.
Closed	Rarely.
Directions	From Poitiers D939 dir. Périgueux; right at r'bout; immediately right into Moulin. Signed.

Alexeline Family
24310 Brantôme, Dordogne
Tel   +33 (0)5 53 05 87 59
Email   contact@moulindevigonac.com
Web   www.moulindevigonac.com

Le Chatenet

Brantôme has been home to man since prehistoric times. The grand Benedictine abbey, carved out at the bottom of the cliffs, overlooks the ribbon of the river Dronne that slowly circles the town. Just up the road, a perfect distance from the hustle and bustle, is Le Chatenet, a Périgord style stone-built house conceived at the end of the 17th century. Jane will show you the sundial they found under the roof marked 1688, William will point the way to the hidden canopy of trees over a path which leads to the centre of town in a ten-minute stroll. Or you may just want to sit on the stone veranda and follow the sun as it sinks pinkly over the walnut trees and green valleys. There are big rooms with stunning fabric on the walls, billiards in the games room, rivers to be canoed and grottos to be explored. There is even a farm down the street with rabbits, chickens and cows, source of your breakfast eggs and milk. Jane and William are super hosts. Brantôme's bell tower is thought to be one of the oldest in France; they say it must be seen from the inside. Add an extra day, you won't regret it.

Price	€110-€135. Suites €135-€175. Extra bed €25.
Rooms	5: 3 twins/doubles, 2 suites.
Meals	Breakfast €12. Restaurant 1km.
Closed	Mid-December to February.
Directions	From Périgueux, D939 to Brantôme; left on D78 for l'Abbaye dir. Bourdeilles; road looks like it ends but cont. on; Le Chatenet 1km out of town. Signed.

Jane & William Laxton
Brantôme,
24310 Périgord, Dordogne
Tel   +33 (0)5 53 05 81 08
Email   lechatenet@gmail.com
Web   www.lechatenet.com

Domaine du Moulin de Labique

Ducks on the pond, goats in the greenhouse and food *à la grande-mère* on the plate – the Domaine glows with warmth and good humour. Shutters are painted with *bleu de pastel* and the 13th-century interiors have lost none of their charm. The new Belgian owners, Christine and Patrick, share dinners (seasonal, local, delicious) in wonderfully relaxed fashion. Bedrooms are a match for the rest of the place and are divided between those in the main building above a vaulted *salle d'armes*, those in the barn, reached via a grand stone stair, and an apartment in the old bread and prune-drying ovens. There are chunky roof beams, seagrass mats on ancient tiles, lovely old iron bedsteads, antique mirrors and papers sprigged in raspberry and jade green. One room has a balcony, the apartment in the barn has a terrace, and some bathrooms have Portuguese tiles: there's much to captivate and delight. Outside, old French roses, young alleys of trees, a bamboo-fringed stream and an exquisite, child-safe pool. Book a long stay, and make time for tastings at the Monbazillac domaines. *Cooking courses in winter.*

Price	€110–€135. Suite €170.
Rooms	6: 3 doubles, 1 twins, 1 apartment for 4.
Meals	Dinner €27. Wine €19–€30.
Closed	Rarely.
Directions	From Cancon N21; D124 for Monflanquin; D153 at Beauregard to St Vivien; on right 1km after St Vivien.

Patrick & Christine Hendricx
St Vivien,
47210 Villeréal, Lot-et-Garonne
Tel   +33 (0)5 53 01 63 90
Email   moulin-de-labique@wanadoo.fr
Web   www.moulin-de-labique.fr

Entry 262   Map 9

Domaine de Pine

Tucked away in 52 acres of rambling cornfields and sweeping woodland lies this beautifully proportioned, pale-stone house. Built for a baron two centuries ago, it's been transformed by an easy-going English couple with impeccable taste into a haven of luxurious comfort and period style. Cathy looks after the 'art du table': at tables adorned with flowers and fine china her breakfasts are fresh and tasty; indulge and ask for smoked salmon and champagne. Soft creams and whites dominate in elegant bedrooms, large and light with beamed ceilings and great views. In winter, perhaps after a day on the slopes, cosy up next to a roaring fire before treating yourself to a specially prepared supper in the gorgeous candlelit blue and white dining room. Summertime calls for lazing on sumptuous wicker loungers, spoiled by exquisite poolside nibbles and a scrumptious dinner on the terrace; views reach to valley and woods beyond. Two spacious courtyard cottages, originally servants' quarters, are available to rent. Step out for medieval town markets, music festivals, horse riding and walks in the grounds – tons of choice.

Price	€80–€175.
	Cottages €595–€1,250 per week.
Rooms	3 + 2: 3 doubles. 2 cottages for 2.
Meals	Breakfast €15. Lunch & dinner by arrangement, from €35.
Closed	Rarely.
Directions	A62 exit to Agen; D656 to Cahors; 25km after St Victor, right, signed Pine; house 1km down road.

Marcus & Cathy Becker
47470 Blaymont,
Lot-et-Garonne

Tel	+33 (0)5 53 66 44 93
Email	ddp@qmh.co.uk
Web	www.ddpine.com

Villa Le Goëland

From the wonderful family bedroom is a *tour d'observation* with the finest view in Biarritz. Villa le Goëland is lush, lavish and inviting. Dominating the ocean, yards from the beaches of glamorous Biarritz, the only privately owned villa of its kind to have resisted commercial redevelopment has opened its arms to guests. Turrets were added in 1903; Paul's family took possession in 1934; now he and his wife, young, charming, professional, are its inspired guardians and restorers. They live in an apartment upstairs and know all there is to know about the pleasures of Biarritz: casino, museums, boutiques, golf, spa. Be ravished by oak floors, magnificent stairs and sunshine-filled balconies that go on for ever; the salon and dining room each have one so fling open the tall French windows. Bedrooms, not cosy but lofty, are panelled and parquet'd, beds are king-size, two suites have terraces, bathrooms date from the 1900s to the 1960s, and breakfasts flourish sunshine and *viennoiseries*, served by Paul with a smile. The final touch: a private parking space for every guest, a godsend in this town.

Price	€150–€270.
Rooms	4: 3 doubles, 1 suite for 3.
Meals	Restaurant 20m.
Closed	November–February.
Directions	From Place Clémençeau in Biarritz centre follow signs for place Ste Eugénie by Rue Mazagran; after pharmacy 1st right Rue des Goélands. House between antique shop & bar, narrow street.

Paul & Elisabeth Daraignez
12 plateau Atalaye,
64200 Biarritz, Pyrénées-Atlantiques
Tel   +33 (0)5 59 24 25 76
Email   info@villagoeland.com
Web   www.villagoeland.com

Maison Garnier

In glamorous Biarritz, playground of royalty and stars, a jewel of sophisticated simplicity. Pristine-white bathrooms have huge showerheads, bedrooms are in off-white, eggshell, cocoa and coffee – and the occasional splash of brilliant colour. The bright breakfast room has Basque floorboards, pale walls, red and white stripes; white linen is a perfect foil for lovely regional tableware in a red and green stripe, and light pours in from great (double-glazed) windows. In 1999 the former boarding house was turned into this smart, hospitable little hotel. There's no hall counter or reception, just a gorgeous wrought-iron stair rail, a 1930s-feel salon with a deep sofa, an original fireplace and a huge oriental carpet – the tone is set the moment you arrive. In 2008 new owners arrived, a delightful pair, interested and interesting, who always dreamed of a hotel by the sea. And the position is superb, on the lively Rue Gambetta, a five-minute walk from the famous surfing beaches, walking distance to everything. A calm relaxing place to stay, a retreat from the street. Book early.

Price	€100–€170.
Rooms	7: 5 doubles, 2 twins.
Meals	Breakfast €10. Restaurants 50m.
Closed	Rarely.
Directions	From A63 exit Biarritz & La Négresse for Centre Ville & Place Clémenceau. Straight ahead for large, white bank building with clock; left onto Rue Gambetta. Free parking on side street.

Joanne Veillot & Patrick Chacoris
29 rue Gambetta,
64200 Biarritz, Pyrénées-Atlantiques

Tel   +33 (0)5 59 01 60 70
Email   maison-garnier@hotel-biarritz.com
Web   www.hotel-biarritz.com

Arguibel

Guéthary is one of the Basque's best-kept secrets. The beaches are charming, the coastal walks breathtaking, there are friendly bars and an artistic history; Debussy, Ravel and Chaplin spent heady summers here. A mile outside the village (with restaurants – but you will need a car), behind a conventional and modest façade, is this surprisingly theatrical hotel, whose boutiquey flourishes are the right side of kitsch and whose bathrooms are pure works of art. Art Deco furniture, 18th-century toile de Jouy, 21st-century sculpture and rock 'n' roll memorabilia inhabit the same space, yet create an astonishingly harmonious whole. Each large bedroom and suite (four reached via the sweeping stair) has its own cocooning luxury (iPods etc) and a balcony with an unbroken view, of rolling hills and mountains beyond. In spite of the vast salon, the chic library/bar, the separate tables at breakfast, there's a personal mood. Fifteen minutes up the coast is grand old Biarritz, paradise for surfers and chic shoppers; south, the atmospheric 'vieille ville' of the port of St Jean de Luz.

Price	€110-€200. Suites €190-€270.
Rooms	5: 3 doubles, 2 suites.
Meals	Breakfast €15. Restaurants 1km.
Closed	5 January-13 February.
Directions	From Biarritz airport, D810 dir. St Jean-de-Luz. At Guéthary follow signs for 'La Table des Frères Ibarboure'. Entrance to Arguibel 50m after 'La Table...' on right.

François Blasselle
1146 chemin de Laharraga,
64210 Guéthary, Pyrénées-Atlantiques

Tel	+33 (0)5 59 41 90 46
Email	contact@arguibel.fr
Web	www.arguibel.fr

Château d'Urtubie

Urtubie is old, very old: built in 1341 with permission from Edward III. The keep is still intact, except for the roof that was changed in 1654 to resemble Versailles. Your host Laurent, generous, charming, passionate about his home, is a direct descendant of the builder of the castle, Martin de Tartas. The castle is classified and even operates as a (fascinating) museum: *The Antiques Roadshow* could run an entire series here. Laurent opened his château hotel in 1996. The whole place is friendly, charming and that includes the rooms, reached by stair or discreet lift. On the first floor are the 'prestige' rooms, light and airy, grand and imposing, in keeping with the age and style. On the second floor are the 'charm' bedrooms, slightly smaller but equally inviting. Bathrooms are a mix of ancient and modern. On the outskirts of this pretty little Basque town, and a five-minute drive from the beach, Urtubie is a sweet retreat in formal gardens with a super pool. Don't be worried it might be stuffy: Laurent couldn't be easier or more welcoming.

Price	€75–€160.
Rooms	10: 1 double, 8 twins/doubles, 1 single.
Meals	Breakfast €11. Restaurant 500m.
Closed	3 November–March.
Directions	A63 Bayonne & St Sebastien, exit St Jean de Luz Sud; 1st on left, N10 for Urrugne. Right just before r'bout entering Urrugne. 3km from St Jean de Luz.

Laurent de Coral
Urrugne, 64122 Saint Jean de Luz,
Pyrénées-Atlantiques

Tel	+33 (0)5 59 54 31 15
Email	chateaudurtubie@wanadoo.fr
Web	www.chateaudurtubie.fr

Les Almadies

On a very pretty shopping street in Saint Jean de Luz, a cool little find. From the discreet street entrance off the tree- and flower-filled square to the understatedly modern furnishings, all is calm, relaxing and quietly stylish. Jean Jacques and Patricia, a young friendly couple, have an eye for clean lines and harmony. The breakfast room – wooden floor, Philippe Starck-style chairs – is a lovely bright space in which to start the day; take your fill of fresh fruits, compotes, yogurts, cheeses and pastries. If it's sunny, eat out on the decked terrace overlooking that charming square. Carpeted, double-glazed bedrooms with fans, the best with (tiny) balconies overlooking the square, have an easy-going simplicity – soft colours, broderie bed covers, white-painted furniture. Bathrooms are a gleaming mix of wood and white tiles. Spend the day at the beach, take the ferry to Bilbao and the Guggenheim, or stay put and explore this lovely old Basque border port. No dinners but wonderful restaurants close by. A simple, stylish spot in the heart of buzzy, busy Saint Jean, run by a brilliant team.

Price	€90–€130.
Rooms	7: 4 doubles, 1 single, 2 triples.
Meals	Breakfast €12. Restaurants in town.
Closed	One month from 11 November.
Directions	In Saint Jean de Luz follow signs for Centre Ville & La Poste; with La Poste on your left, 2nd right on Rue d'Esslissagaraiy which becomes Rue du Midi. New underground parking close by.

Jean Jacques Hargous
58 rue Gambetta, 64500 Saint Jean de Luz,
Pyrénées-Atlantiques
Tel   +33 (0)5 59 85 34 48
Email   hotel.lesalmadies@wanadoo.fr
Web   www.hotel-les-almadies.com

Hôtel Laminak

Smiling and relaxed, Philippe and Chantal are enchanted with their small hotel, the result of a long-cherished dream. They should be: seven years on, it's both intimate and stylish. The setting is delightful too, with all the lush greenery of the Basque countryside at your feet, and mountain views. The hotel is on a quiet road outside the village of Arbonne, with a few discreetly screened neighbours and a big handsome garden filled with mature shrubs and trees; lovely to be served breakfast outside in summer. Rooms are crisp and fresh, a pleasing mix of antique and modern, with harmonious colours and bright walls; we especially like the three opening onto the garden. Above all we like the friendliness and sense of humour of Philippe and Chantal. Settle by the pool in summer and by the open fire in winter, warmed by the easy comfort of the place as you sink into a big bright cushion-strewn sofa. It's a ten-minute hop to the best surfing coast in Europe and the heady charm of Biarritz – and the mountains are worth a week's effort in themselves. Just below them, fish await your line.

Price	€73-€103. Children under two free.
Rooms	12 twins/doubles.
Meals	Breakfast €10. Light dinner €11-€17; book ahead.
Closed	Rarely.
Directions	A63 exit 4 La Négresse & follow signs to Arbonne; signed.

Philippe & Chantal Basin
Route de St Pée,
64210 Arbonne,
Pyrénées-Atlantiques
Tel   +33 (0)5 59 41 95 40
Email   info@hotel-laminak.com
Web   www.hotel-laminak.com

La Maison de Navarre

Two donkeys graze the family's field, beyond which Sauveterre's old rooftops can be seen, against a snow-crested Pyrenean backdrop. Off an unbusy main road, behind the immaculately renovated 18th-century façade, all is comfort and light. Cecile has a love of gentle colours – soft ochres, sage greens, aqua blues – and has picked works by local artists to grace her pastel palette. She speaks good English and makes a charming hostess, while Philippe is the genius backstage. Irresistible aromas float across the garden from the kitchen; the cuisine is a major feature of this small, professionally run hotel and the 18-cover restaurant is loved by the locals. Menus are regional, produce is from the kitchen garden, and the chef's chocolate gâteau with Espelette peppers is a delicious example of his creativity. The lovely spa town of Salies de Bearn is a ten-minute drive, the neighbouring river bounces with salmon and the twice-weekly markets are a pleasure (don't miss the local sheep's cheese, brebis). Return to a garden with a pretty pool – and crisp bedrooms not huge but cosy, each with a spotless bathroom.

Price	€60-€79. Triple €83-€96.
Rooms	7: 5 doubles (2 interconnect), 1 twin, 1 triple.
Meals	Breakfast €8. Lunch & dinner €18.50-€35. Wine €12-€35. Children's meals €10.
Closed	November; 22 February-7 March.
Directions	A64 exit 7; 12km to Sauveterre-de-Bearn; D933. Signed.

Cécile & Philippe Champion
Quartier Saint-Marc,
64390 Sauveterre de Beam,
Pyrénées-Atlantiques

Tel	+33 (0)5 59 38 55 28
Email	infos@lamaisondenavarre.com
Web	www.lamaisondenavarre.com

Entry 270   Map 13

Château de Méracq

Madame will give you a warm welcome in excellent English and is always happy to help or just to chat. She is very proud of her château, her dog, her hens and her husband's cooking. He has established a menu that combines the south-west's predilection for foie gras and duck with exotic sprinklings of spices and rose petals. If you take the half-board option, you can juggle your meals around as you like: even by eating more the next day if you miss one. The pretty château is at the end of a long and inviting driveway through large grounds with chairs under shady trees. One oak is 200 years old, perhaps planted by proud new owners. The eight bedrooms are an unusual mix: some in fresh stripes or flowers, others with bold turquoise or rose walls, with contemporary patterns on the beds. The first-floor rooms are grander, with bath and shower, while those on the second floor are simpler but all have their own shower. Rooms have lace-trimmed sheets and bowls of fruit and flowers. There are no numbers on the doors. As Madame says: "It wouldn't feel like home".

Price	€100–€130. Suites €250.
Rooms	8: 5 doubles, 1 twin, 1 suite for 3, 1 suite for 4.
Meals	Breakfast €13–€15. Casual 'country' meal €18. Lunch or dinner €29–€39; book ahead. Wine €9–€150.
Closed	Mid-December to mid-January.
Directions	D834 for 12km towards Aire from Adour & Bordeaux & Mont de Marsan, then left on D944 through Thèze; 1st right. Château on edge of Méracq.

M & Mme Guerin-Recoussine
64410 Méracq Arzacq,
Pyrénées-Atlantiques

Tel	+33 (0)5 59 04 53 01
Email	chateau-meracq@wanadoo.fr
Web	www.chateau-meracq.com

Limousin • Auvergne

Au Rendez-Vous des Pêcheurs/Fabry

It isn't called Fishermen's Lodge for nothing and there's a spectacular, steep winding decent. The house and its exquisite riverside setting are intimately linked. Fifty years ago, the Fabrys built a house on the banks of the Dordogne; at the same time a dam was started just downstream. Madame opened a kitchen for the site workers – and the house became an inn. This being the Corrèze, food looms as large as the river. The restaurant, a fine room full of light and plants and Limoges china, overlooks the view reaching off to the distant wooded hills of the gorge. A reader describes his meal: "I had a set menu comprising of a *mise en bouche*, a feuilleté of sea scallops, a superb fillet steak with gratin potatoes and asparagus and four types of chocolate dessert that defy description". Bedrooms are differently decorated in simple, pleasing country style with coordinated bathrooms. The terrace is generous, the garden pretty, the view to treasure. Remarkable value in one of France's gentlest, loveliest pieces of countryside. A treasure.
Take a trip down the river in a traditional longboat.

Price	€46-€50. Half-board mandatory in summer €46 p.p.
Rooms	8: 5 doubles, 1 twin, 2 triples.
Meals	Breakfast €7. Picnic available. Lunch & dinner €16-€45. Restaurant closed Sun eve & Mon 20 Sept-15 June.
Closed	12 November to mid-February.
Directions	42km east of Tulle; D978 to St Merd de Lapleau via Marcillac la Croisille, then D13 to lieu-dit Pont du Chambon.

Mme Fabry
Pont du Chambon,
19320 Saint Merd de Lapleau, Corrèze
Tel   +33 (0)5 55 27 88 39
Email   contact@rest-fabry.com
Web   www.rest-fabry.com

La Maison des Chanoines

Originally built for the canons (les chanoines) of Turenne, this ancient restaurant-hotel has been in Monsieur Cheyroux's family for 300 years. No wonder the family held on to it – the 16th-century, mellow-stoned house with its steep-pitched slate roof is one of the loveliest in a very lovely village. Madame, young, charming, gracious, is a fan of fine English fabrics and has used them lavishly for curtains and cushions. Bedrooms are divided between this house and another (equally ancient) opposite, approached via a little bridge from the garden. Well-lit rooms have plain carpets and white walls; bathrooms ooze fluffy towels. The breakfast room is stone-flagged with wickerwork chairs padded in duck-egg blue. The dining takes place in the old cellar – small and cosy, with white-clothed tables and vaulted ceiling – or under a fairylight-strewn pergola in the garden amid honeysuckle and roses. The food is a delight; Monsieur is chef and will use only the freshest, most local produce for his regional dishes. Ask about their three-day gourmet stay. Great value.

Price	€70-€100.
Rooms	5: 2 doubles, 1 twin, 1 family room, 1 triple.
Meals	Breakfast €10. Lunch & dinner €3-€49. Open for lunch Sundays & holidays. Closed Wednesdays in June.
Closed	15 October to week before Easter.
Directions	From Brive D38 to Monplaisir, then D8 for 8km to Turenne. Left uphill following château sign; hotel on left before church.

Chantal & Claude Cheyroux
Route de l'Église,
19500 Turenne, Corrèze

Tel	+33 (0)5 55 85 93 43
Email	maisondeschanoines@wanadoo.fr
Web	www.maison-des-chanoines.com

Auberge de Concasty

Half a mile high stands the river-ploughed plateau: strong air, wild country, immense space. Built 300 years ago, the family mansion stands prouder than ever, and the utterly delightful Causse family have brought everything thoroughly up to date: jacuzzi, hammam and organic or local produce to keep you blooming (veg from the sister's farm next door). The dining room, with its vast inglenook fireplace where some fine plants live in summer, and the covered patio overlooking the pool and the view, are the stage for lovingly prepared shows of foie gras and asparagus, scallops and confits, the supporting cast an impressive choice of estate wines; great breakfasts, too. Guest rooms, some in the main house, some in a restored barn, two in the newly renovated chestnut dryer, are stylishly rustic with space, good floral fabrics and an evocative name each – no standardisation here, except for that view. The magnificent new family room in pale ivory and soft blue is the height of sophistication. You will love the smiling, attentive staff and the warm family atmosphere they generate. *Some rooms with balcony or terrace.*

Price	€63–€159.
Rooms	12: 11 doubles, 1 family room.
Meals	Breakfast €9. Brunch €16. Picnic available. Dinner €32–€42.
Closed	December–March.
Directions	From Aurillac, N122 for Figeac, left to Manhès on D64. From Figeac, N122, then D17 after Maurs.

Martine & Omar Causse-Adllal
15600 Boisset, Cantal

Tel	+33 (0)4 71 62 21 16
Email	info@auberge-concasty.com
Web	www.auberge-concasty.com

Château de Sédaiges

An old creeper-strewn château such as children dream of, Sédaiges has it all: 15th-century turrets and crenellations, stairs and corridors galore, a crazily high neo-Gothic hammer-beamed hall built to house the tapestries given by Louis XVI, and elegant 18th-century drawing rooms, open to the public, where Marie-Antoinette's lookalike holds court. Delightful Bab tells the tales with all her passion for this microcosm of a vanishing way of life – the remote Auvergne is more unspoilt than any other part of old France – and the family chapel bears witness. In the creaky old warren upstairs, beneath aristocratic ceilings, are the endearingly unpretentious family-château bedrooms, two of them just refurbished: marble and muslin, florals and plush frame some fine old pieces. Bathrooms vary in style. A simple damask-clothed, silver-served coffee and croissant breakfast among gleaming copper pans in the kitchen is as atmospheric as it gets. Don't miss the re-engineered Barbie-doll show or the wonderful botanical walk through the park with its stupendous specimen trees.

Price	€110–€150. Extra bed €20.
Rooms	5: 3 doubles, 1 suite for 3, 1 suite for 4 (without sitting area). Overflow room for children.
Meals	Restaurant in village.
Closed	October–April.
Directions	From Aurillac D922 for Mauriac 10km. At Jussac right onto D59 to Marmanhac; signed.

Bab & Patrice de Varax
15250 Marmanhac, Cantal

Tel	+33 (0)4 71 47 30 01
Email	chateau15@free.fr
Web	www.chateausedaiges.com

Domaine de Gaudon - Le Château

The contrast could scarcely be greater. Out in the wilds of deepest Auvergne with nature bounding free all round, you find new Venuses and urns lining the edges of a great park. Inside the 19th-century splendour of glossy oak panelling, ceiling roses and original wall coverings, this totally natural, endearing couple have created a setting of unexpected glamour, all brass and satin and gilt and quilting, for their superb French antiques. Gleaming luxuriously, big bathrooms are in keeping. Alain is a dab hand at wall panels and mouldings, Monique knows exactly what she likes in fabrics and drapes and colour combinations (Prussian blue and gold, canary yellow and gold, green and orange), they simply love having guests and breakfast is designed to dazzle you as your bedroom did. Gaudon is a Gîte Panda in a wildlife conservation area with some superb specimen trees, a wetland observation spot and innumerable frogs, bats, birds and insects (there are samples in frames indoors). Herons fish in the pond, children love the place and your hosts have been breeding Connemara ponies for 40 years. Astonishing.

Price	€110. Singles €90. Suite €130. Extra person €25.
Rooms	5: 3 doubles, 1 twin, 1 suite.
Meals	Supper trays available. Restaurant 4km.
Closed	Rarely.
Directions	A75 from Montpellier exit 9; D229 then D996 to St Dier d'Auvergne. At end of village, D6 for Domaize 3km. Right for Ceilloux, 1km.

Alain & Monique Bozzo
63520 Ceilloux, Puy-de-Dôme
Tel   +33 (0)4 73 70 76 25
Email   domainedegaudon@wanadoo.fr
Web   www.domainedegaudon.fr

Château Royal de Saint-Saturnin

The volcanic Auvergne is the perfect setting for this magnificently turreted and castellated fortress, high on the forested fringes of Saint-Saturnin, one of France's most beautiful villages. Five spacious, sumptuous bedrooms, with regal four-posters and an inspired blend of antique and modern furniture, occupy the oldest wing of this 13th-century 'monument historique': Catherine de Medicis and Marguerite de Valois were once owners and now it is open to the public. Suite Louis XIII, its bathroom tucked into a tower, spans the castle's width; views are to tumbling rooftops and Romanesque church, and to gardens and parkland behind (heaven for weddings). The vaulted dining room, bedecked with polished copper pans, is the background for relaxed breakfast spreads, while dinners are served in true table d'hôtes style, at a table shared with the owners, after aperitifs on the terrace with views. Redolent with regal history, the château has been lovingly, painstakingly returned to its original glory, yet, thanks to friendly, well-travelled Emmanuel and Christine, is not intimidating in any way.

Price	€150–€170. Suites €190–€210.
Rooms	5: 2 doubles, 3 suites.
Meals	Breakfast €13.50. Hosted dinner with wine, €42; book ahead. Restaurant 1.5km.
Closed	November–March.
Directions	From Clermont-Ferrand, A75 dir. Issoire & Montpellier; exit 5 dir. Aydat for 6km; left dir. Saint-Saturnin; left at Rue de la Chantelle; at Fountain Plazza, gate on right.

Emmanuel & Christine Pénicaud
Place de L'Ormeau,
63450 Saint-Saturnin, Puy-de-Dôme

Tel	+33 (0)4 73 39 39 64
Email	chateaudesaintsaturnin@yahoo.fr
Web	www.chateaudesaintsaturnin.com

Château de Maulmont

This extraordinary place, built in 1830 by Louis Philippe for his sister Adélaïde, has long views and architecture: medieval crenellations, 16th-century brick patterning, Loire-Valley slate roofs, neo-Gothic windows, even real Templar ruins – a cornucopia of character. The owners provide activities on 23 hectares of parkland (a golf driving range, riding nearby, fishing, sauna, swimming pools outdoors and in) and cultivate a certain 'formal informality'. They have preserved original features – carved inside shutters, the original spit in the kitchen, the panelled banqueting hall with its stained-glass portraits of Adélaïde in various moods – and collected some impressive furniture. Bedrooms are spacious, all are individually decorated and there's a wonderfully romantic room in the tower reached via a spiral stair. All have very smart bathrooms. The well-established restaurant where classical piped music plays is wood-panelled from top to toe, staff are alert and friendly, and you can arrive by helicopter if you choose. A destination place for grand events, and a super family hotel.

Price	€135-€185. Suites €195-€220. Apartments €200-€275. All prices per night.
Rooms	18 + 2: 9 doubles, 7 twins, 2 family suites for 3-4. 2 apartments for 4-6.
Meals	Breakfast €14-€16. Lunch & dinner €25-€54. Wine €30-€150.
Closed	8 November-31 March.
Directions	N209 for Vichy; D131 for Hauterive; there, right to St Priest Bramefant; D55 then right at r'bout on D59 to Randan.

Ian & Maartje Lawrie
St Priest Bramefant,
63310 Randan, Puy-de-Dôme

Tel	+33 (0)4 70 59 14 95
Email	info@chateau-maulmont.com
Web	www.chateau-maulmont.com

Auberge de Chassignolles

The old village lay untouched in the pure green air, its 1930s inn decaying gently behind the medieval church; then along came two charming, colourful young Londoners, bringing oodles of talent and baby Fred. The place now hums with good looks and seriously delicious food. It is simplicity incarnate: upstairs, light from tall windows falls on herring-bone parquet, bounces off white walls onto perfectly appropriate old furniture – a 1930s carved and inlaid bedroom suite dressed in pure white linen, a deep and friendly armchair – and Ali's artistic eye sees to all the details. One room above the restaurant is a resident's library/sitting room and there's a big private garden over the road. Bathrooms are perfectly adequate with good extras. The pretty, old-style restaurant – country furniture, checked cloths, crinkly lamps, a fascinating mixture of old crockery – is the ideal frame for Harry's finely honed *cuisine de terroir*, all fresh local produce and real taste. An antidote to urban frenzy, with a small grocery shop by the bar, this is a perfect focus for revived community life and a boon for travellers.

Price	€45-€65.
Rooms	8: 6 doubles, 1 family room for 4; 1 twin sharing bathroom.
Meals	Breakfast €7.50. Lunch €24 (Sunday only). Dinner €24 (Tuesday-Sunday only). Picnic €8.
Closed	Mid-October to mid-May.
Directions	From A75 exit 17, left under m'way dir. Jumeaux onto Auzon; D5 for 8km, left onto D52 to Chassignolles. Auberge in main square.

Harry Lester & Ali Johnson
Le Bourg,
43440 Chassignolles, Haute-Loire
Tel   +33 (0)4 71 76 32 36
Email   info@aubergedechassignolles.com
Web   www.aubergedechassignolles.com

Ethical Collection: Environment;
Community; Food.
See page 446 for details

Midi – Pyrénées

Le Domaine de la Borie Grande

The 18th-century house in two hectares of parkland combines understatedly elegant luxury with a country B&B mood – delightful. It is a beautifully kept home where you will find artistic flair and a love of cooking (vegetables from the neighbour, local wines, seasonal produce). A place of friendly proportions and lovingly collected antiques, where soft yellow cushions and gilt-edged fauteuils add sparkle to a palette of taupe, cream and dove grey. Enter a square hall off which lead three reception rooms: a cosy one for contemplation, a tranquil drawing room for tea and a grand salon for aperitifs and conversation. A stunning carved armoire takes pride of place, the deep cream sofa could seat a dozen, a big pale rug softens a terracotta floor and Cordes is perched high on the hill; from here, a magical view. You will be guided up a sweeping stair to large and luminous bedrooms where antique rugs strew polished parquet, crisp linen enfolds new beds and white bathrooms have big mirrors and oodles of towels. The raised garden is delightful, and you may share bikes, tennis court and saltwater pool. *Cash or cheque only.*

Price	€110–€150. Suites €120–€150.
Rooms	4: 1 double, 1 twin, 2 suites.
Meals	Dinner with wine, €38.
Closed	Rarely.
Directions	From Cordes sur Ciel for Laguépie. Right at bend at bottom of hill leaving Cordes; 1km to church in Campes; left for St Amans. On left, 500m from church.

Alain Guyomarch
St Marcel Campes,
81170 Cordes sur Ciel, Tarn

Tel	+33 (0)5 63 56 58 24
Email	laboriegrande@wanadoo.fr
Web	www.laboriegrande.com

Entry 280   Map 15

Le Phénix

Like its namesake, it rose from the ashes: when Tim and Ally bought the old *maison de maître* it had almost burned to the ground. Location is everything though, and it is set in acres of gentle woods and parkland, so they set to with gusto and the results are delightful. The relaxed attitude of the owners gives a homely but stylish feel; the guest sitting room has an open fire, underfloor heating, deep comfy sofas in soft creams and taupes, plenty of books and games. The kitchen is the hub and here you may sit and chat and watch your supper being prepared; enjoy a glass of wine here, or take it to the pretty garden room with its rattan furniture and green outlook. A stone staircase leads to big bedrooms with handmade beech and oak floors, lovely rugs, a mix of florals and stripes, a fresh feel; bathrooms are ultra-modern or vintage, with generous baskets of goodies. There's even a little kitchen should you want to rustle up a picnic and dine by the pool – or lounge in a hammock in a shady corner. Cafés and bustling markets are minutes away by car; this is perfect for families. *No credit cards. Minimum stay two nights in August.*

Price	€75–€95. Suites €120. Triple €100.
Rooms	5: 2 doubles, 2 suites for 5, 1 triple.
Meals	Dinner with wine, €25; book ahead.
Closed	Rarely.
Directions	From Rabastens, left at cinema onto D2 dir. Sálvagnac. 5km then left onto D28 Condel & Grazac; 100m on right. Signed.

Tim & Ally Hewett
Lieu-dit La Riviere,
81800 Rabastens, Tarn
Tel   +33 (0)5 63 33 86 64
Email   info@lephenixfrance.com
Web   www.lephenixfrance.com

Midi – Pyrénées

Hôtel Cuq en Terrasses

Come to the Pays de Cocagne, the brochure says. Where is that exactly, you may ask, have I drunk that wine? It is in fact an imaginary land of pleasure, from the once prosperous pastel-producing Tarn. Philippe and Andonis gave up good jobs in Paris to buy this 18th-century presbytery after falling in love with the region. Perched in beautiful gardens on the side of a hill, midway between Castres and Toulouse, the multi-level mellow stone edifice with white shutters looks – and is – inviting. All the rooms, including the two-floor suite by the saltwater pool, exude character and charm. All are different, with original terracotta floors, hand-finished plaster, exposed beams, a Chinese vase here, an antique bed there. It is worth staying just for the bathrooms, lovely with hand-painted tiles. Evening meals, on the terrace in summer, are a delight to the eye and the palate: something different each day, fresh from the market, beautifully balanced by wines from the region. Readers are full of praise, for the food and the gardens, the pool and cascade, the blissful views, the wonderful hosts.

Price	€95–€150. Suite €190. Half-board €185–€274 for 2 (min. 4 nights).
Rooms	7: 3 doubles, 3 twins/doubles, 1 suite.
Meals	Breakfast €14. Snacks available. Hosted dinner €35; book ahead. Wine €14–€25.
Closed	November–Easter.
Directions	N126 to Cuq Toulza then D45 towards Revel. After 2km on left at top of hill in old village.

Philippe Gallice & Andonis Vassalos
Cuq le Château,
81470 Cuq Toulza, Tarn
Tel +33 (0)5 63 82 54 00
Email cuq-en-terrasses@wanadoo.fr
Web www.cuqenterrasses.com

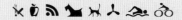

Domaine de Rasigous

The drawing room is the magnet of this exceptional house: gentle colours, fabulous furnishings and, in winter, a log fire in a marble fireplace. The soft yellow and white dining room is full of light; never twee, the tables are beautifully decorated for good-looking varied food and local wines (especially the delicious Gaillac). Natural pale, bare floorboards with fine rugs or luxurious plain carpets give that country-house feel to large, heavenly bedrooms, sensitively decorated with rich colours and interesting furniture. The three suites are elegantly unfrilly. Luxurious bathrooms have been ingeniously fitted into odd spaces – the free-standing bath is most handsome. Even the single room, with its sleigh beds, lovely linen and bathroom in a walk-in cupboard, is on the 'noble' floor, not under the eaves. The courtyard is ideal for summer breakfast; gaze at the water lilies in the water garden, eight different types of frogs will sing and jump for you. The owner's flair and hospitality make this a wonderful place to stay – try to give it at least three nights.

Price	€105. Single €65. Suites €130–€140.
Rooms	8: 4 twins/doubles, 1 single, 3 suites for 2.
Meals	Breakfast €12. Dinner €29 (except Wednesdays). Wine €15–€45. Restaurant nearby.
Closed	15 November–15 March.
Directions	From Mazamet D621 for Soual for 16km; left on D85 to St Affrique les Montagnes. On for 2km on D85; green sign on left.

Emile Navas
81290 St Affrique les Montagnes, Tarn
Tel   +33 (0)5 63 73 30 50
Email   info@domainederasigous.com
Web   www.domainederasigous.com

Château de Séguenville

A dream of a French family château. Restoring it is a perpetual labour of love for Marie; and still it has oodles of character. She is an enthusiastic cook and loves wine, so will happily prepare a menu gastronomique if you ask in advance. This is a 13th-century château, rebuilt in 1653, beautifully run and in the family for 40 years; Marie can tell you all about both house and region. Be charmed by galleried bedrooms with marble fireplaces and creaky floors, big bathrooms that combine the old with the new, a salon Chinois with black leather sofas, a second salon with a vast open fire, and centuries-old trees in the grounds. It's still crumbling in places but you'll love the slightly frayed charm, and Marie, who has children of her own, particularly likes having families to stay. Decoration is simple yet elegant, and full of personality. Outside are a swimming pool and a terrace for breakfast with glorious views. In the summer spin off on a bike – or visit the chateau's windmill, open to visitors and still grinding flour. In stunning countryside – and within easy reach of the airport. *No credit cards.*

Price	€120–€135.
Rooms	5: 3 doubles, 1 suite, 1 family room for 5.
Meals	Dinner, 3 courses, €25. Wine from €7.
Closed	15 December–15 January.
Directions	From Toulouse dir. Blagnac Airport; Cornebarrieu & Cadours; on to Cox, 3rd road on right. Signed 5km after Cox.

	Marie Lareng
	Région de Toulouse,
	31480 Cabanac Séguenville, Haute-Garonne
Tel	+33 (0)5 62 13 42 67
Email	info@chateau-de-seguenville.com
Web	www.chateau-de-seguenville.com

Château de Beauregard

Paul and Angela have created something memorable here. Paul is French, a chef by training and brimful of energy – an entrepreneur – but it is Angela's intuition and imagination that have wrought the magic inside this little hotel. The château, grafted onto a 17th-century dairy farm in 1820, was in a woeful condition when they bought it. Everyone thought them quite mad but they've saved it triumphantly, using reclaimed materials, even finding some massive old radiators; the new central heating looks perfectly at home. The rooms are full of appeal and interest, the old furniture and fabrics that Angela has tracked down have just enough shabby chic to look as though they've been there forever. Each bedroom is named after a French writer, with a corresponding shelf of their work. Breakfast is served in the pretty winter-garden or, in warm weather, out under the wisteria (the grounds are lovely). Dining at L'Auberge d'Antan is a treat: Paul has turned the stables into a rustic restaurant and you can watch the (very good) Gascon-style food being cooked over a wood fire. There's even a new spa.

Price	€60–€80. Suites €80–€200. Apartment €460–€900 per week.
Rooms	10 + 1: 4 twins/doubles, 6 suites. Apartment for 6.
Meals	Breakfast €13. Dinner €33.
Closed	November–March.
Directions	From Toulouse to Tarbes, A20 exit 20 to Salies du Salat; D117 to Saint Girons, Massat.

Angela & Paul Fontvieille
L'Auberge d'Antan,
Avenue de la Résistance,
09200 Saint Girons, Ariège

Tel	+33 (0)5 61 66 66 64
Email	contact@chateaubeauregard.net
Web	www.chateaubeauregard.net

L'Abbaye Château de Camon

Camon… the name conjures up images of pious folk, wrapped in sackcloth and arriving by donkey. History and architecture buffs will swoon trying to work out which bits were built when, but it was first recorded as a Benedictine Abbey in 928. Now Peter, who managed The Samling in Cumbria, and his wife Katie, an interior designer, give you monks' bedrooms with vaulted ceilings and long windows with 28 panes; all look south over the hills and have tiny glistening floor tiles. Rooms on the second floor are squarer; all have soft colours, beautiful fabrics and spoiling bathrooms. On chilly evenings, hang out in the huge salon with its exquisite 18th-century plasterwork, floral ceiling and roaring fire, or take tea quietly in the sheltered cloister garden. Breakfast is served, most elegantly, on a long high terrace running the whole length of the château and overlooking formal park gardens with lawns, mature trees and swimming pool. Chef Tom will thrill bon viveurs with his rather grand menu, the estate wine is superb and you are 30 minutes from grand skiing at Mont d'Olmes. Stunning.

Price	€120–€180. Suites €240.
Rooms	11: 9 doubles, 2 suites for 4.
Meals	Breakfast €18. Dinner €38.
Closed	November–15 March.
Directions	From Carcassonne, N13 to Bram; D4 to Fanjeaux; D119 south to Mirepoix; D625 towards Laroque; D7 for Camon. Signed.

Katie & Peter Lawton
09500 Camon, Ariège

Tel	+33 (0)5 61 60 31 23
Email	peter.katielawton@wanadoo.fr
Web	www.chateaudecamon.com

Hôtel Restaurant Relais Royal

Arrive on a summer afternoon and you'll pass the courtyard tables set for tea. Then through the Renaissance-style gate and into the lobby where terracotta gleams, the grandfather clock ticks away the hours and pretty arched doors lead to a second courtyard and pool. The lofty dining room has a touch of gilt here and there and is a suitable setting for some serious dining (menus include one for young gourmets!). Service is very friendly and unobtrusive. Dine in winter in front of a fire in the old kitchen, its walls lined with copper pans; retire to the clubby Blue Room. Then up the grand ironwork staircase to bedrooms with a modern décor that allows the original features to shine: glorious 18th-century windows and Nespresso machines, high ceilings and beams painted fashionably white. Fabrics are coordinated and bathrooms are large and luxy, some with roll tops. The Midi Pyrénées provide a beautiful (hiking and biking) backdrop to this sweet cathedral town, its medieval square full of tempting cafés, and there's a great pâtisserie around the corner. Magnificent Carcassonne is worth at least a day.

Price	€160-€290. Suites €300-€400.
Rooms	9: 5 twins/doubles, 4 suites for 2-4.
Meals	Breakfast €20. Lunch €22-€90. Dinner €35-€90 (except Mon & Tues). Children's meals €18.
Closed	3 January-10 February.
Directions	From Toulouse A66 to Foix. Exit Pamiers, Mirepoix & Carcassonne. D20 to Mirepoix & Bram. In centre of Mirepoix, near post office.

Gerwin Rutten
& Rogier Van Den Biggelaar
8 rue Maréchal Clauzel,
09500 Mirepoix, Ariège

Tel	+33 (0)5 61 60 19 19
Email	relaisroyal@relaischateaux.com
Web	www.relaisroyal.com

Le Mûrier de Viels

You won't meet a soul on the drive to get here – but you may meet a wild deer. This intimate hotel, made up of a sprinkling of 18th-century buildings on many lush levels, hides amongst the oak woods and gazes down upon the river. Come for a smiling welcome and an atmosphere of relaxed comfort: Josephine and Oz have left stressful lives in the UK to realise their dream of owning a small hotel in France. The layout is charming, with reception, restaurant and guest rooms scattered among terraces, entwined by secret corners. The pool area has a great view, as do most of the rooms; there's space and blissful tranquillity. In the bedrooms, rustic stone walls rub shoulders with white plaster, there is stylish modern French furniture and soothing colours, big walk-in showers and white towels, excellent reading lamps and fat pillows. One suite has a fitted wardrobe with antique doors, a comfy raffia sofa and a stunning view through a huge window. Every room is pristine. Treat yourself to Oz's beautiful cooking on the terrace – or in a dining room bright with yellow leather chairs.

Price	€65–€105. Duplex suite €105–€130. Family rooms €75–€105. Cottage €450–€750.
Rooms	7 + 1: 3 doubles, 1 twin, 1 duplex suite for 3, 2 family rooms for 3. Cottage for 4.
Meals	Breakfast €9.50. Picnic on request. Dinner €25–€30. Wine €9–€30.
Closed	November to mid-March; December-February.
Directions	From Villefranche de Rouergue, cross river then immediately right onto D86 to Cajac. 2km, follow signs.

Josephine & Oz
12700 Causse et Diege,
Aveyron

Tel	+33 (0)5 65 80 89 82
Email	info@le-murier.com
Web	www.le-murier.com

Villa Ric

Jean-Pierre built his house in 1985 – a quarter century ago – high on a hill covered in elegant trees; the panorama from the dining terrace reaches as far as the eye can see. Villa Ric is ideally placed as a stopover for the Auvergne, Dordogne or the journey down to Spain, but why not linger a little longer? The food is a delicious part of your stay and Jean-Pierre discusses the menu each evening with guests (for whom the restaurant is exclusively reserved). The food is fresh, regional and inventive, and you can choose to go half-board. Bedrooms are neat, light, pretty, French with Laura Ashley touches; some have broad striped wallpaper and white wicker chairs, most have polished exposed beams. Bathrooms gleam; each matches its flower-themed bedroom. Elisabeth is rightly proud of her hillside garden; tamed by the creation of triangular grassed terraces, it tumbles prettily down to a sheltered, heated pool. As for the little timbered market town down that steep hill, Saint Cere hosts a well-established music festival in summer: opera, music in the streets, exhibitions – great fun.

Price	€75–€105.
Rooms	5 twins/doubles.
Meals	Breakfast €10. Dinner €36–€40. Wine €22–€50.
Closed	November-Easter.
Directions	From Paris, A20 exit 52 for St Céré, then Leyme. From Toulouse exit 56; hotel 2km from St Céré.

Elisabeth & Jean-Pierre Ric
Route de Leyme,
46400 Saint Céré, Lot

Tel	+33 (0)5 65 38 04 08
Email	hotel.jpric@libertysurf.fr
Web	www.villaric.com

Manoir de Malagorse

You get more than you pay for here, so enjoy it to the hilt. The refined manoir in the idyllic setting was once a farmhouse whose occupants fell on hard times. Now the place smiles again, thanks to Anna and Abel's loving restoration. Off the central staircase, spread over two floors, the bedrooms are statements of simple luxury and the great kitchen is a wonder to behold: a massive fireplace, a vaulted ceiling. This is where you dine at one long table – unless you choose the privacy of the dining room, or the terrace among the immaculate pom-pom hedges. Anna's table decorations are a match for Abel's exquisite food: napkins tied with twine, candles tall and dramatic. Now this delightful pair have twins of their own; they love the idea of entertaining families and have created two contemporary suites in an outbuilding. Colours are muted, bed covers quilted, your hosts are unintrusively present and Anna can offer a professional massage after Abel's demanding wine-tastings. There are cookery courses in summer; in winter they run an Alpine restaurant. Special. *Gastronomic discovery weekends. Wine tasting. Massage.*

Price	€110–€165. Suites €195–€300. Extra bed €25.
Rooms	6: 4 doubles, 2 suites.
Meals	À la carte lunch, from €20. Dinner €39.
Closed	December-April.
Directions	From Souillac 6km, N20 for Cressensac. On dual c'way, 1st right to Cuzance & Église de Rignac; 1st right in Rignac, signed. Detailed directions on booking.

Anna & Abel Congratel
46600 Cuzance, Lot
Tel   +33 (0)5 65 27 14 83
Email   acongratel@manoir-de-malagorse.fr
Web   www.manoir-de-malagorse.fr

Hôtel Relais Sainte Anne

When conversation flounders, *un ange passe*. Perhaps there is one in the tiny chapel of Sainte Anne, in the centre of the beautifully preserved little town of Martel. In the walled garden, with a large pool discreetly tucked away, gravel paths run through high box-edged alleys. It's a place of quiet contemplation whilst taking the air, and inside is as atmospheric: warm old stones and terre cuite tiles, fine wallpapers, fabrics and heavy rugs. Bathrooms are often tiled with black and terracotta and a bit of gilt or candy stripe in blue and white, with flowery friezes. In the old school house is an oriental suite in beige and lacquer red, exuding opulence and space. We loved the lighter, more recently done-up rooms, their beams painted white. All the rooms are scented with lavender and those on the ground floor have terraces. Now there's a menu offering innovative cuisine, served on a veranda'd terrace furnished comfortably in wicker, or in the intimate dining room with big open fire. Sophistication without self-consciousness — a rare treat.

Price	€75–€165. Suites €145–€265.
Rooms	16: 7 doubles, 4 twins, 1 single, 4 suites.
Meals	Breakfast €13–€15. Lunch & dinner €16–€35. Wine €17–€90. Restaurant closed Monday lunchtimes.
Closed	Mid-November to mid-March.
Directions	From Brive A20 for Cahors exit 54 for Martel; Rue du Pourtanel; hotel on right at town entrance.

Ghislaine Rimet-Mignon
Rue du Pourtanel,
46600 Martel, Lot
Tel   +33 (0)5 65 37 40 56
Email   relais.sainteanne@wanadoo.fr
Web   www.relais-sainte-anne.com

La Terrasse

A child might build a castle like this: tall and straight, with a mix of towers round and square. It's actually more fortress than château and has stood guard over the Dordogne since the 11th century; the history is ferocious, the setting dramatic. Today La Terrasse is a wonderfully peaceful, hospitable country retreat, thanks to lovely hands-on owners Gilles and Françoise. Leave the village square, enter the stone-flagged front courtyard, soak up the history. Salon and dining room have vaulted ceilings where tables are beautifully set and in summer you dine on a wide terrace under the vines. A spiral stone staircase takes you up to the bedrooms, the most characterful in the oldest part of the building. Some overlook the road and river, others the swimming pool set high into the walls, unusually private and atmospheric. There's not much of a garden as the land falls down the hill below, but great views. Food is authentically regional, with four menus to make your mouth water. Explore Sarlat, Souillac, Rocamadour – best out of season – and the markets of Gramat and Martel. Or canoe the Dordogne just below.

Price	€80-€125. Triple & suites €135-€230.
Rooms	15: 9 twins/doubles, 1 triple, 2 suites for 3, 3 suites for 4.
Meals	Buffet breakfast €12. Lunch & dinner €28-€50. Restaurant closed Tuesday lunchtimes.
Closed	November-February.
Directions	From Limoges, A20 exit 55; at r'bout 1st right to D803 for Martel. On for 5km, right onto D15 for Meyronne; signed.

Gilles & Françoise Liébus
46200 Meyronne, Lot

Tel	+33 (0)5 65 32 21 60
Email	terrasse.liebus@wanadoo.fr
Web	www.hotel-la-terrasse.com

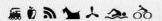

Hôtel Restaurant Le Vert

The alchemy of family tradition – three generations and 25 years for this young couple – has rubbed off onto the very stones of this unpretentious, authentic country inn where Bernard's skills shine from the kitchen. All is simplicity with fresh flowers, glowing silverware and old flagstones leading you from the small lobby to the dining room. Glance at the blackboard for the day's special to get your appetite going and if the weather is as it should be, head for a table on the terrace. The local food cognoscenti are greeted as friends here, always an auspicious sign. You might choose a warm goat's cheese, golden roasted with a lavender honey, then a prune-stuffed quail followed by a cherry-studded tiramisu. This is Cahors wine territory; Eva will advise. The rooms in the garden annexe are big, cool and elegant with beamed ceilings, stone walls and antique furniture lightened by simple white curtains and delicate bedspreads. The pool is hidden on the far side of the garden. In a country where politicians are authors and cooks are philosophers, Bernard's ivory tower is in the kitchen.

Price	€85–€130.
Rooms	6 twins/doubles.
Meals	Breakfast €10. Dinner €28–€45.
Closed	November–March.
Directions	From Villeneuve sur Lot, D811 for Fumel; south of Fumel D139 for Montayral. Past Mauroux towards Puy l'Evêque for approx. 500m. Hotel on right.

Bernard & Eva Philippe
Le Vert,
46700 Mauroux, Lot

Tel	+33 (0)5 65 36 51 36
Email	info@hotellevert.com
Web	www.hotellevert.com

Domaine de Cantecor

Whether you are in the main house or in the outbuilding with its garden-level patio, all the rooms are bright, cheerful, uncluttered, charming. The 18th century property has masses of character and the owners make it clear that they want you to feel at home. On summer nights the floodlit pool is enchanting and during the day you may well be unable to resist a game of boules on the lawn or just relax in the quiet garden. Comfortable sofas around an open fireplace, bookshelves stacked with paperbacks, a country kitchen (the central meeting place) and samples of wine bought from local growers complete this charming picture. Lydi will cook dinner if the group is big enough and if she feels all the guests would enjoy mingling. This is a great base for exploring the subterranean caves or sampling the full-bodied wines from this area. Lydi and René keep a good supply of information on all the activities in the area and, between them, can hold their own in English, German, Spanish and Dutch, of course. Great people, great value. *No credit cards.*

Price	€65-€80. Family room €75-€105.
Rooms	5: 4 twins, 1 family room for 2-4.
Meals	Restaurant 2km. Occasional dinner with wine, on request.
Closed	October-March.
Directions	A20 exit 58, then N20 towards Montauban for 7km; left on D250 for La Madeleine; left after 600m, signed.

Lydi & René Toebak
La Madeleine,
82270 Montpezat de Quercy, Tarn-et-Garonne

Tel	+33 (0)5 65 21 87 44
Email	info@cantecor.com
Web	www.cantecor.com

Hostellerie du Manoir de Saint Jean

Hats off to Anne-Marie, who, after three years, has impressed the locals (we asked around) with her renovations and her cuisine. This might not have been so difficult for another native from the town, but she is a transplant from Nice and an ex-antique dealer to boot. The dining room is, of course, outstanding; soft yellow and cream, full of enormous gilt framed mirrors and beautiful drapes framing huge windows. The terrace is particularly lovely and overlooks the formal garden – gradually establishing itself – and the side of the pool. There is a 'menu of the day' based on seasonal produce with the addition of two choices for each course. Anne-Marie hand-picks her wine suppliers and makes sure that they are among those who are producing the most 'natural' product possible; the same philosophy governs the chef's choice for his local produce. Space and more space – from the entrance hall to the corridors to the bedrooms where well-chosen antiques rest in just the right places adding warmth and colour. Bathrooms are bright and airy. A fine beginning, the patina will come: this is a place to watch.

Price	€100–€120. Suites €150–€200.
Rooms	10: 1 double, 9 suites for 2-4.
Meals	Breakfast €13. Lunch & dinner €38–€70. Restaurant closed Sunday eve & Mondays.
Closed	Rarely.
Directions	A62 exit 9; in Moissac, D7 to Bourg de Visa. 9km; well signed.

Anne-Marie Morgadès
Saint Jean de Cornac,
82400 Saint Paul d'Espis, Tarn-et-Garonne
Tel   +33 (0)5 63 05 02 34
Email   info@manoirsaintjean.com
Web   www.manoirsaintjean.com

Château de Goudourville

Medieval splendour without the draughts and with hot showers. Hughes de Gasques established a stronghold here in the 11th century, Simon de Monfort laid siege to Goudourville – in vain – and it was here, after the battle of Coutras, that Henri IV laid 22 flags at the feet of the Countess of Gramont, 'la belle Corisande'. Bedrooms are vast and dramatic with grand old four-posters (be sure you ask for one of the larger beds). There's Clement V, done up in red silk, Charles IX, all stone walls and cream hangings; d'Andouins, with subtle blue-and-cream wallpaper and a pretty, painted four-poster, Gasques, a lighter room in white and cream with a rosy terracotta floor. Baths are deep, mattresses are pretty firm. Dinner is served at small tables in a stone-vaulted dining room with a huge fireplace and you can choose from a selection of local specialities. There's a tree-filled terrace overlooking the Garonne, a large swimming pool and masses to do and visit once you've jumped in the car. Start with the château's beautifully preserved 11th-century chapel, end with lovely Moissac.

Price	€135–€160.
Rooms	6: 3 doubles, 3 triples.
Meals	Dinner from €46; book ahead.
Closed	Mid-November to March.
Directions	From Valence, D953 towards Lauzerte. Signed.

Jacqueline Bazire
82400 Goudourville,
Tarn-et-Garonne

Tel	+33 (0)5 63 29 09 06
Email	goudourville@wanadoo.fr
Web	www.chateau-goudourville.fr

L'Arbre d'Or

The 'Golden Tree' is Chinese and turn-of-the-century (the previous one); it's a ginkgo biloba and probably the finest in France. David will tell you its story and will explain why he believes Beaumont de Lomagne to be the finest example of a bastide town in south-west France; it's certainly very handsome and the Saturday market is not to be missed. He and Ann obviously love the place and are doing it up little by little and take great care of their guests; they've given thought to disabled access and are happy to look after cyclists and walkers. Ann's a keen cook and has adopted traditional, regional recipes – adding the occasional English crumble – which you can eat outside in the shaded, pretty garden or in the dining room with its exposed beams. A comfortable, old-fashioned atmosphere reigns in the bedrooms too, with their marble fireplaces, large windows, interesting old furniture and pretty decorative touches. Two of the bedrooms have walk-in showers; the quietest overlook the garden at the back. A 17th-century gentleman's residence-turned-hotel with plenty of character.

Price	€60–€70.
Rooms	5: 4 doubles, 1 twin.
Meals	Dinner with aperitif, wine & coffee, €24; book ahead.
Closed	Rarely.
Directions	From A62 exit Castelsarrasin. From A20 exit Montauban. D928 dir. Auch. Hotel opp. Beaumont post office.

Ann Miemczyk & David Leek
16 rue Despeyrous,
82500 Beaumont de Lomagne,
Tarn-et-Garonne

Tel	+33 (0)5 63 65 32 34
Email	info@larbredor-hotel.com
Web	www.larbredor-hotel.com

Entry 297   Map 14

Castelnau des Fieumarcon

Getting there is almost an initiation. Pass through a large Renaissance portal and spot a music stand and a welcome sign; then ring the gong. If all you hear is birdcall, you are in the right place. Built in the 13th century by local feudal lords – who for a time during the Hundred Year War pledged allegiance to the English crown – this stronghold was left to crumble until 25 years ago when the owners moved in. They restored the ramparts, renovated the houses, creating gardens for each one and left much of the creeper-clad old stone untouched. The houses are not 'interior decorated', but simple, clever touches lend sophistication: framed dried herbs on the painted walls, fairy-light baldaquins, terracotta tiles, a massive Louis XV armoire, antique Gascony treasures. Many have their own kitchens. Castelnau is on high ground so the views from every window – and the pool – are astounding, giving off a timeless hazy glow from the low-lying hills and surrounding fields. Stendhal called it the French Tuscany. He would be at home here: no cars, no TVs, no telephones. A rare pearl.

Price	€90-€300 (€800-€2250 per week).
Rooms	13 houses for 2-11.
Meals	Breakfast €15. Restaurant 4km.
Closed	Rarely.
Directions	A61 exit for Auch on N2. From Astaffort right onto D266 after police station; D266 until Castelnau. After 1km left to Lagarde Fieumarcon, on 4.5km; on right after church; ring gong.

Frédéric Coustols
32700 Lagarde Fieumarcon, Gers
Tel   +33 (0)5 62 68 99 30
Email   office@lagarde.org
Web   www.lagarde.org

Château de Pomiro

Vineyards and woods encircle this once prominent hunting lodge of the Marquis and Marquise de Noë. Stone lions survey the entrance leading to a high-ceilinged hallway and handsome oak staircase. Big light-filled bedrooms flaunt distinctly châteauesque flourishes: feathery fin-de-siècle lampshades, ornate repro antiques and gilded accessories. All have garden views. Sip an aperitif in the petit salon or pluck juicy grapes fresh from the overhanging vines in late summer. Very friendly Roy and Rosemary, who owned an Alpine hotel for many years, have turned one of the old barns into a games room; future plans include a polo centre on the château's 200 acres, and Argentinian horses. You breakfast on the terrace overlooking gardens scattered to the horizon with trees… on a clear day you can see the snow-capped Pyrenees. At dinner try the region's famous foie gras or confit de canard accompanied by a glass of the château's Armagnac or Floc – the cellars are still stocked with the stuff! Book in for golf and fishing nearby, or venture out to muse the markets of Gascony's gorgeous villages.

Price	€120–€150.
Rooms	8: 5 twins/doubles. Cottage: 3 doubles.
Meals	Dinner, 4 courses with aperitif & wine, €45 (5 days a week). Restaurants 6km.
Closed	Rarely.
Directions	From Montreal, D15 west dir. Barbotan les Thermes; on 4.5km, D31 south; on 3km, château on right.

Rosemary Neal
32250 Montreal du Gers, Gers

Tel	+33 (0)5 62 69 57 99
Email	enquiries@chateaupomiro.com
Web	www.chateaupomiro.com

Château de Projan

Fascinating is the story of how an eccentric world-traveller and painter restored this 18th-century château to house his art collection. Eclectic and successful is the mix of the original pieces – mirrors, commodes and armoires – with paintings, tapestries and sculpture from the pre-Raphaelite, Cubist and Art Deco periods. Bedrooms are all on the first floor with wide oak boards and tomette tiles at the intersections of the passageways. One fabulously large room has a 15-metre high ceiling with the original mouldings, others have their preserved timber frames, antique writing desks and modern oak. Most astonishing are the 20th-century panelled bathrooms, built for a king's ransom we imagine, designed to harmonise with the rooms: sparkling white porcelain, modern taps, massive mirrors, huge showers. There are two terraces with views across to the Pyrenees for dining, a hall-cum-piano room and fireplaces for chilly evenings. The kitchen opens to the ground-floor hall so you can watch Richard prepare his duck or pigeon specialities for dinner. Perfect for the jazz festival in Marciac.

Price	€100-€150.
Rooms	8: 6 doubles, 1 suite for 3, 1 family room for 4.
Meals	Breakfast €13. Dinner €35-€55.
Closed	February; week before All Saints Day; 21-28 December (open 31 December).
Directions	A64 exit Pau; N134 to Sarron; D646 to Riscle, St Mont & Projan. Signed.

Christine & Richard Poullain
32400 Projan, Gers

Tel	+33 (0)5 62 09 46 21
Email	infos@chateau-de-projan.com
Web	www.chateau-de-projan.com

Le Relais de Saux

Three to five hundred years old, high on a hill facing Lourdes and some dazzling Pyrenean peaks, the house still has a few unregenerate arrow slits from sterner days. You come in through the multi-coloured garden that spreads across lawns and terraces with corners for reading or painting. Bernard Hères inherited Saux from his parents and, with the help of his wife's flair and energy, has opened it to guests. Bernard knows the area well and can guide you to fine walks, climbs or visits. Return to deep armchairs in the dark old-timbered salon with its peaceful garden view. Bedrooms are in the same traditional, elegant mood with draped bedheads and darkish carpeted or flock-papered walls. One has no fewer than four tall windows, another has an old fireplace, the two second-floor rooms are big yet cosy with their lower ceilings; bathrooms are carpeted and well-fitted. Lourdes' torchlit Marian Procession – praying the rosary in all the languages – is a truly moving experience. But a word of warning: vigilance is required on exiting the dual carriageway on your return.

Price	€90–€96.
Rooms	6: 4 doubles, 2 twins/doubles.
Meals	Restaurant 2km.
Closed	Occasionally.
Directions	Left 3km north of Lourdes. Signed but difficult to spot; 1st property 100m from main road.

Bernard & Madelaine Hères
Route de Tarbes, Le Hameau de Saux,
65100 Lourdes, Hautes-Pyrénées

Tel	+33 (0)5 62 94 29 61
Email	contacts@lourdes-relais.com
Web	www.lourdes-relais.com

Languedoc • Roussillon

La Lozerette

In September 1878, Robert Louis Stevenson set off from Le Monastier, accompanied by Modestine the donkey, to walk the 220km path to St Jean du Gard. Towards the end of his journey he stopped off at the Cevennes village of Cocurès, on the river Tarn, just above the National Park. Here Pierrette runs the country inn started by her grandmother and passed on to her by her parents. Laid-back staff, warm and friendly, handle all comers to this busy hotel. Pierrette herself is hands-on, running the reception, taking orders in the (excellent) restaurant, managing the wine cellar: a trained sommelier, she will pick you out just the right bottle. Bedrooms, mostly a good size, colour coordinated but not twee, have wooden floors, oh-so-comfortable beds and a decoration of stripes, checks or flowers. The small bar with its cheerful bucket chairs is charming, the gardens pretty, the balconies bright with flowers. The whole hotel shines. Take a drink to the garden or play boules, walk in the National Park, follow Stevenson's trail – on foot, donkey or horseback. Good value, one of the best.

Price	€63–€88. Half-board €62–€74 p.p.
Rooms	20 twins/doubles.
Meals	Breakfast €8.50.
	Lunch & dinner €17–€47.
	Children's meals €10.50. Rest. closed
	Tues & Wed lunch out of season.
Closed	November–Easter.
Directions	From Florac, N106 for Mende;
	right on D998 for Le Pont de
	Montvert. After 4km hotel on left,
	signed.

Pierrette Agulhon
Cocurès,
48400 Florac, Lozère
Tel +33 (0)4 66 45 06 04
Email lalozerette@wanadoo.fr
Web www.lalozerette.com

Domaine de Marsault

At the end of an avenue of fine planes is a most elegant *maison de maître*: Jean-Pierre Salle has joyfully revived the family mansion and grounds. Step into a stone-flagged hallway and a vast salon, awash with light from high windows overlooking the garden beyond. Red-check armchairs and a fire make this room a winter retreat; for summer there's a Napoleonic 'salon d'été'. Two bedrooms sharing a big bathroom with a wonderful old bath are equally plush – one floral with a huge canopied bed, the other with a draped four-poster – while the big boldly coloured suites have dressing rooms and marble fireplaces, gleaming armoires and pretty chaises longues. Antoine serves a generous, delicious and languorous breakfast at round tables under parasols, or in the dining room at the big polished table. As for the garden, it's large, walled and wonderful, with green swards and cypress trees, sweet roses and elegant round pool. The cherry on the cake? Lovely honey-stoned Uzès awaits at the end of a well-used track through the vines: in 20 minutes you are in *centre ville*. *Wine tasting & Uzès tours. Minimum stay two nights.*

Price	€190. Suites €230.
Rooms	5: 2 doubles, 2 suites; 1 double sharing bathroom (let to same party only).
Meals	Restaurants 2km.
Closed	Mid-October to mid-March.
Directions	A9 exit Rémoulins dir. Uzès; thro' Uzès dir. Alès; 1km, 1st right at r'bout onto Rue Landry; left after 400m; 200m, right at driveway with plane trees. Car park on left.

Jean-Pierre Salle
30700 Uzès, Gard

Tel	+33 (0)4 66 22 53 92
Email	info@domainedemarsault.com
Web	www.domainedemarsault.com

Villa Saint Victor

This frightfully grand looking, 1880s building, all towered and pillared and stone-staircase'd, is actually very friendly and twinkly on the inside. Run as a proper family business, Geoffroy taking great care of you and Stéphane and his wife in the kitchen, the feel is smaller and cosier than you might imagine. A salon with lovely antiques and paintings has space for mingling extroverts as well as corners for cosier chats; the dining area has an arched ceiling, an open fire and big wicker chairs to linger in. Bedrooms on the first floor are grander, with upholstered chairs, views over the park and generous bathrooms, some tower-shaped with bidets like thrones; the rooms above are simpler and more contemporary, with rope carpeting, lighter colours and excellent bedding. Fresh, generous food is beautifully prepared and presented; afterwards you can wander through doors to the garden with its old palm trees and parasols, sloping lawns and silent lily pond. Children will adore the space to run around and you're near to Uzès with its stunning market – and Roman Orange.

Price	€90–€140. Suites €180–€230.
Rooms	17: 7 doubles, 4 twins, 6 suites.
Meals	Breakfast €15. Lunch €18. Dinner €35. Restaurant closed Sun eve & Mon.
Closed	January-February.
Directions	From Uzès D982 to Bagnol sur Cèze for 6km; right on D125 to Saint Victor des Oules. Signed.

Geoffroy & Stéphane Vieljeux
Place du Château,
30700 Saint Victor des Oules, Gard

Tel	+33 (0)4 66 81 90 47
Email	info@villasaintvictor.com
Web	www.villasaintvictor.com

Hôtel Le Saint Laurent

A sparkle of château-living sweeps through this quiet hotel, tucked down one of the village's medieval streets. Not surprising as Christophe, Thierry and Stéphane worked in grand establishments before injecting the 14th-century farmhouse with a sense of élan. There's a salon with red damask and velvet armchairs, a fragrant sun-trapped jasmine'd courtyard for breakfast (great pancakes!), and a veranda invitingly spread with deep sofas. Stone-flagged spaces show off their statues, gilded mirrors and heavy candlesticks, while bedrooms are intimate – some a slight squeeze – yet lavish, rich with antiques, cushions and pretty objets. Some have padded bedheads, others romantic canopies, one has a terrace, another a luscious purple and mauve palette. All very boudoir, and delicious chocolates to welcome you. Large white bathrooms want for nothing. You will be spoilt by the owners and staff, there's a spa (great for winter), a small pool for summer and dinner is a fabulous event. Avignon, Uzès and vineyards are close; enjoy the town's music concerts. Intimate, theatrical, charming. *Secure parking nearby.*

Price	€95–€165. Suites €195–€215.
Rooms	10: 7 doubles, 3 suites (1 with terrace).
Meals	Breakfast €15. Dinner €38. Wine €18–€34. Restaurant 20m.
Closed	Never.
Directions	A9 exit 22 Roquemanne. Left on N58 to Bagnols sur Cèze; left, 4km for St Laurent des Arbres. Hotel in old town centre. Signed.

Thierry Lelong, Christophe Bricaud &
Stéphane Zabotti
1 place de l'Arbre,
30126 Saint Laurent des Arbres, Gard

Tel   +33 (0)4 66 50 14 14
Email   info@lesaintlaurent.biz
Web   www.lesaintlaurent.biz

Domaine du Moulin

The little luxuries of a good hotel and the personality of a B&B in Antoinette's renovated 12th-century mill. She and Otto, both Dutch and multi-lingual, have been respectful of age and style: old parquet floors and doors have been revived, a wooden stair polished to glow. Big modern flower paintings and a Belgian tapestry look good on the walls. The river Nizon flows beneath the house and criss-crosses the grounds, several hectares of them – a mill pond flanked by cherry trees (spectacular in spring), an alley of poplars, a lavender field, a pool. And there are swings and slides for the grandchildren, which yours may share. Breakfast is a Dutch feast of hams, cheeses and cherry jams, served at the big table under the tented pergola, or in the all-white dining room with chandelier. Antoinette is lovely and fills the place with flowers. Bedrooms, named after her daughters, have piles of pillows and fine English florals; all are air conditioned, one has a sun terrace of its own. Bathrooms are swish with big showers or two basins. There's a cosy library full of books, and you and the chef choose the menu for dinner.

Price	€80–€185. Apartment €1,200–€2,200 per week.
Rooms	4 + 1: 4 twins/doubles. Apartment for 7.
Meals	Breakfast €15. Dinner by arrangement. Restaurants nearby.
Closed	Rarely.
Directions	A9 exit 22, Roquemaure for Bagnols sur Cèze. After 4km continue past left turn for St Laurent des Arbres. Left at Rubis, follow road.

Antoinette Keulen
& Otto Van Eikema Hommes
Chemin de la Bégude,
30126 Saint Laurent des Arbres, Gard

Tel	+33 (0)4 66 50 22 67
Email	laurentdesarbres@aol.com
Web	www.domaine-du-moulin.com

La Bastide Sainte Anne

With its chapel and pigeonnier, this Provençal manor looks as venerable as the Pont du Gard's soaring arches. But Sainte Anne, built by master builders, is thoroughly 21st century: its stones are new and its beams are straight! Honeymooning English couple Garry and Amanda fell in love with it in 2008, then moved in. Spacious bedrooms with tiled floors are visually pleasing with their painted furniture, white linen and bouti bedspreads. The first-floor room has its own lift, ground floor rooms have French windows opening to the garden. Big bathrooms have walk-in showers, posh smellies, thick white towels and dressing gowns. Eat a generous breakfast on the terrace to stunning views through olives and truffle oaks of the Pont du Gard, with the Alpilles on the distant horizon. Breakfast in the dining room or lazily in bed; a plethora of local restaurants take care of dinner. The lovely open salon's windows frame more incredible vistas, an indoor heated swimming pool in the Orangerie looks out over the walled garden, jasmine and roses perfume the air, and sunloungers fringe a murmuring fountain. *Beauty treatments available.*

Price	€110–€140.
Rooms	3 twins/doubles.
Meals	Picnic available.
	Restaurants 3-minute drive.
Closed	Rarely.
Directions	A9 exit 23 Remoulins. D1600, then D6086 dir. Bagnoles sur Cèze. At Les Croises, left on D19A dir. Aes 1km. Right on D228 to Castillon du Gard, right Chemin de la Berrette. 1st left, house on right.

Garry & Amanda Andrews
9 chemin de la Garrigue,
30210 Castillon du Gard, Gard

Tel	+33 (0)4 66 81 96 65
Email	labastidesainteanne@hotmail.com
Web	www.labastidesainteanne.com

La Maison

No noise, just the hoot of an owl and a flutter of doves around the roof tops. This 18th-century mellow-yellow stone house sits in the heart of the village. Church, tower and château stand guard over it; beyond are vineyards, fields and woodlands. The views are magical. Back in the house, old vaulted ceilings, shuttered windows and terracotta floors are an understated foil for a contemporary-ethnic décor; Christian and Pierre have infused this grand old house with a very special spirit. Bedrooms, mostly large, have bathrooms to match: the red room with a terrace looking onto the château walls, the suite with a roof terrace and 360° views. There are warm sandy walls, Indonesian wall hangings, ethnic fabrics, painted beams. Breakfast is taken leisurely and blissfully in the walled garden where an ancient tree casts generous shade, or convivially at the long table in the library. There's a piano in the salon and a deeply stylish pool. Choose a restaurant down the hill or strike out further – to Nîmes, Avignon, Arles, Uzès. Original décor, welcoming hosts, heaps of charm. One of the best.

Price	€115–€195.
Rooms	5: 4 doubles, 1 suite for 4.
Meals	Bistros in village.
Closed	Mid-November to mid-March.
Directions	From Nîmes D979 for Blauzac, 16km; after Pont St Nicolas, left for Blauzac; into village, house behind church.

Christian Vaurie
Place de l'Église,
30700 Blauzac, Gard

Tel	+33 (0)4 66 81 25 15
Email	lamaisondeblauzac@wanadoo.fr
Web	www.chambres-provence.com

L'Enclos des Lauriers Roses

The tiny reception gives no clue as to what lies beyond; a hamlet within a village. Step across a sunny dining room, through French windows – and blink. Scattered around three swimming pools is a cluster of cottage rooms. Newly built of pantile and stone recovered from old village houses, most have a private terrace or garden. Large, airy and prettily furnished with painted Provençal pieces and fabulous mattresses, each has a different charm – Mimosa has a finely upholstered yellow bed, Amarilys has big chunky terracotta tiles. Walls are white, ceilings neatly beamed, there might be a bed tucked under a stone arch or extra beds for children on the mezzanine. Bathrooms are modern and marbled and a fridge keeps drinks chilled. Madame Bargeton runs the excellent restaurant, Monsieur does the wine – 500 bottles in the cellar – and their sons take care of the buildings and garden. Eat on the terrace or in the dining room; the cooking is loved by the locals. Nîmes, Avignon and beaches are less than an hour, swim in the Gorges du Gardon, walk amongst the pines. As for the village, it's charming.

Price	€80–€110. Triples €105–€115. Family rooms €130–€160. Half-board €122–€190 for 2.
Rooms	18: 10 twins/doubles, 2 triples, 5 family rooms for 4, 1 family room for 6.
Meals	Breakfast €12. Lunch & dinner €23–€42.
Closed	10 November–10 March.
Directions	A9 exit 24 for N86 to Remoulins. After 3.5km left to St Gervasy for Cabrières. In village centre, signed.

Bargeton Family
71 rue du 14 Juillet,
30210 Cabrières, Gard

Tel	+33 (0)4 66 75 25 42
Email	reception@hotel-lauriersroses.com
Web	www.hotel-lauriersroses.co.uk

Domaine des Clos

When Sandrine and David returned to their Beaucaire roots, they found a worthy vessel for their creativity in an 18th-century wine domaine. All has been authentically and lovingly restored. Every room has a view to the vineyards or the central courtyard lawn, the pool is large and the family – with three children – truly charming. The beautifully designed interiors reveal lots of old beams, vibrant splashes of colour in curtains, bedspreads and tapestries and artefacts galore, many collected during the Aussets' Tunisian travels. Outside are exquisite Italianate gardens and the best of Provence... from among the olive trees, jasmine and bougainvillea, shady stone pergolas and relaxing sitting spots emerge. Consider an aperitif or, in summer, a meal on the terrace of the old ecurié; in winter, keep warm by the fireplace in the communal salon, delightful with its deep fuchsia walls and ceilings hung with handcrafted fixtures. It is hugely original, wonderfully artistic, and the information booklet includes enough markets to keep the picnic bags brimming. Be as active or as idle as you like.

Price	€85-€165.
	Apartments €500-€1,700 per week.
Rooms	8 + 5: 5 doubles, 3 family rooms for 4.
	5 apartments for 2-7.
Meals	Dinner with wine, €30, twice weekly in summer; book ahead. Restaurant 6km.
Closed	January.
Directions	Exit A9 at Remoulins to Beaucaire. On entering Beaucaire 2nd exit at large r'bout, then D38 to St Gilles for 6km. Domaine on left.

Sandrine & David Ausset
Route de Bellegarde,
30300 Beaucaire, Gard
Tel   +33 (0)4 66 01 14 61
Email   contact@domaine-des-clos.com
Web   www.domaine-des-clos.com

L'Auberge du Cèdre

No wonder guests return to this big bustling house. The lively, charming Françoise and her multi-lingual husband Lutz welcome walkers, climbers, cyclists and families. Workshop groups are welcome too: there's a special space for them, separate from the big and comfy sitting room. This is a mellow-stoned auberge, adorned with green shutters, iron balustrades and orangerie windows at the rear. Bedrooms are plain, beamy, white, with the odd splash of ethnic colour and terracotta floors that gleam. Except for the new suites, bathrooms are shared; this is not the place for those looking for luxury. Sharing keeps the prices down and there have been no complaints. On the contrary, the atmosphere is one of good humour and laughter. Meals are chosen from a blackboard menu. A great place for a family to stay: a swimming pool, space to run around in, pétanque under the chestnut trees before you turn in for the night. The auberge sits in the middle of the Pic Saint Loup, one of the best vineyards in the Languedoc; Lutz's excellent wine cellar is another reason to prolong your stay.

Price	€48–€134. Half-board €36–€79 extra p.p. Apartment €790–€1,250 per week.
Rooms	18 + 1: 5 twins/doubles, 7 triples, 3 quads, all sharing 8 bathrooms & 7 wcs; 3 suites, each with separate shower. 1 apt for 6.
Meals	Light lunch €12. À la carte menu €30–€39 at weekends. Wine €9–€88.
Closed	Mid-November to mid-March.
Directions	D17 from Montpellier for Quissac. 6km N of St Mathieu de Tréviers, left to Lauret, 1km. Thro' village; signed.

Françoise Antonin & Lutz Engelmann
Domaine de Cazeneuve,
34270 Lauret, Hérault

Tel +33 (0)4 67 59 02 02
Email welcome@auberge-du-cedre.com
Web www.auberge-du-cedre.com

Bergerie de Fontbonne

This 17th-century bergerie basks among green oaks, garrigue and gnarled vines on a Languedocian hillside, its pale rough-hewn stone walls blending into the sun-kissed landscape. The Passets found the building in ruins, trees breaching the roof. Careful renovation has created an intimate hotel with a trio of bedrooms, one at ground level. Welcoming Madame is an interior designer and her décor is perfect: elegant and rustic not twee. Each spacious room has a bathroom with a stylish free-standing bath and a separate shower. Two salons downstairs team classic French furniture with stone flags, wooden beams and pale plaster, while the dining room's oval table sets the scene for relaxed and generous breakfasts: local breads, pâtisserie and jams, seasonal fruits and yoghurt. Arrange it with Madame and a chef will cook dinner, served on family china, accompanied by local wines. Outdoors, wide paths and the dappled shade of cherry and acacia trees make the lawns a pretty setting for al fresco meals. Blending seamlessly with the landscape, the lovely garden echoes to the calls of nightingales, cicadas, cuckoos and sheep.

Price	€135–€150.
Rooms	3 doubles.
Meals	Breakfast €15. Dinner €40; book ahead. Wine €6.50–€22.
Closed	Rarely.
Directions	A9 exit D34 Lunel dir. Sommières; 1st r'bout dir. Alès, 2nd r'bout D22 dir. St Mathieu de Tréviers. In Campagne, right for D120; cross Garrigues 2km. After riding centre, 1st left, minor road 400m.

Emmanuelle Passet
3105 chemin les Mougères,
34160 Galargues, Hérault

Tel	+33 (0)4 67 92 41 44
Email	contact@bergeriedefontbonne.com
Web	www.bergeriedefontbonne.com

Hôtel de Baudon de Mauny

Here is a very fine *hôtel privé*, its flowery façade in Louis XVI style, its position the cobbled heart of Montpellier. A vast and noble double front door opens onto a courtyard and you enter 18th-century France. Breakfast is served in the elegant hall alongside; a wide stone stair transports you to bedrooms above. On the first floor you will admire the majestic ceilings, the stone floors, the marble fireplaces, the plaster friezes and the vast windows, some with their original panes. Second-floor bedrooms have private salons and brand new shower rooms. It is sophisticated, extraordinary, and the young family whose passion this house is live above; you will be looked after beautifully. Outside the door is grand old Montpellier with its exciting young energy – its sleek designer trams, its car-free Old Town, its farmers' market under the arches, its dance festival in July, its botanic gardens – the oldest in Europe? – and its rich collection of art housed in the just-restored Musée Fabre. Strolling distance is the Jardin des Sens for extravagant dining, and the marvellous old brasserie next to the opera. *Minimum stay two nights.*

Price	€160–€220.
Rooms	5: 1 double, 4 suites.
Meals	Breakfast €15. Restaurants nearby.
Closed	Rarely.
Directions	From North A9, exit Montpellier Centre; follow signs for Le Corum (park here). Hotel 200m walk: right out car park, left up Rue Montpellieret, right Rue de l'Aiguillerie, right, 1st left.

Alain de Bordas
1 rue de la Carbonnerie,
34000 Montpellier, Hérault

Tel	+33 (0)4 67 70 39 69
Email	contact@baudondemauny.com
Web	www.baudondemauny.com

Hôtel de Vigniamont

The townhouse of the Comte de Vigniamont has been revived. Enter a cool flagged entrance, ascend a lovely stone-turned stair – the town is known for them – and step into an elegant, uncluttered, terracotta-tiled salon where stuffed sofas ask to be sunk into and floor-to-ceiling windows overlook 400 years of history. Large, refined bedrooms have sophisticated colours and pretty fauteuils, an antique wardrobe here, a touch of toile de Jouy there, perhaps French windows opening to a central courtyard; each with its own little entrance hall, each beautifully kept. The English McVeighs have worked so hard to restore this place; outgoing and generous, they ran a tea shop, and later a pub, in California. Now they serve excellent breakfasts on the sun-washed roof terrace; and later, as the sun goes down, it's candlelit 'raid the pantry' time – aperitifs, conversation and delectable tapas! Once weekly a mouthwatering meal is produced. A treat to be in lively Pézenas, embraced by antiques and artisans, buildings, balconies, restaurants and bars – and with such warm, generous people.

Price	€100-€150. Suites €120-€140.
Rooms	5: 1 double, 4 suites.
Meals	Hosted dinner with wine, €45 (Mondays only).
Closed	November-March.
Directions	A9 exit 34, D13 to Pézenas centre; left after Carrefour s'market; 2nd left on Rue Louis Blanc; right on Rue Joseph Cambon; left onto Rue Massillon. Street parking possible.

Robert & Tracy McVeigh
5 rue Massillon,
34120 Pézenas, Hérault
Tel +33 (0)4 67 35 14 88
Email info@hoteldevigniamont.com
Web www.hoteldevigniamont.com

Le Clos de Maussanne

This is La Chamberte No.2 – in countryside not town. Surrounded by vineyards just off the main road, the unusual 17th-century house with the clock tower is smaller inside than it looks. Just one room in depth, the house is nevertheless most elegant, and has been furnished as charmingly as its town cousin. The lovely dining room/salon, the heart of the place, looks onto noble old plane trees at the front and a beautiful walled garden at the back; there's a covered terrace full of tables and a super restaurant kitchen downstairs; ask about cookery classes. Staff are delightful. Bedrooms overlook the garden too, and are gorgeous, with sober cream walls, chunky modern furniture, big beds, quilted spreads. The largest room has limewashed beams stretching to the roof, and a pale floor that sweeps from dressing room to terrace. But the biggest inspiration is the food – no menu, and each night a surprise. Visit lovely old Pézenas or stroll the canal bank (seven locks in a row) to Béziers and its pedestrianised old quarter; there's a market on Fridays. Return to a pool surrounded by palms – bliss.

Price	€120-€150.
Rooms	5 doubles.
Meals	Lunch €40. Dinner €45.
	Wine €15-€110.
Closed	Never.
Directions	A9 exit 35 dir. Béziers. 1st r'bout, 2nd exit dir. Pézenas; 2nd r'bout, 1st exit dir. Pézenas. 2km on right.

Bruno Saurel & Irwin Scott-Davidson
Route de Pézenas,
34500 Béziers, Hérault

Tel	+33 (0)4 67 39 31 81
Email	contact@leclosdemaussanne.com
Web	www.leclosdemaussanne.com

Port Rive Gauche

Marseillan is bliss, a little old fishing town down by the great spreading lagoon of Thau, a quiet backwater that the tourist hordes have overlooked. In its heyday 300 years ago, Languedoc wines were brought along the Canal du Midi, which ends in the lagoon, to be shipped from Marseillan and Sète. Two 18th-century wine warehouses have been converted into 11 two-bedroom apartments. Their sober elegance absorbs the waves of light from sea and sky with tranquil grace: every generous living room and every snug bedroom looks over the water, and each has a balcony or a rooftop terrace. The pale plain wood furniture, the natural fabrics, the high-quality equipment breathe rest and reassurance. The little harbour with its boats and cafés is a few minutes' walk away. Collect your fish straight off the boat, prepare it in your perfectly fitted kitchen, then borrow a clutch of bikes and go exploring. Or have a massage and meet others in the tea room. Breakfast will be brought to your suite next morning or you can walk to one of the charming harbourside cafés. Delightful Heather has all the right advice.

Price	€130–€260 for 4 (€735–€1,470 per week).
Rooms	11 suites for 4 (each with kitchen).
Meals	Breakfast from €8. Restaurant 100m.
Closed	January.
Directions	From A9 junc. 34 to Florensac; right D32 to Marseillan (not Marseillan Plage); over 2 r'bouts for 'centre ville'. Left at sign Port Rive Gauche on Rue Jean Bertouy (becomes Rue de Suffren).

Heather Riddoch
Rue des Pêcheurs,
34340 Marseillan, Hérault

Tel	+33 (0)4 67 00 87 65
Email	reservation@garrigaeresorts.com
Web	www.garrigaeresorts.com/rive-gauche

La Chamberte

When Bruno and Irwin set about converting the old wine storehouse the last thing they wanted was to create a 'home from home' for guests; this is far more special! Communal spaces are huge, ceilings high, colours Mediterranean and floors of pigmented polished cement. Bedrooms are simpler than you might expect, TV-free, with big beds (some with a step up), beautiful quilts and warm colours; shower rooms are in ochres and muted pinks, some with pebbles set in cement; thick walls keep you cool in high summer. As for the food, this is Bruno's domain: "not my profession but my passion". He may whisk you off to the hills early one morning, stopping on the way home for a loaf of bread and a paté to accompany pre-dinner aperitifs. In summer you dine on the inner patio, a glorious plant-filled space that reaches up to the original barn roof; in winter you are treated to a dining room with an open fire and stylishly vibrant little tables: one menu, four courses, each delicious. Béziers is a pretty little town surrounded by vineyards, crossed by the Canal du Midi. Wonderful beaches beckon. *Cash only.*

Price	€70–€98.
	Half-board €910 for 2 per week.
Rooms	5 doubles.
Meals	Lunch with wine, €35.
	Dinner with wine, €35–€45.
Closed	Rarely.
Directions	A9 exit 35 Béziers Est for Villeneuve lès Béziers; over canal to town centre; 2nd left after Hotel Cigale; green gate on right.

Bruno Saurel & Irwin Scott-Davidson
34420 Villeneuve lès Béziers, Hérault

Tel	+33 (0)4 67 39 84 83
Email	contact@la-chamberte.com
Web	www.la-chamberte.com

Le Couvent d'Hérépian

Push the heavy doors to sober grandeur: the barrel-vaulted, taupe-painted staircase that faces you is pure 17th-century convent and a candlelit alcove carries today's blackboard menus. You have entered a soft, humane house that breathes a near-maternal security. Fabrice Delprat, a quietly determined eco-warrior, keeps the convent on sustainable rails with humour and care for detail. Big, square, high rooms in the same muted nun's-habit tones display superb eco quality at every turn: natural paints, pure Vosges linens, bamboo duvets, designer bathrooms. Prices reflect desirability. Garden-side rooms glow in the evening sun, their north-facing sisters stay cool, the dearest have private terraces and the two-bedroom suite is stupendous. But come down to the garden and the wild hills rising beyond or to the spa and an essential oils massage. Breakfast at the convivial kitchen table, beneath the ancient vaults, is fresh local goodies and more candles. Don't miss the womb-like bar or the local caterer's traditional dinner specialities. This is one convent that knows about sophisticated hedonism and design. *Wine tasting.*

Price	€120–€355.
Rooms	12: 11 suites for 2, 1 suite for 4 (1 double, 1 twin). All with kitchen, sitting and dining spaces.
Meals	Breakfast €13. Dinner from €20. Wines from €7. Tapas €7–€10, noon–11pm.
Closed	Never.
Directions	From Béziers D909 for Bédarieux 30km; left D909A to Hérépian centre; Rue du Couvent right from central x-roads. Ask about parking.

Fabrice Delprat
2 rue du Couvent,
34600 Hérépian, Hérault

Tel	+33 (0)4 67 23 36 30
Email	herepian@garrigae.com
Web	www.garrigaeresorts.com/le-couvent

Château de la Prade

Lost among the cool shadows of tall sunlit trees, beside the languid waters of the Canal du Midi, is a place of understated elegance and refinement. The 19th-century house is more 'domaine' than 'château', though the vineyards have long gone. It sits in 12 acres… formal hedges, ornamental railings and impressive gates linking château to grounds. Swiss Roland runs the chambres d'hôtes side of things, Lorenz looks after the gardens: generous, kind-hearted, discreetly attentive hosts. Served on pink tablecloths in a light, airy room with a crystal chandelier, dinner is a mix of Swiss, French and Italian cuisine, and breakfast a delicious treat (croissants with homemade apple and rose preserve, exquisitely prepared fruit salads). Bedrooms, too, have tall windows, polished floors and an uncluttered charm; be charmed by traditional armchairs and footstools, huge beds and fresh flowers, white bathrooms with towels to match. You are a half mile from the main road to Carcassonne and yet here there's a feeling of rare calm – disturbed only by the peacocks calling from the balustrades, most vocal in late spring!

Price	€95-€115.
Rooms	4 twins/doubles.
Meals	Dinner €24. Wine €17.50-€23.
Closed	Mid-November to mid-March.
Directions	From A61 exit 22; thro' Bram 2.5km; left D6113 for Villepinte; house signed on left.

	Roland Kurt
	11150 Bram, Aude
Tel	+33 (0)4 68 78 03 99
Email	chateaulaprade@wanadoo.fr
Web	www.chateaulaprade.eu

Château de Cavanac

A peaceful place, with birdsong to serenade you. The château has been in the family for six generations and dates back to 1612; Louis, *chef et patron*, has a small vineyard, so you can drink of the vines that surround you. It's a convivial place, with a big rustic restaurant in the old stables – hops hang from ancient beams and there's an open fire on which they cook the grills; in summer you dine under the stars. It's quiet and friendly, with much comfort and an easy feel; Louis and Anne are justly proud of their food and breakfasts are delicious. The older bedrooms, with Chinese rugs on terracotta tiles, are somewhat dated but the most recently renovated are positively lavish: dramatic canopies, plush fabrics in soft colours, parquet floors, a colonial feel. (Note that the Mimosa room is accessed via the dining room, unlit after hours.) There's a swimming pool outside and a very pretty sunshiney terrace dotted with sunloungers. Beyond the smart wrought-iron gates Languedoc waits to beguile you: horse riding, cellars to visit, incredible Carcassonne close by.

Price	€85–€120. Singles €65–€95. Suites €150–€155. Triples €160.
Rooms	28: 19 doubles, 2 singles, 4 suites, 3 triples.
Meals	Breakfast €12. Dinner from €42 (except Mondays). Restaurants 3km.
Closed	January-February; 2 weeks in November.
Directions	From Toulouse, exit Carsassonne Ouest for Centre Hospitalier, then Route de St Hilaire. Signed. Park in restaurant car park.

	Anne & Louis Gobin
	11570 Cavanac, Aude
Tel	+33 (0)4 68 79 61 04
Email	infos@chateau-de-cavanac.fr
Web	www.chateau-de-cavanac.fr

Montfaucon

A gracious spot for peace and quiet by the river Aude – strolling couples, quacking ducks – yet a short walk from lovely old Limoux with its bars, restaurants and weekend festivals throughout the year: a lively pull for musicians and artists. Enter the huge beautiful doors to this ancient house, parts of which go back to 1324, to discover a fabulous conversion has taken place. Local artisans and master craftsmen have created a stylish entrance lobby with stone walls, marble floors and a sweeping staircase in turned wood. The dining room has beautiful beams, wrought-iron wall lights and huge French doors through which light floods; the terrace, romantically lit at night, overlooks river and town. The atmosphere is one of relaxed elegance, individually designed bedrooms in 19th-century style have floral or striped bedcovers and curtains to match. Sleep deeply in a vast bed with monogrammed sheets; wake to gleaming marble, Persian rugs and walk-in showers. Marvellous. *Minimum stay two nights.*

Price	€170-€220.
Rooms	5: 2 doubles, 2 twins, 1 suite for 2.
Meals	Restaurants 5-minute walk.
Closed	24 December-5 January.
Directions	A61 exit 23 Carcassonne Ouest. Signed.

	Joanne Payan
	11 rue Blanquerie,
	11300 Limoux, Aude
Tel	+33 (0)4 68 69 48 40
Email	joanne@montfaucontours.com
Web	www.montfaucontours.com

Château des Ducs de Joyeuse

The drive up is impressive, the castle even more so: 1500s and fortified, part Gothic, part Renaissance, standing in its own patch of land on the banks of the Aude. A large rectangular courtyard is jolly with summer tables and parasols, the stately dining room has snowy linen cloths and fresh flowers, the staff are truly charming and helpful, and the menu changes daily according to what is fresh. Vaulted ceilings and well-trodden stone spiral stairs lead to formal bedrooms with heavy wooden furniture, some beamed and with stone fireplaces; there's a heraldic feel with narrow high windows, studded doors and smart bedspreads in navy blue and bright red. Ask for a room with a watery view. Bathrooms glow with tiled floors, bright lights and stone walls – some up to two metres thick: perfect sound insulation. Historical information about the building is on display everywhere, manager Philippe is full of ideas and can help you plan your trips out. Hearty souls can knock a ball around the tennis court then cool off in the outdoor pool – or brave that lovely river. Good value.

Price	€90–€135.
	Suites & family rooms €150–€220.
Rooms	35: 10 doubles, 11 twins, 12 suites for 2,
	2 family rooms for 4–5.
Meals	Breakfast €12. Dinner €34–€55,
	June–September only. Wine €20–€80.
Closed	Mid-November to February.
Directions	A61 exit 23 Carcassonne Ouest. D118,
	left D52.

Dominique & Alain Avelange
Allée du Château,
11190 Couiza, Aude
Tel   +33 (0)4 68 74 23 50
Email   reception@chateau-des-ducs.com
Web   www.chateau-des-ducs.com

La Fargo

Pluck a handful of cherries on the way to breakfast; gather up the scents of rosemary and thyme. This centuries-old converted forge sits effortlessly in the unspoilt Corbières countryside. Christophe and Dominique, a gentle, delightful couple, lived the good life rearing goats before rescuing the building years ago. Large, light bedrooms have a charming and simple colonial style – white or stone walls, tiled floors, dark teak, bright ikat bedcovers – and the new block (six huge rooms and a sitting room) is a credit to the craftsmen. Bathrooms are mosaic'd, showers are like rainstorms. Breakfast – just homemade jams and brioches – is on the terrace beneath the kiwi fruit vines. Dine here or in the restaurant where clean modern lines blend with rustic stonework and food is a fabulous mix of Mediterranean and Asian. Corbières is a natural de-stresser: come for birdwatching, walking, fishing, vineyards, Cathar castles, medieval abbeys. Or wander around La Fargo's potager and orchard, pluck some fruit and lie back in one of dozens of wooden loungers. A serene place – and the infinity pool is a dream.

Price	€117–€130. Family rooms €150–€187. Extra bed €15.
Rooms	12: 8 doubles, 2 twins, 2 family rooms for 2-4.
Meals	Breakfast €10. Lunch & dinner €30–€50.
Closed	15 November–15 March.
Directions	A61 exit Lézignan-Corbières, D611 to Fabrezan; D212 to Lagrasse, then St Pierre des Champs. Fargo on right on leaving village.

Christophe & Dominique Morellet
11220 Saint Pierre des Champs, Aude

Tel	+33 (0)4 68 43 12 78
Email	contact@lafargo.fr
Web	www.lafargo.fr

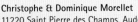

Le Mas Trilles

There's a haphazard feel to the layout of this rambling, honey-coloured 17th-century farmhouse that Marie-France and Laszlo have renovated so well. First greeting you are the sounds of birdsong and rushing water, then, perhaps the head-spinning scent of orange or cherry blossom. There are two comfortable sitting rooms, one high-ceilinged with its original beams, both with cool terracotta tiles and places to read and relax; some of Marie-France's paintings are displayed here. Many of the bedrooms, larger in the main house, are reached by unexpected ups and downs. There are fine antiques and French doors lead onto little terraces; some look onto the pool, some onto woods or mountains. The largest room has magnificent views of the Canigou mountain, the spiritual home of the Catalan nation. Breakfast on the sweet terrace with homemade fig or apricot jam or in front of a crackling fire on chilly day. Then down by the river, there are fine views of the mountains and an intoxicating feeling of space. With its personal welcome, Le Mas Trilles feels more like a home than a hotel.

Price	€92–€216.
	Triples & suites €168–€248.
Rooms	10: 3 doubles, 5 triples, 2 suites.
Meals	Light meals, €15, on request.
	Restaurant 200m.
Closed	8 October–30 April.
Directions	Exit 43 Boulou towards Céret on D115, but do not enter town. House is 2km after Céret towards Amélie les Bains.

Marie-France & Laszlo Bukk
Le Pont de Reynès, 66400 Céret,
Pyrénées-Orientales

Tel	+33 (0)4 68 87 38 37
Email	mastrilles@free.fr
Web	www.le-mas-trilles.com

Rhône Valley – Alps

Le Clos du Châtelet

Washed in barely-there pink, with soft blue shutters, the house was built as a country retreat towards the end of the 18th century by a silk merchant who loved trees. Overlooking the valley of the Saône, with immaculate sweeping lawns, the garden is full of sequoias, cedars, chestnuts and magnolias. To one side of the house, an open outbuilding, home to a collection of antique bird cages, is smothered in flowers. Bedrooms are peaceful havens of elegantly muted colours: Joubert in pink-ochre, its twin wrought-iron four-posters dressed in toile de Jouy; Lamartine in palest aqua with grey and lilac hangings. All have polished wooden floors and gently sober bathrooms. There's much comfort here: an open fire in the sitting room, period furniture, prints, deer antlers on the wall and an delicious air of calm. A harp stands in the corner of the elegant drawing room — we are not sure if it is played but this is the sort of place where it might be. Dinner is by candlelight in an atmospheric dining room with an old terracotta floor and a fountain in the wall. Conveniently close to Bourgogne. *No credit cards.*

Price	€105–€110.
Rooms	4: 3 doubles; 1 double with separate bath.
Meals	Dinner €30; book ahead. Wine €20–€35.
Closed	Rarely.
Directions	A6 exit Tournus for Bourg en Bresse, then to Cuisery. Right at Cuisery for Sermoyer & Pont de Vaux. In Sermoyer follow chambres d'hôtes signs.

Mme Durand Pont
01190 Sermoyer, Ain
Tel   +33 (0)3 85 51 84 37
Email leclosduchatelet@free.fr
Web   www.leclosduchatelet.com

Hôtel Le Cottage Bise

Not many hotels are blessed with such a languid lakeside setting; you could almost imagine yourself in a Wagner opera as you gaze from the terrace at the sun setting over the Roc de Chère. The three buildings that make up this friendly, supremely well-run hotel resemble – quel surprise! – Alpine chalets; what's more, they are set in well-planted gardens with a classy pool and perfectly gravelled pathways. Monsieur and Madame Bise run this relaxed and not-so-small hotel with a quiet Savoyard efficiency, which, at its heart, has a proper concern for the comfort of guests. Rooms are smart, spacious, very French, with patterned carpets and floral prints, navy stripes and polished retro pieces. Every room is different and the balconied suites are splendid, with views to lake and mountains. Talloires has the highest number of Michelin stars per resident than anywhere in the world, and the food here (in the restaurant or on the decked terrace) is first class. You are away from the bustle of Annecy but close enough to dabble if you wish. Sail, windsurf, waterski, pedalo – the lake laps at your feet.

Price	€100–€250.
	Suites & family rooms €300–€350.
Rooms	35: 17 doubles, 15 twins, 3 suites.
	Family rooms available on request.
Meals	Breakfast €17. Lunch €27–€60.
	Dinner €40–€60. Wine €25–€50.
	Restaurants within walking distance.
Closed	10 October–April.
Directions	In Annecy dir. Bord du Lac for Thônes D909. At Veyrier du Lac, D909A to Talloires. Signed in Talloires.

Jean-Claude & Christine Bise
Au Bord du Lac,
74290 Talloires, Haute-Savoie

Tel	+33 (0)4 50 60 71 10
Email	cottagebise@wanadoo.fr
Web	www.cottagebise.com

Auberge Le Chalet des Troncs

Some people get everything right, and without making a lot of noise about it. Jean-François, an architect, has skilfully renovated this wood and stone chalet built around 1780. The style is rustic, the design is contemporary. All walls in the two sitting rooms are the original wood as are ceiling and floor; an old sledge has been converted into a coffee table with a nice scatter of antiques and bric-a-brac about. Original is the design of the handsome leather and pine sofas in front of the big open fire as are the open rough-plank dividers between the beds and bathrooms. He has cleverly fashioned lamps made from branches and kept the light subdued. Christine is busy in the kitchen garden or gathering wild herbs which she uses in her exellent cooking; the pot au feu is prepared over the open fire. The indoor pool feels outside as one wall is a huge picture window onto to the mountain views. You can cross-country ski from the door or catch a free bus 800 metres away for the Grand Bornand. Perfectly quiet, with a lovely rambling garden – grass, shrubs, moss, wild flowers – this is hard to fault.

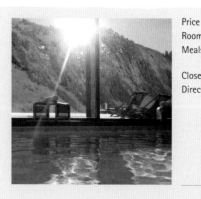

Price	€140-€228.
Rooms	4: 3 twins, 1 family room for 3.
Meals	Breakfast €15. Picnic lunch €10-€20. Dinner from €40.
Closed	Rarely.
Directions	At church in La Grand Bornand, straight on 5km dir. Vallée du Bouchet. In Hameau des Plans, right at little chapel for Hameau.

Christine & Jean-François Charbonnier
Les Troncs, Vallée du Bouchet,
74450 Le Grand Bornand, Haute-Savoie

Tel	+33 (0)4 50 02 28 50
Email	contact@chaletdestroncs.com
Web	www.chaletdestroncs.com

Au Coin du Feu-Chilly Powder

The homeward piste takes you to the door; the cable car, opposite, sweeps you to the peaks. The chalet is named after its magnificent central fireplace… on one side gleaming leather sofas, on the other, red dining chairs at a long table. Everything feels generous here: great beams span the chalet's length, windows look up to the cliffs of the Hauts Forts, high ceilings give a sense of space. There's a reading room on the mezzanine above the living area with books, internet, antique globe and worn leather armchairs, and a small bar made of English oak by a carpenter friend. Bedrooms are Alpine-swish and themed: there's the Toy Room for families, the English Room that sports a bowler hat. The carpets are sisal, one room's four-poster is veiled in muslin and the bathrooms have Molton Brown toiletries and shower heads as big as plates. The chef produces the best of country cooking, and Paul and Francesca can organise everything, including torchlight descents. There's massage, a sauna, a hot tub outdoors, DVDs to cheer wet days – even an in-house nanny. A great spot for families. *New seven-bedroom chalet next door.*

Price	€80. Half-board mandatory in winter (€465–€1,095 p.p. per week).
Rooms	17: 6 doubles, 3 twins, 7 family rooms for 2-5, 1 triple.
Meals	Picnic lunch €5. Dinner with wine, €35.
Closed	Never.
Directions	From Morzine, signs to Avoriaz, then Les Prodains; 2.8 km. On right, just before cable car.

Paul & Francesca Eyre
BP 116, 74110 Morzine,
Haute-Savoie

Tel	+33 (0)4 50 74 75 21
Email	paul@chillypowder.com
Web	www.chillypowder.com

The Farmhouse

The day starts with a breakfast spread in the cattle shed – now a deeply atmospheric dining room – and ends with a slap-up dinner hosted by Dorrien. Eighteen years ago he gave up England for the oldest farmhouse in Morzine – the lovely, steeply pitched Mas de la Coutettaz at the peaceful end of town. Push open the mellow carved door to find a 1771 interior of dark chunky beams, huge polished flags and patina'd pine doors with original mouldings. Big, characterful, comfortable bedrooms, whose bathrooms promise white robes and L'Occitane lotions, are reached via a central stone stair; some have mountain views. And at the end of the garden is an exquisite little mazot: the bedroom is up a steep outside stair. Morzine is the perfect staging post for the Avoriaz and Portes du Soleil, so come for hiking, biking, swimming in the lakes; in winter, a 'ski host' at the farmhouse introduces you to the runs. Return to a hot toddy in the bar and a crackling log fire, lit at the merest hint of chill, even in summer. Final proof (as if you needed it) that you will adore The Farmhouse and hope to return.

Price	€75–€175. Singles €45–€135. Triples €105–€255. Half-board €95–€190 p.p.
Rooms	9: 4 doubles, 1 twin/double, 1 suite for 6, 3 triples.
Meals	Dinner, 4 courses with wine, €30–€40. Half-board only, December-April, on weekly basis.
Closed	May; October-November.
Directions	From Morzine dir. Avoriaz. On Ave Joux Plan, left after Nicholas Sport, then right. 200m on left, signed.

Dorrien Ricardo
Le Mas de la Coutettaz,
74110 Morzine, Haute-Savoie

Tel	+33 (0)4 50 79 08 26
Email	info@thefarmhouse.co.uk
Web	www.thefarmhouse.co.uk

Chalet Odysseus

Chalet Odysseus has the lot: comfort (soft sofas, bright rugs, open fire), swishness (satellite TV, sauna, small gym), a French chef who waves his gourmet wand over the dining table once a week, and English hosts who spoil you rotten. Kate and Barry lived in the village for seven years, then built this chalet. They have the ground floor of this beautifully solid, purpose-built, new chalet, you live above, and it's the sort of place you'd be happy in whatever the weather. Cheerfully pretty bedrooms come with the requisite pine garb, beds are covered in quilts handmade by Kate, two rooms have balconies that catch the sun, and the tiniest comes with bunk beds for kids. The shower rooms and bathroom are airy and light. As for Les Carroz, most skiers pass it by on their way to high-rise Flaine – a shame, for the village has heaps of character and several fine places to eat. Your own 4x4 gets you to the lifts in minutes, tying you in with the whole of the Grand Massif. Dinners are four-course and there's a *grole* night to boot. Great for a family break, whatever the season.

Price	€90. Half-board €100 p.p.
Rooms	5: 2 doubles, 2 twins, 1 family room.
Meals	Dinner with wine, €40.
Closed	Rarely.
Directions	From A40 exit 19 to Cuses; N205 for Sallanches; left D106. 2km before Les Carroz at red & white-shuttered chalet on left; signed.

Kate & Barry Joyce
210 route de Lachat,
74300 Les Carroz d'Araches, Haute-Savoie
Tel   +33 (0)4 50 90 66 00
Email   chaletodysseus@wanadoo.fr
Web   www.chaletodysseuslachat.com

Hôtel Slalom

Right by the Olympic Kandahar run, and opposite the start of the famous Tour du Mont Blanc, is a sparkling hotel. It reopened in 2006 under the inspired stewardship of Tracey Spraggs, whose dream it had been to have a place of her own. Plain on the outside, it is super-stylish within, designer modern but with personality. Bedrooms have fresh white walls, cream carpets and space; curtain-free windows pull in beautiful views. There's a swish little bar, all chrome and polished leather, heaps of restaurants outside the door and a bus a two-minute walk. Best of all, you're 30 metres from the cable car and can ski back to the door. Although this area offers the best tree skiing in the region, the little town of Les Houches – ten minutes from touristy Chamonix – is charming all year round. Take a picnic to the pine-fringed Lac des Chavants and a step back in time on the Mont Blanc Tramway (it opened in 1904 and is still going strong). Sporty types can climb, trek, mountain bike, paraglide, play tennis, have a round of golf and there are good spas nearby, too. Warm, stylish, friendly. *Transfers can be arranged.*

Price	€86–€178.
Rooms	10 twins/doubles.
Meals	Breakfast €10–€12. Restaurants in village.
Closed	May & November.
Directions	From Geneva A401 to Chamonix. N205 & E25 exit Les Houches, right on D213, right on Rue de Bellevue.

Tracey Spraggs
44 rue de Bellevue,
74310 Les Houches, Haute-Savoie
Tel   +33 (0)4 50 54 40 60
Email   info@hotelslalom.net
Web   www.hotelslalom.net

Château Clément

On a wooded hill filled with birds and views – overlooking the spa town of Vals les Bains and the valley beyond – this ornate 19th-century château once saw service as a wartime prison and a holiday centre. Restored to former glory by Éric and Marie-Antoinette, it is now both luxurious eco hotel and young-family home. An extraordinary wooden staircase sweeps you up to airy bedrooms decorated with restrained elegance to complement original features – polished antiques, glowing parquet, tall windows with views to terraced gardens, parkland and the undulating Ardèche. Huge bathrooms have overhead showers attached to free-standing baths, stacks of white towels, organic soaps. House and setting may be grand but the young Chabots are as welcoming as can be, grow their own fruit and veg and eat with their guests in the evening. Éric is an experienced cook and pâtissier-chocolatier and works his magic at dinner. Breakfasts are fabulous too, served on the terrace in summer. Let yourself be enticed from the rose-rich gardens and the elegant salons to the summer pool on the sunny south terrace.

Price	€160-€200. Suite €235-€250. Loft €2,500-€3,800 per week.
Rooms	5 + 1: 4 doubles, 1 suite. 'Loft' for 8-10.
Meals	Dinner with wine, €60.
Closed	January-March.
Directions	A7 exit Le Pouzin for Privas; thro' St Privat; right D578 to Vals les Bains town centre; right at casino, left T-junc., right after hospital; signs to château; gate on left.

Marie-Antoinette & Éric Chabot
La Châtaigneraie,
07600 Vals les Bains, Ardèche

Tel	+33 (0)4 75 87 40 13
Email	contact@chateauclement.com
Web	www.chateauclement.com

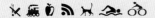

Le Clair de la Plume

Come to feast on the 300 species of old-fashioned and English roses that spill into the winding streets of this 'village fleuri'. Pushing open the wrought-iron gates of the pink-façaded *maison de maître* brings you into something new. Jean-Luc Valadeau has created a feeling of warmth and hospitality: "a home with all the comforts of a hotel". His staff are equally attentive, ushering you through deliciously elegant rooms, antique pieces catching your eye on the way, and the small terraced garden has a natural pool with a lovely view over the town, set in a sea of lavender. Peaceful bedrooms are divided between the main house and a second house 100m away. Find Louis Philippe wardrobes in some, country-style wicker chairs in others, luxurious bathrooms, washed or ragged walls, original floor tiles or shining oak planks – a combination of great taste and authenticity. After a generous breakfast, the garden restaurant is open in summer from noon till late for exotic selections of tea, organic assiettes salées, mouthwatering patisseries, locally made ice cream. Jean-Luc gives you bikes to borrow – explore!

Price	€98–€175.
Rooms	15: 2 doubles, 10 twins/doubles, 3 family suites.
Meals	Breakfast €14. Light lunch €13 (May-September only). Restaurants within walking distance.
Closed	Never.
Directions	From Lyon A7 exit 18 Montélimar Sud dir. Nyons; D133 then D541 to Grignan; signed.

Jean-Luc Valadeau
Place de Mail,
26230 Grignan, Drôme
Tel   +33 (0)4 75 91 81 30
Email   info@clairplume.com
Web   www.clairplume.com

Michel Chabran

Michel Chabran is a delightful man and a prince among restaurateurs, and his little hotel, 50 miles south of Lyon, lies in France's gastronomic heart. In elegant, luxurious surroundings, before a real fire, be seduced by potato purée with Sevruga caviar, poularde de Bresse, hot soufflé of Grand Marnier – food that has won Michel accolades. The à la carte menu stretches to four pages, the set menu two, there are 400 wines and the service is exemplary. It all started in 1937 when Michel's grandfather supplied sandwiches to workers heading south on the first paid holidays to the sun; the rest is history. Bedrooms are deliciously cosy and soundproofed; some face the main road, others the garden – an oasis of beauty and calm. The restaurant and veranda too overlook the lawns, the plane trees, the flowers, the maples. Come for a truffle weekend from November to March; Michel explains the 'black diamonds', then sits you down to a six-course meal. Work it all off the next day in the Vercors National Park, or visit Chave, producer of the Hermitage wines that will have delighted you the night before. €10 supplement for pets.

Price	€110–€175. Single €110–€175. Suite €250–€295.
Rooms	11: 9 doubles, 1 single, 1 suite.
Meals	Breakfast €23. Lunch & dinner €35–€169. Wine from €25.
Closed	Never.
Directions	A7 south of Lyon exit Tain l'Hermitage or Valence North to N7 for Pont de l'Isère. Restaurant & hotel on main street opp. town hall.

M & Mme Chabran
29 avenue du 45 Parallèle,
26600 Pont de l'Isère, Drôme

Tel	+33 (0)4 75 84 60 09
Email	chabran@michelchabran.fr
Web	www.michelchabran.fr

Entry 334   Map 11

La Treille Muscate

It's love at first sight with this jewel of a 17th-century Provençal mas, set in a classified village where pottery and antiques abound. Inside are stone walls, exposed beams, vaulted ceilings and a magnificent ancient fireplace. The views over the Rhône valley and adjoining forests are breathtaking; two of the salons, some of the bedrooms and the highly popular dining terrace all have them. There's also an exquisite enclosed garden for quiet moments. Rooms – four with private terraces – are an inviting and elegant blend of traditional and comfy modern, with choice antiques much in evidence and lots of colour variations, offset by bursts of dazzlingly pure white. The traditional indoor sitting and dining areas are equally welcoming, against a backdrop of stonework and earth tones, and the cuisine regularly gets rave reviews from France's top sources, with the décor sharing the billing. Owner Katy, a former language teacher in France and England, clearly loves her work and greets her guests like old friends. Hiking, horse riding, golf, great markets and summer festivals round out the menu.

Price	€65–€130. Suite €120–€150.
Rooms	12: 8 doubles, 3 twins/doubles, 1 suite.
Meals	Breakfast €11. Dinner €28. Wine €18–€82.
Closed	7 December–12 February.
Directions	From north exit A7 Loriol, south on N7 dir. Montélimar for 1.5km; left on D57, after approx. 3km, D554 to Cliousclat.

Katy Delaitre
26270 Cliousclat, Drôme

Tel	+33 (0)4 75 63 13 10
Email	latreillemuscate@wanadoo.fr
Web	www.latreillemuscate.com

Château de la Commanderie

Grand it appears, and some of the makers of that grandeur – Knights Templar, princes and prime ministers – look down upon you as you eat in the dining room, a favourite restaurant for the discerning palates of Grenoble. Yet the atmosphere is of an intimate family-run hotel. The whole place is awash with family antiques and heirlooms, the breakfasts are delicious, good taste prevails and flowers add that touch of life and genuine attention. And there are massages galore in the sumptuous spa. Bedrooms are divided among four buildings, adding to the sense of intimacy. Rooms in château and chalet are more traditional with carved wooden beds and gilt-framed mirrors, though some of them give onto a small road. The Orangerie's rooms (as you'll discover once you have negotiated the rather plain corridors) look out over fine parkland, and are deliciously peaceful. The least expensive rooms are in the Petit Pavillon, on the roadside. But whichever you choose, you will be beautifully looked after – and you are in a smart suburb of Grenoble. *Signs for 'La Commanderie' indicate an area of town, not the château.*

Price	€102–€190. Singles €92–€180.
Rooms	43 twins/doubles.
Meals	Buffet breakfast €14. Lunch & dinner €27–€70. Restaurant closed Mondays, Saturday lunchtimes & Sundays.
Closed	20 December–3 January.
Directions	From Grenoble, exit 5 Rocade Sud for Eybens, immed. right at 1st lights for Le Bourg; right after Esso garage. Entrance to hotel 300m on left at turning in road.

M de Beaumont
17 avenue d'Echirolles, Eybens,
38230 Grenoble, Isère

Tel	+33 (0)4 76 25 34 58
Email	resa@commanderie.fr
Web	www.commanderie.fr

Collège Hôtel

Who would have thought that a school-themed hotel could be so exhilarating? Combine it with a sleek new design and you have one of Lyon's most exciting places to stay, on the edge of the charming old quarter. Built in the 30s in Art Deco style, the new renovation has introduced a quirky kind of cool and at night optical fibres light the façade all colours of the rainbow. The entrance hall has lovely 'old school' touches, a huge painting of a classroom and a vintage TV running cult school classics. Room prices are chalked onto a blackboard; the reception desk has been created from a gymnasium horse; the brown breakfast room glows with polished wooden tables, leather benches and glass-fronted bookcases. Take the lift clad in school assembly photographs to black and white corridors signposted 'the dorms'… bedrooms are pure symphonies of white (walls, beds, leather armchairs), bathrooms are relentlessly stylish, with several large triangular bathtubs. A graceful roof terrace completes the show, decked in green and jutting like the prow of an ocean liner. Bravo!

Price	€115-€145.
Rooms	40 twins/doubles.
Meals	Breakfast €12. Restaurants nearby.
Closed	Never.
Directions	A6 Paris-Lyon exit Vieux Lyon; after tunnel of Fourière follow river on Quai Fulchiron & Quai Bondy; left at Pont La Feuillée to Pl. St Paul, opp. station. Hotel on left corner (parking €12).

	Chantal Corgier
	5 place St Paul, 69005 Lyon, Rhône
Tel	+33 (0)4 72 10 05 05
Email	contact@college-hotel.com
Web	www.college-hotel.com

L'Ermitage Hôtel Cuisine-à-manger

An ultra-modern sister for Lyon's centrally sited Collège Hotel, 20 minutes away by car. The architecture may be different but the swish interiors are just as cool: pale blonde wood, walls exposed brick or bright white, mocha leather sofas, a crisp dining room, beautifully designed chairs. But the big plus here is the panorama: views sweep over the city to the green foothills beyond and locals negotiate the twisty road up just for the view; catch it from the terrace with its shady trees and lime green seating, or from the all-weather pool with immaculate decking. The old streets of Lyon teem with good restaurants but you have a couple here, too, one with sliding glass doors to a terrace; we hear good reports of the food. Indulge in a gentle game of pétanque, puff around the fitness trail, return to minimalist bedrooms short on decoration, just oak floors, excellent mattresses, flat-screen TVs… and retro fridges in the corridors. Some rooms look onto the street; others have the stunning views – at their most dramatic during the Festival of Light, when Lyon's monuments and bridges are floodlit.

Price	€135–€185. Suite €225.
Rooms	28: 27 doubles, 1 suite for 4.
Meals	Breakfast €12. Lunch & dinner from €30.
Closed	Never.
Directions	From Paris A6 exit 33; follow signs for Limonest; Route de la Garde, Route du Mont Verdun, Route du Mont Thou, Route des Crètes. Free parking.

	Nicolas Vainchtock
	Chemin de L'Ermitage, Mont Cindre,
	69450 Saint Cyr au Mont d'Or, Rhône
Tel	+33 (0)4 72 19 69 69
Email	contact@ermitage-college-hotel.com
Web	www.ermitage-college-hotel.com

Entry 338   Map 11

Château de la Charmeraie

Nestled into the deep quiet of the Lyonnais hills, this 19th-century estate welcomes you with fine craftsmanship into reception rooms panelled in walnut and wild cherry and exquisite even to the detail of silver door handles. The outside is beguilingly simple, a deep apricot and ochre-pink, where a long sun terrace unfolds, furnished in appealing wickerware and forming a neat lip above the pool. On fine days breakfast is served here, comprising homemade jams, breads and pastries. From its seat in a dell, the house enjoys a marvellous vista of private lake, parkland and a drive flanked by horse chestnut. Within, bedrooms are sumptuous, traditional and feminine in style, matching enticing beds and perfectly upholstered armchairs with marble or brass-framed log fires, ingeniously paired at eye-level with flat-screen televisions. One comes with a pretty conservatory, another with a bed swathed in fluffy apple-green netting – wondrously amorous. Bathrooms have sheer class. It's easy to get caught up in Brigitte's enthusiasm for her own home, particularly while seated at her excellent table d'hôtes.

Price	€70–€155.
Rooms	6: 4 doubles, 1 twin, 1 suite.
Meals	Dinner with wine, €30. Restaurant 10km.
Closed	Never.
Directions	A6 from Paris exit Portes de Lyon dir. Rouanne, L'Arbresle, Clermont-Ferrand. Entering St. Laurent de Chamousset, r'bout 4th exit dir. 'Complexe sportif'. Right at Virgin Mary statue; 1st left, 1st right.

Brigitte & René Trégouët
Domaine de la Bâtie,
69930 Saint Laurent de Chamousset,
Rhône

Tel	+33 (0)4 74 70 50 70
Email	contact@chateaudelacharmeraie.com
Web	www.chateaudelacharmeraie.com

Château de Pramenoux

Climb up into the Mont du Beaujolais hills above Lyon for a stunning panorama. Rivers pulse down on either side and great Douglas pines clean the air. As you round a curve, a pair of Gothic pepperpot turrets pop surprisingly into view. The château sits in a natural clearing and views from the terrace and bedrooms sweep splendidly down the valley; a small pond in front anchors the eye. Emmanuel, a young escapee from the corporate world, charming, engaging, passionate about this place, will point out the bits that date from the 10th century up to the Renaissance; he has patched and painted much of it himself. Rooms are big, hugely comfortable and have simple, elegant bathrooms. Recline in the cherrywood panelled room with its a gold and white striped bed and Louis XVI chairs in eau-de-nil; slumber in a canopied bed surrounded by blue and gold fleur-de-lys, a textile re-created by Emmanuel with the weavers of Lyon. Sheer beauty, sweet peace, wonderful dinners hosted by Emmanuel and Jean-Luc, and opera in the summer in the vast reception hall. It is unforgettable. *Cash or cheque only.*

Price	€125–€140.
Rooms	5 doubles.
Meals	Hosted dinner with wine & aperitif, €35; book ahead.
Closed	Rarely.
Directions	From A6 exit Belleville D37 for Beaujeu to St Vincent; left D9 to Quincié, Marchampt, Lamure; at end of Lamure, lane opp. 'terrain de sport' for Pramenoux.

Emmanuel Baudoin
69870 Lamure sur Azergues, Rhône

Tel	+33 (0)4 74 03 16 43
Email	emmanuel@pramenoux.com
Web	www.pramenoux.com

Provence – Alps – Riviera

Le Mas de Peint

In the heart of the Camargue, live as a Camargue 'cowboy' – book in for an energetic, gastronomic short break! Lucille and Jacques are warm, kind and proud of their beautiful farm. Five hundred bulls, 15 horses and swathes of arable land keep Jacques busy; Lucille deals with the rest. She has introduced an elegant but sober French country-farmhouse feel – no flounces or flummery, just impeccable style. Bedrooms are deep green or old rose; generous curtains are checked dove-grey; floors come tiled or wool-carpeted. There's eye-catching quirkery everywhere – a collection of fine pencil sketches, an antique commode – and some rooms with mezzanine bathrooms under old rafters. Breakfast royally in the big family kitchen or on the wisteria-draped terrace, then drift across to the secluded pool, encircled by teak loungers, scented with jasmine. We recommend demi-pension: there's a fabulous new chef who delivers elegant, regional, innovative food, served under a muslin canopy at tables aglow with Moroccan lamps. Follow with coffees and cognacs in the clubby cigar room or the seductive salon.

Price	€235–€295. Suites €375–€435. Half-board €72 extra p.p.
Rooms	12: 2 doubles, 6 twins/doubles, 2 suites for 2, 1 suite for 3, 1 suite for 3-4.
Meals	Breakfast €22. Lunch €35–€58. Dinner €58. Restaurant closed Wednesdays.
Closed	5 January-19 March; 13 November-17 December.
Directions	Arles to St Marie de la Mer D570; 2km after 2nd r'bout, D36 for Salin de Giraud & Le Sambuc. On left 2km after Le Sambuc; signed.

Jacques & Lucille Bon
Le Sambuc,
13200 Arles, Bouches-du-Rhône

Tel	+33 (0)4 90 97 20 62
Email	hotel@masdepeint.net
Web	www.masdepeint.com

Grand Hôtel Nord Pinus

An Arlesian legend, where Spain meets France, ancient Rome meets the 21st century – the hotel is hugely atmospheric. Built in 1865 on Roman vaults, it came to fame in the 1950s when a clown and a cabaret singer owned it: famous bullfighters dressed here before entering the arena and the arty crowd flocked (Cocteau, Picasso, Hemingway...). Anne Igou keeps the drama alive today with her strong personality and cinema, fashion and photography folk – and bullfighters still have 'their' superb Spanish Rococo room. The style is vibrant and alive at this show of Art Deco furniture and fittings, great bullfighting posters and toreador costumes, North African carpets and artefacts, fabulous Provençal colours and ironwork. Colour and light are deftly used to create a soft, nostalgic atmosphere where you feel both warm and cool, smart and artistic. Rooms are big, ceilings are high, the top floor suite has a covered terrace and views over the rooftops. A well-known chef has created a gourmet menu and breakfast is a festival of real French tastes – more magic, more nostalgia. As Cocteau said: "An hotel with a soul".

Price	€170–€240. Suites €295. Apartment €570.
Rooms	26: 9 doubles, 9 twins, 6 suites for 2, 1 suite for 4, 1 apartment for 4 (without kitchen).
Meals	Breakfast €15–€20. Lunch & dinner from €35.
Closed	January-February.
Directions	From A54 exit Arles Centre for Centre Ancien. Boulevard des Lices at main post office; left Rue Jean Jaurès; right Rue Cloître, right to Place du Forum.

Anne Igou
Place du Forum,
13200 Arles,
Bouches-du-Rhône

Tel	+33 (0)4 90 93 44 44
Email	info@nord-pinus.com
Web	www.nord-pinus.com

La Riboto de Taven

Have you ever slept in a cave, in a canopied bed with an ornate cover and hangings, and a luxurious modern bathroom next door? Here you can – if you book far enough ahead; just make sure you stay for more than a night. The Novi-Thème family – Christine, Philippe and Jean-Pierre – have farmed for four generations and are guardians of a most magical place. Their 18th-century *mas* faces the spectacular cliff-top village of Les Baux de Provence – perhaps the most beautiful village in France – and, as the house is built onto the limestone, the rock forms the ceilings of two of the bedrooms. Outside, up the stone steps from the gardens (magnificent formal French, full of hidden corners) is a sprawling, sun-dappled terrace with a wonderful view; watch the light change on the cliffs with each passing hour. Excellent is the food, delightful is the welcome; you arrive as guests and leave as friends. A supreme oasis of peacefulness, history and light, strategically placed for Arles, Avignon, Orange, the Pont du Gard, the Côtes du Rhône, and festivals galore. *Children over ten welcome. Minimum stay two nights.*

Price	€190–€240. Troglodyte suites €290. Apartment €275. All prices per night.
Rooms	6: 3 doubles, 2 troglodyte suites, 1 apartment for 4 (without kitchen).
Meals	Breakfast €18. Poolside lunch €23. Dinner €55. Restaurant closed Wednesdays.
Closed	Early January–early March.
Directions	From St Rémy de Provence D5 to Maussane & Les Baux. Past entrance to village & head towards Fontvieille. Hotel on D78G; signed.

Novi–Thème Family
Vallon de la Fontaine,
13520 Les Baux de Provence,
Bouches-du-Rhône

Tel	+33 (0)4 90 54 34 23
Email	contact@riboto-de-taven.fr
Web	www.riboto-de-taven.fr

Mas de l'Oulivié

Having fallen in love with the olive groves, lavender fields and chalky white hillsides of Les Baux de Provence, the family built the hotel of their dreams some years ago: a creamy-fronted, almond green-shuttered, Provence-style structure, roofed with reclaimed terracotta tiles, landscaped with cypress and oleander. The owners' taste is impeccable, and every last detail has been carefully crafted, from the local oak furniture and the painted and waxed walls to the homemade tiles around the pool. And what a pool! It is curvaceous and landscaped, with a jacuzzi and a gentle slope for little ones. Furnishings are fresh, local, designed for deep comfort. Bedrooms are gorgeously coloured, country-style with an elegant twist. The bar/living-room has a rustic fireplace, filled with flowers in the summer. The Achards love to provide guests and their children with the very best and that includes a superb well-being and massage room and delicious lunches by the pool; they also sell their own lavender and oil. One of the crème de la crème of Provence's small, modern country hotels – near oh-so-pretty Les Baux.

Price	€110-€280. Suites €340-€470. Extra bed €25.
Rooms	27: 25 doubles, 2 suites.
Meals	Breakfast €14. Poolside lunch €8-€35 (booking advisable). Wine €12-€29. Restaurants 2km.
Closed	Mid-November to mid-March.
Directions	From north A7 exit 24 for St Rémy de Provence & Les Baux. Mas 2km from Les Baux on D78 towards Fontvieille.

Emmanuel & Isabelle Achard
Les Arcoules,
13520 Les Baux de Provence,
Bouches-du-Rhône

Tel   +33 (0)4 90 54 35 78
Email   contact@masdeloulivie.com
Web   www.masdeloulivie.com

Mas des Comtes de Provence

Homesick for the south of France, looking for a life change after a busy career in Paris, Pierre fell for this historic hunting lodge and settled in happily after a huge restoration. The mellow-stone *mas* belonged to King René whose château is up the road; some say the Germans blocked the underground tunnel that connected them. A soberly elegant stone exterior dating from the 15th century protects a large interior courtyard overlooked by pretty shuttered windows. As for the bedrooms, they are regal and awesomely huge – the Royal Suite measures 100m^2. Roi René comes dressed in tones of ivory, brown and beige, Garance is in terracottas and yellows; bathrooms have huge towels. The vast pool (no steps) heated by the Provence sun is well hidden in the two-hectare park, majestically treed with 300-year-old planes, pines, cypresses and cedars; swings and authentic boulodrome, too. Pierre and Elisabeth may prepare a barbecue here, but there's a different menu every day. Hiking, cycling, riding – all are minutes away. A lovely property full of history, charm and cachet. *Weddings & quilt-making courses.*

Price	€140-€200. Suites €240-€380.
Rooms	9: 6 twins/doubles, 3 suites for 4-6.
Meals	Breakfast €12.50. Lunch €25-€40. Dinner with coffee, €40-€50; book ahead. Wine €25-€45.
Closed	Never.
Directions	From Tarascon D970 dir. Arles. 200m after Tarascon, D35 on right 'Petite Route d'Arles'; on 800m, road on left. Mas 600m on left.

Pierre Valo & Elisabeth Ferriol
Petite Route d'Arles,
13150 Tarascon,
Bouches-du-Rhône

Tel	+33 (0)4 90 91 00 13
Email	valo@mas-provence.com
Web	www.mas-provence.com

La Maison du Paradou

Those lucky enough to wash up at this honey-stone 'mas' in sleepy Paradou will find intimacy and luxury combined. This charmingly converted coaching inn has a stupendous vaulted salon with a roaring fire and books galore, making it one for all seasons; in good weather you decamp onto the terrace for delicious communal breakfasts. You'll find a boules pitch, two rather swish pools, white sun loungers and a super garden. As for the rooms, expect the best: fabulous linen on the comfiest beds, delicious colours to keep you smiling (emerald, fuchsia, lemon) and bathrooms that go the whole way. A TV/computer in each room is packed with music and movies, but downstairs walls are crammed with art, some of it sensational: Nick's father was a collector. Communal dinners are served twice weekly, and the legendary Bistro du Paradou (Terrance Conran's favourite restaurant) is around the corner. Michelin stars aplenty wait up the hill. Arles is close for all things Van Gogh, as is St Remy for its ever-popular market, and don't miss the magical Cathédrale d'Images at Les Baux. Special place, special people.

Price	€265–€285.
Rooms	5 doubles.
Meals	Lunch €35. Dinner €75. Restaurants nearby.
Closed	Rarely.
Directions	From Nice, A8 to A7 north; 1st exit after toll station at Lançon de Provence; A54, 1st exit dir. St Martin de Crau. Right at major junc. in St Martin to Les Baux; on for 7km. Signed.

Andrea & Nick Morris
Route de Saint-Roch,
13520 Paradou, Bouches-du-Rhône
Tel   +33 (0)4 90 54 65 46
Email   reservations@maisonduparadou.com
Web   www.maisonduparadou.com

Hôtel Le Cadran Solaire

A soft clear light filters through the house, the light of the south pushing past the smallish windows and stroking the light-handed, rich-pastelled décor where simple Provençal furniture, stencil motifs and natural materials – cotton, linen, organdy and seagrass – give the immediate feel of a well-loved family home. The simplicity of a pastel slipcover over a chair, a modern wrought-iron bed frame and an authentic 'boutis' quilt is refreshing and restful – and the house stays deliciously cool in the summer heat. The solid old staging post has stood here, with its thick walls, for 400 years, its face is as pretty as ever, calmly set in its gentle garden of happy flowers where guests can always find a quiet corner for their deckchairs. You can have delicious breakfast on the shrubby, sun-dappled terrace, under a blue and white parasol, or in the attractive dining room where a fine big mirror overlooks the smart red-on-white tables. A wonderful atmosphere, relaxed, smiling staff all of whom are family. Linden, olives, figs, roses in the garden, and an excellent little restaurant in the village.

Price	€70-€110. Family suite €145.
Rooms	12: 5 doubles, 3 twins/doubles, 1 twin, 2 triples, 1 family suite (1 double, 1 twin).
Meals	Breakfast €9. Restaurants in village.
Closed	November-March. Call for out of season reservations.
Directions	A7 exit Avignon Sud for Châteaurenard; D28 to Graveson. 1st right into village; through village almost to end; small sign on right. Right for 200m to end of 1st block; through gates on right.

Elisa & Jean-Claude Rastoin
5 rue du Cabaret Neuf,
13690 Graveson, Bouches-du-Rhône

Tel   +33 (0)4 90 95 71 79
Email   cadransolaire@wanadoo.fr
Web   www.hotel-en-provence.com

Hôtel Gounod

Madame and Monsieur Maurin are experienced and enthusiastic hoteliers, rightly proud of their smart little hotel. On the main town square, Hôtel Gounod lies at the very heart of lively, artistic, much sought-after St Rémy, and takes its name from the composer Charles Gounod. His work informs the theme of the entire hotel. His music plays (softly) in the elegant communal areas, a statue of the Virgin Mary reflects his religious persuasion, and each very different bedroom, reached along a labyrinth of corridors, has been decorated to reflect a phase of his life. The effect is theatrical, colourful, diverting, eccentric, bordering at times on the kitsch. Beds are voluptuous and the quietest rooms look onto the garden, an oasis of calm with a lazy pool. For a gastronomic treat, pad over to the salon de thé, where Madame Maurin – an excellent patissière – serves her masterful creations, alongside giant ice creams and sandwiches. A very pleasant place in which to hang your Provençal hat – and make sure you're around on a Wednesday: market day!

Price	€145–€195. Duplex & suites €230.
Rooms	34: 20 doubles (10 with terrace), 10 twins, 1 duplex, 3 suites.
Meals	Tea room snacks & light supper, from €13.
Closed	Rarely.
Directions	A7 exit Cavaillon to St Rémy, signs for 'centre ville'. On main square opp. church. Free taxi service to local station/airport.

M & Mme Maurin
18 place de la République,
13210 Saint Rémy de Provence,
Bouches-du-Rhône

Tel   +33 (0)4 90 92 06 14
Email   contact@hotel-gounod.com
Web   www.hotel-gounod.com

Entry 348   Map 16

Le Mas des Carassins

You'll be charmed by the gentle pink tiles and greige shutters of the *mas* turned hotel, which settles so gently into the greenery surrounding it. The garden is massive and bursts with oleanders, lavender and lemons. Carefully tended patches of lawn lead to a pool and barbecue; after a swim, pétanque and badminton to play. Or spin off on bikes – charming St Rémy is at the end of the peaceful road. This is Van Gogh country (he lived for a time nearby) and an ancient land: the hotel lies within the preserved area of the Roman town of Glanum. In the pretty dining room, oil paintings by a friend add a splash to white walls, while meals are a fine feast of market produce accompanied by excellent local wines. Bedrooms are dreamy, washed in smoky-blue or ochre shades; dark wrought-iron beds are dressed in oatmeal linens and white quilts; those on the ground floor open to small gardens or wooden decks. The young owners have thought of everything: pick-up from the airport or train, car rental, tickets for local events. Perfect. *New summer/winter swimming pool. Children over 12 welcome.*

Price	€99–€189. Suites €202–€212.
Rooms	14: 12 twins/doubles, 2 suites.
Meals	Breakfast €12. Dinner €29.50. Half board €26.50 extra p.p. Restaurants 5-minute walk.
Closed	January–early March.
Directions	From St Rémy de Provence centre, over Canal des Alpilles on Ave Van Gogh, then right into Ave J. d'Arbaud. Hotel entrance on left after 180m.

Michel Dimeux & Pierre Ticot
1 chemin Gaulois,
13210 Saint Rémy de Provence,
Bouches-du-Rhône

Tel	+33 (0)4 90 92 15 48
Email	info@masdescarassins.com
Web	www.masdescarassins.com

Mas de Cornud

Guest house, cookery school and wine courses combine in a typical farmhouse where two majestic plane trees stand guard over the boules pitch and the scents and light of Provence hover. Nito, chef and nature-lover, cares about how colour creates feeling, how fabrics comfort: she and David, the sommelier, have done a superb restoration. Discover hangings from Kashmir, old French tiles, a piano you may play, and bedrooms big and varied, warm and simple. The atmosphere is convivial and open: you are a member of a family here, so join the others at the honesty bar, choose a cookbook to drool over, take a dip in the cool pool. The kitchen is the vital centre of Cornud: here you eat if the weather is poor (otherwise the garden has some lovely spots). And there are cookery lessons for the enthusiastic: the teaching kitchens have granite work stations, wood-fired and spit-roast ovens. Direct from artisan suppliers come olive oils and cheeses; the garden provides herbs, vegetables and fruits. Come and be part of Provence. *Minimum stay two nights. Children over 12 welcome. Credit cards accepted via PayPal only.*

Price	€150-€230. Suite €240-€395.
Rooms	6: 5 doubles, 1 suite for 2-5.
Meals	Picnic €40. Lunch €21-€35. Hosted dinner with wine, €55-€65.
Closed	November to week before Easter.
Directions	3km west of St Rémy de Provence on D99 dir. Tarascon. D27 for Les Baux 1km, left at sign for Mas de Cornud on D31. House 200m on left after turn.

Ethical Collection: Environment; Community; Food.
See page 446 for details

David & Nitockrees Tadros Carpita
Petite Route des Baux (D31),
13210 Saint Rémy de Provence,
Bouches-du-Rhône
Tel   +33 (0)4 90 92 39 32
Email mascornud@live.com
Web   www.mascornud.com

Mas du Vigueirat

A small pool cascading into a larger pool, a walled garden with quiet corners, wisteria, honeysuckle, trees of all sorts… and nothing to disturb the view but meadows, woods and horses. You'll find it impossible to leave this tranquil, scented spot – although St Rémy (galleries, Van Gogh museum) is just up the road, and Arles, Avignon, the lavender fields and olive groves of Baux de Provence are not much further. High plane trees flank the drive to the dusky pink, blue-shuttered Provençal farmhouse and inside all is light, simplicity and gentle elegance. Bedrooms are uncluttered spaces of bleached colours, limed walls and terracotta floors. Views are over the garden or meadows; ground-floor Maillane has a private terrace. The high-beamed dining room/salon is a calm white space with a corner for sofas and books. If the weather's warm you'll take breakfast under the plane tree; after a dip in the pool or a jaunt on the bike, enjoy one of Catherine's delicious lunches, fresh from the vegetable garden. No suppers, but the helpful Jeanniards will recommend local places.

Price	€130–€155.
	Suite €185 (July/August only).
Rooms	4: 3 doubles, 1 suite.
Meals	Picnic available. Poolside meals in summer €15–€20. Restaurants 3km.
Closed	Christmas.
Directions	From Lyon A7 exit Avignon Sud to Noves. In St Rémy, right at 5th r'bout to Maillane. After 3km, right at sign for pepinières.

Catherine Jeanniard
Chemin du Grand Bourbourel, Route de Maillane,
13210 Saint Rémy de Provence,
Bouches-du-Rhône

Tel	+33 (0)4 90 92 56 07
Email	contact@mas-du-vigueirat.com
Web	www.mas-du-vigueirat.com

Mas Doù Pastré

It's a charming place, gypsy-bright with wonderful furniture, checked cushions, colourwashed walls, fine kilims. Built at the end of the 18th century, this lovely old *mas* belonged to Grandpère and Grandmère: nine months of the year were spent here, three up in the pastures with the sheep. Albine and her sisters have turned the old farmhouse into a hotel to keep it in the family – and she and her talented handyman husband, Maurice, have succeeded, brilliantly. Bedrooms have wooden or tiled floors, antique doors and comfortable beds; all are big, some with their own sitting areas. Bathrooms are original with stone floors and beautiful washbasins picked up at flea markets; a claw-foot bath peeps theatrically out from behind striped curtains. Breakfast is a delicious feast and if you want a lie-in, light meals are served all day long in the new restaurant gastronomique. The garden is the best room with long views over the Alpilles: lounge on a chaise-longue with a bright awning, swim in the dreamy pool, drift off in the jacuzzi, or have a shaitsu treatment in the hamman. Bliss. *Minimum stay three nights July/August. Unsupervised pool.*

Price	€125-€180. Suite €240. Gypsy caravans €80-€150. All prices per night.
Rooms	16: 10 doubles, 2 twins, 1 suite for 4. 3 gypsy caravans for 2.
Meals	Breakfast €15. Light meals €12-€13 (1-8pm). À la carte available.
Closed	15 November-15 December.
Directions	From A7 exit Cavaillon for St Rémy for 10km, then left for Eygalières. House on route Jean Moulin (dir. Orgon), opp. Chapelle St Sixte.

Albine & Maurice Roumanille
Quartier St Sixte,
13810 Eygalières, Bouches-du-Rhône
Tel   +33 (0)4 90 95 92 61
Email   contact@masdupastre.com
Web   www.masdupastre.com

Mas de la Rabassière

Fanfares of lilies at the door, Haydn inside and Michael smiling in his chef's apron. Rabassière means 'where truffles are found' and his epicurean dinners are a must; wines from the neighbouring vineyard, and a sculpted dancer, also grace the terrace table. Cookery classes using home-produced olive oil along with advice on what to see and where to go, jogging companionship and airport pick-ups are all part of Michael's unflagging hospitality; nobly aided by Thévi, his Singaporean assistant. Michael was posted to France by a multi-national and on his retirement slipped into this unusually lush corner of Provence. The proximity of the canal keeps everything green: revel in the well-treed park with its grassy olive grove, roses galore, lilies, jasmine, and white and blue wisteria. There's a large library in English and French, and bedrooms and drawing room are comfortable in English country-house style: generous beds, erudite books, a tuned piano, fine etchings and oils, Provençal antiques. Come savour this charmingly generous house – and Michael's homemade croissants and fig jam on the shady veranda.

Price	€135. Singles €85.
Rooms	2 doubles.
Meals	Dinner with wine, €47.
Closed	Rarely.
Directions	A54 exit 13 to Grans on D19; right on D16 to St Chamas; just before r'way bridge, left for Cornillon & up hill for 2km; house on right before tennis court. Map sent on request.

Michael Frost
2137 chemin de la Rabassière,
13250 Saint Chamas, Bouches-du-Rhône
Tel   +33 (0)4 90 50 70 40
Email   michaelfrost@rabassiere.com
Web   www.rabassiere.com

Ethical Collection: Food.
See page 446 for details

Château de la Barben

The castle, all towers, turrets and terraces, is majestic; as is its position, high on impregnable rock, overlooking a lush valley. Join the museum visitors and enter to discover guardrooms, subterranean passages and watchtowers with pulleys, arrow slits, coats of arms and innumerable tapestried rooms. Madame is as elegant as you would hope her to be, Monsieur looks after the guests, with charm, and their daughter, a talented cook, delivers dinners to the big table in the 11th-century kitchen, shared with your hosts – or to the balustraded terrace for dinner à deux. Bedrooms range from Diane, a (relatively) modest symphony in celestial blue, to the Suite des Amours in the tower, its four-poster dating from the Renaissance, its canopies of cream linen, its stone fireplace vast... take a bottle of bubbly to the private terrace and toast that exceptional view. Bathrooms are mostly huge, and scattered with L'Occitane potions. Heaps to do, from exploring the orangeries, topiaries and ornamental ponds in the gloriously historic grounds to discovering the sights, tastes and smells of delicious Provence.

Price	€130–€230.
Rooms	5: 3 doubles, 2 suites.
Meals	Dinner, 3 courses, with wine, €50.
Closed	December–February.
Directions	A7 then A54 exit 15 (Pélisanne); D572 to La Barben village.

Bertrand Pillivuyt
Route du Château,
13330 La Barben, Bouches-du-Rhône
Tel   +33 (0)4 90 55 25 41
Email   info@chateau-de-la-barben.fr
Web   www.chateaudelabarben.fr

Bastide Le Mourre

Victorine fell in love with this lovely 17th-century bastide years before it came on the market. Now she has her little piece of paradise, a blue-shuttered hamlet in the heart of the Luberon encircled by vines, olives, jasmine and roses. Attached to the house are the gîtes: the pigeonnier, the silkworm house, the wine stores, two barns and, at the top of the garden, secluded and shaded by an ancient oak, the little round Moulin for two. All have their own private entrance and terrace where breakfast is served, all are filled with light and colour, all will delight you. Imagine big sisal rugs on ancient terracotta floors, fine Provençal ceilings and painted wooden doors, open stone fireplaces and whitewashed stone walls, a piqué cotton cover on a baldaquin bed, a dove-grey dresser in a sweet, chic kitchen. Victorine was an interior designer and her love of texture, patina and modern art shines through. The pool is set discreetly on a lower level away from the house, the grounds are large and open with seductive views, the peace is a balm. Heavenly place, delightful owner. *Minimum stay three nights.*

Price	€160–€265 (€880–€1,700 per week).
Rooms	6 houses, each with kitchen: 2 for 2, 3 for 4, 1 for 5-6.
Meals	Breakfast €15. Restaurants 5km.
Closed	Rarely.
Directions	Avignon dir. Apt to Coustellet; on to Oppède Le Vieux, 1st right Chemin du Mourre. Big house with blue shutters on left.

Victorine Canac
84580 Oppède, Vaucluse
Tel   +33 (0)4 90 76 99 31
Email   lemourre@aol.com
Web   www.lemourre.com

Entry 355 Map 16

Lumani

Minutes from the Pope's Palace and the mythical Pont d'Avignon, tucked into the medieval ramparts, is this handsome, blue-shuttered, 19th-century house. Walk off the street into a cool, lush garden with 100-year old plane trees, hammocks, striped chairs, sculptures, and shady spots for reading or contemplating; it is beautifully designed and blissfully peaceful (just the splashing of a fountain, the chirruping of birds). Inside are light-filled, minimalist rooms with abstract paintings on white or vibrant walls, tiled floors, clever lighting. Bedrooms are just as beautiful and truly restful; all look over the garden. Your hosts, Elisabeth (an artist) and Jean (an architect), encourage creative pursuits: they give you a sound-proofed music studio, provide tours and guidebooks on architecture and art, and offer classes in cookery. Allow them to look after you in the ochre red salon... or you may rent the whole house and do your own cooking. You are in the heart of Provence so explore the lavender fields, stride the hills and visit the delightful villages and their markets. Peaceful, creative, special.

Price	€90–€140. Suites €140–€170. Whole house available.
Rooms	5: 3 twins/doubles, 2 suites for 2-4.
Meals	Restaurants 3-minute walk.
Closed	Mid-November to mid-December; 6 January-March.
Directions	A7 exit north for town centre; left at ramparts. Right at Café Lazare. Under portway to St Lazare, immediately right onto Rempart St Lazare for 200m. Signed.

Elisabeth & Jean Béraud-Hirschi
37 rue du Rempart Saint Lazare,
84000 Avignon, Vaucluse

Tel	+33 (0)4 90 82 94 11
Email	lux@avignon-lumani.com
Web	www.avignon-lumani.com

La Bastide du Bois Bréant

Step into a corner of paradise. This is a jewel of a 19th-century truffle farm, renovated with
equal parts of imagination and stylish good taste. Viviane and Philippe spoil you with a big
welcome, and more: superb cuisine Provençal, grounds filled with flowers, rooms aglow
with antiques, and a delicious décor. Some rooms have fireplaces, one has a terrace,
the garden views are dreamy and there's every mod con. White boutis quilts and
diaphanous bed curtains provide the perfect background for chocolate throws, and other
contemporary shades. Time seems to stand still as you wander the vast heavily treed
park and its gardens, laze on one of several terraces, take a plunge in the heated pool.
The wood-beamed dining room is bright and spacious, with garden views on two sides; for
quiet evenings you have two comfy sitting rooms, with piano, library and fireplaces.
The Luberon bursts with markets every day of the week, Avignon's summer festival is one
of many and there's sport for all: cycling, rock climbing, golf, guided walks – just ask the
advice of your hosts. No wonder guests book months in advance.

Price	€100–€202. Suite €202.
	Treehouse €100–€120.
Rooms	14: 8 doubles, 4 twins/doubles,
	1 suite for 4, 1 treehouse for 2.
Meals	Dinner €27; book ahead.
	Restaurants 200m.
Closed	4 November–15 March.
Directions	From A7, exit Avignon Sud dir. Apt;
	on to Coustellet; right at lights to
	Cavaillon; left after 2km. Hotel signed.

Viviane & Philippe Duminy
501 chemin du Puits du Grandaou,
84660 Maubec en Luberon, Vaucluse
Tel   +33 (0)4 90 05 86 78
Email   contact@hotel-bastide-bois-breant.com
Web   www.hotel-bastide-bois-breant.com

Ethical Collection: Environment.
See page 446 for details

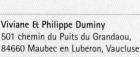

Entry 357   Map 16

La Bastide de Voulonne

This bastide sits in splendid isolation in the lavender fields stretching beneath the ancient hilltop villages perched on the Luberon mountains. It matches our dream of the perfect Provençal farmhouse. As you swing into the circular driveway, there are ancient plane trees, a spattering of cyprus, tufts of lavender and blue shutters against golden ochre walls. The heart of this 18th-century farm is an inner courtyard where you can breakfast to the soothing sound of the fountain with staircases leading off each corner. The bedrooms (and beds) are huge, done in natural local colours, with tiled or parquet floors. The garden – more like a park – is vast, with a big pool not far from the house. The owners have refreshed the herb garden for the kitchen and menus centre round local food, while cherries, apricots, pears, figs and raspberries come from their orchards. After an aperitif with guests, dinner is served at separate tables, or at a communal one, in a big dining hall where the centrepiece is the carefully restored bread oven. *Two-day truffle courses in winter.*

Price	€125-€150. Family suites €180-€265.
Rooms	13: 10 twins/doubles, 3 family suites for 3-5.
Meals	Breakfast €12. Dinner €32. Wine €28.
Closed	Mid-November to December (open January & February by arrangement).
Directions	From south exit A7 Cavaillon; at Coustellet D2 to Gordes for 1km; right after white fence of Ets Kerry La Cigalette; 600m on left. Not in the village of Cabrières d'Avignon.

Penny & Julien Hemery
Cabrières d'Avignon,
84220 Gordes, Vaucluse

Tel	+33 (0)4 90 76 77 55
Email	contact@bastide-voulonne.com
Web	www.bastide-voulonne.com

Le Mas des Romarins

Michel and Pierre bought this hotel in 2002 and it overlooks one of France's most beautiful villages. Forget the buildings on either side: the secluded pool and pretty garden will tug you away from it all and there's a private path (ten minutes) into town. That fabulous hilltop view of Gordes, with its distant misty-blue mountains and surrounding plains, will ensure you linger long over a delicious breakfast buffet. The sitting room is comfortable without being over-lavish. The ochres and smoky rusts of the bedrooms contrast with the oatmeals and creams of the two-tone walls, while Parisian linens and soft furnishings link arms with traditional cotton prints. The bedrooms are small, cool, comfortable and quiet; in summer, choose one with a terrace. Best of all is the food, extremely good four-course dinners, served at pretty white-clothed tables, or in the garden in summer. Should you happen to stay when the kitchen closes, the friendly staff will book you a table in Gordes. Great walking, fine dining, easy living.

Price	€99–€197. Quadruples €175–€211.
Rooms	13: 10 twins/doubles, 3 quadruples.
Meals	Dinner €30 (except Tues, Wed & Thurs). Restaurants 10-minute walk.
Closed	3 January–5 March; 28 November–17 December.
Directions	From Avignon, east on N7; left onto N100 for Apt; left to Gordes. Route de Sénanque on left entering Gordes. Hotel 200m on right.

Michel Dimeux & Pierre Ticot
Route de Sénanque,
84220 Gordes, Vaucluse

Tel	+33 (0)4 90 72 12 13
Email	info@masromarins.com
Web	www.masromarins.com

Entry 359   Map 16

Château La Roque

The first-known stronghold dominating the valley from this craggy lookout held back the Saracens in the eighth century; ceded to the Papal States in the 13th century, it was again an important strategic outpost. In 1741 it settled into peace as a private household. The peace remains blissful, the only interruption coming from the bees buzzing in the acacias; the views remain long and stretch over the floor of the valley. Jean, who knows his history, can tell you (in French) about the golden ratio used to build the castle. Bedrooms are huge, simple, bordering on spartan, but never cold. One has a big deep coral bed under high vaulted ceilings, and two antique chairs as bedside tables. Floors are terracotta, interspersed with polished ochre cement in some rooms. Bathrooms continue the theme: roomy, simple, each with big double basins — on old pedestals or perhaps set on tables. The evening's menu might be monkfish with a saffron sauce on a bed of green asparagus followed by a millefeuille with strawberries and marscarpone served on the vine dappled terrace or below in the garden. *Children over 11 welcome.*

Price	€120–€170. Suites €240.
Rooms	5: 2 doubles, 3 suites.
Meals	Breakfast €18. Dinner €40 (except Sundays); book ahead.
Closed	4 January–10 February.
Directions	From Lyon, A7 exit Orange Sud for Carpentras; on to Pernes les Fontaines, then St Didier, then La Roque 2km.

Chantal & Jean Tomasino
Chemin du Château,
84210 La Roque sur Pernes, Vaucluse

Tel	+33 (0)4 90 61 68 77
Email	chateaularoque@wanadoo.fr
Web	www.chateaularoque.com

Le Clos du Buis

The gorgeous 'village perché' of Bonnieux has somehow avoided the crush of unchecked tourism. Le Clos sits in its old heart, overlooking the town and the surrounding hills. Part of the structure used to be the town bakery; the original front and the oven remain. Time and loving care have been allocated without restraint – Monsieur longed to return here – and everything appears to have been just so forever: Provençal country cupboards that rise to the ceiling, ancient cement patterned tiles, a stone staircase with an iron bannister leading to crisp, clean, uncluttered bedrooms, another bannister leading to the garden. One side of the house is 'in' town, the other side opens to stunning hill views – snow-topped in season. Provence is here on all sides, from the pretty checked cotton quilts on the beds to the restaurant's excellent food, served by Monsieur. The beautiful garden frames the large, delightful terrace/pool and new summer kitchen. If wine or weather keep you from the hills, days can be spent browsing the books by the old stone hearth – or playing the baby grand. *Sawday's self-catering also.*

Price	€84–€120. Family rooms €117–€135. Extra bed €15.
Rooms	8: 2 doubles, 4 twins/doubles, 2 family rooms for 3.
Meals	Dinner €28. Restaurants within walking distance.
Closed	Mid-November to mid-February (open Christmas & New Year).
Directions	A7 to Aix exit 24 Avignon Sud; D973 to Cavaillon; left on D22 to Apt 30km; right on D36. In village centre.

M & Mme Maurin
Rue Victor Hugo,
84480 Bonnieux, Vaucluse
Tel   +33 (0)4 90 75 88 48
Email   le-clos-du-buis@wanadoo.fr
Web   www.leclosdubuis.fr

Auberge du Presbytère

They say "when the wind blows at Saignon, tiles fly off in Avignon": the Mistral can blow fiercely down from the mountains to the Mediterranean. This fairytale 11th-century village of 100 inhabitants lies deep in the Luberon hills and lavender fields; the auberge sits deep in Saignon, half hidden behind an ancient tree near the village's statue-topped fountain. Delicious meals are served under this tree, or in a pretty terraced garden, glassed in for the winter months. The bedrooms are simple, but truly charming colourwashed walls, country pieces, no TVs but Roger & Gallet soaps in lovely bathrooms with Italian stone block tiles. In Blue, a huge fireplace and a stone terrace looking out onto the hills… views from some of the rooms are breathless. A log fire burns on chilly days in the informal arched stone sitting area. Gerhard, the new, young owner, will be faithful to the spirit of this hotel and is in love with his new surroundings. A secret, splendid place from which to visit the hill towns. Or, if you are fit, rent a bike and follow the cycling signs. Outstanding value.

Price	€60–€145.
Rooms	16: 14 twins/doubles; 2 twins/doubles with separate shower/bath. Some rooms interconnect.
Meals	Breakfast €10.50. Lunch & dinner €20–€38. Restaurant closed Wednesdays.
Closed	Mid-January to mid-February.
Directions	From Apt D900 to Saignon village. At r'bout with 1 olive & 3 cypress trees to start of village, left lane marked 'riverains' to Place de la Fontaine.

Anne-Cécile & Gerhard Rose
Place de la Fontaine,
84400 Saignon, Vaucluse

Tel	+33 (0)4 90 74 11 50
Email	reception@auberge-presbytere.com
Web	www.auberge-presbytere.com

Le Mas des Grès

A party atmosphere reigns at this spotlessly maintained roadside hotel, where Nina looks after you and Thierry conjures up superb food from an open-plan kitchen; inspiration comes from his Italian grandmother. Join in with the preparations or simply settle down to enjoy it all, in the big beamed dining room or, in summer, under the lovely plane trees and vine-clad terrace, accompanied by twinkling lights and candles. Children eat what the adults eat and then potter around to their hearts' content. Plainish bedrooms vary in size, with neat quilts on firm beds and views over the fields; bathrooms are tiled top to toe; some have superb Italian showers. Nina knows everyone in the area and can rustle up almost anything from wine tastings of Châteauneuf du Pape to bike trips through the Luberon, trout fishing with the family and golf at one of the 15 courses in the area. A favourite is a guided nature hike to gather culinary plants and herbs, and, for collectors of brocante, the popular L'Isle sur la Sorgue is up the road. Return to a playground for little ones and a family-happy pool. *Cookery classes for children (& adults on request).*

Price	€80–€230. Suites €210.
	Half-board €90–€145 p.p.
Rooms	14: 12 doubles, 2 suites for 4.
	Some rooms interconnect.
Meals	Breakfast €12. Picnic lunch €15.
	Buffet lunch €20 (July & August only).
	Dinner €36.
Closed	11 November–15 March.
Directions	A7 Apt & Avignon Sud, D33 for 13km; cross Petit Palais on D24. At T-junc. of D901, right to Apt. Hotel after 600m on right.

Nina & Thierry Crovara
Route d'Apt,
84800 Lagnes, Vaucluse

Tel	+33 (0)4 90 20 32 85
Email	info@masdesgres.com
Web	www.masdesgres.com

Entry 363   Map 16

Château Talaud

Lavish and elegant – a stunning place and lovely people. Hein has a wine export business, Conny gives her whole self to her house and her guests. Among ancient vineyards and wonderful green lawns – an oasis in Provence – the ineffably gracious 18th-century château speaks of a long-gone southern way of life. Enter and you will feel it has not entirely vanished. Restored to a very high standard, the finely proportioned rooms have been furnished with antiques, many of them family pieces, and thick, luxurious fabrics. Windows reach from floor to ceiling and frame a stand of plane trees or fine landscaping. The big bedrooms mix old and new (Directoire armchairs, featherweight duvets) with consummate taste and bathrooms are old-style hymns to modernity. The pool is an adapted 17th-century irrigation tank: one goes through an arch to the first, shallow cistern, leading to a deeper pool beyond – ingenious. Guests may laze in the lovely gardens and listen to the caged love birds, but Conny is happy to help you plan visits in this fascinating area. An exceptionally fine, well-kept guest house. *Minimum stay two weeks in cottage July/August.*

Price	€190–€240. Cottage & apartments €1,400–€1,600 per week.
Rooms	5 + 3: 3 doubles, 2 suites. 1 cottage for 5, 2 apartments for 2.
Meals	Dinner, €45, twice weekly; book ahead.
Closed	1-13 January; 17 February-3 March; 15-31 December.
Directions	D950 for Carpentras; at r'bout at Loriol du Comtat right on D107 for Monteux. 500m, small sign 'Talaud' on right marks road to château.

Conny & Hein Deiters-Kommer
D107, 84870 Loriol du Comtat,
Vaucluse

Tel	+33 (0)4 90 65 71 00
Email	chateautalaud@gmail.com
Web	www.chateautalaud.com

Château Fort Guet

Searching for somewhere with character for a beach based holiday? Look no further than Pere Heures' 'on the beach' rooms. With never-ending dunes as a backdrop and stunning uninterrupted views out over the Med, the vista and smooth sandy beaches here are magnificent. The Château Fort Guet complex was built in the late 1930s when functionality rather than glitz was in vogue. It owes much of its charm and quality to its German designer and prominent position on the coastline. The Riviera can serve up some pretty rough weather at times, but this complex was built to withstand the weather and much, much more. They say that time stands still for no man, and Père Heures and his rooms certainly move forward. They manage to avoid that clinical, modern chain hotel feel with its low ceilings, uneven floors and unpredictable outside showers. Meals are served in the central dining room. Menus are simple but *fruits de la mer* is always available. Eating to the sound of crashing waves is a pleasure not to be missed.

Price	€39-€45.
Rooms	3 doubles.
Meals	Need to be caught in advance.
Closed	Only at high tides.
Directions	Directions on booking. He has moved over the years, but Père Hueres is invariably waiting for you.

	Monsieur Père Heures
	Sur La Plage,
	Boulet de Cannes
Tel	+00 (0)1 19 39 02 08

Château du Martinet

Although Napoleon could hardly have slept in this magnificent château – it was built in 1712, burned down during the French Revolution, and rebuilt only in 1846 – one can almost see his ghost, legs stretched out before a blazing fire in the 18th-century salon, sipping a well-aged cognac named in his honour. Dutch Ronald and French Françoise left busy lives in Holland to move into and lovingly revive this superb, listed monument, set in a vast, heavily treed parkland. Their dedication shows in their friendly, sincere welcome, and in their choice of elegant decoration and 18th- and 19th-century antiques. High ceilings, tall windows and subtle colours create a light, gracious and airy feel, while special touches abound: a marble ionic column here, a tapestry there, an exquisite wood-panelled ceiling with leather insets in the dining room, sumptuous chandeliers and gilt-edged mirrors throughout. Bedrooms are luxurious; colours range from fuchsia to soft blue. Outside are swimming pool, tennis court, pétanque and a fitness run; inside, elegance, tradition and refined opulence. Special.

Price	€190–€295. Suite €270. Cottages €1,000–€1,200 per week.
Rooms	5 + 2: 2 doubles, 2 twins, 1 suite for 2-3. 2 cottages for 2-3.
Meals	Pool lunches €20. Hosted dinner, with wine, €50; book ahead. Restaurant 3km.
Closed	January-March.
Directions	A7 exit Orange Sud or Avignon Nord to Carpentras; D942 for Sault & Mazan. 2km after r'bout leaving Carpentras, château on left at bend.

Françoise & Ronald de Vries
Route de Mazan,
84200 Carpentras, Vaucluse

Tel   +33 (0)4 90 63 03 03
Email   contact@chateau-du-martinet.fr
Web   www.chateau-du-martinet.fr

Le Château de Mazan

The father and uncle of the Marquis de Sade were born here – an unexpected connection, given the luminosity of the place. Though the infamous Marquis preferred Paris, he often stayed at Mazan and organized France's first theatre festival here in 1772. The château sits in an appealing little town at the foot of Mont Ventoux. Floors are tiled in white-and-terracotta squares that would drown a smaller space, ceilings are lofty, windows are huge with the lightest of curtains. This is a family hotel, despite its size, and Frédéric, who speaks good English, runs an efficient staff. Each room is an ethereal delight: pale pink walls, a velvet settee, a touch of apricot taffeta, a flash of red. Ground-floor bedrooms have French windows opening to a private sitting area; a couple of the rooms in the annexe across the road have private terraces. There are beautiful palms and secluded spots in the gardens – doze in the shade of the mulberry trees – and a large terrace for dinner; the chef has worked in starred restaurants and is keen to win his own. Stay on a Friday and catch Carpentras market. *Car park down hill.*

Price	€98–€275. Suites €320–€400. Family rooms €220–€275. Extra bed €40.
Rooms	31: 14 doubles, 3 suites for 4, 14 family rooms for 3-4.
Meals	Breakfast €17. Lunch & dinner from €35. Restaurant closed Tuesdays; Mondays out of season.
Closed	January-February.
Directions	From Carpentras D942 for Sault & Ventoux, 7km. In Mazan, 1st right near town hall, then left. Signed.

Danièle & Frédéric Lhermie
Place Napoléon,
84380 Mazan, Vaucluse

Tel	+33 (0)4 90 69 62 61
Email	reservation@chateaudemazan.com
Web	www.chateaudemazan.fr

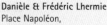

Château Juvenal

From the entrance hall, peep through the double doorways at the sitting and dining rooms on either side. Stunning! With two glorious lit chandeliers reflecting in the gilt-edged mirrors at each end of this long reception suite, you are transported back a couple of centuries. Surely the chamber orchestra will be tuning up any minute for a post-prandial concert with notes floating among the exquisite period furniture, high ceilings, tall windows. Yet this 19th-century gem is lived in and loved every day, thanks to delightful Anne-Marie and Bernard, who also produce an award-winning wine and delicious olive oil from their 600 trees. The traditional bedrooms are all on the first floor and range from cosy to spacious: Iris the smallest in pure white and grey, Cerise, larger, with deep pink spread, Raisin with Louis XIII chairs and marble-top dresser, Les Genêts, sunny yellow with a roll top bath. Grab your shopping basket and visit the local market, there is a summer kitchen next to the pool. There are wine visits, a pony for the kids, annual tango events, a spa and two lovely apartments for longer stays.

Price	€110-€150. Family suite €130-€170. Apartments €900-€1,600 per week.
Rooms	4 + 2: 1 double, 2 twins/doubles, 1 family suite for 2-3. 2 apartments for 4-6.
Meals	Hosted dinner with wine, €36, twice weekly.
Closed	Never.
Directions	From Carpentras dir. Vaison La Romaine, Malaucène on D938 for 8km. Left to D21, to Baumes de Venise for 700m; right just before cemetery in St Hippolyte.

Ethical Collection: Environment.
See page 446 for details

Anne-Marie & Bernard Forestier
Chemin du Long Serre,
84330 Saint Hippolyte le Graveyron,
Vaucluse

Tel	+33 (0)4 90 62 31 76
Email	chateau.juvenal@wanadoo.fr
Web	www.chateau-juvenal.com

Les Florets

The setting is magical, the greeting from the Bernard family is heartfelt and the walks are outstanding. Les Florets sits at the foot of the majestic Dentelles de Montmirail – a small range of mountains crested with long, delicate fingers of white stone in the middle of Côtes du Rhône country. Over 40km of clearly marked paths wind through here so appetites build and are satiated on the splendid terrace under the branches of plane, chestnut and linden; the low stone walls are bright with busy lizzies and the peonies were blooming in March. You'll also be sampling some of the wines that the family has been producing since the 1880s. Bright blue and yellow corridors lead to well-organised rooms that are simply and florally decorated, all with big tiled bathrooms but without mozzie meshes and air con. We liked the tiny 50s reception desk topped with a big bouquet from the garden; a ceramic *soupière* brightens one corner, a scintillating collection of glass carafes stands in another. All this and the wine list a work of art. Book well ahead, people return year after year.

Price	€100–€140. Apartment €160.
Rooms	15: 14 doubles, 1 apartment for 2-4 in annexe (without kitchen).
Meals	Breakfast €15. Lunch & dinner €29–€45. Restaurant closed Wednesdays.
Closed	January; 1 week in February.
Directions	From Carpentras, D7 for Vacqueyras. Right on D7 to Gigondas for 2km; signed.

M & Mme Bernard
Route des Dentelles,
84190 Gigondas, Vaucluse

Tel	+33 (0)4 90 65 85 01
Email	accueil@hotel-lesflorets.com
Web	www.hotel-lesflorets.com

Entry 369   Map 16

L'À Propos

It's like stepping through the looking glass into another world: one of refined French taste and modern elegance, where heels click on polished parquet and the smell of fresh coffee drifts through salons warmed by log fires. If the house weren't so full of 19th-century period features you'd say parts were wacky – such as the walls clothed in black-and-white postcard blow-ups of the town. In other parts white predominates, softened by earthy fabrics and oil paintings. The fantasy continues into three private parks through which one wanders in the shade of ancient cypresses and palms. Discover a heated pool, a balneotherapy, a Buddha to encourage peace and harmony. There's harmony in the bedrooms, too: spacious, beautifully arranged rooms, with fabulous bathrooms attached. All feels classic yet contemporary. Take afternoon tea or a glass of Rhône wine, savour lunch or dinner in the popular restaurant, browse the boutique. If only the dream didn't have to end… but beyond are ancient ruins and vibrant markets, canoeing on the Ardèche and wine tastings in vignobles. Perfection in Orange.

Price	€110-€155. Suites €170-€245.
Rooms	5: 1 double, 4 suites for 1-4.
Meals	Lunch €21. Dinner à la carte, €30; book ahead. Wine €18-€50. Restaurants 150m.
Closed	Never.
Directions	Exit A7 at Orange Centre. Follow signs for Vaison la Romaine Hospital; left at corner with Police station. Bear left, hotel 150m on right.

Estelle Godefroy-Mourier
15 avenue Frédéric Mistral,
84100 Orange, Vaucluse

Tel	+33 (0)4 90 34 54 91
Email	info@lapropos.com
Web	www.lapropos.com

Villa Noria

The garden sets the scene, a delightfully exclusive enclave of mature cedars, palms, cherries, roses and manicured lawn. Within it is an elegant 18th-century house, run by a couple who speak three languages with ease and look after guests with immaculate professionalism. Madame greets you politely then ushers you up the stone farmhouse stair to beautiful bedrooms decorated in Provençal style, the finest on the first floor. Tiled floors are cool underfoot, walls are polished with pigmented wax (cerise, blue, raspberry), overheads are beamed, beds opulently swathed in white linen and bathrooms boldly, diagonally tiled. You breakfast in an elegant, wraparound conservatory where fauteuils are dressed in red and white checks and the long oval dining table sits beneath a huge weeping fern. In summer you're under the trees. Noria rests on the edge of the peaceful village of Modène, near several burgeoning villas, and the views sweep over vineyards to mountains beyond; recline by the saltwater pool on a handsome wooden lounger and drink them in. For urban evacuees, a stylish retreat. *No credit cards.*

Price	€65–€110. Suite €130–€150.
Rooms	5: 3 doubles, 1 twin, 1 suite for 4.
Meals	Hosted dinner with wine, €35. Restaurant 1.5km.
Closed	Never.
Directions	D974 Carpentras to Bedoin; after 7.5km, left onto D84 to Modène. House on left on entrance to village. Signed.

Phillipe Monti
84330 Modène, Vaucluse

Tel	+33 (0)4 90 62 50 66
Email	post@villa-noria.com
Web	www.villa-noria.com

Entry 371   Map 16

Hostellerie du Val de Sault

This landscape has been called "a sea of corn gold and lavender blue": from your terrace here you can contemplate the familiar shape of Mont Ventoux, the painter's peak, beyond. The charming, communicative Yves has gathered all possible information, knows everyone there is to know on the Provence scene and is full of good guidance. He creates menus featuring truffles or lavender or spelt, or game with mushrooms for the autumn perfectly served in the formal atmosphere of the light, airy restaurant. And… children can eat earlier, allowing the adults to savour their meal in peace. Perched just above the woods in a big garden, this is a modern building of one storey; wooden floors and pine-slatted walls bring live warmth, colour schemes are vibrant, storage is excellent; baths in the suites have jets. Each room feels like a very private space with its terrace (the suites have room for loungers on theirs): the pool, bar and restaurant are there for conviviality; the fitness room, tennis court and boules pitch for exercise; the jacuzzi space for chilling out. *Ask for a room with a view. Spa.*

Price	€60-€135. Suites €233. Duplexes from €290. Half-board approx. €125 p.p.
Rooms	21: 6 twins/doubles, 11 suites, 4 duplexes for 2 (without kitchen).
Meals	Breakfast €14. Lunch & dinner €28-€92. Half-board only, May-Sept. Restaurant closed April-May and Sept-Oct.
Closed	November-April.
Directions	A7 exit 23; D942 for Carpentras Mazan Sault, then for St Trinit & Fourcalquier. Left after r'bout, by fire station.

Yves Gattechaut
Route de St Trinit, Ancien chemin d'Aurel,
84390 Sault, Vaucluse
Tel   +33 (0)4 90 64 01 41
Email   valdesault@aol.com
Web   www.valdesault.com

Auberge de Reillanne

The solid loveliness of this 18th-century house, so typical of the area, reassures you, invites you in. And you will not be disappointed: you'll feel good here, even if you can't quite define the source of the positive energy. Monique clearly has a connection to the spirit of the place and has used all her flair and good taste to transform the old inn into a very special place to stay. Bedrooms are large and airy, done in cool restful colours with big cupboards and rattan furniture. There are beams, properly whitewashed walls and books. Bathrooms are big and simple too. Downstairs, the sitting and dining areas are decorated in warm, embracing colours with terracotta tiles and flame-coloured curtains. This would be a place for a quiet holiday with long meditative walks in the hills, a place to come and write that novel under the shade of the century-old trees, or simply to get to know the gentle, delicate, smiling owner who loves nothing better than to receive people in her magical house. One of our favourites.

Price	€70-€75. Singles €55. Half-board €68 p.p.
Rooms	6: 3 doubles, 3 triples.
Meals	Breakfast €8.50. Dinner €23. Wine €20.
Closed	20 October-April.
Directions	N100 through Apt & Céreste. Approx. 8km after Céreste, left on D214 to Reillanne. Hotel on right.

	Monique Balmand
	04110 Reillanne,
	Alpes-de-Haute-Provence
Tel	+33 (0)4 92 76 45 95
Email	monique.balmand@wanadoo.fr
Web	www.auberge-de-reillanne.com

Villa Morelia

Nine years ago, in a delightful Alpine village with breathtaking views, Robert and Marie-Christine, a charming couple who know quite a bit about cuisine, opened a small restaurant and intimate hotel. It is now a sumptuous and award-winning place to stay, run by owners whose welcome could not be more generous or sincere. You will love everything inside: high airy ceilings, walnut windows and doors, bathrooms with multi-jet showers and all the right touches, big bedrooms which manage the trick of looking both elegant and welcoming, views over the huge and beautiful grounds. On top of this, the chef Laurent Lemal is a poet with a magic touch transforming the freshest ingredients into pure delight; our dessert consisted of three dishes based on three red fruits in season. Table linens are impeccable, wines are wonderful, the service is exceptional and Robert will pick you up if you don't want to drive. It is, in his words, "une grande maison de famille". In other words, not just a place to hang your hat for a couple of days. Great hiking and biking, and Italy a hop over the pass. *Cookery courses. Spa & new rooms open 2010.*

Price	€150–€190. Single €120. Suites €280–€350. Family rooms €190-€225.
Rooms	10: 4 doubles, 1 single, 3 suites, 2 family rooms for 3.
Meals	Breakfast €20. Picnic lunch available. Dinner €68.
Closed	12 November-27 December; April.
Directions	7km from Barcelonnette on D900 Gap-Cuneo road. Villa in centre of village.

Marie–Christine & Robert Boudard
04850 Jausiers,
Alpes-de-Haute-Provence
Tel   +33 (0)4 92 84 67 78
Email info@villa-morelia.com
Web   www.villa-morelia.com

Le Moulin du Château

A sleepy place – come to doze. Your silence will be broken only by the call of the sparrowhawk or the distant rumble of a car. This 17th-century olive mill once belonged to the château and stands at the foot of an ancient grove; the vast pressoir is now a reception area where modern art hangs on ancient walls. The Moulin is a long, low, stone building with lavender-blue shutters and the odd climbing vine, and stands in its own gardens surrounded by lavender and fruit trees. In the bedrooms light filters though voile curtains, shadows dance upon the walls. The feel is uncluttered, cool, breezy, with vibrant colours: turquoise, lilac, lime – luminous yet restful. This is an easy-going 'green' hotel where the emphasis is on the simple things of life. Edith and Nicolas use regional and organic food, boules is played under the cherry tree, poppies grow on an old crumbling stone staircase and views stretch across fields to village and château. There are bikes for gentle excursions into the countryside, and further afield are the Cistercian abbey of Le Thoronet, the Verdon Canyon and Digne Les Bains.

Price	€105-€137. Half-board €165-€197 for 2.
Rooms	10: 5 doubles, 2 twins, 1 triple, 1 quadruple, 1 suite.
Meals	Breakfast €9. Picnic lunch €10. Dinner €30 (except Mon & Thurs). Wine €6-€30. Restaurants nearby.
Closed	November-March.
Directions	From Gréoux les Bains D952 to Riez, then D11 for Quinson; head for St Laurent du Verdon; take road after château. Signed.

Edith & Nicolas Stämpfli-Faoro
04500 Saint Laurent du Verdon,
Alpes-de-Haute-Provence
Tel   +33 (0)4 92 74 02 47
Email   info@moulin-du-chateau.com
Web   www.moulin-du-chateau.com

Ethical Collection: Environment; Food.
See page 446 for details

Entry 375   Map 16

Hôtel du Vieux Château

Once a hill fort on the Roman road linking Fréjus to Grenoble, tiny Aiguines, overlooking the Lac de Ste Croix, has never stopped being a place of constant passage. It is also a place with 'soul', intrinsically French. Frédéric, affable and smiley, came home to roost after a busy and peripatetic youth. He is taking his time restoring the hotel, once part of the village's castle. "I want to get it right," he says. Getting it right means no fuss and frills, but a crisp refreshing simplicity. A good sense of colour marries yellow, blue and old rose with Provençal or tartan-patterned curtains, and bathrooms have rich hued Salernes tiles: deep turquoise, royal blue, salmon, grass-green. High rooms at the front have those views over the rooftops to the lake, the eye travelling unhindered over the lavender-covered plateau towards the blue mountains in the distance. Others catch a glimpse of the pretty village square and castle. Bedrooms at the back, looking over a village street, may well be cooler in a searing summer. Close by is the Domaine Saint Jean de Villecroze – a must-visit for lovers of red wine.

Price	€55–€75.
Rooms	10: 7 twins/doubles, 1 single, 2 family rooms for 3-4.
Meals	Breakfast €7. Lunch from €6.50. Dinner €22–€28. Restaurants in village.
Closed	November–March.
Directions	From A8, exit for Draguignan, then D557 through Flayosc & Aups for Moustiers Ste Marie to Aiguines. Ask about parking.

Frédéric Ricez
Place de la Fontaine, 83630 Aiguines, Var

Tel	+33 (0)4 94 70 22 95
Email	contact@hotelvieuxchateau.fr
Web	www.hotelvieuxchateau.fr

Une Campagne en Provence

Water gushes and flows throughout the 170-acre estate. In spring, streams and rivers abound; the 12th-century Knights Templar created a myriad of irrigation channels. The stunning bastide keeps its massive fortress-like proportions and bags of character and charm. Martina and Claude love their Campagne and their sense of fun makes a stay a real treat. The main house is arranged around a central patio, with stairs leading to the bedrooms above. Simple Provençal furnishings are lit by huge windows, floors are terre cuite, there are cosy 'boutis' quilts and sumptuous towels and linen, and bathrooms cleverly worked around original features. Breakfasts are scrumptious, and fun; dinners – meet the other guests – put the accent on wonderful local produce and their own wine. In the cellar find music and a mini cinema – great for kids; there's table football and a pool with a view (open May to October), a sauna and a Turkish bath. Beyond are tracks leading to the hills, and Provençal villages. An isolated paradise for all ages, overseen by a charming young family, two geese and one dear dog.

Price	€95–€115. Suite €110–€120. Studio €110–€130.
Rooms	5: 3 doubles, 1 suite, 1 studio for 2 with kitchenette.
Meals	Hosted dinner with wine, €33. Restaurant 7km.
Closed	January to mid-March.
Directions	A8 Aix-Nice exit St Maximin la Ste Baume; thro' town centre, right at small r'bout with monument; 1st right on D28 to Bras & Le Val. After 9km, right & follow signs.

Martina & Claude Fussler
Domaine le Peyrourier, 83149 Bras, Var

Tel	+33 (0)4 98 05 10 20
Email	info@provence4u.com
Web	www.provence4u.com

Ethical Collection: Environment; Food.
See page 446 for details

Hostellerie Bérard & Spa

Bags of atmosphere, stunning gardens, exquisite gastronomy, a magical spa and possibly the best breakfasts in France. René is Maître Cuisinier de France of the Michelin-starred restaurant, aided by son Jean-François; Danièle is an expert in local wines. In both restaurant and bistro the emphasis is on Provençal gastronomy using organic seasonal produce and herbs from the kitchen garden, and the food is pure joy. Madame and Monsieur are true belongers: they grew up in this hilltop village, opened in 1969 and have respectfully restored a complex of highly evocative buildings, an 11th-century monastery; a blue-shuttered bastide, a *maison bourgeoise*, an artist's pavilion. The views are framed visions of olive groves, of vines in their serried choreography and Templar strongholds on mountain tops in the distance. Each bedroom is a lovely French surprise – a delicate wrought-iron four-poster, a snowy counterpane, curtains in toile de Jouy. Daughter Sandra, full of friendly enthusiasm, handles the day-to-day running of this perfect hotel. *Ask about cookery courses with René.*

Price	€94–€174. Suites €251–€291.
Rooms	40: 36 doubles, 4 suites for 4.
Meals	Buffet breakfast €21. Lunch & dinner €43–€146. Wine from €26.
Closed	4 January–11 February.
Directions	A50 towards Toulon exit 11; follow signs to Cadière d'Azur. Hotel in centre of village.

Bérard Family
Rue Gabriel Péri,
83740 La Cadière d'Azur, Var
Tel   +33 (0)4 94 90 11 43
Email   berard@hotel-berard.com
Web   www.hotel-berard.com

Le Pré aux Marguerites

No bell, no sign, but don't give up: the place is a gem. Built in the 1950s in Provençal style, the house was the family's holiday home when Frédéric was a child. Your captivating, cultured, well-travelled host was an interior designer in New York; now he is passionately engaged in the region, as well as running this exquisitely positioned cliffside B&B, bang in front of the sea. Breakfasts are convivial and copious, served on the terrace or by the pool. And what a pool! Under the pines, free of chemicals, overlooking the sea. You could spend all day here, up among the mimosas and palms, the benches and pathways; there's a small playground too and, best of all, a path that meanders down to a totally private beach. The largest suite, facing the sea, has a big bed enveloped in fawn cotton, a beautiful antique day bed and a matching armoire, and a bathroom with bright blue tiles. Cosier Colombier comes with a sloped beamed ceiling and a sprinkling of as-lovely antiques. Escape Cavalaire, upscale family resort with a huge marina, to hilltop villages Ramatuelle and Gassin – popular with visitors but ever enchanting.

Price	€150–€300.
Rooms	2 suites, each with kitchenette.
Meals	Dinner €45. Wine from €15.
Closed	January-March.
Directions	Ave des Alliers, 1st left Ave Neptune, 1st right Ave des Amphores, 1st left Ave des Triton, 1st right Ave du Corail.

Frédéric Jochem
1 avenue du Corail,
83240 Cavalaire, Var

Tel   +33 (0)4 94 89 11 20
Email   fjochem@aol.com
Web   www.bonporto.com

La Ferme d'Augustin

A 13th-century gateway heralds your arrival to the olive farm that opened to guests (just a few wanderers and celebrities) in the early days of Brigitte Bardot... she still lives near by. Fifty years on: fabrics from Provence, tiles from Salernes and objets stylishly scattered by owner Ninette. The décor is wonderfully relaxed, the pool is discreet and the place is filled with garden roses. The farm rests in a relatively untouched spot of this legendary peninsula, a minute from Tahiti Beach – and two miles from St Tropez, reached by a road known only to the locals, or a 15-mile coastal path: the position is among the best on the Riviera. Couples, families, foodies flock. Organic veg from the potager, wines from the vines, fruits from the orchard and their own olive oil structure a cuisine that is as authentic as it is simple; savour the flavours of Provence from the terrace or the pergola. Bath soaps and gels, exclusive to the hotel, express the same Provençal spirit; bedrooms in apartments are cosy and characterful, some with whirlpool baths and sea views. A rich, relaxed Riviera retreat. *Hydrotherapy pool.*

Price	€150–€660.
Rooms	46: 16 doubles, 28 suites, 2 apartments for 2-4.
Meals	Breakfast €14. Lunch à la carte €15–€50. Dinner à la carte €30–€60.
Closed	Mid-October to April.
Directions	From Nice, exit Le Muy dir. St Tropez; on to Chemin de la Belle Isnarde. Hotel on road before Tahiti Beach on left. Secure parking.

Ethical Collection: Food.
See page 446 for details

Vallet Family
Route de Tahiti, Saint Tropez,
83350 Ramatuelle, Var

Tel	+33 (0)4 94 55 97 00
Email	info@fermeaugustin.com
Web	www.fermeaugustin.com

Hôtel des Deux Rocs

A charming old French townhouse/inn at the top of an enchanting little hillside town: Seillans is a gem. Julie and Nicolas, a young and talented team, share time spent in the company of the greats – Paul Bocuse, Michel Troigros, Michel Guérard; you eat very well here. The interiors too are a delight, with polished antiques and portraits of noble heads up the stairway; note the rich fabrics on 18th-century chairs, the 17th-century sedan chair, a well-travelled suitcase here and there. New bathrooms are in ageless British style: white porcelain basins, reissued vintage fittings, roll top tubs... perfection. Bedrooms, from small to large, are all distinctive, all polished. Hard to choose between the room with the red and white checked Pierre Frey fabric or the 'toy soldier' theme in bold red and blue. Some overlook the valley, others the wide spread of a splendid terrace with a cinematographic view. The splashing of the fountain accompanies fabulous food served under majestic plane trees; candlelit tables are set with small bouquets of rose, lilac and hortensia.

Price	€75–€135. Family rooms €125–€165.
Rooms	14: 11 doubles, 2 family rooms for 3, 1 for 4.
Meals	Breakfast €13. Lunch & dinner €36–€62. Restaurant closed Sun eve, all day Mon & Tues lunchtimes Oct-April.
Closed	Rarely.
Directions	From A8 exit 39 Les Adrets; follow signs to Fayence, then Seillans. Hotel at top of village.

Julie & Nicolas Malzac-Heimermann
Place Font d'Amont,
83440 Seillans, Var

Tel	+33 (0)4 94 76 87 32
Email	hoteldeuxrocs@wanadoo.fr
Web	www.hoteldeuxrocs.com

Bastide Saint Mathieu

This is where you want to be: near enough to the coast for a stroll along the Croisette, far enough from the hordes. Wrought-iron gates open to a stunning 18th-century bastide with gardens and a huge park, fully treed and with all the exotica of the region – grapefruit, figs, cherries, almonds, heaps of flowering shrubs – while the outside terraces, replete with a cuisine d'été, are ideal for receptions and weddings. Of massive stone and elegantly shuttered, the bastide overlooks fields and hills of olive and lemon trees. Serene surroundings combine with prime pampering inside and bathrooms are decadently gorgeous (but never flashy). Fragrances and soaps may be from Molinard, Fragonard or Galimard: Saroya is fair to all the Grasse houses. The luxuries continue: cashmere blankets, DVD players, a contemporary four-poster facing the window to catch the morning sun. Breakfast, watched over by a painted angel by the fireplace – or on the terrace – is as late as you like. There's a huge heavenly pool, a boules piste, spa treatments on request. They've even launched their own opera festival.

Price	€270–€330. Suites €360–€380.
Rooms	5: 1 double, 2 twins/doubles, 2 suites.
Meals	Restaurants nearby.
Closed	Rarely.
Directions	A8 exit 42 Grasse Sud; cont. to r'bout (4 Chemins); exit at MacDonald's; left at r'bout; over next r'bout; cont. to Elephant Bleu car wash; exit r'bout for St Mathieu; under 2 bridges; left at T-junc.; right into Chemin de Blumenthal.

Soraya Colegrave
35 chemin de Blumenthal,
06130 Grasse, Alpes-Maritimes

Tel	+33 (0)4 97 01 10 00
Email	info@bastidestmathieu.com
Web	www.bastidestmathieu.com

Les Rosées

A short drive down from hilltop Mougins (galleries, restaurants, a photographic museum) are terraced gardens, four divine bedrooms and a secluded pool. In spite of close neighbours (a couple of houses) it's lovely and tranquil here in the hills, close yet far from tourist bustle, and beautiful. Which is why Kilperick and Canadian Jenny bought the 400-year-old *mas*, transformed it and turned it into a haven of rusticity and romance. The large luxurious suites display colour-washed walls, old terracotta tiles and a rare attention to detail; pillows and towels are lined with hand-sewn tassels, raw silk and linen curtains tumble to the floor, bathrooms have paintings, candles line your path to the door. Sainte Marguerite has its own terrace, Serguey its own fire and Isadora gets the breezes; but all stay cool in summer. Best of all is the service: warm, personal, professional, unostentatious – five star without the fuss. Breakfast is served wherever you like it and if they can't do you dinner you can march up to the village – the 25-minute climb is a delight.

Price	€200–€310.
Rooms	4 suites.
Meals	Breakfast €15. Restaurant 500m.
Closed	Never.
Directions	A8 exit 42 to Mougins & Grasse; right onto D3 to Tournamy; 2nd exit at r'bout onto Ave de Font Roubert; thro' lights, right at Lavoir up narrow lane. Hotel 350m on right.

Kilperick Lhobet
238 chemin de Font Neuve,
06250 Mougins, Alpes-Maritimes

Tel	+33 (0)4 92 92 29 64
Email	lesrosees@yahoo.com
Web	www.lesrosees.com

Hôtel Le Cavendish

The hotel is a joy. Some people have it and some don't, but Madame Welter has more of it than most, and her talents show in every corner of this splendid rebirth of a Napoleon III edifice. Subtle are the modern comforts and splendid are the rooms, many with balconies or terraces. Sensuous, exuberant and almost edible is the choice of fabric and colour: crunchy raspberry taffeta, tasselled pistachio green, golden apricot silk, twilight mauve – yet never over the top. On the contrary, one feels as though one is a guest in the grand home of a *grand homme*, such as its namesake, Lord Cavendish. How convivial to have a complimentary open bar for guests in the evening, how attentive to offer leaf teas for breakfast, how sexy to dress the curvy Carrara marble staircase with candles at dusk, how delightful to slip between the lavender-scented sheets of a turned down bed at night. Freshly baked croissants, cakes and crumbles, homemade jams and a cheery staff make mornings easy, especially if you are attending one of the events at the Festival Hall, ten minutes away. Superb. *Private beach nearby, €15 p.p. Valet parking €20. Breakfast included for Sawday guests.*

Price	€130-€295.
Rooms	34 twins/doubles.
Meals	Breakfast €20.
	Complimentary bar 5-11pm.
Closed	Never.
Directions	From Nice A8; left at r'bout on Boulevard Carnot; follow signs for Palais des Festivals. Signed.

Christine & Guy Welter
11 boulevard Carnot,
06400 Cannes, Alpes-Maritimes
Tel   +33 (0)4 97 06 26 00
Email   reservation@cavendish-cannes.com
Web   www.cavendish-cannes.com

Hôtel La Jabotte

Why is La Jabotte so special? Is it the courtyard scented with oranges or the bedrooms the colours of jewels? Or is it Claude and Yves, Belgians who came to the Cap one summer and fell for a small faded hotel. Today it is an exquisite jewellery box, an explosion of colour, beautifully clean and inviting. Yves is the artistic one, Claude oversees all, both are generous and kind. Tucked down a small side street, 60 metres from the beach, are polished stone floors and cherry-red walls, pots of roses and bright parakeets, a wagging white Westie, Tommy, lavender and glasses of champagne. Pass the deep aubergine sofa, enter the gliding wall of glass and you find the enchanting pebbled courtyard off which bedrooms lie. Each has its table and chairs outside the door and pots of plants lovingly labelled; this feels more home than hotel. Bedrooms – Lavender, Citron, Papillon – are small but charming, shower rooms have L'Occitane lotions and fulsome towels. After fresh jams, oranges and croissants, saunter into Old Antibes – or drift down to the free sandy beach and your own parasol. *Limited parking, book ahead.*

Price	€91–€123. Suite €134–€175.
Rooms	10: 9 twins/doubles, 1 suite for 2-4.
Meals	Restaurants within walking distance.
Closed	15 October–15 March.
Directions	Follow signs for Antibes Centre then Cap d'Antibes, Les Plages, La Salis. In small street 60m from La Salis beach.

Yves April & Claude Mora
13 avenue Max Maurey,
06160 Cap d'Antibes, Alpes-Maritimes

Tel	+33 (0)4 93 61 45 89
Email	info@jabotte.com
Web	www.jabotte.com

Villa Val des Roses

You could drive here, park the car and not touch it until you leave. A sandy beach with a view to old Antibes is a minute away, the old town and market are ten minutes and the shops five. Filip is young, Flemish, and found the Art Deco villa 100 metres from the sea after searching for the 'perfect place'. Filip has all the necessary diplomas and the family, Maman included, are charming. They do everything themselves and put on a very good breakfast; enjoy it in your room, on the terrace or by the pool. They will also do light lunches to have by the pool. For dinner, they can recommend a restaurant, phone ahead and make sure you get a good table. It's not cheap but this is the Côte d'Azur – and the mini bar is free, there's a laptop for each room and four bikes to borrow. The gracious white house with white shutters is enclosed in its garden by high walls in a quiet little road. Fabrics and walls are white too – cool and tranquil. Note the bedrooms are open-plan, each with a large oval bath for a sybaritic touch. The setting is fabulous. *Children over 14 welcome.*

Price	€140–€295.
Rooms	4 suites: 2 for 2, 2 for 2-3.
Meals	Poolside snacks available.
Closed	Rarely.
Directions	From Antibes dir. Cap d'Antibes, les plages, to Salis Plage. Keep shops on right. Immediately after Hotel Josse, at old stone archway, Chemin des Lauriers on right. Ring bell on gate.

Filip Vanderhoeven
6 chemin des Lauriers,
06160 Cap d'Antibes, Alpes-Maritimes

Mobile	+33 (0)6 85 06 06 29
Email	val_des_roses@yahoo.com
Web	www.val-des-roses.com

Hôtel Restaurant Le Grimaldi

You don't have to go to Haute Provence to find Provençal style: it's all here. The cobbled village of Haut de Cagnes – Brigitte Bardot had a house here in the 60s – oozes character, restaurants and artists' studios. With sweeping views, Hotel Grimaldi is high up on the main square, where locals play boules and meet for a chat, children bring bikes and tourists wander. On Friday evenings in summer, concerts draw people from miles around; there's quite a buzz. Rick was a New York banker who used to come here on holiday, then he decided to stay. Now he runs a jazz club in the basement too – but the hotel is so well-insulated you won't hear a thing. Bedrooms, in elegant shades of grey, off-white and cream, are uncluttered yet cosy, with russet floor tiles, reclaimed antique doors, Egyptian cotton, super beds. Snug bathrooms are white-tiled and stocked with fluffy towels. The beamed restaurant offers delicious food in chic, simple surroundings, spilling out to an enchanting terrace on the square. And there's a free navette to ferry you down to restaurants, markets and sea. *Parking close by, €10.*

Price	€115–€140. Suite €155–€180.
Rooms	5: 4 doubles, 1 suite for 2.
Meals	Lunch €12–€35. Dinner €26–€60. Wine €25–€100. Restaurant closed January–February.
Closed	Never.
Directions	From Aix exit 47 Cagnes sur Mer, 'centre ville'; up hill to Haut de Cagnes. Follow signs to Château Musée. Ask hotel about parking.

Rick Fernandez
6 place du Château, Haut de Cagnes,
06800 Cagnes sur Mer, Alpes-Maritimes

Tel	+33 (0)4 93 20 60 24
Email	contact@hotelgrimaldi.com
Web	www.hotelgrimaldi.com

Villa Saint Maxime

On a site facing hilltop St Paul de Vence is a retreat of white spaces, a contemporary gem. The house was built by a British architect during the first Gulf War and, in a modern echo of eastern dwellings, the main atrium has a retractable roof allowing breezes to waft through (and affords thrilling night-sky views). Be wowed by bold sweeping lines, pale marble and gleaming terracotta, pillared halls and, in the central stairwell, a broken-glass garden that sparkles like Ali Baba's jewels. Each air-conditioned room has a balcony or terrace to make the most of the views, the bath and shower rooms are spectacular, and you lounge beneath exotic palms and parasols by a very large pool. Ann and John spent their early married life in this summer-busy village beloved of Picasso, Miro, Chagall. Ann collects modern art; discover a piece or two in your room, more in the legendary Fondation Maeght. Breakfast, with champagne if you wish, is any time at all, while an orange aperitif here sets the mood for dinner at an immaculate restaurant up the hill. Fabulous. *Unsupervised pool. Children over 12 welcome.*

Price	€155–€240. Suites €190–€380.
Rooms	6: 4 doubles, 2 suites.
Meals	Restaurants within walking distance.
Closed	Rarely.
Directions	A8 exit Cagnes sur Mer for Vence then St Paul. Nearing village, left at blue sign for villa. At end of road, blue gate, on left.

Ann & John Goldenberg
390 route de la Colle,
06570 Saint Paul de Vence, Alpes-Maritimes

Tel	+33 (0)4 93 32 76 00
Email	riviera@villa-st-maxime.com
Web	www.villa-st-maxime.com

Hôtel Windsor

A 1930s Riviera hotel with a pool in a quiet palm grove and exotic birds in cages? All that… and much more. The Windsor has brought the Thirties into the 21st century by asking contemporary artists to decorate some of their rooms. The result: many gifts of wit, provocation, flights of fancy, minimalist sobriety, with Joan Mas's *Cage à Mouches* and cosmopolitan Ben's writing on the walls. The Antoine Beaudoin's superb frescoes of Venice, Egypt, India – all our travel myths – and Tintin, everyone's all time favourite. Plain white beds have contrasting cushions or quilts; furniture is minimal and interesting; delightful little bathrooms, most of which have been redone, some directly off the room, are individually treated. All clear, bright colours, including the richly exotic public areas: the much-travelled owners chose an exquisitely elaborate Chinese mandarin's bed for the lobby, panelling and colourful plasterwork for the restaurant, a fine wire sculpture, stone and bamboo for the hall. Light filters through onto warmly smiling staff. Spoil yourself and opt for one of the superior or traditional rooms.

Price	€90–€175.
Rooms	57 twins/doubles.
Meals	Breakfast €12. Dinner à la carte, with wine, €29–€40. Restaurant closed Sundays.
Closed	Never.
Directions	In centre of Nice, 10-min walk from train station. A8 exit Promenade des Anglais. Left at museum on Rue Meyerbeer; right on Rue de France; 1st left Rue Dalpozzo.

Odile Redolfi-Payen
& Bernard Redolfi-Strizzot
11 rue Dalpozzo,
06000 Nice, Alpes-Maritimes

Tel	+33 (0)4 93 88 59 35
Email	contact@hotelwindsornice.com
Web	www.hotelwindsornice.com

Entry 389   Map 16

Hôtel Les Deux Frères

Only the rich and famous have this view so go ahead, be brave, rise at the crack of dawn and wonder at the beauty of the light coming up over the ocean and along the coast. All terrace dining tables have views but you will be able to pick a favourite for hot coffee and croissants and linger even more. Willem, the Dutch owner who combines Provençal comfort with an exotic flavour – down to the seven languages he speaks and his restaurant's innovative dishes – is full of ideas. There is a tea room next door for refreshments and he has added two refurbished apartments: you can either sleep in the old village store, with its bright yellow façade and the vintage set of scales in the window, oak floors and new beds, or in the old bakery. And there are views of the coastline, mountainside or the old village square from every small, sparkling hotel room. Choose between an oriental blue and gold ceiling, a stylish lime green or a nautical blue. After parking in the village you will follow a short, fairly steep path. Ideal for the young and fleet of foot. Rooms may be small, but views are enormous.

Price	€100–€110. Singles €75.
Rooms	12: 10 doubles. 2 apartments for 2 (microwave & fridge).
Meals	Breakfast €9. Lunch from €28. Dinner from €48. Rest. closed Mon & Tues lunch in summer; Sun eve; mid-Nov to mid-Dec.
Closed	Never.
Directions	From Nice A8 exit 57 La Turbie then Roquebrune Cap Martin. Left at Roquebrune & Vieux Village. Stop at municipal car park & walk, 50m.

Willem Bonestroo
Place des Deux Frères,
06190 Roquebrune Cap Martin,
Alpes-Maritimes

Tel	+33 (0)4 93 28 99 00
Email	info@lesdeuxfreres.com
Web	www.lesdeuxfreres.com

If you have any comments on entries in this guide, please tell us. If you have a favourite place or a new discovery, please let us know about it. You can return this form or visit www.sawdays.co.uk.

Existing entry

Property name: _____

Entry number: _____ Date of visit: _____

New recommendation

Property name: _____

Address: _____

_____

Tel/Email/Web: _____

Your comments

What did you like (or dislike) about this place? Were the people friendly? What was the location like? What sort of food did they serve?

_____

_____

_____

_____

Your details

Name: _____

Address: _____

_____

_____ Postcode: _____

Tel: _____ Email: _____

Please send completed form to:
FH6, Sawday's, The Old Farmyard, Yanley Lane, Long Ashton, Bristol BS41 9LR, UK

Many of you may want to stay in environmentally friendly places. You may be passionate about local, organic or home-grown food. Or perhaps you want to know that the place you are staying in contributes to the community? To help you we have launched our Ethical Collection, so you can find the right place to stay and also discover how each owner is addressing these issues.

The Collection is made up of places going the extra mile, and taking the steps that most people have not yet taken, in one or more of the following areas:

• Environment Those making great efforts to reduce the environmental impact of their Special Place. We expect more than energy-saving light bulbs and recycling – in this part of the Collection you will find owners who make their own natural cleaning products, properties with solar hot water and biomass boilers, the odd green roof and a good measure of green elbow grease.

• Community Given to owners who use their property to play a positive role in their local and wider community. For example, by making a contribution from every guest's bill to a local fund, or running pond-dipping courses for local school children on their farm.

• Food Awarded to owners who make a real effort to source local or organic food, or to grow their own. We look

for those who have gone out of their way to strike up relationships with local producers or to seek out organic suppliers. It is easier for an owner on a farm to produce their own eggs than for someone in the middle of a city, so we take this into account.

How it works
To become part of our Ethical Collection owners choose whether to apply in one, two or all three categories, and fill in a detailed questionnaire asking demanding questions about their activities in the chosen areas. You can download a full list of the questions at www.sawdays.co.uk/about_us/ethical_collection/faq/

We then review each questionnaire carefully before deciding whether or not to give the award(s). The final decision is subjective; it is based not only on whether an owner ticks 'yes' to a question but also on the detailed explanation that accompanies each 'yes' or 'no' answer. For example, an owner who has tried as hard as possible to install solar water-heating panels, but has failed because of strict conservation planning laws, will be given some credit for their effort (as long as they are doing other things in this area).

We have tried to be as rigorous as possible and have made sure the questions are demanding. We have not checked out the claims of owners before making our decisions, but we do trust them to be honest. We are only human, as are they, so please let us know if you think we have made any mistakes.

The Ethical Collection is still a new initiative for us, and we'd love to know what you think about it – email us at ethicalcollection@sawdays.co.uk or write to us. And remember that because this is a new scheme some owners have not yet completed their questionnaires – we're sure other places in the guide are working just as hard in these areas, but we don't yet know the full details.

Ethical Collection online

There is stacks more information on our website, www.sawdays.co.uk. You can read the answers each owner has given to our Ethical Collection questionnaire and get a more detailed idea of what they are doing in each area. You can also search for properties that have awards.

Ethical Collection in this book

On the entry page of all places in the Collection we show which awards have been given.

A list of places in our Ethical Collection is shown below, by entry number.

Environment

22 • 101 • 160 • 192 • 222 • 244 • 279 • 353 • 357 • 368 • 375 • 377

Community

22 • 192 • 228 • 279

Food

16 • 22 • 128 • 160 • 192 • 215 • 222 • 244 • 279 • 350 • 353 • 375 • 377 • 380

Photo: Domaine du Moulin d'Eguebaude, entry 16

Climate Change Our Warming World   £12.99

Climate Change – Our Warming World provides a concise and easy to understand summary of climate change covering the causes and impacts of, and solutions to, this global crisis. With powerful images and testimonials written by those already affected, this book offers a critical insight into our changing climate and underlines the need to take action today.

Climate Change aims to inform and inspire immediate action to safeguard our planet, with an introduction by Archbishop Desmond Tutu, a preface by Dale Vince, founder of Ecotricity, and quotes from Dr Pachauri, Chairman of the UN's Intergovernmental Panel on Climate Change, Sir David Attenborough and Susan Sarandon.

Also available in the Fragile Earth series:

Ban the Plastic Bag A community action plan **£4.99**
One Planet Living A guide to enjoying life on our one planet **£4.99**
The Little Food Book An explosive account of the food we eat today **£6.99**

To order any of the books in the Fragile Earth series call +44 (0)1275 395431 or visit www.fragile-earth.com

Money Matters
Putting the eco into economics   £7.99

This well-timed book will make you look at everything from your bank statements to the coins in your pocket in a whole new way. Author David Boyle sheds new light on our money system and exposes the inequality, greed and instability of the economies that dominate the world's wealth.

Do Humans Dream of Electric Cars?   £4.99

This guide provides a no-nonsense approach to sustainable travel and outlines the simple steps needed to achieve a low carbon future. It highlights innovative and imaginative schemes that are already working, such as car clubs and bike sharing.

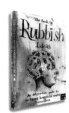

The Book of Rubbish Ideas   £6.99

Every householder should have a copy of this guide to reducing household waste and stopping wasteful behaviour. Containing step-by-step projects, the book takes a top-down guided tour through the average family home.

The Big Earth Book
Updated paperback edition   £12.99

This book explores environmental, economic and social ideas to save our planet. It helps us understand what is happening to the planet today, exposes the actions of corporations and the lack of action of governments, weighs up new technologies, and champions innovative and viable solutions.

What About China?   £6.99
Answers to this and other awkward questions about climate change

A panel of experts gives clear, entertaining and informative answers arguing that the excuses we give to avoid reducing our carbon footprint and our personal impact on the earth are exactly that, excuses.

Special places to stay, slow travel and slow food

The Slow Food revolution is upon us and these guides celebrate the Slow philosophy of life with a terrific selection of the places, recipes and people who take their time to enjoy life at its most enriching. In these beautiful books that go beyond the mere 'glossy', you will discover an unusual emphasis on the people who live in Special Slow Places and what they do. You will meet farmers, literary people, wine-makers and craftsmen – all with rich stories to tell. *Go Slow England, Go Slow Italy* and our new title *Go Slow France* celebrate fascinating people, fine architecture, history, landscape and real food.

"*Go Slow England* is a magnificent guidebook" *BBC Good Food Magazine*

RRP £19.99. To order either of these titles at the Readers' Discount price of £13.00 (plus p&tp) call +44(0)1275 395431 and quote 'Reader Discount FH'.

Have you enjoyed this book? Why not try one of the others in the Special Places series and get 35% discount on the RRP *

British Bed & Breakfast (Ed 14)	RRP £14.99	Offer price £9.75
British Bed & Breakfast for Garden Lovers (Ed 5)	RRP £14.99	Offer price £9.75
British Hotels & Inns (Ed 11)	RRP £14.99	Offer price £9.75
Devon & Cornwall (Ed 1)	RRP £9.99	Offer price £6.50
Scotland (Ed 1)	RRP £9.99	Offer price £6.50
Pubs & Inns of England & Wales (Ed 6)	RRP £15.99	Offer price £9.75
Go Slow England	RRP £19.99	Offer price £13.00
Ireland (Ed 7)	RRP £12.99	Offer price £8.45
French Bed & Breakfast (Ed 11)	RRP £15.99	Offer price £10.40
French Holiday Homes (Ed 4)	RRP £14.99	Offer price £9.75
French Châteaux & Hotels (Ed 6)	RRP £14.99	Offer price £9.75
French Vineyards (Ed 1)	RRP £19.99	Offer price £13.00
Go Slow France	RRP £19.99	Offer price £13.00
Paris (Ed 1)	RRP £9.99	Offer price £6.50
Italy (Ed 6)	RRP £14.99	Offer price £9.75
Go Slow Italy	RRP £19.99	Offer price £13.00
Spain (Ed 8)	RRP £14.99	Offer price £9.75
Portugal (Ed 4)	RRP £11.99	Offer price £7.80
India & Sri Lanka (Ed 3)	RRP £11.99	Offer price £7.80
Green Europe (Ed 1)	RRP £11.99	Offer price £7.80
Morocco (Ed 3)	RRP £9.99	Offer price £9.10

*postage and packing is added to each order

To order at the Reader's Discount price simply phone +44 (0)1275 395431 and quote 'Reader Discount FH'.

Photo: istock.com

① Provence – Alps – Riviera B&B ②

③ ④ **Une Campagne en Provence**

Water gushes and flows throughout the 170-acre estate. In spring, streams and rivers abound; the 12th-century Knights Templar created a myriad of irrigation channels. The stunning bastide keeps its massive fortress-like proportions and bags of character and charm. Martina and Claude love their Campagne and their sense of fun makes a stay a real treat. The main house is arranged around a central patio, with stairs leading to the bedrooms above. Simple Provençal furnishings are lit by huge windows, floors are terre cuite, there are cosy 'boutis' quilts and sumptuous towels and linen, and bathrooms cleverly worked around original features. The four apartments are close by, well-stocked and with knockout views across vineyards or fields; heated floors too, so you'll not be chilly. Breakfasts are scrumptious, and fun; dinners put the accent on wonderful local produce and their own wine. In the cellar is music and a mini cinema – great for kids; there's table football and a pool with a view, a sauna and a Turkish bath. An isolated paradise for all ages, overseen by a charming young family, two geese and one dear dog.

Price	€95–€115. Suite €110–€120. Studio €110–€130. ⑤
Rooms	5: 3 doubles, 1 suite, 1 studio for 2 with kitchenette. ⑥
Meals	Breakfast & dinner for self-caterers by arrangement. Hosted dinner with wine, €33. Restaurant 7km. ⑦
Closed	January to mid-March. ⑧
Directions	A8 Aix-Nice exit St Maximin la Ste Baume; thro' town centre, right at small r'bout with monument; 1st right on D28 to Bras/Le Val. After 9km, right & follow signs. ⑨

⑩ Ethical Collection: Environment; Food.
See page 445 for details

Martina & Claude Fussler
Domaine le Peyrourier, 83149 Bras
Tel   +33 (0)4 98 05 10 20
Email   info@provence4u.com
Web   www.provence4u.com

⑫ Entry 377   Map 16   ⑪ ✗ 🐕 🔊 ⌇ 🚴   ⑬